GIVING VOICE TO LOVE

Giving Voice to Love:

SONG AND SELF-EXPRESSION FROM THE

TROUBADOURS TO GUILLAUME DE MACHAUT

Judith A. Peraino

OXFORD
UNIVERSITY PRESS

OXFORD
UNIVERSITY PRESS

Oxford University Press, Inc., publishes works that further
Oxford University's objective of excellence
in research, scholarship, and education.

Oxford   New York
Auckland   Cape Town   Dar es Salaam   Hong Kong   Karachi
Kuala Lumpur   Madrid   Melbourne   Mexico City   Nairobi
New Delhi   Shanghai   Taipei   Toronto

With offices in
Argentina   Austria   Brazil   Chile   Czech Republic   France   Greece
Guatemala   Hungary   Italy   Japan   Poland   Portugal   Singapore
South Korea   Switzerland   Thailand   Turkey   Ukraine   Vietnam

Copyright © 2011 by Oxford University Press

Published by Oxford University Press, Inc.
198 Madison Avenue, New York, New York 10016

www.oup.com

Oxford is a registered trademark of Oxford University Press

Library of Congress Cataloging-in-Publication Data
Peraino, Judith Ann.
Giving voice to love : song and self-expression from the troubadours
to Guillaume de Machaut / Judith A. Peraino.
p. cm.
Includes bibliographical references and index.
ISBN 978-0-19-975724-4 (hardcover : alk. paper)
1. Troubadour songs—History and criticism.   2. Trouvère songs—History and criticism.
3. Descorts—History and criticism.   4. Motets—14th century—History and criticism.
5. Music and literature—History—To 1500.   I. Title.
ML182.P44 2011
782.4'30944—dc22   2011007498

...lication of this book was funded in part by the Otto Kinkeldey Endowment of the American Musicological
...ciety, the Margarita Hanson Endowment of the American Musicological Society, and the Publications
...ment of the American Musicological Society, supported by the National Endowment for the Humanities.

1 3 5 7 9 8 6 4 2

...in the United States of America
on acid-free paper

For
Richard Crocker

Acknowledgments

THE TROUBADOURS AND trouvères often ended their songs with an acknowledgment, naming the patrons, peers, friends, and loved ones who helped give them a voice. I begin with my *envoi*, and with deep gratitude to all those named in the following paragraphs for their significant contributions to my own voice.

I have dedicated this book to Richard Crocker, whose model of creative thought, passionate engagement, and elegant writing I always strive to emulate. In keeping with his generous spirit, Richard offered his comments on some of the chapters. And it was Richard who introduced me to Hunter Hensley, Professor of Voice at Eastern Kentucky University, and suggested that he record the examples. Thus began a two-year collaboration with Hunter (and at times with Richard too) studying, rehearsing, and deliberating nearly thirty songs note for note, word for word. Working with Richard and Hunter to record these songs was invaluable, and shaped my thoughts about expression in secular monophony. The fruit of this collaboration can be heard on the companion website, and can be read throughout the pages of this book.

Chuck Raniewicz was the sound engineer for the recordings. I thank him for his technological expertise, keen ear, patience, and sense of humor during the many long days of the editing process. I would also like to thank Chris Munson at Eastern Kentucky University, who recorded songs "from afar" when needed.

I am particularly grateful to Alice Colby Hall for her philological expertise, and for reviewing my translations of Occitan and Old French, and to Rupert Pickens, who coached Hunter on the pronunciation and performance of these languages. I would like to thank the Department of Music at Cornell University and particularly the chair,

Roberto Sierra, for supporting this project financially. While writing this book I had the opportunity to teach a graduate seminar on the secular music of Guillaume de Machaut, and another on the music of the troubadours and trouvères; I thank the graduate students who participated in these seminars for invigorating conversations.

I have benefited from the comments offered by many outstanding scholars of medieval music and literature, especially William Burgwinkle, Ardis Butterfield, Emma Dillon, John Haines, Cary Howie, Sarah Kay, and Elizabeth Randell Upton. I am particularly grateful to Monica Roundy, who provided expert proofreading and suggestions for the entire manuscript. Bonnie Blackburn served as the copyeditor for this book. I have long admired her scholarship and writing, and I was privileged to have the assistance of her extensive knowledge and critical eye. This book shows the indelible mark of many conversations with art historian Kate Morris. I thank her for inspiring me to pursue the idea of medieval expressionism, and for reading chapters and excerpts as requested.

Friends and family contributed in many ways, sometimes with ideas born of casual conversation, but more often with much-needed food, drink, and respite. I thank Barb Blom, Bronwyn Evans, Jason Frank, Becky Givan, Jerry Johnson, Yael Kropsky, Tracy McNulty, Carl and Nancy Peraino, Camille Robcis, Sara Shenk, Penny VanSchoik, and Gwen Wilkinson.

To my partner Carmen Enid Martínez, I owe both my words and my quiet.

Table of Contents

About the Companion Website

THE COMPANION WEBSITE to this book contains sound clips for the music examples, the majority of which were recorded for the first time expressly for this project. A symbol ⊙ OXFORD WEB MUSIC will alert the reader to the sound clip that accompanies the transcribed example. Expanded transcriptions and performances of a number of the songs appear on the website as well. Readers can access the companion website using this web address: www.oup.com/us/givingvoicetolove, and the username Musici and access code Book5983. Please note that these are case-sensitive.

List of Figures

List of Tables

Abbreviations

BIBLIOGRAPHIES, DICTIONARIES, AND ESSAY ANTHOLOGIES

B-ref, B-rond   Nico H. J. van den Boogaard, *Rondeaux et refrains du XIIIe siècle au début du XIVe* (Paris: Klincksieck, 1969)

Frank   István Frank, *Répertoire métrique de la poésie des troubadours*, 2 vols. (Paris: Librairie Ancienne Honoré Champion, 1953)

FS   *Fauvel Studies: Allegory, Chronicle, Music, and Image in Paris, Bibliothèque Nationale de France MS francais 146*, ed. Margaret Bent and Andrew Wathey (Oxford: Clarendon Press, 1998)

Gen   Friedrich Gennrich, *Bibliographie der ältesten französischen und lateinischen Motetten*, Summa musicae medii aevi 2 (Darmstadt: n.p., 1958)

HT   *A Handbook of the Troubadours*, ed. F. R. P. Akehurst and Judith M. Davis (Berkeley: University of California Press, 1995)

LR   François-Just-Marie Raynouard, *Lexique roman ou dictionnaire de la langue des troubadours*, 6 vols. (Paris: Silvestre 1844)

ML   *Medieval Lyric: Genres in Historical Context*, ed. William D. Paden (Urbana and Chicago: University of Illinois Press, 2000)

PC   Alfred Pillet and Henry Carstens, *Bibliographie der Troubadours* (1933; repr. New York: Burt Franklin, 1968). Bibliographic entries will be given in the form PC (author number)-(song number), as in PC 70-43.

PDP   Emil Levy, *Petit Dictionnaire provençal-français*, 4th ed. (Heidelberg: Carl Winter, 1966)

PSW   Emil Levy, *Provenzalisches Supplement-Wörterbuch: Berichtigungen und Ergänzungen zu Raynouards Lexique Roman*, 8 vols. (Leipzig: Reisland, 1915)

RS   Hans Spanke, *G. Raynauds Bibliographie des altfranzösischen Liedes* (1955; repr. Leiden: E. J. Brill, 1980)

TI   *The Troubadours: An Introduction*, ed. Simon Gaunt and Sarah Kay (Cambridge: Cambridge University Press, 1999)

EDITIONS OF LYRICS AND MUSIC

Adam   *The Lyrics and Melodies of Adam de la Halle*, ed. Deborah Hubbard Nelson and Hendrik van der Werf (New York: Garland, 1985)

Aimeric   *The Poems of Aimeric de Peguilhan*, ed. William P. Shepard and Frank M. Chambers (Evanston, IL: Northwestern University Press, 1950)

Anthology   *Anthology of Troubadour Lyric Poetry*, ed. Alan R. Press (Edinburgh: Edinburgh University Press, 1971)

Bernart   *The Songs of Bernart de Ventadorn*, ed. Stephen G. Nichols, Jr. and John A. Galm et al. (Chapel Hill: University of North Carolina Press, 1962)

Jaufre   *The Poetry of Cercamon and Jaufre Rudel*, ed. George Wolf and Roy Rosenstein (New York: Garland, 1983)

Marcabru   *Marcabru: A Critical Edition*, ed. Simon Gaunt, Ruth Harvey, and Linda Paterson (Cambridge: D. S. Brewer, 2000)

Raimbaut   *The Poems of the Troubadour Raimbaut de Vaqueiras*, ed. Joseph Linskill (The Hague: Mouton and Co., 1964)

Songs   *Songs of the Troubadours and Trouvères: An Anthology of Poems and Melodies*, ed. Samuel N. Rosenberg, Margaret Switten, and Gérard Le Vot (New York: Garland, 1998)

Thibaut   *The Lyrics of Thibaut de Champagne*, ed. and trans. Kathleen J. Brahney (New York: Garland, 1989)

William   *The Poetry of William VII, Count of Poitiers, IX Duke of Aquitaine*, ed. and trans. Gerald A. Bond (New York: Garland, 1982)

OTHER ABBREVIATIONS

B   designates folio numbers from the facsimile of trouv. *M*, ed. Jean and Louise Beck. See the list of facsimile editions in the Bibliography for full citation.

troub.   Troubadour manuscript

trouv.   Trouvère manuscript

TROUVÈRE MANUSCRIPT SIGLA

A   Arras, Bibliothèque Municipale, 657 (1278, Artois)

I   Oxford, Bodleian, Douce 308 (early 14th century, Lorraine)

K   Paris, Bibliothèque de l'Arsenal, 5198 (1270s, Picardy or Artois)

M   Paris, Bibliothèque nationale de France, f. fr. 844 (original corpus: 1250s–1270s, Artois and possibly elsewhere)

Mt Paris, Bibliothèque nationale de France, f. fr. 844 (collection of songs by Thibaut de Champagne)

N   Paris, Bibliothèque nationale de France, f. fr. 845 (1270–80, Picardy or Artois)

O   Paris, Bibliothèque nationale de France, f. fr. 846 (1280–90, Burgundy)

P   Paris, Bibliothèque nationale de France, f. fr. 847 (1270–80, Picardy or Artois)

R   Paris, Bibliothèque nationale de France, f. fr. 1591 (early 14th century, Artois)

T   Paris, Bibliothèque nationale de France, f. fr. 12615 (1270s–1280s, Artois)

U   Paris, Bibliothèque nationale de France, f. fr. 20050 (ca. 1231, Lorraine)

V   Paris, Bibliothèque nationale de France, f. fr. 24406 (after 1266, Artois)

W   Paris, Bibliothèque nationale de France, f. fr. 25566 (end of the 13th century, Artois)

X   Paris, Bibliothèque nationale de France, n.a. fr. 1050 (1270s–1280s, Artois or Arras)

a   Vatican City (Rome), Biblioteca Apostolica Vaticana, Reg. lat. 1490 (late 13th or early 14th century, Artois)

TROUBADOUR MANUSCRIPT SIGLA

A   Vatican City (Rome), Biblioteca Apostolica Vat. lat. 5232 (13th century, Italy)

B   Paris, Bibliothèque nationale de France, f. fr. 1592 (13th century, Italy)

C   Paris, Bibliothèque nationale de France, f. fr. 856 (14th century, southern France)

D/ Dᵃ Modena, Biblioteca Estense, α. R. 4. 4 (1254, Italy)

E   Paris, Bibliothèque nationale de France, f. fr. 1749 (14th century, southern France)

F   Vatican City (Rome), Biblioteca Apostolica Vaticana, Chigiana L. IV 106 (14th century)

G   Milan, Biblioteca Ambrosiana, S.P. 4 (*olim* R 71 sup.) (14th century, Italy)

H   Vatican City (Rome) Biblioteca Apostolica Vat. lat. 3207 (late 13th century, Italy)

I   Paris, Bibliothèque nationale de France, f. fr. 854 (13th century, Italy)

K   Paris, Bibliothèque nationale de France, f. fr. 12473 (13th century, Italy)

M   Paris, Bibliothèque nationale de France, f. fr. 12474 (14th century, Italy)

Mª Madrid, Academia de la Historia, MS 9-24-6/4579 (14th century, Catalonia)

N   New York, Pierpont Morgan Library, MS 819 (14th century, Italy)

O   Vatican City (Rome), Biblioteca Apostolica Vat. lat. 3208 (early 14th century)

P   Florence, Biblioteca Mediceo Laurenziana, Plut. XLI cod. 42 (early 14th century)

Q   Florence, Biblioteca Riccardiana, MS 2909 (14th century, Italy)

R   Paris, Bibliothèque nationale de France, f. fr. 22543 (14th century, southern France)

S/S^i Oxford, Bodleian Library, Douce 269 (13th century, Italy)

Sg   Barcelona, Biblioteca de Catalunya 146 (14th century, Catalonia)

T   Paris, Bibliothèque nationale de France, f. fr. 15211 (14th–15th century)

U   Florence, Biblioteca Mediceo Laurenziana, Plut. XLI cod. 43 (14th century)

V   Venice, Biblioteca Nazionale Marciana fr. App. cod. XI (1268, Catalan)

W   Paris, Bibliothèque nationale de France, f. fr. 844 (original corpus: 1250s–1270s, Artois and possibly elsewhere)

X   Paris, Bibliothèque nationale de France, f. fr. 20050 (ca. 1231, Lorraine)

a   Florence, Biblioteca Riccardiana, MS 2814 (1598, Italy)

a^1 Modena, Biblioteca Estense, Campori γ.N.8.4 (16th century copy of early 14th century MS)

c   Florence, Biblioteca Mediceo Laurenziana, Plut. XC inf. 26 (15th century, Italy)

e/e^b/e^3 Vatican City (Rome), Biblioteca Apostolica Vaticana, MS Barb. lat. 3965 (18th-century copy of early sources, Italy)

f   Paris, Bibliothèque nationale de France, f. fr. 12472 (14th century, southern France)

MOTET MANUSCRIPT SIGLA

Mo   Montpellier, Bibliothèque Inter-Universitaire, Section Médecine, H 196 (1270s–early 14th century, Paris)

W2   Wolfenbüttel, Herzog August Bibliothek, Guelf. 1099 Helmst. (Heinemann catalogue 1206) (mid-13th century, Paris)

OTHER MANUSCRIPT SOURCES AND ABBREVIATIONS

Fauvel   Paris, Bibliothèque nationale de France, f. fr. 146
P-BnF   Paris, Bibliothèque nationale de France

MACHAUT MANUSCRIPTS

MS A   Paris, Bibliothèque nationale de France, f. fr. 1584 (early 1370s, possibly
        Reims)
MS C   Paris, Bibliothèque nationale de France, f. fr. 1586 (ca. 1356, Paris)
MS Vg   Ferrell-Vogüé MS, on loan to the Parker Library, Corpus Christi,
        Cambridge (*olim* New York, Wildenstein Collection, MS without
        shelfmark) (ca. 1370)

Map of France ca. 1270.

E fol quet.

on chan tan mauen amen ber
cho queu cug chan tan oblit
dar avas percho chan quo bli
ves la dolor El mal damor Er
on plus chan plus men souen
dala bocha nulla res no ma ues
cuas tan merce per ques uerta
es em bla be Quins el cor port
dom na uostra faitbon Quem
castia queu no uir mararon

GIVING VOICE TO LOVE

Introduction

LOVE, SELF, AND SONG

LOVE SONGS OF every epoch, from the Middle Ages to the present day, embody this paradox: they often fuse the most personal emotion with the most banal language. But some love songs may stand in relief against a background of formulaic music, clichéd lyrics, conventional scenarios; they may seem more expressive or subjective than others, presenting not a common language of love but rather a point of view rooted in a specific time, place, psychology, and vocabulary. Furthermore, this subjective voice may be more evident in the musical setting than in the hackneyed sentimentality of the words. We expect music to be in some way mimetic of the emotions expressed in the words, either through iconic melodic gestures linked to words ("word painting"), or through a system of affective associations attached to certain modes (such as major and minor) or chord progressions (such as the twelve-bar blues).[1] But medieval love songs do not show any systematic affective associations with modes, finals, intervals, or pitch collections. In the Middle Ages, the relationship between music and words often seems purely structural: the words—their form and genre, their sonic patterns of rhyme and meter—provide a framework for strophic or sequential construction, for the use of refrains, and sometimes also for the choice of notation and melodic contours. Moreover, the lyrics of medieval love songs are notoriously moody—stanzas of praise follow those of blame, self-deprecation alternates with boasting—yet the music is most often strophic, repeating

---

1. The classic study of music and emotion is Meyer, *Emotion and Meaning in Music*. For a recent study of the meaning of church modes in the Renaissance madrigal see McClary, *Modal Subjectivities*.

the same melody from one stanza to the next.[2] If an iconic melodic gesture aligns with a word or phrase for the first stanza, it is ill-suited to the words in subsequent stanzas.[3] This does not mean, however, that the sentiment "love" plays no part in the composition of melodies, or that music does not represent "self-expression," or is not somehow mimetic of subjectivity. We simply have yet to understand fully what medieval music expresses, and how, and for whom. This study attempts to make a contribution toward understanding musical self-expression in medieval love songs. The most robust and self-conscious repertories of medieval love songs appear in the vernaculars of Occitan and French from the beginning of the twelfth century to the last decades of the fourteenth century, notated as single lines of melody. Thus I focus on these monophonic vernacular repertories in what follows.[4]

REASONS TO SING

Sometime in the late twelfth century the troubadour Folquet de Marselha (fl. 1178–95) composed a love lyric that begins with a dilemma regarding the intended purpose and actual effect of song:

En chantan m'aven a membrar	In singing it befalls me to remember
so qu'ieu cug chantan oblidar,	what I expected in singing to forget,
mas per so chant qu'oblides la dolor	but I sing in order to forget the pain
e·l mal d'amor.	and the anguish of love.
Et on plus chan plus m'en sove,	And yet the more I sing, the more
	I remember,
que la boca en al re non ave	for my mouth can say naught else

---

2. Following convention in literary scholarship, I will use the word "stanza" specifically to describe the units of lyric and music organized by a principle of structural repetition, and "strophic" to describe that structural repetition. The word "strophe" refers generically to segments of lyrics and music that may or may not repeat; thus I will use "strophe" for units that do not repeat poetic structure or melody, and "heterostrophic" to describe that structural diversity. See Turco, *The New Book of Forms*, 6. See also the discussion of "strophe" in chapter 1.

3. See Margaret Switten, "Music and Versification," esp. 148.

4. John Haines has revealed a robust practice of singing *cantica amatoria* centuries before the first troubadour entered the picture; and he further deduces from the condemnatory description of churchmen that women played a significant, if not central, role in their performance in the round dances of festivities. Haines admits, however, that these early vernacular amorous songs represent a tradition distinct from—though sometimes intersecting with—the complex explorations of subjectivity and self-expression that "love" came to signify for the troubadours and trouvères. See Haines, *Medieval* Song, 51–82. Secular love lyrics appear in Latin as well as other European vernaculars, notably the German *Minnesang*, the Iberian *cantiga d'amor*, and the Italian *ballata* and *canzone*. These vernacular lyrics—very few of which survive with musical notation—and to some extent the Latin lyrics as well, are indebted to the construction and diffusion of the troubadours' concept of *fin' amors*, the origins of which are discussed below. For more on indigenous Spanish song forms see chapter 5; see also the relevant articles on German, Spanish, and Italian lyric traditions in *HT* and *ML*.

mas en: "Merce!"

Per qu'es vertatz e sembla be

qu'ins e·l cor port, Dona, vostra faisso,

que·m chastia qu'ieu no vir ma razo.

but "Mercy!"

That's why it is true and seems fitting

that in my heart, Lady, I carry your image,

which chastises me so that I do not change my subject.[5]

The troubadour sings to forget, yet the song causes him to remember. Along with the pains of love the troubadour also remembers his lady, whose image, embossed on his heart,[6] further enjoins him not to deviate from his *razo*. The Occitan word *razo* derives from the Latin rhetorical term *ratio* (f.), which refers to the justifying motive of an action, or the reason for an oration.[7] In the context of troubadour lyric, *razo* can mean the song's motivation, origin, or subject matter.[8] The *chant* is the product of the troubadour's craft, yet the conceit of the lyric is the troubadour's lack of control, encapsulated in his cry "mercy." Both mouth (*boca*) and exclamation become metonyms for the song itself—something the mouth does by force of love. As love buffets and subordinates the troubadour, he implores the lady: "Do with the body then what you will, and preserve

---

Although scholars at one time emphasized the priority of Latin over vernacular lyrics, citing shared forms and love themes, more recent assessments call attention to their differences—especially the heavily scholastic and Ovidian influence in the Latin repertory. Winthrop Wetherbee notes that the Latin love lyric generally shows less subtle self-analysis, and that many of them seem to have been written in response to the lyrics of the troubadours and trouvères. See the discussion of the origins of the medieval love lyric below; see also Dronke, *Medieval Latin and the Rise of European Love-Lyric*; Stevens, *Words and Music in the Middle Ages*, esp. 48–52, 63–73; Wetherbee, "The Place of Secular Latin Lyric." In 1932, musicologist Friedrich Gennrich argued that vernacular song forms developed from four basic Latin models—litany, rondel, sequence, and hymn. See his *Grundriss einer Formenlehre des mittelalterlichen Liedes*. Both his reductive typology and his historical interpretation were criticized two years later by Hans Spanke; see his review of Gennrich's study, reprinted in *Studien zur lateinischen und romanischen Lyrik des Mittelalters*, 440–54. The major extant sources for secular monophony in all European languages are described in Fallows et al., "Sources, MS, §III: Secular Monophony."

5. PC 155-8. All editions and base translation of this lyric are from *Songs*, 145–46; in all cases I have modified the translations. I have also consulted Folquet de Marselha, *Le Troubadour Folquet de Marseille*, ed. Stroński, 27–31, and Schulman, *Where Troubadours Were Bishops*, 196–99.

6. This idea of an image impressed or held in the heart, which is thematically developed in the remaining stanzas of the song, links this song to the medieval arts of memory, which emphasized visualization of images. See Huot, "Visualization and Memory," 11.

7. For the use of *ratio* as a rhetorical term see *Rhetorica ad Herennium*, 50–53 (I, 16.26), 121–25 (II, 22.35); see also Poe, *From Poetry to Prose*, 35; Burgwinkle, *Razos and Troubadour Songs*, xvii; and Patterson, *Troubadours and Eloquence*, 11–13. Both Poe and Burgwinkle cite *ratione* as the Latin etymon, while Patterson cites *ratio*.

8. An early use of *razo* to mean the subject or theme of a composition appears in a lyric by Marcabru (fl. 1130–49), *Auias de chan com enans' e meillura*, line 3 (PC 293-9); see *Marcabru*, 134–35 for text and translation; and see Raynouard, *LR* 5:51. Sometime in the thirteenth century *razo* came to designate a prose introduction to specific songs. For more examples and a detailed discussion of *razo* as a term used in lyrics and as a prose genre see Poe, *From Poetry to Prose*, 35–65.

the heart as your dwelling," playing on the homonyms *cors* (body) and *cor* (heart).[9]
While the heart in courtly lyrics figures as the organ of emotions, memory, thought, and
intention,[10] the body could signify either the corporeal self, or the holistic self, including
temperament, behavior, and status.[11] In Folquet's lyric, the *cor* and *cors* are at odds: the
heart functions as both a dwelling place for the lady and as an antagonist for the body,
as the third stanza expresses:

Qu'el guarda vos e·us ten tan car	For it [the heart] keeps you and holds you so dear
que·l cors en fai nesci semblar,	that it makes the body look like a fool,
que·l sen hi met, l'engienh e la valor,	for it uses sense, skill and merit
si qu'en error	so that in error
laissa·l cors pe·l sen qu'el rete;	it leaves the body while it retains the reason;
qu'om mi parla, manthas vetz s'esdeve,	it often happens that someone speaks to me,
qu'ieu no sai que,	and I know not about what,
e·m saluda qu'ieu no·n aug re;	or greets me and I don't hear a thing;
e ja per so nuls hom no m'ochaizo	and so no man may ever accuse me
si·m saluda et ieu mot non li so.	if he greets me and I don't say a word.

The very condition of the heart that forces the troubadour to sing also renders the body
mute and foolish, robbing the troubadour of sensible responses to the external world—
the *cors* that is also temperament and behavior.

Cor, cors, and boca—the subjugating heart, the subjugated self, and the singing mouth—
together comprise the *razo* of this song, its subject matter and cause. The *razo* driving
most medieval love songs can be distilled to the dynamic tension among *cor*, *cors*, and
boca, or, in other words, among love, self, and expression through song. Scholars have
identified similar triangulated relationships at work in these lyrics: Elizabeth Poe
identifies the "dynamic coequivalence" of the experience of love, the process of song,

---

9. "Empero faitz del cors so que·us er bo / e·l cor gardatz si qom vostra maizo" (lines 19–20).

10. For a discussion of the heart's involvement in memory, see Carruthers, *The Book of Memory*, 48–49. For a
good summary and bibliography of medieval "pectoral psychology," see Jager, "The Book of the Heart," 2–4.
See also Wack, *Lovesickness in the Middle Ages*, 78–79, 94–95. For a discussion of the many valences of *cor* in
troubadour verse see Cropp, *Le Vocabulaire courtois des troubadours*, 254–64.

11. In *Non es meravelha s'eu chan* (PC 70–31), Bernart de Ventadorn describes the lady (or possibly himself) as
"francs cors umils, gais et cortes" (noble person, humble and courtly), line 54. For text and translation see
Bernart, 132–33. (I have substituted the word "person" for "figure"). For a discussion of *cors* in troubadour
poetry see Cropp, *Le Vocabulaire courtois des troubadours*, 45–46, 160, 258. In the northern lyrics and romances
the word *cors* appears frequently to mean physical body or "person," and "self"; according to Norman Susskind
" 'cors' provides a frequent reminder of the physical aspect of love." See Susskind, "Love and Laughter in the
Romans Courtois."

and the poetic "I" (that is, the "I" within the lyric as distinct from the ego of the author);[12] looking at the northern trouvère repertory, Paul Zumthor argues that the semantic constellations of *aimer, trouver* (which yields *trouvère*), and *chanter* create a tautology such that "each of the terms implies both of the others in an endless chain welded together by the 'song.' "[13] While in poetry love, self, and song may have porous semantic boundaries, allowing for many games of self-reference, in practice—in the setting of words to melodies, in their transmission, and in their performance—love, self, and song may become radically dissociated and counterposed.

Folquet de Marselha was a historical figure about whom much is known. A troubadour born into the merchant class, Folquet suddenly abandoned singing and composing in 1195, entered a Cistercian monastery, and later became the Bishop of Toulouse during the Albigensian Crusade. He died on Christmas day, 1231. References to persons and events in his lyrics allow some to be located to a specific place and time. The above-quoted song *En chantan m'aven a membrar*, for example, mentions Lord Guillem (the VIIIth) and the destination Montpellier in its two *tornadas*, and these suggest composition between 1187 and 1191, when Folquet was associated with the courts at both Marseille and Montpellier.[14] *En chantan m'aven a membrar* appears in over twenty sources, the earliest of which (troub. *D*) is dated 1254 (the earliest written source for troubadour and trouvère lyrics is dated ca. 1231), but only one source preserves music—a north Italian manuscript from around 1300.[15] The historical coordinates for the famous early troubadour Jaufre Rudel can also be determined with some confidence: his name is found in a charter from Tenaille Abbey in 1120, and references within his own lyrics, and in one by Marcabru, place him in the Second Crusade (ca. 1147).[16] Yet, as with Folquet, the written records for his songs are far removed in time from his presumed flourishing dates of 1125–48. Jaufre's lyric *Lanqan li jorn son lonc en mai* with the famous phrase *amor de lonh* (love from afar) survives in fourteen sources, including troub. *D* from 1254, while music survives in only three sources. The three melodies are remarkably similar to one another, though their lyrics

---

12. Poe, *From Poetry to Prose*, 4. This distinction was first made in 1946 by Leo Spitzer, and has been variously modified but generally accepted by later medievalists. The poetic "I" is sometimes called the lyric "I" or the lyric *je*. See Spitzer, "Note on the Poetic and the Empirical 'I' in Medieval Authors."

13. See Zumthor, *Toward a Medieval Poetics*, 167; id., *Essai de poétique médiévale*, 214.

14. See Folquet de Marselha, *Le Troubadour Folquet de Marseille*, ed. Stroński, 13–15, 71–72, 153–58.

15. The source with music is troub. *G* (p. 15); for a description see Aubrey, *The Music of the Troubadours*, 43–46. For a discussion of troubadour sources in general see Burgwinkle, "The *Chansonniers* as Books." Burgwinkle notes that only nine troubadour sources date from the thirteenth century, and most of these are Italian-made (247). The earliest exclusively troubadour source is the first part of troub. *D*, dated 1254. Two other mid-thirteenth-century sources, troub. *W* and *X*, are primarily collections of northern trouvère lyrics (trouv. *M* and *U*, respectively), which include a section of southern composers. The earlier and more modest of these two sources, trouv. *U*, was possibly commissioned in 1231 for a wedding; on this see Lug, "Katharer und Waldenser in Metz." See also Aubrey, "Sources, MS, §III: Secular monophony, 4: French."

16. See *Jaufre*, 96–101; see also Rosenstein, "Retour aux origines du troubadour Jaufre Rudel."

are remarkably dissimilar, with different numbers and ordering of stanzas, and different languages: in two of the three the lyric is translated from Occitan into French![17]

Thus Jaufre's song of "love from afar" took on temporal and cultural dimensions for his later medieval audience—a beloved object of the distant past, anthologized and translated, redacted and scrambled. I want to linger on this point, for it is here that we can perhaps find a relationship between the troubadours' concept of love as perpetual desire and the material traces of their songs. Paul Zumthor describes the historian's relationship to medieval texts as a relationship of desire across an unbridgeable distance—a temporal *amor de lonh*. He writes:

> [W]e speak well only about things we know concern us personally, about things we love, perhaps. Every relationship we maintain with a text involves some latent eroticism. Only this dynamism puts a critical reader in a situation comparable to that of the medieval reader or listener, whose whole body, not only his visual and auditory faculties, was engaged in the reception of the text.[18]

Carolyn Dinshaw, too, uses passionate and sensual language to describe the practice of "doing" medieval history: "The historian manages thus, by writing, to 'touch' bodies across time," making partial connections that are affective and pleasurable.[19] If hearing, reading, and studying a text are considered embodied acts of desire, then certainly the compiling, writing, rubricating, and illuminating of those manuscripts that first transmit these texts were no less labors of love. Scribes, like performers, interpreted and preserved the songs, expressing a cultural (if not also personal) desire for the distant Other, removed in space (à la Jaufre Rudel) and time (à la Zumthor). With pen on parchment, the "touch" between scribes and authors is actual as well as metaphorical: the scribe embodies the words and music with his gestures on the page.

But what subjectivity, and what about subjectivity, might we be able to read in these corporately created songs that advertise a sincere expression of individuality? How, specifically, do the musical settings of love lyrics enter into the questions about subjectivity and self-expression posed by the lyrics? One goal of this project is to bring philosophical and theoretical notions about the self and subjectivity to bear on the nuts and bolts of music.

Words have subjects: the subject matter or topic of paragraphs; the grammatical subject in a sentence—the "doer" who acts. In philosophical discourse, especially in the Enlightenment era of the eighteenth century, "the subject" (L. *subjectum*) refers to

---

17. PC 262-2. For a comprehensive discussion and edition of the lyric's many versions see Pickens, *The Songs of Jaufré Rudel*, 150–213. Music is preserved in troub. *R, W,* and *X* (the latter two MSS contain the lyric in its French translation; troub. *W* attributes the song to Gossiames Faidins [Gauclem Faidit]). See *Jaufre*, plates 1–6 for facsimiles and transcriptions of the melodies.

18. Zumthor, *Speaking of the Middle Ages*, 22.

19. Dinshaw, *Getting Medieval*, 47; see also 1–54 and 34–47.

the self's actively reflective dimension (the "I think…"), or "the mind," which was the starting point of inquiry and knowledge—hence subjectivity (the sense or condition of the self as reflective, or "what is in the mind"), and subjective (of the mind or self).[20] Post-Enlightenment philosophers such as Friedrich Nietzsche, and later theorists such as Jacques Lacan, Louis Althusser, and Michel Foucault, overturned the agency of the subject: for them, "the subject" refers to one who is *subjugated* by pre-existing language and similar "discursive practices" that perpetuate ideology.[21] In a much-cited article from 1969, Althusser coined the term "interpellation" to describe the way ideology creates self-reflecting "subjects" out of "individuals" by calling to or hailing them through language (which he represented as a policeman's hail). This use of "subject" in fact brings the word back to its medieval—pointedly political—meaning: a subject is a person living under the dominion of a king, lord, or government. Subjects must pay allegiance, service, or tribute to the ruling power and submit to its laws in exchange for protection, and in hope of generosity.[22]

Is the self or individual wholly exhausted in the discursive formation of the subject? While Althusser would answer "yes," most scholars of literature, art, and music envision a dialectic between ideology and the individual that allows for a modicum of freedom to resist or counter total conscription by ideology.

Music has subjects too, but it quickly becomes difficult to form a list of predicates. What is the subject matter of music? Who is the "doer" of or within music?[23] Is music a function of self-inquiry? How does music subjugate or interpellate individuals? Words enjoy a seemingly immediate access to thought, communication, meaning, and understanding; music, with or without words, enjoys a seemingly immediate access to emotions and to embodied reactions (swaying, tapping, chills)—but less obviously to

---

20. See Seigel, *The Idea of the Self*, 14–17. See also Altieri, *Subjective Agency*, 1–26, esp. 25; Davidson, *Subjective, Intersubjective, Objective*, 39–52 (for subjectivity defined as "what is 'in the mind' " see 43).

21. Nietzsche writes of "the seduction of language…which conceives and misconceives all effects as conditioned by something that causes effects, by a 'subject'.… [But] there is no 'being' behind doing, effecting, becoming; 'the doer' is merely a fiction added to the deed—the deed is everything.… [o]ur entire science still lies under the misleading influence of language and has not disposed of that little changeling the 'subject' (the atom, for example, is such a changeling, as is the Kantian 'thing-in-itself')…." See *On the Genealogy of Morals*, 45. Art Berman, summarizing Lacan's theory of subject formation, writes: "the subject, an ego, [is] *created by* a language that pre-exists the child and that accordingly determines not only how the world shall in the future be known but also what the knower, the subject, *is*." See Berman, *From the New Criticism to Deconstruction*, 186. For a discussion of the subject as "subjugation" in Althusser and Foucault, see Butler, *The Psychic Life of Power*.

22. S.v. "Subject," I.1–3, *Oxford English Dictionary Online*; for examples in medieval Occitan sources see also Raynouard, *LR*, III, 472, and 584; Levy, *PSW*, 7:685. Under "Subject" II, the *OED* lists the "senses derived ultimately (through L. *subjectum*) from Aristotle" including the grammatical meaning of "a word or group of words setting forth that which is spoken about and constituting the 'nominative' to a finite verb" (II.8), and the philosophical meaning of "the thinking or cognizing agent" (II.9). See also Seigel, *The Idea of the Self*, 14–15.

23. This line of inquiry intersects with the much debated question of narrative in music. On this see Nattiez, "Can One Speak of Narrativity in Music?"; and Maus, "Classical Instrumental Music and Narrative"; Almén, *A Theory of Musical Narrative*.

meaning and understanding. For Romantic philosophers of nineteenth-century Europe, the principal subject of music was exactly that which could not be expressed by words—the ineffable condition of being. For medieval philosophers in the speculative tradition of Pythagoras and Plato, the principal subject of music was also the condition of being: music (in theory) expresses the proportional balance, the "harmony," that describes the universe of God's perfect design. Medieval musicians working outside the church also contemplated the subject of music in words and in notes. These musical meditations (in practice) may have had little to do with the "harmony of the spheres,"[24] but they were no less philosophical in their attempts to express the complex, often paradoxical experience of being in the world—the experience of autonomy and agency on one hand, and of interdependence and subjugation on the other. Once again, Folquet de Marselha offers a concise depiction of this tension in song, here aligned with emotion (heart) and reason (mind):

Qu'aissi·l sui subjetz et aclis	How subjugated and abased
	I am to her
de bon talen,	from sincere desire,
qu'en lieis amar an pres conten	for in loving her contend
mos ferms coratges e mos sens,	my steady heart and my mind,
c'usquecx cuj'amar plus fortmens.	for each believes that it loves the strongest.[25]

"Love" here, and elsewhere in this repertory, functions as an expedient way to name the experience of being both passive and active in thought and deed, of being "subject to" desire, and the "subject of" desire.[26] The song, then, becomes a means of exploring and expressing this subjectivity.

WHAT'S LOVE GOT TO DO WITH IT?

Medieval love songs (and perhaps all love songs) present themselves as urgent self-expressions. "Amors me fet conmencier une chançon nouvele" (Love makes me begin a

---

24. John Stevens brings the medieval speculative tradition to bear on medieval song, arguing that the underlying aesthetic of songs is numerical proportion. See Stevens, *Words and Music in the Middle Ages*, 13–47. Robert R. Edwards argues that the speculative concept of a rationally ordered universe has aesthetic and thematic implications for medieval lyric and narrative in their construction of "ideal landscapes" and "dream visions"; though, unlike Stevens, Edwards does not make an argument for actual numerical ratios in the metrical design of lyrics. See Edwards, *Ratio and Invention*, esp. xi–xxi, 3–33.

25. Lines 32–36 of *Tan mou de corteza razo* (PC 155-23); text and translation (modified) from Schulman, *Where Troubadours Were Bishops*, 190–91.

26. Sarah Kay also discusses the "double position of the subject as both *subject of* and *subject to* the medium which delineates it." See *Subjectivity in Troubadour Poetry*, 43.

new song). This line, which opens a lyric by the trouvère Thibaut de Champagne (fl. 1220–53), swiftly and emphatically proclaims the inextricable bond between the sentiment "love" and its musical, vocal expression.[27] Similarly, the troubadour Bernart de Ventadorn (fl. 1147–70) famously boasted:

Non es meravelha s'eu chan	It is no wonder that I sing
melhs de nul autre chantador,	better than any other singer,
que plus me tra·l cors vas amor	for my heart draws me more toward love
e melhs sui faihz a so coman	and I am made better suited to its command.[28]

Loving and singing are practically synonymous here: the better the lover, the better the singer, and vice versa. Yet the boast is an odd one, for the troubadour celebrates his exceptional skill in subservience. Love, or the heart, acts as an overlord commanding the troubadour, and the song represents the principal manifestation or product of the "service," which is itself a distinguishing feature of this type of "courtly love."[29]

Scholars have noted the seeming "love explosion" in twelfth-century France. Writings on love flourished in monasteries, cathedral schools, and secular courts alike, though depending on the context, love could be chaste or erotic, directed to a celestial or terrestrial beloved, harmonizing or disorienting, unilateral or reciprocal, a means to an end or an end in itself.[30] The dissemination of Islamic and Christian mysticism, the rise of Mary as a figure of veneration, socio-economic shifts that necessitated a "civilizing" of the military class, the increased influence of clerics in court life, the patronage of powerful noblewomen in Occitan—all these have been cited as factors in the twelfth-century emergence of the troubadours' *fin'amors* and its peculiar mix of profane desire and ascetic practices.[31]

---

27. RS 1268. For a complete edition and translation of the poem see *Thibaut*, 2–5.

28. Text and translation from *Bernart*, 132–33.

29. In 1883 Gaston Paris coined the term "courtly love" to refer to the peculiarities of this type of love-service. Drawing on the Arthurian romances of Chrétien de Troyes (fl. 1170–90), themselves narrative renditions and critiques of lyric sentiments, Paris constructed a paradigm of "courtly love": a knight becomes enamored of a woman of a higher social position, and he must earn the favor of his beloved through courageous acts and courteous behavior. See Paris, "Études sur les romans de la Table Ronde: Lancelot," 518–19. For historiographic discussion of the invention of "courtly love," see Bloch, "Romance, Philology, and Old French Letters"; and Hult, "Gaston Paris and the Invention of Courtly Love". The term "courtly love," once widely adopted in the scholarly literature, has been roundly criticized and has fallen out of use.

30. For a summary of these different contexts and meanings of love see Moore, *Love in Twelfth-Century France*; and Leclercq, *Monks and Love*.

31. For a summary and bibliography for the many theories of origin for *fin' amors* see Bond, "Origins"; see also Lazar, "*Fin' amor*"; and Ruth Harvey, "Courtly Culture in Medieval Occitania." For a historical and contextual study see Paterson, *The World of the Troubadours*. For the civilizing trends and the influence of clerics in court life see Jaeger, *The Origins of Courtliness*. Sandra Resnick Alfonsi traces what she believes to be the definitive theme of masculine submission to feminine superiority in classical, Arabic, and Latin literary sources; see her

The *fin'amors* (pure love) of the troubadours and trouvères contains elements of earlier and contemporaneous love theories and expressive practices derived from classical, biblical, and Hispano-Arab sources. From classical Greek and Roman writers the troubadours inherited the theory that love and desire are instigated through the eyes, while the melodious conjuring of a distant beloved can be traced to the Song of Songs.[32] (It is noteworthy that the voice or "I" of the Song of Songs is female, speaking of, or imagining, the voice of a male beloved.) Treatises on love and lovesickness by Arab writers describe love as self-discipline or psychosomatic disturbance.[33] Ovid's love literature, widely disseminated in the twelfth century, provided a model for some key features of medieval love lyrics—namely, the lover as a cultural ideal (replacing the hero of epic poetry), the artful resistance to desire that perpetuates desire, and the sense that love poetry's true end is its own production.[34]

Yet despite this background, "love" between two human beings in medieval Europe prior to the twelfth century was not usually ascribed to relationships of mixed gender;[35] rather, love existed between aristocratic men, between the king or bishop and a peer or a member of his court. Thus some of the earliest "courtly love" poems—replete with dramatic "wounds" and "flames" of love, and desire for embraces and kisses—were composed for Charlemagne and other male companions by the abbot of Tours, Alcuin of York. Scholars debate whether this rhetoric of passionate love between men, often drawn from the Song of Songs, lies on a continuum with private homosexual practices, or represents a specifically public, non-sexual homosocial relation.[36] Regardless, troubadour and trouvère lyrics retain from this tradition a fusion of ardent love with the court economy of service and favor; they also frequently reveal an underlying bid for the attention of a

---

Masculine Submission in Troubadour Lyric, 3–91; she gives particular weight to the rise of the cult of Mary in Occitania (59–73).

32. For a discussion of the classical origins of the medieval "love through the eyes" see Walsh, introduction to *Andreas Capellanus on Love*, 16; Wack, *Lovesickness in the Middle Ages*, 7–8. For a discussion of the medieval visual representations of "love through the eyes" see Camille, *The Medieval Art of Love*, 26–49. For a discussion of the Song of Songs and twelfth-century love literature see Leclercq, *Monks and Love*, 27–61.

33. See Wack, *Lovesickness in the Middle Ages*, and Boase, *The Origin and Meaning of Courtly Love*, 62–75.

34. See Haahr, "Justifying Love"; Cahoon, "The Anxieties of Influence"; Leclercq, *Monks and Love*, 62–85. Manuscripts containing Ovid's amatory poetry proliferated in the twelfth century. See Hexter, *Ovid and Medieval Schooling*, 4, 15. Peter Dronke argued in 1965 that what was novel about the love literature in the Middle Ages was not the theme of "courtly love," which he believed was "at least as old as Egypt of the second millennium B.C.," but rather "the variety of sophisticated and learned *development* of *courtois* themes," which he believed "were made possible through the influence of Latin learning." More specifically, Dronke saw mystical and theological worshipful love language of twelfth-century writers as a "background of ideas," although the routes of influence were left unclear. See Dronke, *Medieval Latin and the Rise of European Love-Lyric*, vii–xii (quotation p. ix), 57–97, and n. 37 below.

35. The famous love letters of Abelard and Heloise are possible exceptions, though they date from the early twelfth century—roughly the same time as the first troubadour lyrics.

36. For these contrasting views see Boswell, *Christianity, Social Tolerance, and Homosexuality*, and Jaeger, *Ennobling Love*, esp. 43–50 for a discussion of Alcuin's love poetry.

male benefactor or another troubadour. This homosocial desire, triangulated or veiled by a real or fictional "lady," perhaps drove the production of many medieval love songs.

Early twentieth-century scholars implicitly pursued self-expression in troubadour songs by focusing on lyrical content and the origin and meaning of love. Writing in the 1940s, Alexander J. Denomy and Leo Spitzer both considered *fin'amors* as the sincere expression of an interior condition that shaped actual behavior, though they proposed different origins. According to Denomy, *fin'amors* had roots in Arab culture and Neoplatonic philosophy, and denoted a profane sensual desire purified of carnality (one technical meaning of *fin* is "distilled").[37] The true objective of this pure love was courtliness (*cortezia*)—a personal ethical development.[38] Leo Spitzer believed this paradoxical, purified love stemmed from Christian asceticism and mysticism; *fin'amors* signified a conversion of carnal passions into redemptive, Christ-like suffering through an internal visionary reality (*réalité de songe*) encapsulated by Jaufre Rudel's phrase *amor de lonh*.[39]

In these early studies, the troubadours' "love" ultimately describes not a relation between two people, but rather a deliberate turning inward in the service of an artistic or spiritual self-discipline. In contrast to this expression of an individual interior condition, Erich Köhler, writing in the 1960s and influenced by Marxist and hermeneutic theory,

---

37. See Zumthor, "An Overview: Why the Troubadours?," 15. Zumthor posits that *fin* maybe a term borrowed from alchemy. See also Zumthor, *Toward a Medieval Poetics*, 159.

38. Denomy believed this paradoxical concept of frustrated sensual desire that leads to "pure love" (*fin'amors*) stems from Muslim roots, specifically the writings of Avicenna (980–1037) on the striving of the rational soul for pure love (though permitting embraces and kisses), the asceticism of orthodox Sufism, and Andalusian poetry transmitted through Spain to southern France. See Denomy, "*Fin'amors*: The Pure Love of the Troubadours," quotation from 174; see also Denomy, "Courtly Love and Courtliness," and Lazar, *Amours courtois et fin'amors*. For a more recent argument for the "Arab origins" of the troubadour lyric tradition see Menocal, *The Arabic Role in Medieval Literary History*. For a summary of scholarship on "courtly love" from 1500 to 1975 see Boase, *The Origin and Meaning of Courtly Love*. Boase offers a chronology of scholarship, as well as a summary of theories of "origin" versus theories of "meaning," giving considerable weight to the theory of Hispano-Arabic origin.

39. See Spitzer, *L'Amour lontain de Jaufré Rudel*, 34, 37; see also 10–11. Spitzer is bolstering earlier studies by Lot-Borodine, Casella, and Auerbach, and arguing against Grace Frank's theory that "*l'amour lontain*" was an allegory for the Holy Land, and Appel's theory that "*l'amour lontain*" was an allegory for the Virgin. Spitzer argues that Jaufre and the other troubadours participated in a general *Geist* that was a priori Christian and, importantly, Augustinian in its valuation of asceticism and interior reality over bodily desires and exterior display. Sarah Spence has also discussed the relationship between Augustinian rhetoric and the troubadours in *Rhetoric of Reason and Desire*, esp. 103–27. In a more recent study Simon Gaunt has revived the a priori Christian milieu, along with Lacanian psychoanalysis, as an interpretive approach to courtly literature. See his *Love and Death in Medieval French and Occitan Courtly Literature*.

With regard to mysticism, Spitzer cites Bernard of Clairvaux (1090–1153), who described with sensual language the soul's love and desire for God. Jean Leclercq argues, however, that Bernard's theology of love was a response to the secular literature of the day, which adult recruits to Cistercian monasteries would have known. "In the circles of knighthood and nobility, love literature had begun to flourish, and Bernard could hardly fail to determine to create a corresponding love literature, which he did with steady continuity." See Leclercq, *Monks and Love*, 21–22; see also 8–26.

argued that this "love" was a group expression of an exterior condition: the *"paradoxe amoureux"* encodes class-based social tensions. More specifically, Köhler read the tension between desire and decorum as an analog to the tensions between the petty nobility and the aristocracy within the community of the court. The songs and the ideal social behavior they espoused (couched in terms of service, recompense, and generosity) helped neutralize those tensions and integrate the two groups.[40] In Köhler's view, "courtly love" was a psychology born of social structure: "Our sociological analysis of the courtly love psychology (*psychologie amoureuse courtoise*) revealed to us that we were dealing with a structure of integration, integration never perfect, which retains by consequence the value and the fascination with the ideal."[41]

As studies focused on troubadour love turned from individual internal convictions to external social structures, literary scholars writing in the 1960s and 1970s—most notably Roger Dragonetti and Paul Zumthor—made a similar turn to structure, approaching love lyrics as manifestations of an a priori system that precludes sincere expression.[42] In so doing they transformed questions about the nature of troubadour love into questions about the nature of troubadour subjectivity—ironically, by denying any trace of subjectivity in the lyrics. Zumthor writes:

> The subjectivity that formerly inhered in the text, deriving from the presentation of a living subject, has been lost to us. This is probably not the simple result of the obscuring effects of time, but may actually derive from some specific feature of the texts involved. It seems to be related to a sort of linguistic 'soft focus' in the underlying poetic technique.[43]

---

40. Köhler, "Observations historiques." Some of these ideas also appear in his earlier essays collected in Köhler, *Trobadorlyrik und höfischer Roman.*

41. "Notre analyse sociologique de la psychologie amoureuse courtoise nous a révélé que nous avions affaire à une structure d'intégration, intégration jamais parfaite, et qui garde par conséquent la valeur et la fascination de l'idéal." See Köhler, "Observations historiques," 46. Though Köhler's socio-economic readings have had lasting impact on troubadour scholars, historical investigations reveal vassalage relationships in the south to be more egalitarian and contractual in comparison to the rigid hierarchies of dependency and submission in the north. See Ruth Harvey, "Courtly Culture in Medieval Occitania," 10, 18.

42. Structuralism was a reaction to the metaphysical and humanist presumptions of historical studies. Structuralist approaches to language, psychology, kinship, and other cultural practices pushed the traditional human "subject" of history out of the center, and focused instead on structure as pre-existing differential relationships. The forefathers of structuralism in literary criticism are generally listed as linguist Ferdinand de Saussure (*Course in General Linguistics*, 1916), anthropologist Claude Lévi-Strauss (beginning with *Elementary Structures of Kinship*, 1949), and psychoanalytic theorist Jacques Lacan (beginning with his paper "The Rome Discourse," delivered in 1953), though structuralism's differential relations and decentered human converges with ideas formulated within philosophy of the nineteenth century—Nietzsche's concept of genealogy (as opposed to history), and Hegel's dialectic between subject and object. See Dosse, *The History of Structuralism*; Culler, *Structuralist Poetics*; and Sturrock, *Structuralism.*

43. Zumthor, *Toward a Medieval Poetics,* 49.

Dragonetti and Zumthor directed their hard focus on the poetic techniques of the later northern trouvère repertory, usually faulted for being derivative of the troubadour tradition, even more full of clichés, vague abstractions, and limited in vocabulary and formal procedures.[44] Dragonetti, however, sought to recuperate the trouvère repertory by changing the terms of engagement from questions of sincerity and originality (which he argued were Romantic and therefore anachronistic aesthetic values) to questions of the mastery of rhetorical and stylistic conventions. He writes:

> Indeed, in the courtly poem, the work of invention requires a total submission, or almost total, to a tradition of style that imposes commonplaces and technical formulas onto the trouvères.…In the Middle Ages, rhetoric designated the art or the method of mastering (*de conquérir*) a style, or at least, of advancing its success.[45]

Drawing on commentaries by Dante, and noting the exalted position of such "classic" yet abstract poets as Gace Brulé and Thibaut de Champagne, Dragonetti argues that, far from prizing originality, the medieval audience for trouvère songs took pleasure in the "play of commonplaces"—topics that expressed their shared sentiments and ideals.[46] According to Dragonetti, the rhetorical form (*exordium, argumentatio, conclusio*), the parameters of style (word choice, figures of speech), standard topics (such as images of nature in the introductory stanza), and versification (rhyme scheme and syllable count) provide a ready-made, even ritual-like structure within which the trouvère must partially *subordinate* his own voice or self-expression to the desires of his public.[47] In Dragonetti's formulation, the trouvère is simultaneously servile and heroic—one who submits to style but also conquers it.

The topic of sincerity is arguably the foundational rhetorical convention upon which the whole edifice of the love song depends; the lady is a "poetic object" or "myth that incarnates an aspiration." Both lover and beloved are publicly authorized fictions, authenticated by the song's technical merit:

> If by his chanson the trouvère succeeds in communicating the stimulation that brings this myth to life for the duration of its performance, and if, moreover, the

---

44. See, for example, Nelson, "Northern France."

45. "En effet, dans le poème courtois, le travail d'invention requiert une soumission totale ou quasi totale à une tradition de style qui impose aux trouvères, lieux communs et formules techniques.…Au moyen âge, la rhétorique désignait l'art ou la méthode de conquérir un style, ou tout au moins, d'en favoriser la réussite." Dragonetti, *La Technique poétique des trouvères*, 539.

46. See ibid., 10, 541–53. The "classic" trouvères, Dragonetti argues, "drew the poetic substances of their poems from pure fiction" ("tiré de la fiction pure, la substance poétique de leurs poèmes" (550).

47. Ibid., 61. Scholars commonly refer to the introductory stanza that evokes the natural world—most often springtime—by the German term *Natureingang*; see Werner, "Über den sogenannten Natureingang der Trobadours."

chanson itself is capable of arousing it, owing to its intrinsic quality, then the fiction becomes plausible and the poem authentic, for it implies then that the trouvère, during the time of the song's creation, lived this fiction, that is to say his artistic self, his *mythical self*...had actually experienced the ideality of *fin amour*.[48]

Dragonetti here offers a fascinating account of the perception—indeed, the vivification— of authenticity based on formal techniques and, importantly, as marked out in time by performance. I will return to these points later. For now I want to call attention to the notion of an "artistic self" and "mythical self" that experiences *fin'amors*, and an audience that temporarily suspends its disbelief. Unlike Denomy, Spitzer, and Köhler, Dragonetti does not offer a meaning or function for these lyrics beyond "poetic pleasure" and a reflection of "the tastes of a category of listeners." Meaning stays within the confines of the song, its performance, and its "veil of fictions."[49]

Dragonetti's "veil of fictions," which prevents us from comprehending the social or individual truths encoded within these songs, becomes for Paul Zumthor the "mists of time" that completely obscure our view of the medieval text in anything other than formal terms.[50] "There is a vast and unbridgeable gap between us and the Middle Ages," Zumthor writes. "Economic history, or the history of institutions or ideas, helps us to reconstruct a general frame of reference for the content of each text, but the essence of that content remains beyond the reach of such approaches."[51] By "essence" Zumthor seems to mean a magical (prelapsarian?) union of text and audience, only available within a synchronic relationship. In discussing his motivations for his structuralist approach, Zumthor cleverly figures the medieval text as an *amor de lonh*—a temporally distant beloved Other:

> What I needed was to recognize myself in the Other—the texts—without making myself a mere learned catalog and without renouncing my taste for literature and my need to enjoy the text for its own sake; I needed to see my equal in the Other, to enter into dialogue with it, and, at moments of intense emotion, to experience the by no means innocent pleasure of a love capable of providing the motive for critical study.[52]

---

48. "Si le trouvère réussit à communiquer par sa chanson l'exaltation qui fait vivre ce mythe pendant la durée de son exécution, et si d'autre part, la chanson elle-même est apte à la susciter en raison de sa qualité intrinsèque, la fiction devient vraisemblable et le poème authentique, car il implique alors que le trouvère, durant le temps de la création, ait vécu cette fiction, c'est-à-dire que son moi d'artiste, son *moi mythique*...ait véritablement éprouvé l'idéalité du fin amour." Ibid., 560.

49. Ibid., 544–55 and 243.

50. Chapter 1 in Zumthor's *Essai de poétique médiévale* bears the title "La nuit des temps"—"nuit" meaning "darkness" or "obscurity," and translated by Bennett in *Toward a Medieval Poetics* as "mists" with the author's approval.

51. Zumthor, *Toward a Medieval Poetics*, 3.

52. Zumthor, Introduction to *Toward a Medieval Poetics*, xii.

Not wanting to renounce his pleasures in the text, but not wanting to do violence to it either, Zumthor, like the troubadours, turns to discipline—a rigorous method of empirical description that will not distort the text with "interpretation." Zumthor holds that while we cannot hope to recover the "living experience" of these songs, we can perhaps decode that experience for our time from the text itself. Through a careful accounting of vocabulary, syntax, and form we can discern the unity and synchronicity of "textual time"— a micro-scale of past, present, and future perceived via repetitions, echoes, and correspondences within and across trouvère songs.[53]

The courtly love lyric, reduced to the lower and higher orders of language use, offers the modern critic equal footing with the medieval listener; both can appreciate the "circularity of meaning" and the "endless variety of nuance" to the "poetic manifestations of *fin'amors.*" *Fin'amors*, for Zumthor, is "a system of well-documented oppositions"— courtly/boorish, sense/madness, truth/falsehood, joy/sorrow, and above all presence/ absence, which doubles back to self/other (or subject/object) encoded grammatically in the omnipresent "I" and its reflective opposition in "you" or "she."[54] These binary oppositions, which already double back onto themselves, mingle with the semantic convergences of *aimer*, *trouver*, and *chanter* to create a "system" that is, in fact, a hall of mirrors. Taking a cue from Bernart de Ventadorn's famous reference to Narcissus in *Can vei la lauzeta mover*, Zumthor writes: "yet the singer does not lose himself in living waters, but in the mirror of Her eyes, which are Love, the song, a beloved You made song, universalized like the voice that sings You." And finally this: "The song is therefore its own subject and has no predicate.... The poem is a mirror of itself."[55] Zumthor's analyses of the medieval love lyric thus result in a collapse of structure into tautologies and mirrors. This, ironically, allows "love" to slide inexorably (back) into the field of an expression of "self" and "subjectivity."

WHAT'S IN A NAME? THE SUBJECT AND THE SELF

Reviving the lost subject became the focus of troubadour scholars in the wake of the monumental formalist studies of Dragonetti and Zumthor, which voided the self-expression of the songs by rendering the author and love nothing more than literary motifs. Armed with "close readings" of specific songs, the studies of L. T. Topsfield,

---

53. See his comments on "reading" versus "interpretation," *Toward a Medieval Poetics*, xxi, xxiii, 4–6, and "textual time," 11.

54. Zumthor, *Toward a Medieval Poetics*, 4, 11, 158–61. The reference to Narcissus appears in lines 21–24 of *Can vei la lauzeta mover* (PC 70-43) as edited in *Bernart*, 166–68: "Miralhs, pus me mirei en te / m'an mort li sospir de preon. / C'aissi.m perdei com perdet se / lo bels Narcisus en la fon" (Mirror, since I saw myself reflected in you / deep sighs have been killing me. / I have destroyed myself just as / the beautiful Narcissus destroyed himself in the fountain).

55. Zumthor, *Toward a Medieval Poetics*, 170.

Linda M. Paterson, Ruth Harvey, Jörn Gruber, Simon Gaunt, and Rouben Cholakian explicate particularities rather than universals, finding multiple complex ways in which one troubadour differentiated himself from another.[56] "Love," here, is neither a warm-hearted sentiment nor a cold-hearted slippery signifier, but rather a stable element against which individuality and originality can be measured in the variables of rhetorical style, conceptions of *fin'amors*, intertextual referencing, uses of irony, and even treatment of women. With chapter titles such as "Guilhem IX of Aquitaine and the Quest for Joy," "Peire d'Alverhnhe, First of the 'Vulgares Eloquentes,'" "Master of Words and Women: Arnaut Daniel," or simply "Raimbaut d'Aurenga,"[57] each of these scholars presumes a historically real, singular, coherent "author" behind each name attached to a particular lyric. Furthermore, as Gruber argues, these medieval authors participated self-consciously in a literary tradition that involved emulation and competition among themselves. Where Dragonetti sees "commonplaces," Gruber sees quotations and dialogue; rather than lyrics being "self-regarding," it is the troubadours who are so.[58]

Indeed, in no other medieval musical repertory do we find the cultural necessity of attaching names to song. We have a handful of names of high-standing clerics or members of religious communities associated with sacred song composition—Saint Ambrose, Notker Balbulus, Adémar de Chabannes, Hildegard of Bingen, Adam and Hugh of St. Victor, Philip the Chancellor, Leonin, Perotin. But these sacred repertories do not insist on a *self* in their expression, nor do any of the songs boldly proclaim authorship, as in this troubadour song:

VIII

Lo vers es fis e naturaus	The song is pure and natural
e bos celui qui be l'enten,	and good for those who understand it,
e melher es, qui·l joi aten	and it is better for those who wait
	for joy.

---

56. These studies are: on rhetorical style, Paterson, *Troubadours and Eloquence*; on conceptions of *fin'amors*, Topsfield, *Troubadours and Love*, and Ruth Harvey, *The Troubadour Marcabru and Love*; on intertextual dialogue, Gruber, *Die Dialektik des Trobar*; on irony, Gaunt, *Troubadours and Irony*; on women, Cholakian, *The Troubadour Lyric*.

57. Chapter titles are from (respectively), Topsfield, Paterson, and Cholakian; the simple author-chapter title "Raimbaut d'Aurenga" appears in Topsfield, Paterson, and Gaunt.

58. In his review of Gruber's study, Frederick Goldin writes "The book thus sets itself squarely against the widely held opinion...that the medieval courtly lyric was a self-regarding, self-generating structure of commonplaces...composed solely for the pleasure of formal variation." See Goldin, review of *Die Dialektik des Trobar*, 422. See also Gruber, *Die Dialektik des Trobar*, 1–7, 256–57. In their summary of troubadour scholarship Gaunt and Kay remark, "If...troubadour lyric had often been held up as the most refined and moving celebration of heterosexual love (Lewis, Topsfield), prevailing wisdom by the late 1980s saw it as a sophisticated game men played with each other." See their introduction to *TI*, 6.

IX

| Bernartz de Ventadorn l'enten; | Bernart de Ventadorn understands it; |
| e·l di e·l fai e·l joi n'aten. | he recites it, he composes it, and he waits for joy from it.[59] |

About 460 names of troubadours survive in the song anthologies and other sources, and 264 trouvère names; about sixty of these are considered major figures who can be matched with historical persons documented in other sources, or who, like Bernart de Ventadorn, have a substantial number of attributed lyrics such that a single person (or seemingly coherent "voice") emerges from the songs themselves. Yet, a tenth of the troubadour lyrics (about 250 of more than 2,500), and well over half of trouvère lyrics (1,750 of 2,130), are anonymous compositions—a substantial collection of seemingly "lost" subjects who nevertheless claim subjecthood, or at least its likeness, as one anonymous *devinalh* (a riddle poem) proclaims: "I am and am not, I was and was not."[60]

To what extent, then, is this "I" produced in secular love songs (even anonymous ones) an expression or contemplation of the self? Theological writings from late antiquity (the *Confessions* of Augustine) to the twelfth century (the *Meditations* by Hugh of St. Victor and Guigo I the Carthusian; and the *Ethics* of Abelard) increasingly emphasize contemplation and personal responsibility, and rely on a concept of the self figured by individuality, introspection, intentionality, and coherence.[61] Yet, as Zumthor and Dragonetti argue, the generalities and tautologies of the vernacular lyric throw all these markers of the self into question, revealing a poetic system rather than sincere self-expression. Michel Zink echoes this skeptical assessment of the lyric in *The Invention of Literary Subjectivity*. Although it would seem that the lyric "I" fits his description of "literary subjectivity" as "what marks the text as the point of view of a consciousness,"[62] he maintains that "sung poetry, which is a poetry of rhetorical formalization and ethical generalization, contrasts with recited poetry [thirteenth-century *dits* and *romans*], which is a poetry of the

---

59. From *Chantars no pot gaire valer*, PC 70-15, lines 50–54. Text and translation from *Bernart*, 81–82.

60. "Sui e no suy, fuy e no fuy." This is the opening line of PC 461-226. For an edition of the lyric see Appel, *Provenzalische Chrestomathie*, 82. The song statistics are culled from the inventories of Pillet-Carstens (PC), and Linker, *A Bibliography of Old French Lyrics*.

61. See Stock, "The Self and Literary Experience in Late Antiquity and the Middle Ages." See also the discussion of the twelfth-century "individual" versus "self" in Bynum, *Jesus as Mother*, 82–109. Bynum argues that medieval concepts of the self included knowing an inner spiritual core or soul that was shared by all rather than particular to the individual (see esp. 87); Stock argues that the importance of reading and writing to self-contemplation strengthened the idea of the self as autonomous and individual (see esp. 842). Stephen G. Nichols argues that in Augustine's *Confessions* 11.27–28, "the performative subject becomes aware of itself as an autonomous consciousness through hearing its own voice raised in [psalm] recitation. This is, for Augustine, just the first step in an education which moves progressively toward the discovery of the transcendent ego, a necessary condition for conversion" (147). See Nichols, "Voice and Writing in Augustine and the Troubadour Lyric."

62. Zink, *The Invention of Literary Subjectivity*, 4.

anecdote of the self." It is in these later poetic anecdotes and confessions, Zink asserts, that we can with confidence say the "I" refers to none other but the author.[63]

Following Michel Zink, three scholars, Sarah Kay, Gerald A. Bond, and Peter Haidu, have produced major studies of medieval subjectivity, all of which argue in various ways for a distinction between the self and the subject. Sarah Kay, in *Subjectivity in Troubadour Poetry*, defines "subjectivity" as "the elaboration of a first-person (subject) position in the rhetoric of courtly poetry," but, *contra* Zumthor, she also revives the "autobiographical assumption" in her readings.[64] For Kay, autobiography refers not to "individualistic narrative which is anecdotally true, but rather to self-representations in which discursive generality is tempered by a sense of historical specificity."[65] In other words, the "I" in troubadour lyrics hovers between generalized grammatical subject and particularized historical self.[66] Given this indeterminacy, Kay comes to a twofold conclusion: "the subject," she writes, "can be read not just as a grammatical position, but as articulating [an autonomous] self," while "the 'self' with which the subject allies does not habitually maintain this position of autonomy with any confidence."[67]

Gerald A. Bond, in *The Loving Subject*, traces the development of the twelfth-century "private secular self" that emerged in Romanesque France. This new self takes shape within a dialectic between the subject (the self as formed by Christian ideology) and the secular lyric *persona* (the self formed by desire and eloquence, modeled on Roman authors).[68] In the courts and schools of the Loire Valley region, Bond argues, "various problems of secular identity seem to have condensed quickly onto *amor*." This is due in large part to the scholastic interest in Roman texts that treated love, friendship, and rhetoric, coupling the "subject of desire" with the "subject of eloquence" (as both topic and ideological construct).[69] The "Loire School" of literature saw the emergence of the first troubadour Guilhem IX from Poitiers.

In Bond's formulation, the self is not wholly absorbed by becoming a subject. Even the "loving subject" that ushers in the new private secular self is not stable, susceptible

---

63. Ibid., 38 (quote); see also 22. More recently, A. C. Spearing takes the contrary view that medieval "textual subjectivity" marks "not the presence but the absence of human subjects," insofar as words call attention to themselves as artifice and not a window onto a human consciousness. See Spearing, *Textual Subjectivity*, 30–31, 174, 197, 247.

64. *Subjectivity in Troubadour Poetry*, 1 and 4.

65. Ibid., 16. Kay does not make a clear distinction between this autobiographical self-representation and the "subjectivity" she reads in troubadour lyric, though the latter seems to be confined to the lyric itself and is "inseparable from rhetorical complexity," while the former can stretch across or point outside lyrics.

66. "The boundaries of self and subject...are here thoroughly imprecise." Ibid., 61; see also 49 and 62.

67. Ibid., 213.

68. Bond, *The Loving Subject*, 1–17; for "the loving subject" as liberatory from the church see 99–100. The notion of an adopted persona in writing separate from the person of the author has a long history in literary studies, notably T. S. Eliot's influential essay *The Three Voices of Poetry*.

69. See Bond, *The Loving Subject*, esp. 2–9, 42–69; quotation from 4.

as it is to competing interpellations and the agency of the individual to adapt or refuse. Peter Haidu, in *The Subject, Medieval/Modern*, also argues that competition between ideologies provides the possibility of autonomy and agency. Haidu finds traces of "freedom" in the moments when a subject must choose between warfare and peace, or between loyalty to the overlord and the support of another emerging ideological superstructure, that of an overarching state power, which could discipline the historical violence of the military class. The pondering of such choices can be gleaned from the texts of vernacular culture, which formed an "ideological workspace for medieval society." Haidu sees the love lyric as one such workspace, disseminating the image of male submission to an absent sovereign power—the Lady, who also stands for the state.[70]

While Zink and Kay (to some degree) see subjectivity as a personal monologue with a more or less stable referent—the act of saying "I" by the author (perhaps through a performer)—Bond and Haidu see subjectivity as produced in a dialogue with ideologically-driven discourses, where the referent for the "I" is neither stable, singular, nor altogether sovereign. But neither is this subjectivity altogether conditioned by, or derived from, the terms of being a subject. Haidu describes subjectivity as the flickering experience of agency that exists outside interpellation: "subjectivity is a phase of existence, a moment of disquieted freedom, of hesitation and choice."[71] Here subjectivity is the awareness of one's own capacities as a political subject, including the capacity (however fleeting) to resist, or at least to change, the terms of becoming a subject. Thus, according to these scholars, while the self exceeds the subject, subjectivity seems to encompass both self and subject: in other words, the self is not identical to the subject, but subjectivity is identical to *self*-awareness.[72]

Thus the love song emerges in the interstices between the subject and the self as an artistic utterance that offers at least the representation of self-awareness (Kay), if not also its real possibility for ideological resistance (Bond, Haidu). But in these modern theories of medieval subjectivity, words and their complexity of meaning provide the privileged access to subjectivity to the neglect of the musical language of love songs, which engages the actual voice and, by extension, the body. While the body is traditionally figured in theology as something to be denied, and in philosophy as a source for empirical data, it took on particular significance in cultural theory in the 1970s and 1980s, in part due to feminist writing that interrogated the ways in which bodies,

---

70. Haidu, *The Subject, Medieval/Modern*, esp. 1–6, 11, 78 (quotation), 81–94, and 341–64.

71. Ibid., 347.

72. It is remarkably difficult to find clear definitions of "subjectivity" in the studies discussed above; frequently one finds only sentences that imply a qualitative difference between subjectivity and the abstracted sense of being a subject, such as in Bond, *The Loving Subject*, 14: "Understanding subjects in this way [i.e. responding to multiple interpellations] makes it easier to theorize about subjectivity without losing the agency of a conscious and concrete individual."

gender, and sexuality constrained women's position as subjects of their own actions, as well as subjects of history. Bodies are readable, subjected to ideological spin, most obviously in hierarchical gender assignments and systematic racist practices. Yet psychoanalytic theory teaches us that bodily drives (for food and sex), which belong in the realm of objective "nature," also impact subjectivity; they bring the self into confrontation with an "Other" who gratifies (mother) or frustrates (father) our desires. These drives, then, are necessarily heavily processed to comply with social mores—the restriction of the father that takes ideological form.[73] Augustine knew these drives as well, and his pursuit of self-knowledge involved his own constant interrogation of the influence of his body on his thoughts and intentions, and thus on his subjectivity.

The association of the body with words has biblical origins—the Word made flesh (John 1:14). But this is not a body of Freudian or Augustinian drives and desires: it is a vessel of creation and resurrection. Christ, as the body and voice of God, represented for Augustine and others pure expression that brought creation full circle, allowing man to return to his origins in God. Paul Gehl remarks "parallel and directly analogous to the doctrine of the Incarnate Word, Augustine offered a theory of words, which also embody the Word."[74] Thus by virtue of the Word, all words held some generational potential; names of objects and names of people were inextricably bound to the material and the bodies they labeled. Medieval writers understood the mutually charged, mystical relationship between bodies and words, where the *corpus* of the author leaves its trace in the corpus of uttered words, and where the corpus of words offers an alternative body for the author to inhabit.[75]

The surviving music for troubadour and trouvère songs bears witness to the embodiment of this literature, or at least a representation of that embodiment. In the material history of secular song, however, there are many more bodies and voices to consider than those of the author and his or her texts. Here Zumthor's notion of a collective "love of text" that traverses temporal distance is relevant: performer, compiler, scribe—each of these bodies (selves, subjectivities) left their mark on the words, but also, importantly, on the music. In fact, these may be the only subjective voices to be heard in medieval song.

---

73. For an excellent discussion of key feminist writings and theories of this era see Moi, *Sexual/Textual Politics*.

74. Gehl, "*Competens silentium*," 129. Gehl goes on to write: "It is true Augustine several times implied that the underlying truth of God's message is silent, interior thought, or more precisely the words spoken by the Word in the inner ear of the soul. The crucial and wonderful fact of salvation, however, is the incarnational act, to which the act of preaching and learning about God is the precise analogue."

75. For comments on the relationship of body to text in the Middle Ages see Spence, *Text and the Self in the Twelfth Century*, esp. 1–17, 63–66; Jaouën and Semple, "The Body into Text." For the creational power of words analogous to the Word see Bloch, *Etymologies and Genealogies*, esp. 36, 60–61; and Holmes, *Assembling the Lyric Self*.

LOVE FROM AFAR: BELATED SONGS AND SELF-EXPRESSION

Many scholars have noted that the great push to anthologize troubadour and trouvère songs around 1250 was a nostalgic enterprise, a self-conscious preservation of a musical past. John Haines writes:

> It was at the very point of the waning of the troubadour and trouvère art in the late thirteenth century that patrons commissioned their songs to be collected in what would later be called chansonniers. Medieval editors culled these prestigious poems from raw sources and presented them in sanitized, ornate versions to readers for whom Guilhem de Poitiers and the Châtelain de Coucy were already distant figures.... Increasingly, they were being written down for posterity in books of fine parchment: songs once sung, now stilled by the quill, laid out in long columns of elegant scripts sprinkled with musical notation.[76]

In their own attempts to bridge the temporal gap some medieval compilers wrote prose introductions to the troubadours' songs in the form of biographies (*vidas*) and back stories (*razos*), interpolating newly created narratives within lyric anthologies.[77] We may well ask if such creative writing extended to the music as well. The belated records of these love lyrics and their melodies could at times preserve the past, and at other times reconfigure and even dismantle it in ways that offer a glimpse of notions about the self, about creative agents, and about desire for the Other.

For medieval love songs the temporal gap between the date of composition and the date of the written record for any given song interferes with a neat identification of the named author with his or her creation. This temporal gap closes for troubadours and trouvères composing after 1250, contemporaneous with the written compilations of secular love songs. Carefully ordered song collections of the troubadours Uc de Saint Circ and Guiraut Riquier, and the trouvères Thibaut de Champagne and Adam de la Halle, suggest the authors' direct oversight in compilation, or at least a scribal practice that worked to forge a stronger connection between the authors' selves and their lyric personas.[78] Yet despite the greater possibilities for artistic control over the written record in the second half of the

---

76. Haines, *Eight Centuries of Troubadours and Trouvères*, 14. Haines goes on to say that "[t]he chansonniers' first readers were just as motivated by an antiquarian curiosity as later readers. Seeking to affirm their status with trophy-books, the emerging *nouveaux riches* as well as the old landed class had chansonniers custom made, books which flattered their ethnic heritage with songs in Occitan and French rather than Latin" (15). For an excellent discussion of the cultural function of troubadour collections, see Burgwinkle, "The *Chansonniers* as Books."

77. See Poe, *From Poetry to Prose*; and Burgwinkle, "The *Chansonniers* as Books," 250.

78. For the northern tradition from the trouvère *chansonniers* to Guillaume de Machaut see Huot, *From Song to Book*; for the southern tradition, including the troubadour Uc de Saint Circ, Petrarch, and Dante, see Holmes, *Assembling the Lyric Self*.

thirteenth century, the later trouvère repertory shows an explosion rather than constriction of musical variants, causing one scholar to remark that "since the manuscripts often attribute to the same trouvère a poem surviving with different melodies, one may conclude that the rubrics refer primarily to the poet and not the composer."[79]

Given that the lyrics emphasize the act of singing, and complexly intertwine the concepts of love, self, and song, the inconsistency of musical transmission, or the division of labor between poet and composer, may seem an astonishing feature of the repertory. Indeed, literary scholars tend to ignore the vagaries of the musical transmission, often resorting to romantic, as well as dismissive, treatments of the music, such as this by Dragonetti: "although strophe and melody with the trouvères form an inseparable whole, however, the submission of both to different technical conventions permits the metrical analysis of the strophes without taking into account their melody."[80] In performance, however, the melody may in fact hinder a perception of the poetic structure. Verbal rhymes are rarely given parallel musical settings, paroxytonic rhymes are not musically distinguished from oxytonic rhymes, melismatic extensions create musical phrases of different lengths from poetic lines that have identical syllable counts, melodic contours may override poetic caesuras, and while the common musical repetition scheme (ABAB CDEF) does help to mark the mid-point syntactic break of the stanzas, there is no poetic reason why one half of the stanza should receive parallel musical settings and the other not. The existence of multiple distinct melodies for a single lyric casts further doubt upon the "inseparable whole" of music and words, as well as the unity of expression.[81]

---

79. See Karp, "Troubadours, trouvères, §III, 1: Music: Manuscript sources." Given the considerably smaller sample of surviving troubadour melodies with multiple concordances (about 50 out of 300 extant melodies) as compared to over well over 1,000 trouvère lyrics with multiple musical settings, a comparison of the relative stability of musical settings cannot be made.

80. "Bien que strophe et mélodie forment chez les trouvères un tout inséparable, cependant, la soumission des deux à des conventions techniques différentes, permet l'analyse métrique des strophes sans tenir compte de leur mélodie." Dragonetti, *La Technique poétique des trouvères*, 561; Zumthor echoes and elaborates: "the most important, but also the most elusive, feature of the chanson is its musical aspect. Words and music proceed from a single source of inspiration and generate each other in a reciprocal relationship, which is so close that any analysis must inevitably take simultaneous account of both. Unfortunately, far too few texts have come down to us with their music, and in any case the interpretation of the latter poses far more difficult problems even than the establishment of the former. It is therefore inevitable that, except in a few cases, I shall concentrate my remarks on the linguistic aspects of the chanson, in the hope that this will allow us to see in negative, as it were, the original, positive, harmonic design" (*Toward a Medieval Poetics*, 144). Zumthor does not mention that about 300 troubadour melodies and over 2,000 trouvère melodies survive. He assumes that melodies were "normally composed at the same time of the text" though he acknowledges the problem of the historical remove of lyric-text from song-text; see "An Overview: Why the Troubadours?," 13.

81. For a good illustration of radically different melodies for the same lyric, see the comparative transcriptions of Bernart de Ventadorn's *Can par la flor justa·l vert fuelh* (PC 70-41) in Aubrey, *The Music of the Troubadours*, 152–53. These melodies also illustrate the variety of syllabic extensions. For her part, Aubrey argues that the "inseparability [of words and music] cannot necessarily be recognized word by word and note by note, but rather through larger constructs of theme, structure, and style" (*The Music of the Troubadours*, xviii). Although she includes a detailed discussion of the melodic forms of troubadour songs (146–94), she offers only a brief

There is yet another complication to be considered: the musical settings of troubadour and trouvère lyrics show a relative paucity of information when compared to the written record of contemporaneous repertories. The thirteenth century witnessed the emergence of modal and mensural rhythmic notation in conjunction with the growth of contrapuntal genres such as organum, conductus, and the motet. Yet despite the availability of these other vocabularies of notation and polyphonic musical formats, the music scribes recorded each troubadour and trouvère song as a single line of melody in "undifferentiated" note shapes—that is, note shapes that do not encode relative rhythmic values. Nor are there indications for instrumental accompaniment, planned or improvised. All in all, the *chansonniers* depict a curiously conservative musical practice for these secular love songs, one that seems conceptually at odds with the virtuosity of the words. Are these monophonic songs to be read literally, as indicative of actual musical practice? Or might they be distilled, schematic, or symbolic in nature?

These questions funnel into one central problematic for medievalists: how do we "read" the manuscripts—as faithful historical records or artful historical constructions? Taken as faithful records, text variants become evidence of scribal error, or scribal fidelity to an oral transmission that has strayed from the mouth or pen of the composer. Since the nineteenth century, philologists have tidied up textual variants based on one of two principles: either they construct an ideal text based on a genealogy of versions, or they designate one authoritative "best text" from the manuscripts. Both approaches effectively render the manuscripts transparent, creating the illusion of a single, "original" text (and a single, original creator) behind the diffuse information of the sources.[82] For the sake of convenience, most literary critics still rely on these editions for their close readings, even when their interpretation argues for an unstable subject.[83]

Ironically, the "best"—or perhaps only—text for the music is often not the best source for the words, as is the case for Jaufre Rudel's *Lanqan li jorn son lonc en mai*. Yet musicologists often make a leap of faith that the melodies retain something of their "essence" first created by the named composer. For example, Elizabeth Aubrey asserts:

> The songs of the troubadours existed as definite "pieces" whether in written form or not. In most cases, where there are two or more readings of a troubadour's melody, they share elements that enable us to recognize in each a version of the same melody.... Such melodic stability derives at least in part from the coherence and consistency *designed by the composer*. The musical elements that make stability

discussion of their relationship to poetic structure (194–97), concluding that "A direct concord between specific poetic elements and the musical elements that resemble them—like poetic rhyme and musical cadences—is rare. Music and poetry followed their own rules, and in the area of structure this is particularly true" (194).

82. See Nichols, "Introduction: Philology in a Manuscript Culture."

83. See those studies by Topsfield, Paterson, Ruth Harvey, and Kay mentioned above.

possible are difficult to identify.... [b]ut they are the elements that both restricted variation by scribes and singers whose *aim was to transmit the essential song*, and freed them to recreate the song without fear of losing that essence.[84]

On one hand Aubrey mystifies troubadour melody with references to hard-to-identify elements and "essences," while on the other hand she attempts to demystify Zumthor's "mists of time" that obscure the subjectivity of the song: the essence is the design of the composer, and the aim of the scribes and singers is to render that essence faithfully.

But how can we know the aims (or the skill level) of the singers who carried the tune for as many as one hundred years? Some literary scholars concede that oral transmission does challenge the privileged status of the composer and the "work," while others argue for a cooperative model that always keeps the troubadour's hand in play, so to speak.[85] Zumthor coined the word *mouvance* to describe the mobility and instability of the songs produced by transmission, which, along with their homogeneity, further evacuated the subject or "I" of the songs.[86] Amelia Van Vleck saw *mouvance* as something the troubadours themselves invited or discouraged with simple or complex rhyme patterns and metaphorical vocabulary.[87] Sarah Kay, who argues for a fundamentally oral conception of the songs, nevertheless restores the supremacy of the troubadour's subjectivity by hypothesizing that "the body of the performer, enacting the 'character' of a troubadour, offers a possible visible correlative of the first-person voice, and connects it, at least temporarily, with social experience."[88] The songs, then, are like dramatic soliloquies; for Kay, the singer becomes transparent much like the manuscripts, as he or she makes visible (and audible) the subjective voice of the troubadour. Thus all performance becomes a mimesis of the troubadour's subjectivity.

Yet scholars in the late 1980s began to look *at*, rather than *through*, the sources, focusing on the emergent "manuscript culture" in which writing itself became an artful practice, evincing its own "poetics" and "mimesis." As Stephen G. Nichols explains:

> The apparently straightforward act of copying manuscripts is not free from mimetic intervention, either. In the act of copying a text, the scribe supplants the original poet, often changing words or narrative order, suppressing or shortening some sections, while interpolating new material in others....Recalling that almost all

---

84. Aubrey, *The Music of the Troubadours*, 32 (emphasis added).

85. See Gaunt, "Orality and Writing." For a thorough discussion of oral and written transmission with regard to the trouvère repertory see O'Neill, *Courtly Love Songs*.

86. See Zumthor, *Essai de poétique médiévale*, 65–75, and the definition in the index; *mouvance* is translated as "instability" in *Toward a Medieval Poetics*, 41–49.

87. Van Vleck, *Memory and Re-Creation*; see also Pickens, "Jaufré Rudel et la poétique de la mouvance."

88. Kay, *Subjectivity in Troubadour Poetry*, 170; see 132–38 for her argument that a song's performance is akin to swearing oaths and bearing witness.

manuscripts postdate the life of the author by decades or even centuries, one recognizes the manuscript matrix as a place of radical contingencies: of chronology, of anachronism, of conflicting subjects, or representation.[89]

Within the "new philology," textual and musical variants are viewed as potentially meaningful; they point to acts of creation and self-assertion by compilers and scribes into the written (re)construction of a performance tradition. In this way, writing is both a mimesis and a performance of subjectivity.

Musicologists and contemporary performers have long grappled with the meaning of the written musical record for troubadour and trouvère songs.[90] Early opinions held that the notation was schematic and incomplete, demanding a heavy interpretive hand. This led to the transcription of melodies with modal or mensural rhythms, and, in audio recordings, to the inclusion of instrumental accompaniment, preludes, and interludes. Such schematic, music-oriented views were eventually challenged by a literal interpretation of the manuscripts' conservatism: the authentic sound of troubadour and trouvère songs was a single voice singing a melody in a rhythmically flexible delivery that would complement in some way the poetic structure of the words. Most proponents of this literal, word-oriented view see melodies as supplemental rather than integral to the expression of the song. Hendrik van der Werf argues for a declamatory performance in which rhythm is guided by the dramatic meaning of the words; John Stevens argues for an isosyllabic performance, based on speculative notions of the numerical harmony between the "music" of the words and the "music" of the melody. Christopher Page, however, argues for a "rhapsodic" performance based on an ethos he derives from the rhetoric of the lyrics themselves, specifically their "high seriousness" and oratory quality. He writes:

> Whence the characteristic manner of the High Style song: neither gregarious in impulse nor indulgent towards its listeners, it usually lacks any choric refrains which might invite us across the space that separates us from the singer and draw us into the song.... Indeed, the idea of the song as the composition of a self-conscious artist is constantly kept in the listener's mind and is a crucial element of the *grand chant* manner.

In addition to refrains, Page argues that meter and instruments also break the barrier between singer and audience with their appeal to the body.[91]

---

89. Nichols, "Introduction: Philology in a Manuscript Culture," 8. Key studies that pursue this line of argument include Huot, *From Song to Book*; Kendrick, *The Game of Love*; Gaunt, "Discourse Desired."

90. An excellent summary and discussion of these positions appears in Aubrey, *The Music of the Troubadours*, 237–73. Aubrey herself maintains an agnostic position and suggests an eclectic approach to performance. See also the careful considerations of van der Werf, *The Chansons of the Troubadours and Trouvères*, 14–21, 26–45; and Leech-Wilkinson, *The Modern Invention of Medieval Music*.

91. Page, *Voices and Instruments*, 15; see also 38–39. Zink proposes exactly the opposite of Page: that the "circularity of the chansons...[and] the presence of melody, through which they were turned over to their performers—all

Although the idea of the troubadour as the serious artist who stands apart from the crowd is tinged with romanticism, underlying Page's argument for rhapsodic monophony is a notion of performance similar to that of Kay, namely that the performance of love songs amounts to a mimesis of the troubadour's subjectivity, the illusion of which is maintained by the insistence on autonomy from the audience. Thus monophony itself is mimetic of monologue, the way one says "I" in purely musical terms. But not all monophony, for the monophony of sacred chant represents the opposite ethos—the joining of many voices into one for the unified praise of God.[92] In the context of chant, monophony emphatically represents the collective voice, not the subjective voice. Given the unrecoverable practices of music-making that took place in courts, encampments, outdoor festivals, clerical quarters, and private homes, it is unlikely that secular monophony was everywhere and always performed monophonically. The greatest significance of the monophony of secular love songs, then, may be its symbolic function—the representation of autonomous self-expression, of the individual voices of troubadours and trouvères.

The word "voice" has literal and metaphorical meanings: the literal voice performs sound and words in real time, but an imagined or metaphorical voice can also be "heard" in the written word, which may or may not be imitative of speech. The privileging of speech over writing and visa versa has been much disputed in post-structuralist theory as well as medieval literary history, though in the medievalists' circles a consensus has been reached that oral and written procedures were coterminous and interdependent, especially within the medieval art of memory.[93] In modern pedagogical literature concerned with writing style and rhetoric, the metaphor of "voice" has been used variously—to designate verb modalities (as in "active voice" or "passive voice"); to describe adopted literary personas or narrative stances (as in T. S. Eliot's "three voices of poetry" or Wayne Booth's reliable or unreliable authorial voice); to mean unique personal expression in expository prose (finding an "authentic voice" or "one's own voice" in writing).[94] Stephen G. Nichols argues that thirteenth- and fourteenth-century *chansonniers* clearly link the voice to writing with depictions of flowing scrolls that drape from the hands of the composer in the act of writing, or singing, or perhaps both at once. Thus writing is charged with the significance of embodiment analogous to the act of singing—a blurring of the literal and the literary voice that is an axiom of the lyrics.[95] With medieval love songs, then, ascertaining

this allowed the audience to take total possession of the poem and locate its own subjectivity behind an 'I' having little to do with that of the poet"; *The Invention of Literary Subjectivity*, 45.

92. On the theological ideal of the unanimity of spirit in singing *quasi una voce* (as if one voice) that underlies sacred chant see Crocker, *An Introduction to Gregorian Chant*, 24–25.

93. See Carruthers, *The Book of Memory*; Berger, *Medieval Music and the Art of Memory*.

94. Bowden, "The Rise of a Metaphor." In *The Composer's Voice*, Edward T. Cone applied the concepts of authorial voice and persona from Eliot and Booth to musical composition.

95. Nichols, "Voice and Writing," 141, and 151–53.

the "voice" is both a crucial and elusive enterprise: it is crucial to understanding the expressive gamut of these songs, and elusive insofar as "voice" is always already "voices."

In the performance of songs we can readily hear what we call "expression" in the manipulation of the voice—phrasing, articulations, mannerisms that are mimetic of emotional speech. Yet for medieval music, we have only the visual text from which to glean expression. In art historical terms, "expressive" and "expressionist" refer to a rendering of interior or psychological reality, as opposed to representing the external world, through an exploitation of the materials of the medium itself; in painting, expression resides in blobs or drips of paint, obvious brush strokes, unnatural coloring, flattened perspective, and stylized, distorted, or abstract forms.[96] Likewise, critics speak of an "expressive" use of space, punctuation, and capitalization in the poems of Emily Dickinson, Ezra Pound, and E. E. Cummings—a concern not only with the visual form of the written word on the page, but also with the transfer from the eye to the mind's internal voice and ear.[97] These features are expressive because they stray from or disrupt tradition or norms, and they turn our attention to the particulars of the given medium and artistic process itself: a "painterliness" and "writerliness" marks the artist's or writer's subjective, idiosyncratic language.

In this book I strive to hear self-expression—the subjective, personal voice—as recorded in the music of some medieval love songs, in their handling of melody, rhythm, form, and genre. Each chapter concerns manipulations of these musical materials in ways that expose a self-consciousness about musical composition—in other words, an expressive "composerliness" that is akin to the artful self-consciousness about the creative process that is so characteristic of the lyrics. But I also strive to understand how melody, rhythm, form, and genre give voice to the complex issues of self and subjectivity encoded in medieval love. It is not my intention to create an overarching system for pinpointing personal styles of named composers.[98] Indeed, the music of these love songs, having

---

96. Shulamith Behr observes that "nowadays, any artist may be deemed 'expressionist' if they exaggeratedly distort form and apply paint in a subjective, intuitive and spontaneous manner"; as a movement in art, Expressionism emerged in various communities of avant-garde artists in Germany prior to and between the World Wars, and was later modified as Abstract Expressionism in the United States after World War II. See Behr, *Expressionism*, 6. See also Gordon, *Expressionism*; Crawford and Crawford, *Expressionism in Twentieth-Century Music*, esp. 1–22; and Donahue, introduction to *German Expressionism*. The conclusion will say more about modern and medieval "expressionism."

97. One critic remarks that early editions of Emily Dickinson "normalized her expressive punctuation"; see Cotter, "My Hero, the Outlaw of Amherst," 28. Regarding Ezra Pound's "Canto 74," Richard Sieburth writes about the confluence of musical rhythm and the particular technology of the typewriter: "Pound's retyping of his notebooks…resulted in a more precise and expressive scoring of its words on the page—each vocable, each punctuation mark zoned by two thumps (or musical rests) on the space bar, which the publisher had difficulty transcribing." See Sieburth's introduction to Ezra Pound, *The Pisan Cantos*, xxvi. On E. E. Cummings see Tartakovsky, "E. E. Cummings's Parentheses," 215–47.

98. For such composer studies see O'Neill, *Courtly Love Songs*, 93–131 (Gautier de Dargies), 136–52 (Minot de Paris), and 181–205 (Adam de la Halle); see also Aubrey, *The Music of the Troubadours*, 203–36 for a discussion

retained the marks of performers, compilers, and scribes along the way of transmission, troubles the notion of a unified authorial "self" as the overarching expressive agent. Thus with the songs I examine here, I hope to elaborate the sprawling nature of their subjective voices, and their density of selves that is a direct function of their music.

Chapter 1, "The Turn of the Voice," begins this study with the concept of "the turn" in Althusser's theory of the subject, and its musical mimesis in *tornadas* and refrains. *Tornadas* are the terminating lines of a lyric; in most cases they are fragmentary half-stanzas or semi-strophes that break the formal and thematic structure of the strophic song with an abrupt change of voice and address, from the "timeless" idiomatic language of courtly love to a sudden rooting in the author's present. Filled with concerns of patronage, transmission, and reputation, *tornadas* expose the interpellative force of language and song. Yet this moment of transparent subjectivity is to be rendered musically, returning the singer to the second half of the melody, recycling rhymes, notes, and sometimes words in a way that resembles refrain procedures. In the trouvère repertory, repeated refrains in the context of dance songs are allegedly group responses, while in the context of *chansons*, motets, and narratives, they often represent a quotation or reported song—a repetition of a different order. *Tornadas* and refrains, then, change "voice" in the sense that the singing voice of the performer takes on a different manner of address aligned with the formal or implied return of music. These musico-poetic turns create possibilities for self-expression: they formalize and thus authorize the disruption of the conventional voice, signaling the fissures between the self and the subject, as well as subjective and collective voices.

The theme of turns or returns permeates this study, as a theoretical construct, an element of musical form, and a temporal relation. Most of the pieces I will consider in the subsequent chapters have the quality of belatedness, the condition of being delayed: they are mono-phonic songs written at a moment when such monophony was going out of style and being replaced by refrain songs such as the *rondeau*, the *virelai* or *dansa*, and the *ballade*, and by polyphonic motets. In the ongoing development of monophony, composers (mostly unnamed) combined backward- and forward-looking characteristics, fusing newer melodic, rhythmic, and refrain procedures with older monophonic idioms and genres of the troubadours and trouvères to construct a unique musical voice. These late, "marginal" melodies, often neglected by scholars, have much to tell us about musical responses to the

---

of developments in musical style through the generations of troubadours. I do not treat the trobairitz and women trouvères separately or specifically. Although this repertory raises fascinating questions regarding gender and expression, there are few extant notated examples from named women composers (one in Occitan, and five in French), and the anonymous songs, and songs attributed to men that belong to the category *chanson de femme*—songs that employ a female protagonist attached to specific themes (*aube, chanson d'ami, chanson de mal mariée, chanson de croisade, chanson de toile, chanson d'ami*)—do not show marked differences in melodic style or in their treatment by the compilers and scribes. I do discuss issues of gender and the appearance of women protagonists, interlocutors, or addressees, throughout, and especially in chapters 4 and 5. For studies of the trobairitz and women trouvères see *Songs of the Women Troubadours*; and *Songs of the Women Trouvères*.

courtly *chanson* tradition. In their turning back—within form and within time—they can be considered *tornadas* writ large, concluding the long *chanson* tradition. One manuscript in particular serves as an exceptional document of such medieval musical expression, and thus as a keystone linking all the chapters in various ways: trouv. *M* (also troub. *W*) contains a wide array of repertories (monophonic and polyphonic, northern and southern) and many chronological layers of additions that bridge the thirteenth and fourteenth centuries; its unique collection of *descort* melodies, early *formes fixes* songs, and idiosyncratic recomposed *chansons* expose the processes of using musical genres, melodic forms, and notation in expressive ways over time. In no other manuscript can we observe such clear and persistent grappling with the musical parameters of the classic vernacular love song.[99]

Chapter 2, "Delinquent *Descorts* and Medieval Lateness," focuses on the emergence of the *descort* in troubadour and trouvère repertories and its particularly self-conscious play with form, genre, and performance. Disruption and belatedness define the *descort*, which is a heterostrophic lyric genre that expresses the idea of "discord" in formal and melodic ways by orchestrating conflicts between sense and sound. Only four Occitan *descorts* survive with music, and three are late additions to trouv. *M*, which contains the largest single collection of notated French *descorts* as well. Here we can see an exchange of ideas among various scribes who "interpreted" *descorts* at different stages of the manuscript's production. Musical and paleographical evidence further suggests that the influence of the *descort*, its non-strophic structure and its principle of discord and disruption, can be seen in the *lais* and *chansons* added to the manuscript at some point after the Occitan *descorts*. Thus the *descorts* began a domino effect of musical composition within trouv. *M* that seems to be self-consciously discordant with the musical tradition of the *chanson*, long before the presumed "autumn" of the Middle Ages or the decline of chivalric culture.

Chapter 3, "Changing the Subject of the *Chanson d'amour*," investigates cross-temporal relationships of voice between anonymous scribes and compilers and the named authors whose songs and identities they recorded. The chapter first considers the discrete *libelli* of songs by Thibaut de Champagne and Adam de la Halle preserved at either end of the *chansonnier* trouv. *T*. Through *compilatio* over time, scribes assembled the individual authorial voices of these two trouvères and created a genealogical line from the early-century Champagne noble to the late-century Artesian cleric. The second part of this chapter looks at the dismantling effects of continued *compilatio* by examining three more late additions to trouv. *M*, specifically three strophic *chansons* by named trouvères whose music has been radically recomposed by later scribes "under the influence" of the *descort*, but also influenced by popular refrains and refrain songs. The unusual forms, melodic behavior, and mensural notation betray an estrangement from the conventions of the

---

99. Henceforth I will identify this source as trouv. *M* since the bulk of its contents is trouvère songs. Other *chansonners* contain examples of what I call expressive uses of mensural notation, chromatic notes, melodic variants, genre, and even organization—especially trouv. *N, O, R, T, V,* and *a*; these sources will be discussed throughout this study.

repertory, and can be read as conscious distortions or parodies—unauthorized versions engaged in an open-ended musical debate about the expressive confines of the aristo-cratic courtly *chanson*.

Chapter 4, "The Hybrid Voice of Monophonic Motets," examines a subgenre of mono-phonic songs labeled *motet enté* (meaning "grafted motet") in some medieval sources. These songs were conceived and crafted from the fusing of the single-voiced *chanson* and the multi-voiced motet. The term "motet" is itself multivalent, for medieval sources often refer to refrains as "motets." Refrains conceptually multiply and blur voices; thus they encapsulate in a figurative way the literal, aural effects of polyphonic motets. Composers, with the horticultural technique of grafting in mind, worked the many guises and voices of the motet into single-stanza, free verse songs that strongly resemble triplum or mote-tus parts, but which are emphatically monophonic. As a compositional practice, grafting has an analog in present-day "sampling" found in popular music; both grafting and sam-pling create musical hybrids that ask readers and listeners to access their knowledge of multiple musical and literary contexts. The medieval "monophonic motet," as both a product of grafting and a graft onto the central *chanson* repertory, calls attention to the cross-genre, and in some cases cross-gender, dialogues contained within a single voice.

Chapter 5, "Machaut's Turn to Monophony," continues the discussion of the refrain as a vehicle for deriving a personal voice from a public one, and returns to belated and discor-dant melodic styles as a means of signifying authentic self-expression. It begins with the question: Why did Guillaume de Machaut write so many monophonic *virelais*? Machaut composed the bulk of his *chansons* in the new *formes fixes* as polyphony, yet he retained monophony for twenty-five of his thirty-three *virelais*. These monophonic *virelais* consti-tute the second most numerous genre in his musical oeuvre. The chapter examines the expressive meaning of both monophony and the *virelai* form, which is the only *forme fixe* to feature a substantial refrain, in the context of the *Remede de Fortune*, the *Voir Dit*, and his "collected works" manuscripts; and it considers their possible genealogical ties to Occitan *dansas*, and their relationship to Machaut's other monophonic—and decidedly archaic—genre, the *lai*. Furthermore, a series of Machaut's *lais* alternate male and female voices, and a few but significant examples of his *virelais* follow suit. As both nostalgic and new, the monophonic *virelai* participates in Machaut's programmatic exploration of the expressive lyric voice that also involves an exploration of the gendered voice.

With the *virelais* of Guillaume de Machaut we do not exactly come "full circle" to the *tornadas* of chapter 1; rather, we find ourselves on a spiral staircase, constantly turning round, though moving to new locations. Formal and temporal turns and returns, the dis-ruption of sense with sound, the troubling of genre and gender with hybrid subjectivi-ties—these are some of the means by which medieval musicians differentiated their voices within the corporate language of the love song, and used music to explore the possibility of self-expression.

1

The Turn of the Voice

Reconogut	I have recognized you,
t'ai, Pan-Perdut,	Pan-Perdut,
e cuiavas ton nom celar:	and you thought you could hide your name from me:
qan tornaretz	when you return
segurs seretz	you can be sure
de seignor et jeu de joglar.	of a master and I of a minstrel.

Thus ends the song *[A]d un estrun* ("In a hurry"), one of two linked lyrics in a seeming exchange of poetic insults between Marcabru and his patron Audric. Both lyrics, however, are attributed to Marcabru and appear successively in most sources.[1] In *[A]d un estrun* Audric addresses Marcabru by name in the first stanza, where he is depicted as in a hurry to leave the court, and by the *senhal* or code name Pan-Perdut, meaning "Vagabond," in the last. The themes of leaving and returning appropriately open and close the song, perhaps representing a cycle in the life of a musician, but also the returns of the song itself—its repeat of the melody with each stanza of words, and its repeat performances that ensure Marcabru's recognition.

---

1. PC 293-20. For text and translation see *Marcabru*, 282–83. The companion lyric is *Seigner n'Audric* (PC 293–43). They appear in succession and with attributions to Marcabru in troub. *A, C, I, K, R*. In troub. *a¹* the two lyrics are headed with the rubric "la tenzon de marcabrus e de segner nenrics" (the *tenso* of Marcabru and Lord Audric). See the commentary for both lyrics in *Marcabru*, 278–79 and 530–31.

The verb *tonaretz* relates directly to the name given by late thirteenth- and early four-teenth-century treatises to the final stanza or half-stanza of lyrics: the *tornada*, meaning the "turn" or "return."[2] *Las Leys d'Amors*, which contains the only detailed description of *tornadas*, prescribes that *tornadas* should have the same meter as the last half of the final stanza, and that they should address the recipient or messenger with one or more *senhals*.[3] Thus Marcabru's stanza seems to announce its function within the lyric, to close the lyric with a marked return, here not a return to the mid-point as became the norm for later *tornadas*, but with an explicit reference to the act of returning.

We can also read *tornaretz* as "turn," and thus find resonances with another act of Marcabru as presented in the manuscripts: he turns his own voice into that of his lord and pointedly marks the relationship of power: "when you (re)turn, you can be sure of a master, and I of a minstrel." Although *[A]d un estrun* is not a love lyric per se, we can rec-ognize the same themes in play, such as the interdependence of self and song, and the assumed (perhaps pretended) dynamic between agency and subordination that animates the troubadour's subjective voice.

In 1970, Louis Althusser, influenced by Marx and Lacan, published a compelling alle-gory of the subject that describes the inaugural moment of subjectivity—the psychic experience of autonomy and agency—as a turn. Althusser used the term "interpellation" to describe the way ideology creates "subjects" out of "individuals." He illustrated inter-pellation with the narrative of "the most commonplace everyday police (or other) hail-ing: 'Hey, you there!'"

> Assuming that the theoretical scene I have imagined takes place in the street, the hailed individual will turn round. By this mere one-hundred-and-eighty-degree physical conversion, he becomes a *subject*." Why? Because he has recognized that the hail was "really" addressed to him, and that "it was *really him* who was hailed" (and not someone else).[4]

In contrast to medieval personification allegories, populated by abstractions such as Love or Reason, here quotidian human characters (the police, the individual on the street) per-sonify large abstract categories—namely, the dominating force of ideology and its state or linguistic apparatuses, and its subjects who are made self-reflective only as a condition of being addressed by an apparatus of ideology.

---

2. For a discussion of the origin and medieval use of *tornada* and related terms, see Mölk, "Deux remarques sur la tornada."

3. For an edition and translation into modern French see Gatien-Arnoult, ed., *Las Leys d'Amors*, 1:338–41; for an edition and discussion of version C, see Anglade, ed., *Las Leys d'Amors*, esp. 2:176–77 for the passage on the *tornada*.

4. See Althusser, "Ideology and Ideological State Apparatuses," 48.

Elaborating Althusser's famous allegorical scene of the policeman's hail, Judith Butler argues that the consequent "turn" of the person who hears the hail signals the paradoxical condition wherein this subordinating interpellation by power can seem the deployment of power:

> [P]ower that at first appears as external, pressed upon the subject, pressing the subject into subordination, assumes a psychic form that constitutes the subject's self-identity. The form this power takes is relentlessly marked by a figure of turning, a turning back upon oneself or even a turning *on* oneself.... That this figure is itself a "turn" is rhetorically, performatively spectacular; "turn" translates the Greek sense of "trope." Thus the trope of the turn both indicates and exemplifies the tropological status of the gesture.[5]

Butler goes on to link this "turn" through its Greek etymon "trope" or *tropos*, which connotes a directional "turn" as well as a "manner" of behavior or speech, to figurative language, such as metaphor, which deviates from customary uses of language to generate meanings that are "irreducibly mimetic and performative."[6] This concept of the trope allows Butler to mark a condition of being prior to subjecthood that is impossible to describe grammatically.[7] The figure who makes the turn, and the gesture of the turn itself, are tropological in that they are outside customary language; in other words, and for my purposes, this key moment that generates subjectivity is a poetic one. Furthermore, this moment takes a musical, even balletic form of call and response. The call is the direct address by power, the response is the 180 degree turn of the hearer. By turning to respond, the subject enacts not only the tropes of poetic language, but also the strophes of sung poetry. In ancient Greek choral lyrics, the demarcation of the metrical segment called the *strophe*—meaning "turn," like *tropos*, but with a twist of the body as a wrestler, horse, or snake might make—coordinated with a physical turning of the chorus.[8] Thus, with respect to interpellation, the poetic turns of strophe and trope, of form and content, inscribe the turn of the subject, the moment of imminent subjectivity.

In this chapter, I want to bracket questions about what subjectivity "is"—monologue, discursive formation, or dialectic—as pursued by the various medievalists discussed in the introduction. Instead, I will examine the places in medieval song where subjectivities

---

5. Butler, *The Psychic Life of Power*, 3–4.

6. Ibid., 4, and 201–202n1; also s.v. τρόπος Liddell and Scott, *A Greek–English Lexicon*. Nathaniel B. Smith notes that the anonymous classical treatise *Rhetorica ad Herennium*, a primary source for rhetorical theory throughout the Middle Ages, "inventoried forty-five figures of speech (including ten later labeled 'tropes,' that is, 'turnings' of the ordinary meaning of words)"; see Smith, "Rhetoric," 402.

7. On the relationship between grammar and ontology see Butler, *Psychic Life of Power*, 10–11, 117–18, and 124.

8. The strophe was performed in one direction, and its metrical equivalent, the antistrophe, was performed in another direction. S.v. στροφή, Liddell and Scott, *A Greek–English Lexicon*. See also Ley, *The Theatricality of Greek Tragedy*, 167–73.

emerge in concerted formal and thematic ways—specifically, in the "irreducibly mimetic and performative" turning points that are *tornadas*, *envois*, and refrains.

RECOGNITION AND SELF-CONSCIOUSNESS IN MUSICAL FORM

Subjective expressions are marked as such by the contingencies of time, place, and person reflected somehow in the utterance. Music indexes time, place, and person with sound organized by patterns of repetition (of key pitches, motives, phrases, sections) that prompt the listener to track time through the contrast of the familiar with the unfamiliar. The return of familiar phrases not only marks progress forward through time, but also refers back in time, pressing the past into the present moment. Literal repetition creates the feeling of stasis; varied repetition creates the feeling of development, of a dynamic or dramatic process. The more literal repetition there is, the more structured and stylized the expression seems and the further away from spontaneity, independence, and singularity—those things that evoke the individual. In the *canso* and *chanson d'amour*, the principal genres of the troubadours and trouvères, the words are structured into isometric stanzas, that is, the number of lines and their syllable counts repeat without variation from one strophe to the next (the rhymes may or may not repeat strophically). Since the *chansonniers* usually set only the first stanza of words to music, we assume that the whole melody repeats with the subsequent stanzas, more or less decorated by the performer, but not enough to lose the sense of the return of familiar music with changing sets of words.

Strophic repetition of melody, though somewhat inflexible for reflecting shifts of mood, nevertheless highlights the words by giving our ears a minimum amount of new musical information to process over time. The repeating melody sets up a control by which we can appreciate the different shades of meaning and subtle sonorities of words intoned over the same notes. Strophic repetition no doubt brought particular challenges and pleasures to the singers of *cansos* and *chansons*. With lyrics consisting of as many as seven or eight stanzas, monotony becomes a critical issue, at least for modern-day performers and their audiences. If no other "orchestration" is used to change up the texture or color of the sound and refresh the ear, the event of the song becomes focused on the voice. It may be that our present-day tastes are less tolerant of strophic songs: we like to dress up our repetitions with dramatic changes that grab our attention in order to create the illusion of a dynamic process.

Christopher Page argues against instrumental accompaniment for the troubadour *canso*. For Page, the "self-conscious artistry" of these songs "forbids us to sing or to do anything which will remove the song and the singer from the centre of our attention"; such distractions from the singer include instrumental accompaniment, metric regularity, and even narrative.[9] This focus on the voice, intensified by strophic repetition,

---

9. Page, *Voices and Instruments*, 14; see also 15–16 and 38.

becomes a focus on the psychology of self, or a mode of self-consciousness fundamentally opposed to the physicality and participatory nature of choral refrains or dance. Paul Zumthor, however, imagines a lost medieval aesthetic that places dance and a communal voice at the center of medieval texts. Zumthor writes: "The point of departure for a medieval poetics ought to be the consideration of that inner beauty in the human voice.... This beauty can, it is true, be conceived of as being particular or special to the individual who gives it vocalization.... But it is conceivable also as a social and historical beauty in that it unites all human beings and, by the use we make of it, shapes a shared culture."[10] The vocality of medieval texts is encoded in "discursive recurrences"—from the repercussion of sounds and words, to refrains and strophic repetition—that construct a "spatiotemporal experience" within which the audience can participate.[11] The pleasure of repetition, here extending to repeat performances, is described in a *tornada* ending Bernart de Ventadorn's song *Ges de chantar no·m prem talans*:

Lo vers aissi com om plus l'au	The song, the more one hears it,
vai melhuran tota via.	improves continually.
E i aprendon per la via	They will learn it on the way,
cil c'al Poi lo volran saber.	those in Puy who want to know it.[12]

Bernart's song draws the audience into its orbit—or, as Zumthor describes, into an ideal, communal dance (perhaps an unmarked reference to the ancient choric "strophe") that unites the voice and gestures of the performer with recognition and response by the audience. Thus the audience is not passive, but also performing. For Zumthor, this performing audience includes present-day medievalists: "we, as medievalists, come as *interpreters*. But here I should like to attach to this word those connotations which are linked to it when applied to the musician or the actor: the idea of producing something, or a special knowledge that is active and capable of bringing about a transformation—and why not, too, the idea of dance?"[13]

Dance as a model for involvement with a text neatly replaces that of psychological identification or emotional empathy: it suggests an embodied engagement without questions of sincerity, interiority, and self-expression. Hearing, learning, and performing are separate activities from composing, however, and medieval love lyrics frequently maintain this distinction. The act of composing itself runs alongside the common poetic themes of unrequited love and political intrigue in troubadour songs. For the troubadour, "composing"

---

10. Zumthor, "The Text and the Voice," 73–74.

11. Ibid., 87 and 85 respectively.

12. PC 70-21. *Ges de chantar no·m prem talans* translates roughly as "I have no desire for singing," thus setting up a contrast with the mood of the *tornada*. Text and translation (modified) from *Bernart*, 98–99. Zumthor quotes this *tornada* in "The Text and the Voice," 85.

13. Ibid., 89–90.

involved two stages: the first was "to find" (*trobar*) the raw material, the second was "to perfect" it (*afinar*).[14] The troubadour worked "to file" (*limar*), "to plane" or "smooth" (*aplanar*), "to polish" (*polir*), "to refine" or "temper" (*refranher*) the raw material of the song. This process generated a rich vocabulary of craftsmanship, mostly taken from woodworking, metallurgy, and with the trouvères, horticulture (discussed in chapter 4). In contrast to these technological and craftsmanship metaphors, composition was also associated with natural temporal cycles, especially the arrival of spring. The first stanza of *Qan lo rius de la fontana,* attributed to Jaufre Rudel, begins with a conventional "springtime" introduction that associates composing or singing a song with the natural revival of life.

Qan lo rius de la fontana	When the stream from the fountain
s'esclarzis si cum far sol,	runs clear as it is wont to do,
e par la flors aiglentina,	and the wild rose blooms,
e·l rossignoletz el ram	and the little nightingale on the bough
volv e refraing et aplana	turns and returns (refines) and polishes
son doutz chantar, et afina,	his sweet song, and perfects it,
dreitz es q'ieu lo mieu refraigna	it is right that I return to (refine) my own (song).[15]

Poetic invocations of nature have deep roots in ancient Greek and Latin literature; in the Middle Ages they fuse with Christian Eastertide symbolism of the Resurrection, and, from the twelfth century on, with Mary as an agent in salvation.[16] Thus Jaufre

---

14. Simon Gaunt remarks: "The composer of a troubadour lyric was not an *autor*, but a *trobador*, one who 'finds'.... The text does not emanate from the troubadour, but antecedes him or at the very least exists independently, a notion that is reinforced by the metaphors used to articulate the troubadour poetics: the poem is an artefact that is bound up, planed, filed or polished." See Gaunt, "Orality and Writing," 234. For an early use of *trobar* to mean "compose" see *Farai un vers de dreit nïen* by Guilhem IX (PC 183-7), lines 5–6: "qu'enans fo trobatz en durmen / sus un chivau" (for it was composed earlier while [I was] sleeping on a horse); and *No sap chantar qui so non di* by Jaufre Rudel (PC 262-3), line 2: "ni vers trobar qui motz no fa" (nor can he compose songs who makes no words). For editions of the poems see *William,* 14–15; *Jaufre,* 134–35. Some scholars have conjectured a semantic link between the Occitan "*trobar*" and the Latin rhetorical term "*inventio*," which refers to the finding of subject matter, perhaps also a linked to Latin *tropus* (figurative speech) and *tropare* (to compose poetry or music). See Smith, *Figures of Repetition,* 43; see also the etymology presented by Zumthor, "An Overview: Why the Troubadours?," 13.

15. PC 262-5. Text and translation (modified) from *Jaufre,* 138–41; I have also consulted the edition in *Songs,* 57–58. For another translation and detailed historical exposition of this song see Rosenstein, "New Perspectives on Distant Love." For more examples of works with references to technical craftsmanship see Paterson, *Troubadours and Eloquence,* 189n4, for a list of lyrics that use terms of polishing, filing, sculpting, and gilding); and Smith, *Figures of Repetition,* 54–57.

16. For the "spring time" topos in literature see Curtius, *European Literature,* 92–94; see also Wilhelm, *The Cruelest Month*; and Rothenberg, "The Marian Symbolism of Spring, ca. 1200–ca. 1500." For a general discussion of topoi in troubadour lyric see Schulze-Busacker, "Topoi," esp. 422–25. For a detailed analysis of springtime vocabulary in trouvère lyric see Dembowski, "Vocabulary of Old French Courtly Lyrics."

combines images of natural creation (with its attendant implications of a divine hand in the making) with artificial, artisanal creation; and he further inflects these commonplaces with his own word games of turns and returns and refinement, which emphatically and artistically link the cycle of nature to the fabrication of the song.

The words *refraing* in line 5, and *refraigna* in line 7 are obviously etymologically related to the word "refrain," which for most musicians refers to a structurally repeating segment of melody and words. The Occitan verb *refranher* bears the meanings "to repeat" and "to temper" (with reference to metallurgy); it is derived from the Latin root *frangere*—to break, to separate, to shatter.[17] Stanzas 2, 3, and 4 of this lyric offer the tempering effects of repetition. The metrical construction is a virtuosic *coblas doblas*. Jaufre weaves together pairs of stanzas by recycling and shuffling rhyme sounds (see table 1.1). But the preponderance of lines ending with the vowel -a- (-ana, -ina, -aigna) does indeed moderate the effect of the shuffle, just as the strophic melody mollifies the agitation of "love from a distant land" with a reassurance of return.

II

Amors de terra loindana,	Love from a distant land,
per vos totz lo cors mi dol;	for you my whole self aches;
e non puosc trobar meizina	and I can find no remedy
si non vau al sieu reclam,	unless I go at her call,
ab atraich d'amor doussana,	with the lure of sweet love,
dinz vergier o sotz cortina	in a garden or beneath a curtain
ab desirada compaigna.	with a desired companion.

III

Pois del tot m'en faill aizina,	Since I get no relief at all,
no·m meravill s'ieu m'aflam,	I am not surprised if I am aflame,
car anc genser Crestiana	for there was never a nobler Christian woman,
non fo, que Dieus non la vol,	for God does not wish there be,
Juzeva ni Sarrazina;	nor a Jewess nor a Saracen;
et es ben paisutz de manna	and whoever gains any of her love
qui ren de s'amor gazaigna.	is well fed with manna.

IV

De desir mos cors non fina	I do not cease desiring
vas cella ren q'ieu plus am,	her whom I love most,

---

17. S.v. "refranher, refragner," in *LR* 3:388. Raynouard lists the meanings "to relieve" (*soulager*), "to moderate" (*adoucir*), "to temper" (*tempérer*). See also "refranher" in *PSW* 7:153. Levy uses lines 5 and 7 from *Qan lo rius de la fontana* as an example of the meaning "to repeat" (*wiederholen*). Levy also includes the meaning "to repress" (*unterdrücken*). Raynouard lists "refranher" under the Occitan root "franger" from the Latin "frangere," *LR* 3:385. See also Switten, "*Versus* and Troubadours around 1100," 97–99.

e cre que volers m'engana	and I think my will deceives me
si cobezeza la·m tol;	if lust takes her away from me;
que plus es pongens q'espina	and the pain which is relieved by enjoyment
la dolors que ab joi sana,	is more piercing than a thorn,
don ja non vuoill c'om m'en plaigna.	and I want no one to pity me for it.

The melody preserved for *Qan lo rius de la fontana* (see example 1.1 🔊 OXFORD WEB MUSIC) sets up a dynamic between two "home" pitches: the D that launches the opening of each large melodic section, and the C that alternates with E as an ending pitch. Only in the second half of the melody does the C acquire the sense of a final, and only really with the last line of music, with its sudden tonicization of C from below. It is a curiously perfunctory and

EXAMPLE 1.1 Jaufre Rudel, *Qan lo rius de la fontana*, stanza I, melody from troub. *R*, fol. 63ᵛ

TABLE 1.1

Recycling of rhymes in *Qan lo rius de la fontana*

Stanzas 1 and 2		Stanzas 3 and 4		Final stanza	
7'	-ana	a ⤬ c	-ina	c	-ina
7	-ol	b ⤬ d	-am	d?	-an [-am]*
7'	-ina	c ⤬ a	-ana	a	-ana
7	-am	d ⤬ b	-ol	b	-ol
7'	-ana	a ⤬ c	-ina	c	-ina
7'	-ina	c ⤬ a	-ana	a/e	-aigna [-ana]*
7'	-aigna	e	e	-aigna	e/a	-ana [-aigna]*

* Corrected rhymes from modern editions are shown in brackets; otherwise from troub. *A*.

ambivalent ending, one that seems to leave the listener hanging despite the finality of the cadence. We might hear the themes of distant love, of frustrated desire, reinforced by each stanza's awkward closure; or perhaps our attention turns momentarily to the local event of the song—the melody and the singer's voice.

The shattering effect of repetition occurs with the final stanza, which features an abrupt change of tone and theme, much like the sudden cadence of the melody:

v

Senes breu de pargamina,	Without a letter of parchment
tramet lo vers en chantan [chantam]	I transmit this song while singing
plan et en lenga romana,	plainly and in the romance tongue,
a·N Hugon Brun per Fillol.	to Lord Hugo Brun, by Fillol.
Bon m'es, car gens Peitavina,	I am pleased because the people of Poitou,
de Beirui et de Bretaigna [Guianna]	of Berry, and of Guyenne
s'esgau per lui, e Guianna [Bretaigna].	and of Brittany, are delighted by it.[18]

The rhetoric shifts from the timeless, conventional language of *fin'amors* to a rootedness in the author's present, explicitly addressing the practical issues of transmission, patronage, and reception. Sarah Kay argues that such particularizing, subjective discourse provides

18. Pickens discerns two written traditions for this lyric, the *x* group (troub. MSS *ABDIKSgE*) with five stanzas (showing the unbalancing effect of the *tornada*); and the *y* group (troub. MSS *CMe^b*), which adds "slot" stanzas to create a balanced six stanzas. Other manuscripts, such as troub. *R* (with music) and troub. *U*, show replacement stanzas and lack the *tornada*. See Pickens, *The Songs of Jaufré Rudel*, 88–135.

a personal signature and a hint of autobiography, such that the subject of the lyric (the lyric "I") merges with the identity of the author, Jaufre Rudel.[19] This coherence of authorial ego and lyric subject, however, comes at a formal cost. Poetically, the large-scale balance of the metrical scheme, divided into pairs of stanzas, is decidedly unbalanced by this final one, which repeats the scheme just prior, resulting in a two plus three grouping of *coblas* (and confusion on the part of many scribes).[20] This sonic return coupled with the decided turn away from ideal love, toward real life, defines the *tornada*, which is the moment when the formal return becomes itself an expressive gesture.

In *Qan lo rius de la fontana* Jaufre's turn to song is hailed by nature's own turning, and Jaufre, literally in turn, in the *tornada*, hails Fillol. Both subjects are subordinate, yet rendered articulate by that subordination. But Jaufre's and Fillol's turns do not stop at 180 degrees, for Jaufre declares that the song has not been written down, and designates Fillol as his vocal proxy in the court of Lord Hugo. Jaufre also boasts that the song already enjoys widespread fame from the repeat public performances by countless other proxies in Poitou, Guyenne, Berry, and Brittany. Thus Jaufre's status as the subject (of his song, of his fame) is spun out by multiple voices in an entanglement of agency and subordination, call and response.

THE TORNADA-REPRISE

Pos vezem de novel florir by Guilhem IX places this metatextual call and response within the text itself, with an actual *respond*—that is, a repeated section of words and melody. After six six-line stanzas that catalog the abstract virtues requisite for loving well (obedience, acquiescence, patience, and refinement), the seventh and final full stanza unexpectedly breaks from the theme and calls attention to the song as a sounding object; its melody (*sonetz*), its strophic construction (*tug per egau*), and its reception (understanding and praise) themselves epitomize *fin'amors* in their good musical behavior. Two nearly identical four-line *tornadas* follow, varying in their initial directive phrases, but otherwise answering the lyric's reference to sound with compressed and insistent sonic returns:

VII

Del vers vos dic que mais ne vau	About this song I tell you that it is worth more
qui be l'enten, e n'a plus lau;	if someone understands it well, and receives more praise;

---

19. Kay, *Subjectivity in Troubadour Poetry*, 145–53.

20. Of the seventeen sources for this lyric, seven manuscripts show a stable set of five stanzas in the same order; four manuscripts add a penultimate stanza (not the same one), which either adds a third shuffle of the rhyme sounds, or further unbalances the *coblas doblas* with another iteration of the second pattern; six present a wide range of redactions including replacement lines and replacement stanzas. The other more popular "distant love" song *Lanqan li jorn son lonc en mai*, with eighteen sources, shows far less stability in order and integrity of stanzas. See the critical notes in *Jaufre*, 159–63 and 165–67 respectively.

que·ls motz son faitz tug per egau	for the words are made in equal groups [*or* all equally]
comunalmens,	each and every one [*or* as is common]
e·l sonetz, ieu meteus m'en lau,	and the melody, I myself praise it
bos e valens.	good and worthy.

VIII

A Narbona—mas jeu no·i vau—	At Narbonne—but I am not going there—
sia·l prezens	let my song be a present to him [*or* her]
mos vers, e vueill que d'aquest lau	and I want it to be the guarantee
me sia guirens.	of this praise for me.

IX

Mon Esteve—mas jeu no·i vau—	My Steven—but I am not going there—
sia·l prezens	let my song be a present to him [*or* her],
mos vers, e vueill que d'aquest lau	and I want it to be the guarantee
me sia guirens.	of this praise for me.[21]

The *tornadas* make explicit the song's function as a stand-in for Guilhem (or "the composer," since one of the song's three sources attributes it to Bertran de Pessars); indeed, the interjection "mas jeu no·i vau" (but I am not going there) insists on the composer's absence, leaving the song alone to do the necessary work of guaranteeing his presence and praise in the minds of his song's audience. Words and music together export Guilhem (Bertran?): a subjective voice seems to emerge as the song itself comes to the fore of the lyric. The doubly marked repetitions—the twin fragmented stanzas, the varied particulars of place and person—index the end of the song as they index the (absent) self.

In the lyrics of Guilhem IX, four of the eight extant *tornadas* do not reference the song or messengers or recipients; rather, they literally return to the sentiments of the prior stanza and repeat or paraphrase key lines. In *Campaigno, non pus mudar qu'eu no m'effrei*, the *tornada* repeats the last lines of the previous stanza almost word for word, though subtly changing the meaning:

21. PC 183-11. Text and translation from *William*, 30–31. For a slightly different translation of these lines and a discussion of the whole lyric as an early example of the typical formulation of love, song, and social worth see Paterson, "*Fin'amor* and the Development of the Courtly *Canso*," 28–31. Paterson translates "que·l mot son fait tug per egau / comunalmens" as "for the words are all fashioned evenly to complement each other" and the last semi-strophe as "Let my *vers* be presented to my Stephen, since I am not going to him in person, and I wish him [*or* it] to vouch for this judgement." Paterson believes Esteve is the recipient of the song rather than its bearer. Of the song's three sources, both *tornadas* appear in troub. *E* and *a¹* (where the song is attributed to Bertran de Pessars); only the second *tornada* appears in troub. *C*. In neither source are the two *tornadas* wholly identical; some of the parallel lines show word omissions or substitutions that change the syllable count and even rhyme words. For philological details see Guilhem IX, *Poesie*, ed. Pasero, 198.

VII

Non i a negu de vos ja·m desautrei,   There is not one among you who would
                                                          ever deny to me,

S'om li vedava vi fort per malavei,   if a man were refused strong wine because
                                                          of sickness,

Non begues enanz de l'aiga   He would not sooner drink water
    que·s laisses morir de sei.   than allow himself to die of thirst.

VIII

Chascus beuri'ans de l'aiga   Everyone would sooner drink water
    que·s laises morir dessei.   than allow himself to die of thirst.[22]

This *tornada*-reprise (to coin a term)[23] references a well-known line from Ovid's *Amores* (3.4.17–18), which illustrates desire for the forbidden: "thus the sick man longingly hangs over forbidden water" (*sic interdictis inminet aeger aquis*).[24] With slight changes to a few words, the *tornada* repeats the sounds but not the sense of the preceding lines, from the folly of a sick man to the common sense of everyone else. The *tornada* does not seem at all subjective or autobiographical; indeed, the *tornada* is a proverb—words with no specific subjectivity behind them.

In rhetorical terms, the *tornada*-reprise functions as a figure called *conduplicatio* or *reduplicatio*, "the repetition of one or more words for the purpose of Amplification or Appeal to Pity" according to the *Rhetorica ad Herennium* (IV, 28.38). The *Rhetorica ad Herennium* explains that *conduplicatio* "makes a deep impression on the hearer and inflicts a major wound upon the opposition—as if a weapon should repeatedly pierce the same part of the body."[25] Such repetition for affective—even embodied—impact is to

---

22. PC 183-4. Text and translation from *William*, 8–9; see also 61n22 for a discussion of the irregular spelling. I have slightly modified the translation to reflect the wording of the Occitan. This song survives in one source, troub. *N* from the fourteenth century.

23. To a certain extent this is a redundant name; Mölk notes that the term "*repreza*" appears earlier than "*tornada*" as a technical term to designate the final couplet or semi-strophe. See "Deux remarques sur la tornada," 4–6.

24. See *William*, 61n20–21. This proverb is listed in Cnyrim, *Sprichwörter, sprichwörtliche Redensarten und Sentenzen*, 46, proverb 766. Guilhem also quotes a proverb in *Pos vezem de novel florir*; see Pfeffer, *Proverbs in Medieval Occitan Literature*, esp. 35–43 for a discussion of the proverbs in Guilhem IX and Marcabru. Pfeffer discusses two lyrics that use proverbs in their *tornadas*: Folquet de Marselha's *Ben an mort mi e lor* (PC 155-5)—a song full of proverbs—and Bertran de Born's *Un sirventes que motz no·ill faill* (PC 80-44) (see 47-48 and 58-59 respectively). In general, Pfeffer argues that the widespread use of proverbs in troubadour lyrics provides evidence for a high degree of literacy among both the composers and their audience (107), although she calls proverbs "a profoundly oral medium" (27). Spearing, in *Textual Subjectivity*, describes a "subjectless subjectivity," which could apply to proverbs (30). Peire Vidal, *Baron de mon dan covit* (PC 364-7) cites a proverb in the *tornada*: "Plus que non pot ses aigua viure·l peis, / non pot esser ses lauzengiers domneis, / per qu'amador compron trop car lur joc" (No more than the fish can live without water, love-service cannot be without slanderers; hence lovers pay most dearly for their joy). See *Anthology*, 198–201, for the text and translation of this song.

25. *Rhetorica ad Herennium*, 325.

be distinguished from other figures of repetition such as *repetitio* (also *anaphora* or *epanaphora*), the repetition of the initial word or words in successive phrases; *conversio* (also *antistrophe* or *epiphora*), the repetition of the ending word or words in successive phrases; *conplexio*, the union of both *repetitio* and *conversio*; and *traductio*, the use of the same word for different functions or in different locations. These four figures, according to the *Rhetorica ad Herennium*, produce an elegance of style whose principal function is to appeal to the ear rather than the emotions.[26]

Conduplicatio is not especially associated with conclusions in classical and medieval rhetorical theory, though one can easily associate the wounding metaphor of *Rhetorica ad Herennium* with "the final blow." The *tornada*-reprise appears as a closing rhetorical option mostly in the lyrics of the earliest troubadours. Guilhem IX, Marcabru, and Jaufre Rudel all use it upon occasion, though their contemporary Cercamon not at all. Examples of *repetitio*, *conversio*, and *traductio* can be found in the *tornadas* of Peire d'Alvernha, Bernart de Ventadorn, Giraut de Bornelh, and Arnaut Daniel; a few scattered lyrics among these authors reprise whole lines and might be counted as *tornada*-reprises.[27] Given the early practice of *conduplicatio*, we could understand the other decorative figures of repetition found in the *tornadas* as also bearing a trace of *conduplicatio* and its reiterative amplification of emotions.

The verbal and musical echo of the *tornada*-reprise momentarily resembles a refrain, though refrains indicate song with their cyclic returns, while *tornada*-reprises indicate finality with their singular return. But this is not to say that *tornadas* bear no relation to refrains. If *refranher* means to temper and refine as well as to repeat, then we might look for such operations in the *tornada*-reprises. With the *tornada* from *Pus la fuelha revirola*, Marcabru carves out and polishes the gem of an aphorism from the last three lines of the final stanza:

IX [...]

No sai si so ditz per mal:	I do not know if this is wrongly said:
que·l cor [a] sotz l'emborilh,	that he has his heart beneath his navel,
bar que per aver sordeya.	the baron who debases himself through money.

---

26. Ibid., 274–81. See also Smith, *Figures of Repetition*, 74–76. *Las Leys d'Amors* calls the repetition of whole lines *bordo tornat*, and considers it a vice characteristic of the new poetry, unless it occurs for reasons of measure, intention, or necessity. See Gatien-Arnoult, ed., *Las Leys d'Amors* 3:104–105.

27. Songs that contain a *tornada*-reprise are: Guilhem IX, PC 183-4, -5, -11, -12; Jaufre Rudel, PC 262-2, Marcabru, PC 293-8, -14, -17, -18, -22, -31, -33, -38. For word and phrase echoes see Arnaut Daniel PC 29-5, -18; Bernart de Ventadorn, PC 70-2, -4, -7, -9, -15, -22, -43; Giraut de Bornelh, PC 242-43, -63, -78, -29, -79, -55, -73. Peirol's *tenso Senher, qual penriaz vos* (PC 366-30) cleverly uses a *tornada*-reprise form at the end of the exchange such that the Senher takes Peirol's words and with a slight shift transforms their meaning. See *Peirol*, ed. Aston, 148-50. See also the remarks about word and phrase repetition in *tornadas* in Smith, *Figures of Repetition*, 113-16. Bernart de Ventadorn PC 70-25, Giraut de Bornelh PC 242-25, and Peire d'Alvernha PC 323-9 reprise or paraphrase one or more full lines.

x

| Que·l cor a sotz l'emborilh | For he has his heart beneath his navel, |
| bar que per aver sordeya. | the baron who debases himself through money.[28] |

With the line "no sai si so ditz per mal" (I do not know if it is wrongly said) Marcabru calls attention to the phrase as if it preexisted his saying it, although the aphorism does not appear in any list of proverbs of the time.[29] Marcabru thus creates a proverb from his own words with their repetition in the *tornada*; the formal site where subjectivity can emerge becomes instead the place where the singular voice is refracted into a chorus.

With this *tornada*—its repetition that is also quotation—we get the first inkling of the sophisticated refrain techniques developed fully by the trouvères. Few troubadour songs contain structurally repeating refrains; in his catalogue of troubadour metrical patterns, István Frank lists sixty-four songs with refrains, the majority attributed to late troubadours such as Cerverí de Girona (fl. 1259–85) and Guiraut Riquier (fl.1254–92), and representing later genres such as the *balada*, *dansa*, and *retroncha*. Women's songs, including *albas* (dawn songs), however, regularly use refrains, and here I want to note the coincidence of the female subject and refrain songs—both uncommon "voices" within the troubadour tradition.[30] Far more common throughout this repertory are refrain words or phrases, such as Jaufre Rudel's "amor de lonh" in *Lanqan li jorn son lonc en mai*, or Marcabru's sharp imperative "Escoutatz!" (listen) in *Dirai vos vuoill ses duptansa* (PC 293-18) which regularly interrupts the flow of eight-syllable lines mid-stanza with a clear admonishment to his audience, rather than an invitation.[31]

In the religious *canso Vera vergena, Maria* by Peire Cardinal (fl. 1205–72), a relatively late song in the troubadour repertory, refrains and the *tornada*-reprise intersect. Each stanza ends with the refrain: "De patz, si·t plai, dona, traita, / qu'ab to filh me sia fiata"

---

28. PC 239-38. Text and translation (modified) from *Marcabru*, 480–81. The first four lines of the final ninth stanza are syntactically connected to the eighth stanza as part of a long sentence complaining about the heir of a Sir Richart or Guiscart (depending on the manuscript).

29. For a discussion and list of proverbs in Marcabru's lyrics see Goddard, "Marcabru, *'li proverbe au vilain'*"; and Dinguirard, "*So ditz la gens anciana*." Aphoristic statements of general truths were called *sententiae* in classical rhetoric.

30. This observation may reflect the legacy of women as key participants in the festive round dances that produced the earliest known tradition of secular songs in Romance vernaculars. In thirteenth-century French sources, round dances such as the *rondet de carole* feature refrains. See Haines, *Medieval Song in Romance Languages*, 51–82.

31. For a list of troubadour songs with refrains see Frank 2:58; for a list of songs with refrain words, see 62–67. For a discussion of refrain usage in troubadour songs see also Switten, "*Versus* and Troubadours around 1100"; and Newcombe, "The Refrain in Troubadour Lyric Poetry." The word *refrim* in troubadour songs most often refers to bird song, as in Arnaut Daniel's *Chansson do·il mot son plan e prim* (PC 29-6), who lists it among the song elements he hears in nature in line 10: "Pel bruoill aug lo chan e·l refrim" (Through the woods I hear the song and the refrain); see Arnaut Daniel, *The Poetry*, ed. Wilhelm, 6–7. Given the short repetitive phrases of bird songs, "refrain" would indeed be an appropriate appellation. See *LR* 5:61 and *PSW* 7:160.

(For peace, if you will, *Dona*, intercede so that with your son it would be granted to me).
The *tornada* repeats this refrain with a slight variation, shifting the language further away
from the courtly register of *Dona* to the sacred register of *Dieu*: "Quar al latz Dieu estas,
traita, / que·m si patz de luy faita" (Because you are at the side of God, intercede, so that
peace will be granted to me from him).[32]

How does music affect the perception of the *tornada*-reprise? Jaufre Rudel's famous
Lanqan li jorn son lonc en mai is the only song that survives with a melody and a *tornada*-
reprise. Although the *tornada* survives in only two of the song's sixteen sources (neither
with music), let us assume that the *tornada* was sung, and observe the musical and rhetor-
ical effect of the reprise (see example 1.2 ● OXFORD WEB MUSIC).

VII

Ver ditz qui m'apella lechai	He speaks the truth, whoever calls me greedy
ni desiron d'amor de loing,	and desirous of a distant love,
car nuills autre jois tant no·m plai	for no other joy pleases me as much
cum gauzimens d'amor de loing;	as the enjoyment of a distant love;
mas so q'eu vuoill m'es tan taïs	but what I want is so kept from me
q'enaissi·m fadet mos pairis	for my godfather fixed my fate
q'ieu ames e non fos amatz.	that I should love and not be loved.

VIII

Mas so q'ieu vuoill m'es tan taïs:	But what I want is so kept from me:
toz sia mauditz lo pairis	cursed be the godfather
qe·m fadet q'ieu non fos amatz!	who fixed my fate so that I should not be loved![33]

As mentioned in the introduction, music for this song survives in three sources—troub.
R and *X* (in French), and trouv. *M* (in French, attributed Jossiames Faidins [Gaucelm
Faidit], and mutilated). All three versions are close in pitch content and melodic contour,
differing mostly in low-level decorations; the melodies in troub. *X* and trouv. *M* are clos-
est (both are primarily trouvère collections), though the latter is written a fifth higher,
while the melody in troub. *R* is a bit more florid. The melody for example 1.2 is based on
the version preserved in trouv. *M*; the missing phrase, indicated with the dotted-line
bracket, has been taken from troub. *R*.

The melody adheres to the *pedes–cauda* structure (to use Dante's terms) typical of
about a third of troubadour *cansos* and most trouvère *chansons*:[34] the first four lines of

32. PC 335-70. The *tornada* appears only in troub. *C*. See Peire Cardenal, *Poésies complètes*, ed. Lavaud, 236–37.

33. Text and translation (modified) from *Jaufre*, 148–49.

34. See Aubrey, *The Music of the Troubadours*, 146–49. Dante's analysis of the troubadour melodic forms have
been widely adopted by musicologists; it appears in *De vulgari eloquentia*, Bk. II, 10–13.

EXAMPLE 1.2 Jaufre Rudel, *Lanqan li jorn son lonc en mai*, final stanza and *tornada*, melody from
trouv. *M*, fol. 189ᵛ/B179ᵛ; words from troub. *A*, fol. 127

poetry are set to identical pairs of phrases (ab ab, forming the *pedes* or "feet") followed
by three or more lines (forming the *cauda* or "tail") that generally do not repeat melodic
phrases schematically or literally. (Dante calls the imaginary dividing line between the
pedes and the *cauda* the "turning point"—*diesis*, or *volta* in the vernacular.) In this song,
however, the last musical line begins in the same manner as each line of the *pedes*—that
is, with a minor third leap from A (sometimes decorated with the lower neighbor-note G)
to the central recitation pitch C. Also typical is the shift to a higher tessitura in the
cauda, which usually corresponds to the beginning of a new syntactic unit. Hendrik

van der Werf notes that the *pedes* of troubadour melodies tend to be more stable than the *caudae*, which is borne out in his comparative transcriptions of this song.[35] All three melodies begin the *cauda* by shifting the recitation pitch a fifth higher, and all three end the tune with the hint of melodic rounding. But the three *caudae* diverge radically in the penultimate line, each throwing our ear off the structuring pitches of the melody with restless undulating contours that span an octave. Leo Treitler has suggested that, in all three versions, the melody is "polarized" away from the principal structuring pitches (A–C–E in the example) to a secondary, competing set (G–B–D), and that this unsettling tension translates into melodic form the ironic theme of an ideal "distant love."[36] The melody in trouv. *M* amplifies this tension, destabilizing even the principal A–C–E chain by introducing a gratuitous, exotic-sounding B♭ in the ending flourish of line 7; the B♭ initially appears as an upper semitone neighbor-note to A, but it returns in the last line of the tune with emphasis, as an undecorated note that sets the fifth syllable of the line. This reiterated moment of "chromatic beauty" effectively keeps the melody unmoored until the very end, setting up the final G as a launching point for the strophic return rather than a landing point or resolution.[37] As with *Qan lo rius de la fontana*, Jaufre's other song of distant love, the melody of *Lanqan li jorn son lonc en mai* resists closure with a surprising sonorous detail that pulls the listener's attention away from the words and toward their performance. The repetition of the *cauda* melody for the *tornada* and the near repetition of words function as an extended, rhetorical flourish—a peroration that returns to the "high point" of the melody as well as to its arcane chromatic inflection.[38]

Turning to the lyrics, the subtle word changes in the *tornada*-reprise do not alter the meaning of the preceding lines; nor do they turn subjective words into a subjectless proverbial statement. Rather, the *tornada* (in accordance with *conduplicatio*) amplifies the meaning and intensifies the emotions by asserting a cause of the subject's suffering that is external to the lyric itself—not the faraway love, the internal refrain and the impetus for the composition, but the mysterious figure of the "godfather." In the Middle Ages, godfathers presented and named their godchild at the baptismal font, and later oversaw the child's spiritual life and education. It was also believed that the life of the godfather influenced the destiny of the godchild. Literary scholars speculate that the "godfather" in Jaufre's lyric refers to Guilhem IX, who declared "quar vueill so que non puesc aver"

---

35. For comparative transcriptions and discussion of melodic features see van der Werf, *The Chansons of the Troubadours and Trouvères*, 83–89; see also 28.
36. See Treitler, "The Troubadours Singing their Poems," 24–26. I have transposed the pitches in Treitler's discussion to reflect my transcription of the melody from trouv. *M*.
37. For a discussion of the use of *musica ficta* for beauty rather than necessity, see Brothers, *Chromatic Beauty*. Brothers begins his study with a discussion of accidentals in the redaction of trouvère melodies found in trouv. *O*; see esp. 11–15.
38. Dragonetti links the lyric *envois* with classical and medieval Latin *peroratio* or *conclusio*; both are conventions that announce the end of the work. See Dragonetti, *La Technique poétique des trouvères*, 309.

(I want what I cannot have),[39] to be echoed in Jaufre's *tornada*: "mas so q'ieu vuoill m'es tan taïs" (but what I want is so kept from me). Thus Guilhem as godfather, Jaufre's fictional spiritual guide, fixes the fate of Jaufre by fixing the terms—of love, of language—into which he is baptized as a poet.[40] The temptation, which I will succumb to for the moment, is to see this as a medieval corroboration of Althusser's "interpellation" whereby preexisting language fixes the terms of subjectivity. Moreover, "godfather" here returns us to the *tornada* of *Qan lo rius de la fontana*, where the name of the jongleur "Fillol" can also be translated as "godson."[41] Read together, Jaufre, the godson in one poem, becomes, in the other, the godfather to the named and nameless performers. Yet another interpretation could understand Jaufre himself as Fillol, the "godson," merging the identities of author and performer. With the *tornada*-reprise of *Lanqan li jorn son lonc en mai*, the thematic return to inherited fate (the mediated terms of subjectivity) coincides with the musical return to the expressive gestures of the *cauda*: thus the singular performing voice is showcased at the moment when the lyrical voice becomes diffuse.

If, as Butler describes, the inaugural moment of subjectivity is "a turning back upon oneself or even a turning *on* oneself," then Jaufre's filiations of voice spin him backward and forward, to the past and future conditions of his self-expression. But this is not a turning *on* oneself in Butler's sense of self-subjugation; rather, Jaufre turns *to* the kinship ties that both subjugate and enable his own voice.

From the thirteenth century on, however, compilers and scribes become important and consequential enablers of troubadour voices. The analysis given above depends on an imagined situation that a performer would know both the *tornada* and that particular melody. The *chansonnier* trouv. *M* preserves just enough of the lyric (four stanzas) with its characteristic refrain word (here *loig* for *lonh*) to render the song recognizable as the troubadour "classic" that it already was by the thirteenth century; in this source, however, the song had drifted some distance from the name "Jaufre Rudel" and the specter of the "godfather."

---

39. From *Pos vezem de novel florir* (PC 183-11), line 20; *William*, 28–29.

40. Lejeune, "La Chanson de 'l'amour de loin' de Jaufré Rudel," 403–42, esp. 434–36. The reference points to poetic filiation and obligation, but also perhaps to the historically tense relationship of vassalage between his House of Blaye and the House of Poitiers. See the commentary in *Jaufre*, 148–49, and 167; for a discussion of the relationship between the Houses of Blaye and Poitiers, see 96–97. For a list of Jaufre's possible borrowings from Guilhem, see *Jaufre*, 102–103. In addition to those cited by Wolf and Rosenstein, Jaufre's *Non sap chantar qui so non di* shares many images with Guilhem's *Farai un vers de dreit nïen*, such as loving a woman whom the troubadour has never seen (Guilhem, line 26: *c'anc no la vi*; Jaufre, line 10: *que anc no vi*), and the thematic contrast between sleeping and waking. For discussions of the role of godparents in the Middle Ages see Lynch, *Godparents and Kinship*, and Jussen, *Spiritual Kinship as Social Practice*, esp. 39 on their role in education. For another discussion of "godfather" in troubadour poetry see Lewent, "Old Provençal *Desmentir sos pairis*."

41. Wolf and Rosenstein translate "Fillol" as "godson" and suggest leaving the name untranslated in a footnote. See *Jaufre*, 149.

THE SCRIBES' TURN

What role might compilers and scribes have played in the preservation and transmission of *tornadas*? The following four tables present a selection of songs and their sources, showing the distribution of sources according to the transmission of the songs' *tornadas*. Tables 1.2 and 1.3 list all the songs with *tornada*-reprises by the earliest troubadours; table 1.4 lists selected non-reprise *tornadas* from the earliest troubadours; tables 1.5 and 1.6 list selected songs from the oeuvre of Bernart de Ventadorn.

The distribution of *tornadas* in the troubadour sources yields a few tendencies but no clear patterns: every source contains nearly as many examples of songs with their *tornadas* as without. *Tornadas* may have either a strong or a weak attachment to the lyric, and they may have different levels of independence when paired. The single *tornada*-reprises of the earliest troubadours (see table 1.2) appear to be weakly attached to the lyric; few manuscripts preserve them, many more do not. Most of the single *tornada*-reprises have a unique manuscript source, and troub. a^1, a sixteenth-century copy of a lost thirteenth-century manuscript from southern France, is solely responsible for a third of these. In contrast to the weak attachment of the single *tornada*-reprises, the few examples of double *tornada*-reprises (where the second *tornada* repeats all or some of the first) appear stronger in their attachment to the lyric, surviving in most or all sources for a given song

TABLE 1.2

Songs with a *tornada*-reprise		MSS with *tornada*	MSS without *tornada*	Alternate *tornada*
Guilhem IX				
4	Compaigno no pus mudar	N		
5	Companho, tant ai agutz	E		
12	Farai un vers, pos mi sonelh	V	CN	
Jaufre Rudel				
2	Lanqan li jorn son lonc	AB	CDEIKMMª RSSgWX	a^1 (lines 22–25 in C)
Marcabru				
8	Assatz m'es bel	A	IKa¹	
17	Dirai vos e mon latin	a¹	ACINR	
18	Dire vos vuoill	a¹	ACDIKMR	
31	L'iverns vai e·l temps	a¹	ACDKNR	
38	Pus la fuelha revirola	R	ACEIKa¹	

TABLE 1.3

Songs with a double *tornada*-reprise

		Tornada A only	*Tornada* B only	Both
Guilhem IX				
11	Pos vezem de novel florir		C	Ea[1]
Marcabru				
14	Contra l'ivern			C
22	Emperaire per mi mezeis			AIKa[1]

TABLE 1.4

Selected songs with non-reprise *tornadas* by the earliest troubadours

		MSS with *tornada*	MSS without *tornada*
Guilhem IX			
7	Farai un vers de dreit nïen[†]	CE	
8	Mout jauzens me prenc[†]	CE	
10	Pos de chantar m'es pres talenz	CDIK	NRa[1]
Jaufre Rudel			
1	Belhs m'es l'estius e·l temps[†]	e[3]	C
3	No sap chantar*	CE Ra[1] e[3]	M
6	Qan lo rius de la fontana[†]	ABCDEIKMSga[1]e[b]	RSUX
Marcabru			
5	El son d'esviat chantaire	AIKa[1]	
15	Cortesamen vuoill comensar[†]	ACKNR	Ga[1]
20	[A]d un estrun[†]	ACDIKRz	a[1]
24	En abriu	AEKNR	
32	Lo vers comenssa	ACIKR	N
35	Per savi teing ses doptanza*	DNa[1]	AIK
40	Pos mos coratges esclarzis*	E	ACIK

[†] Full strophe.
* Last full strophe also functions as a *tornada*.

(see table 1.3). Thus we may surmise that some songs of the earliest troubadours lost their *tornada*-reprises in transmission; or, on the contrary, perhaps they gained them upon occasion. In any case, this option for composing a *tornada* was clearly the less favored one. For these early lyrics, the transmission of single *tornadas* that do not repeat words of the prior stanza is most robust, especially *tornadas* that are full stanzas, such as the one for Jaufre's *Qan lo rius de la fontana* (see table 1.4).

TABLE 1.5

Selected songs with a single *tornada* by Bernart de Ventadorn

		MSS with *tornada*	MSS without *tornada*
10	Bel m'es qu'eu chan	DIKN	
13	Be·m cuidei de chantar sofrir	R	CDIKMSᵢa
17	En cossirer et en esmai*	ACDGIKLMNQ	ORV
23	La dousa votz ai auzida	CV	DGIKRX
25	Lancan vei la folha*†	ABDGIKLPRSᵢT	CMQSgVa
31	Non es meravelha s'eu chan	CG	ADFIKLMNOPQRSUVWa
33	Pel doutz chan que·l rossinhols	ACDGIKNa	QR
39	Can l'erba fresch' e·lh folha	CO	ADIKMNRVa
43	Can vei la lauzeta mover	ACEGLOPQSU	DFIKMNRVWXa

* Last full strophe also functions as a *tornada*.
† *Tornada*-reprise.

TABLE 1.6

Selected songs with double *tornadas* by Bernart de Ventadorn

		Tornada A only	*Tornada* B only	Both	Neither
1	Ab joi mou lo vers	ABIKLMMª PRSUa		C	DGQTV
4	Amors, e que·us	DEIKMNa	Lf	AC	RS
6	Era·m cosselhatz*	Mf	RSᵢ	EO	ABCDIKQV
7	Ara no vei luzir	M	R	ABCGIK	DOPQSW
8	A, tantas bonas			C	DIKNR
15	Chantars no pot			ACDGIKPa	
29	Lo rossinhols	C		ABSa	DFIKMNQRV
41	Can par la flors	ABGIKNPSU		CMOSga	DEQRW
42	Can vei la flor	ACGIKMNVa		P	DRQX

* Last full strophe also functions as a *tornada*.

The *tornadas* of Bernart de Ventadorn yield an even more complicated picture of transmission. In general, the more robust the transmission of the song, the greater the likelihood that the *tornada(s)* will be preserved across more sources. But this is not always the case. Among the sample of his single *tornadas* listed in table 1.5, the *tornadas* for songs 13, 23, 31, and 39 appear to be much weaker than those for songs 10, 17, and 25. The *tornada* for song 10 might be considered the strongest in its attachment to the lyric for the lyric does not appear without it, although the relative paucity of sources probably is a factor. For his most famous song *Can vei la lauzeta mover*, however, the number of sources with and without the *tornada* is nearly equal. Among the double *tornadas* (see table 1.6), the same varying and inconclusive conditions hold true: both *tornadas* for song 6 seem to be weak, while the first *tornadas* for songs 1, 4, 41, and 42 are strong and independent compared to the first *tornadas* for songs 7 and 15, which appear most often in a pair.[42] The double *tornadas* for song 29, although stronger as a pair, are nevertheless weakly represented in the sources. The independent appearance of the second *tornada* from a pair is rare but not impossible; similarly, the order of the two *tornadas* is generally stable, although for song 41 the two are switched in troub. *Sg* and *a*. Given the strength and independence of the first *tornada* of any given pair, we could speculate that the second *tornada* attached to the lyric at a later date.

A few sources point to the condition of exemplars as a factor in *tornada* transmission, though, again, no clear pattern emerges in terms of date or geography. Of the thirty-eight songs by Bernart de Ventadorn with *tornadas*, only five (songs 8, 13, 23, 31, and 39) have dramatically weak transmissions of *tornadas* compared to the song proper (that is, the *tornadas* survive in one or two sources out of seven or more sources for the song itself). Troub. *C* is a common source for the *tornadas* in four of these five cases, suggesting the compilers' efforts toward completeness and consistency.[43] This is a fourteenth-century southern French source that tends to preserve *tornadas* for Bernart's songs (twenty-five out of thirty-three songs); in contrast, troub. *D*, a mid-thirteenth- to fourteenth-century Italian source, often does not preserve *tornadas* (fifteen out of thirty-three songs). Turning to the two southern manuscripts with music, troub. *G*, a fourteenth-century Italian source, tends to preserve *tornadas* (twenty out of twenty-three songs), while troub. *R*, a fourteenth-century southern French source, does not (twelve out of thirty songs). The thirteenth-century northern French sources, troub. *X* (trouv. *U*) and *W* (trouv. *M*) do not transmit any *tornadas* for the troubadours listed in the above tables.

---

42. Note that song 15 survives with both *tornadas* in all its sources. Although the two *tornadas* in song 4 are linked by word echoes, they only appear together in two of the thirteen sources.

43. The *tornadas* for song 8 appear in troub. *C*; the *tornada* for song 13 in troub. *R*, for song 23 in troub. *C* and *V*; for song 31 in troub. *C* and *G*, for song 39 in troub. *C* and *O*. All but one of these *tornadas* directly address a person (Bel Vezer, Cortes, Corona), or name a place (Ventadorn, Narbonne, La Mura); song 39 uses the generic phrase "Messatger, vai" (messenger, go). Since the majority of Bernart's *tornadas* are specific rather than generic (see table 1.8 below), the specificity of content is probably not a deciding factor in the weak transmission of these five *tornadas*.

What does all this tell us? Why do some *tornadas* have a robust transmission record while others do not? The survival of *tornadas* seems not to be a function of scribal procedures; rather, the relative strength or weakness of the attachment of one or more *tornadas* to a song may depend on the extent to which a given *tornada* seemed integral to the expressive concept of the song. Two of Bernart's songs, *En cossirer et en esmai* (song 17) and *Lancan vei la folha* (song 25), offer good examples of how the last stanza and the *tornada* can display an expressive coherence—a coherence that does not necessarily pertain to the relationship among the other stanzas, for one curious feature of troubadour and trouvère love songs is their lack of connection or narrative flow from one stanza to the other, resulting in a frequent shuffling of stanza order.[44] *Lancan vei la folha* (song 25) ends with the following full stanza and *tornada*-reprise:

VII

Encontra·l damnatge	a	Against the loss
e la pena qu'eu trai,	b	and pain which I suffer
ai mo bon uzatgel,	c	I have my good habit,
c'ades consir de lai.	b	that I always think about the place where she is.
Orgol e folatge	a	There is pride, madness,
e vilania fai	b	and villainy
qui·n mou mo coratge	a	in whoever diverts my heart
ni d'alre·m met en plai,	b	and involves me with something else,
car melhor messatge	a	for I have no better messenger
en tot lo mon no·n ai	b	in all the world (than my heart)
e man lo·lh ostatge	a	and I send it to her as a hostage
entro qu'eu torn de sai.	b	until I return from here.

VIII

Domna, mo coratge,	a	Lady, my heart,
·l melhor amic qu'eu ai,	b	the best friend that I have,
vos man en ostatge	a	I send to you as a hostage
entro qu'eu torn de sai.	b	until I return from here.[45]

While the stanza announces the heart as the troubadour's messenger, the *tornada* enacts this metonym, literally replacing *messatge* with *coratge* in the return of the last four rhymes.

---

44. For the sources and their stanza order see Bernart de Ventadorn, *Seine Lieder*, ed. Appel, 98 and 144 respectively. For *Lancan vei la folha* (song 25), nine sources (of eighteen) are uniform in their stanza order and completeness, while the other nine show a variety of conditions with many missing and shuffled stanzas. For *En cossirer et en esmai* (song 17), nine of thirteen sources transmit the same order of stanzas and the *tornada*.

45. Text and translation (modified) from *Bernart*, 112–13.

Thus in the *tornada* the heart becomes a personified messenger—the *melhor amic*—
who takes the place of the jongleur. In medieval literature, the heart, in addition to being
an organ of emotion, thought, and memory, was also a place of writing akin to parch-
ment, where God inscribes his commandments and his new covenant, and where the
troubadour inscribes his desires, or has engraved an image of the beloved.[46] The heart as
messenger and message thus becomes identical with the song itself. In good song-fashion,
the *conduplicatio* of the last two lines recapitulates the melodramatic images of the
previous stanza—the heart as a willing hostage, the displacement of the troubadour, and
the promise of return encoded in the return of the words.

In *En cossirer et en esmai* (song 17), the final stanza and the *tornada* also form an
extended expressive moment:

VII

Pois messatger no·lh trametrai	a	Since I will not send a messenger to her	
ni a me dire no·s cove,	b	and since for me to speak is not fitting,	
negu cosselh de me no sai.	a	I see no help for myself.	
Mais d'una re me conort be:	b	But I console myself with one thing:	
el sap letras et enten.	c	she knows and understands letters.	
Et agrada·m qu'eu escria	d	I would gladly write	
los motz, e s'a leis plazia,	d	the words, and if it pleases her,	
legis los al meu sauvamen.	c	let her read them for my deliverance.	

VIII

E s'a leis autre dols no·n pren,	c	And if no other grief besets her,	
per Deu e per merce·lh sia	d	for God and mercy's sake let her not take away	
que·l bel solatz que m'avia	d	the beautiful kindness nor the sweet talk	
no·m tolha ni· seu parlar gen.	c	she had for me.[47]	

The ending of *En cossirer et en esmai* is remarkable for the evidence it presents of a written
tradition of songs, and for the vernacular literacy of young noblewomen.[48] It also suggests
an erotics of writing and reading that replaces singing and listening—the beloved's

---

46. Jager, *The Book of the Heart*, 65–86.

47. Text and translation (modified) from *Bernart*, 87–88.

48. The *tornada* of Jaufre Rudel's *Qan lo rius de la fontana* suggests a written tradition of song by way of the neg-
    ative: "Senes breu de pargamina, tramet lo vers en cantan" (without a letter of parchment, I send this verse
    while singing). For commentary and more evidence of a written tradition of transmission see Kendrick, *The
    Game of Love*, 37–40. See also Van Vleck, *Memory and Re-Creation*, 43–55.

potential pleasure in reading, Bernart's cathartic pleasure (his *sauvamen*) in being read. Yet the penultimate full stanza and the *tornada* are linked by contrasting images of vocal performance, specifically, the troubadour's self-imposed silence (*ni a me dire no·s cove*) with the beloved's ability to speak (*seu parlar gen*). This opposition calls into question the expressive potential of the written word, for according to this lyric, the written word does not speak or sing as a messenger can, and therefore cannot expose or imitate the troubadour's subjectivity. Given the frequent self-referentiality of troubadour lyrics, however, we assume that what the beloved reads is the troubadour's song. And does that mean she also reads its music? I will return to this question later; for now, I simply want to call attention to the circular exchange of this extended *tornada*-complex—the denial of speech, the substitution of writing, and the reward of sweet words. One can imagine that the economy of writing presented here offered the scribe a point of identification with the subjective voice of the song.

Poetic construction and musical setting also determine a *tornada*'s expressive contribution to the lyric. *Tornadas* that are a full stanza, and thus fully expressive of the poetic structure of rhymes and line lengths, tend to have robust records of transmission. Most semi-strophe *tornadas* reinforce the pattern of rhyme-scheme segmentation, usually coinciding with syntactic segmentation, set up in the previous stanzas. For example, if the stanzas have seven lines, the pattern may be 4+3 (see Bernart's song 12 with the rhyme scheme abab/aab) or 3 + 4 (see song 18, with the rhyme scheme abb/cbbd), then the *tornada* will usually replicate the last segment. Only a few *tornadas* in Bernart's oeuvre break this pattern,[49] and one of these is the *tornada* for *Non es meravelha s'eu chan*, which survives in only two of nineteen sources for the song. The lyric consists of seven eight-line stanzas concluded by a three-line *tornada*; each line contains eight syllables. The *coblas unissonans* (the same rhyme sounds for each stanza) offer an intricate weave of related (-an, -en) and contrasting (-or, -es) and sounds. The last stanza and *tornada* are as follows:

VII

Bona domna, re no·us deman	a	Good lady, I ask nothing of you
mas que·m prendatz per servidor,	b	but that you take me as a servant,
qu'e·us servirai com bo senhor	b	for I will serve you as a good lord,
cossi que del gazardo m'an.	a	whatever my reward.
Ve·us m'al vostre comandamen,	c	Behold me at your command,
francs cors umils, gais e cortes.	d	noble person, humble, gay, courtly.
Ors ni leos non etz vos ges	d	You are not at all a bear or lion
que·m aucizatz s'a vos me ren	c	that you would kill me if I gave myself up to you.

---

49. Song 40 contains eight-line stanzas with the rhyme scheme abba/abba, and a *tornada* of five lines, thus ending the song with the rhymes aabba; song 16 contains eight-line stanzas with the rhymes scheme abba/cdcde, and two *tornadas* of three lines each, thus ending the song with three non-rhyming lines.

VIII

A mo Cortes, lai on ilh es,	d	To my Cortes, where she is,
tramet lo vers, e ja no·lh pes	d	I send the song, and may it never burden her
car n'ai estat tan lonjamen.	c	that I have been away so long.[50]

A strong syntactic break cuts all the stanzas neatly into two symmetrical halves, which also resonates with the symmetrical rhyme scheme: abba/cddc. The three-line *tornada* disrupts the syntactic and sonic symmetry of the stanzas, sending the ear back to the harsher -es rhyme mid-pattern. This poetically awkward return also has melodic ramifications (see example 1.3 ◉ OXFORD WEB MUSIC).

The melody and *tornada* for this song appear together in troub. *G*, though the address is to "A ma tortre," which means "to my turtledove"; in the other source that preserves the *tornada* (troub. *C*) the address specifies "A mo Cortes"—a *senhal* roughly translated "to My Courtly One," which is a masculine substantive adjective that could refer to a jongleur.[51] In troub. *G*, the scribe notated two successive stanzas of *Non es meravelha s'eu chan*; though nearly identical, the musical setting of the second stanza appears several notes out of phase with that of the first, suggesting that the music scribe did not actually know the song.[52] Nevertheless, the melody reinforces the symmetry of the lyric by setting the first and fifth lines with nearly identical musical material: the leap of a fourth or third to the recitation pitch G, followed by a short stepwise descent to an open cadence on F. Each of these key structural phrases is succeeded by phrases that have distinct and contrasting functions: the second line of music forms an antecedent–consequent pair with the first, and together they project the recitation note G as a tonic; in mid-stanza, the sixth line follows the fifth with an angular, and tonally open-ended, phrase that pushes the melody along to the next line. The *tornada* routes the singer to this angular, unstable sixth phrase of music, forcing a dramatic leap of a fifth from the final D up to A instead of returning to the structurally logical fifth line, which would have reinforced the symmetry of the words and music. But it is this musical illogic of the *tornada* that heightens its expressive effect, for the song is sent over the treacherous hills and valleys of that sixth melodic phrase, somewhat wayward yet compelled forward to the end by its own restlessness.

---

50. Text and translation (modified) from *Bernart*, 133–34.

51. See Bernart de Ventadorn, *Seine Lieder*, ed. Appel, 191; and Kaehne, *Studien zur Dichtung Bernarts von Ventadorn*, 2:195. In Example 1.3 I have used the text edition from *Bernart*, which prefers the *tornada* from troub. *C*. The *senhal* "mo Cortes" does not appear in any other lyric by Bernart de Ventadorn, though the *tornada* of *Pel doutz chan que·l rossinhols fai* (song 33) addresses "Huguet mos cortes messatgers" (Hugh, my courtly messenger). The *tornada* in troub. *G* reads as follows:

A ma tortre, lai on ilh es,	To my turtledove, where she is,
tramet lo vers, e no·il q'il pes	I send the song, and may it not burden her
qar eu no la vei plus souen.	that I do not see her often.

52. For a discussion of this manuscript and scribal procedures see Aubrey, *The Music of the Troubadours*, 43–46.

EXAMPLE 1.3 Bernart de Ventadorn, *Non es meravelha s'eu chan*, final stanza and *tornada* from troub. *G*, fol. 9

Though expressive, the poetic and musical misfit of the *tornada* for *Non es meravelha s'eu chan* may account for its weakness, though such awkwardness does not necessarily characterize the other four examples of weak *tornadas*; all of those correspond to some logical poetic and musical segmenting of the stanza proper.[53] In the end, as with the seemingly random preservation of troubadour melodies, the sources present no consistent reason for the strength of one *tornada* and the weakness of another except for the

---

53. Songs 8, 23, 39 have melodies in troub. *R*, but not their *tornadas*.

vagaries of oral and written transmission. But one thing is clear: most songs have *tornadas* in one or more sources (especially the later fourteenth-century sources troub. *C* and *G*), and the expressive contribution of *tornadas* has something to do with their melodic turns as well as their textual and subjective turns.

DIMINISHING RETURNS

In a short but insightful article, Chantal Phan argues that *tornadas* and later *envois* represent a collision (*entrechoque*) between two universes, the fictional one inside the lyric, denoted by the lover (the lyric "I," the lady, and the "song"), and the real one exterior to the lyric, denoted by names of poets, jongleurs, recipients, and places. According to Phan, this collision has a musical analog: "The final strophe lengthens the last part of the *chanson* with the dynamic elements: the tension between reality and fiction and the ambiguity between the lover and the poet, which corresponds to the formal surprise of the shortened strophe and the reprise of the melody from the middle."[54] The element of surprise may be overstated here, as is the generalization that all *tornadas* and *envois* point outside the lyric. Even the specifying *tornadas* can further a fiction, as Phan also suggests.[55] Just as the *vidas* and the *razos* created extra-lyrical fictions of a single "author" and a sincere, expressive "work," so did the names and places in the *tornadas* help late thirteenth- and early fourteenth-century readers and audiences conjure up the earlier world of the troubadours.

But what do the performances conjure up? What interests me about Phan's remark is the idea that *tornadas* poetically and musically participate in a key element of troubadour lyrics, namely, the ambiguity of the subjective voice as lover or poet, and, I might add, performer. The turn back to the mid-section melodically announces this ambiguity, regardless of the lyric's content, with a formal disruption. The semi-strophe *tornadas* themselves lie outside the formal dimensions of the lyric proper, and with their reprise of rhyme sounds, phrases, or lines, they call attention to the lyric as composed song rather than spontaneous utterance. Multiple *tornadas*, however, signal the ending of the song not with a grand finale, but rather with the medieval version of the "fade out." Sometimes the *tornadas* in a pair have different, decreasing lengths, such as those in Bernart de Ventadorn's *Can vei la flor, l'erba vert e la folha* (song 42) as it survives in troub. *P*; a melody for this song survives in the northern source troub. *X* (see example 1.4 below ● OXFORD WEB MUSIC).[56] After a springtime opening stanza that establishes Bernart's renewed

---

54. "[L]a strophe finale rallonge la dernière partie de la chanson par des éléments dynamiques: les tensions entre réel et fiction et l'ambiguïté entre amant et poète, qui correspondent aux surprises formelles de la strophe écourtée et de la mélodie reprise au milieu." Phan, "La tornada et l'envoi," 61.

55. Ibid., 59.

56. Troub. *P* preserves all seven stanzas and two *tornadas*; the stanza order is fairly consistent in the manuscripts. Troub. *X* transmits only the first three stanzas of the song; the opening line reads *Quant vei parer l'erbe vert*

desire for love and joy, the song goes on grimly to consider the folly of such desire, which has led Bernart to love the "wrong woman"—the one who rejects him most—and to spurn the woman who is generous. The final stanza and two *tornadas* are as follows:

VII

L'aiga del cor c'amdos los olhs me molha	The tears from my heart that moisten my eyes
m'es be guirens qu'eu penet mo folatge.	are surely a pledge that I repent my folly.
E conosc be midons en pren damnatge	I know for sure that my lady will regret it
s'ela tan fai que perdonar no·m volha.	if she goes so far as to refuse to pardon me.
Pois meus no sui et ilh m'a en poder,	Since I am not my own, and she has me in her power,
mais pert s'ela qu'eu el meu dechazer,	she has more to lose from my downfall than I do,
per so l'er gen s'ab son ome plaideya.	therefore it would be good for her to negotiate with her vassal.

VIII

Mo messatger man a mo Bel Vezer,	I send my messenger to my Bel Vezer,
que cilh que·m tolc lo sen e lo saber,	for the one who robbed me of my wit and intelligence
me tol midons e leis que no la veya.	takes away my lady and her, so that I may not see her.

IX

Amics Tristans, car eu no·us posc vezer,	Friend Tristan, because I cannot see you,
a Deu vos do cal que part que m'esteya.	I give you over to God wherever I may be.[57]

Both *tornadas* contain proper names, though only the second is a direct address. The first *tornada* directs the song-as-messenger to Bel Vezer, a *senhal* that appears in seven of Bernart's lyrics (twice in *Can vei la flor, l'erba vert e la folha*; see stanza V, line 33, transcribed and performed on the companion website). In most cases, as in this song, Bel Vezer is clearly distinguished from the beloved (here *midons*), thus naming a recipient

---

e la fuelle. See Bernart de Ventadorn, *Seine Lieder*, ed. Appel, 240. The words for Example 1.4 are taken from the edition in *Bernart*.

57. Text and translation from *Bernart*, 163–65.

of the song who is outside the lover–beloved dyad, but not outside the economy of desire. Perhaps the code name for a particular patroness,[58] the tangle of pronouns in the final line of this first *tornada*—"[the one who] takes away my lady and *her* (*leis*) so that I may not see *her* (*la*)"—separates and confuses Bel Vezer and the beloved. Yet Bel Vezer also represents the listeners, who truly bear witness to the troubadour's song, and who constitute the other necessary component for self-expression. The name Tristan appears in five of Bernart's lyrics, and in at least one of these as the legendary lover of Iseult (song 44). Scholars have proposed various possible identities for this *senhal*, even suggesting multiple referents, including an unidentified beloved and the troubadour Raimbaut d'Aurenga.[59] Another pairing of Bel Vezer and Tristan in *tornadas* of diminishing length occurs in song 29, *Lo rossinhols s'esbaudeya*, which ends with the dramatic declaration "Tristan, si no·us es veyaire / mais vos am que no solh faire" (Tristan, even if it does not seem so to you, I love you more than I used to). The second "Can vei" lyric, *Can vei la lauzeta mover* (song 43), ends more melodramatically:

Tristan, ges no·n auretz de me	Tristan, you shall have nothing more from me
qu'eu m'en vau, chaitius, no sai on.	for I depart, wretched, I know not whither.
De chanter me gic e·m recre,	I forsake and renounce singing,
e de joi e d'amor m'escon.	and I seek shelter from joy and love.[60]

In all three of these rhetorically related *tornadas* Tristan is the last to be addressed; and in each we encounter a final crisis of communication sharply focused by the direct address to Tristan, who is not present (song 42), not comprehending (song 29), and who is finally rejected as the recipient of future songs, which symbolizes Bernart's silence (song 43). Tristan seems to evoke the diminishing returns of love—an inverse relationship to the ever increasing efforts of the troubadour-lover.[61]

This inverse relationship is at the heart of *Can vei la flor, l'erba vert e la folha*: the impossibility of love is what the lover seeks: "I follow the woman who is most arrogant towards

58. See Bernart de Ventadorn, *Seine Lieder*, ed. Appel, xlii–xlvii. Songs 1, 8, 12, 28, 29, 41, and 42 mention Bel Vezer. For commentary on the possible identity and location of Bel Vezer see also Mouzat, "De Ventadorn à Barjols," 426. On Tristan and Bel Vezer, see also Kaehne, *Studien zur Dichtung Bernarts von Ventadorn*, 1:52–57, 76–77.

59. See Bernart de Ventadorn, *Seine Lieder*, ed. Appel, xlvii–xlviii. Songs 4, 29, 44, 42, and 43 refer to Tristan in their *tornadas*. The two *tornadas* of song 4 strongly link the name Tristan with the *domna* by repeating the phrase *gabar e rire* (mock and laugh) in association with both. The phrase frames the *tornada* complex, thus structurally connecting the two. See *Bernart*, 52–53. W. T. Pattison identifies Bernart's Tristan as referring to Raimbaut d'Aurenga; see *The Life and Works of the Troubadour Raimbaut d'Orange*, 24–25.

60. Text and translation from *Bernart*, 167–68.

61. I am not proposing a "cycle" of Bernart's Tristan lyrics, as earlier scholars have, although I do note the shared disposition and thematic use of Tristan in these *tornadas*. See also Kaehne, *Studien zur Dichtung Bernarts von Ventadorn*, 2:246–48 for a consideration of their thematic relationships.

me / while fleeing the lady who was full of goodness."[62] Despite the troubadour's repentance for his folly, the gradual reduction of words at the end of his song—from seven lines, to three lines, to two lines—enacts the robbery of the troubadour's "wit and intelligence" (*lo sen e lo saber*) perpetrated by the paradox of his desire. As the troubadour is robbed of his words, he is also robbed of seeing Bel Vezer ("Pleasing Vision" or "Fair Sight"—here the *senhal* is made ironic), his lady, and Tristan.[63]

The melody for *Can vei la flor, l'erba vert e la folha*—an *oda continua*—is remarkably beautiful: phrases float in the upper half of a G octave, linked by opening gestures and motifs that are nevertheless unpredictable in their recurrence. (See example 1.4 🔊 OXFORD WEB MUSIC). Although G provides the structural ambitus, as marked out by the first line with its full octave descent, the melody often gently pulls our ear to C or F, as the does the second line with its opening recitation motif on repeated Cs and the cresting of the contour on F. More than half of the phrases (lines 2, 4, 5, and 7) begin with this striking recitation motif—four or five repeated pitches followed by a descending line—which contrasts with the sweeping gestures that open phrases 1, 3, and 6. The two internal lines (4 and 5) transpose the recitation motif from the C of line 2 to F, which we hear again in the last line of the stanza. Such frequent halting of the melodic flow enforces a meditative pause on C, and especially F; this last pitch is an unstable plaintive tone caught between the pull of C and G. We are meant, it seems, to meditate on these notes that keep us suspended in a pleasurable tension, building desire for melodic resolution. It is an apt musical analog to the troubadour's meditation on the folly of his misplaced desire, which has held him hostage.

The two *tornadas* amplify this sense of folly and capture between the "right" and the "wrong" objects of desire. The first *tornada* cycles back from the cadence on G to the repeated Fs in line 5 with the leap of a minor seventh, echoing the internal melodic juncture between lines 4 and 5 heard with each strophic repetition. Given the multiple lines that start with repeated Fs, we may not be sure at first if the melody has returned to line 4, 5, or simply repeated the last line; and in a short time we do hear the last line again, which echoes where we have just been at the head of the *tornada*. The momentary melodic disorientation that we may feel with the first *tornada* continues with the surprising return to line 6 of the second *tornada*. Although this *tornada* resolves the tonal conflict somewhat with an octave leap that emphasizes G, the ear has been saturated by the returns to F, and unsettled by the deferral of closure. We simply do not trust our ears that we have come to the end. In performance, the diminishing returns of the two *tornadas* create a unique five-line melody assembled from fragments of the song, thus radically altering the strophic melody, its number of phrases, its play of motifs and structuring pitches, and the listener's orientation within these.

---

62. "Eu sec cela que plus vas me s'ergolha / e cela fuih que·m fo de bel estatge" (lines 22–23).

63. For an interpretation of Bel Vezer within the discourse of vision and desire in troubadour poetry see Gaunt, *Love and Death*, 180–91.

EXAMPLE 1.4 Bernart de Ventadorn, *Can vei la flor, l'erba vert e la folha*, final stanza and *tornadas*, melody from troub. *X*, fol. 88

With example 1.4 I have reconstructed a performance practice from admittedly weak links between the *tornadas* and the verse. By way of contrast, Bernart's *Chantars no pot gair valer* (song 15) is remarkable in that the two diminishing *tornadas* are strongly bound to the stanzas; the lyric does not survive without them.[64] They are quoted below:

---

64. See also songs 29 and 42. Related to these may be the full + semi-strophe *tornada* complexes discussed above. Text from *Bernart*, 81, translation my own.

VIII

Lo vers es fis e naturaus	This song is true and natural
e bos celui qui be l'enten,	and good for whomever understands it well,
e melher es, qui·l joi aten.	and it is better for him who waits for joy.

IX

| Bernartz de Ventadorn l'enten | Bernart understands it, |
| e·l di e·l fai e·l joi n'aten. | he sings it, he composes it, and he waits for joy from it. |

Not only does the final *tornada* repeat the same rhyme words as the first, but it also harks back to the final two lines of the opening stanza:

| qu'en joi d'amor ai et enten | for the joy of love I have and devote |
| la boch' e·ls olhs e·l cor e·l sen. | the mouth, the eyes, the heart, and mind. |

Nouns of the body that end the first stanza become at the end of the song verbs definitive of the troubadour's craft, linked by the melodious enclitic construction *e·l*, which can be either pronoun or article. Neither *tornada* casts the listener to the world outside the lyric; together the semantic content of the *tornadas* fold Bernart into the lyric, shoring up the identity of the author with the lyric "I" while the procedure of the song itself works to discriminate between author, lover, and performer. Unfortunately, no melody survives for this lyric, but we can imagine the dramatic expressive effect of these literally diminishing returns, where the performer's voice falls silent just as the author's voice comes to the fore.

With each melodic return that is not a complete return, and with each echo of *e·l* that is not quite the same as before, sound and sense compete for attention, and this casts the name "Bernart" itself into the realm of pure sounds that have a tenuous purchase on meaning. But does this ambivalence between sound and sense also pertain to the written word? Here I want to consider the scene of reading the song that the *tornadas* of *En cossirer et en esmai* invite us to imagine. Recall that Bernart foregoes the usual oral delivery through a messenger in favor of a written text that the beloved will read. A. C. Spearing argues that "textual subjectivity," which he observes in medieval English literature, marks "not the presence but the absence of human subjects" insofar as written words call attention to themselves as artifice and not a window onto a human consciousness.[65] Poetic conceits and figurative language also work to evacuate the self; the subject qua person is replaced by the subject qua text, thus leaving the grammatical subject "I" open to interpretation. The evacuation of the human subject seems an explicit maneuver at the end of *En cossirer et en esmai*, which utilizes a common topos in the troubadour *canso*—the fear of speech or the

---

65. See Spearing, *Textual Subjectivity*, 1–17, 30–31, 174, 197, 247 (quotation).

renunciation of song. R. Howard Bloch observes that this topos is "contrary to the manifest presence of the song" and that the resulting paradox signifies "an impossible relation of speaker to voice."[66] When a written document, rather than a vocal performance by the troubadour or his proxy the jongleur, provides the "manifest presence of the song," the "relation of speaker to voice" shifts to the relation of reader to writing.

Laura Kendrick argues that troubadour songs were conceived in writing, and she points to the creation of puns in the oral phonetic realization of the written text as evidence.[67] Kendrick focuses on erotic word games that can arise from variant spellings and different parsings of syllables, but in her general arguments for the performativity of writing and the orality of reading we may also understand better how the written word can be mimetic of subjectivity. *En cossirer et en esmai* appears in troub. *G* with musical notation for the first stanza (the *tornada* does appear at the end of the lyric in this source). We could understand this assertion of music as an insistence on the primacy of performance, as Sarah Kay would argue, despite the abject silence and recourse to writing that the lyric expresses. Or we could understand music as a further textualization of the subject. Notation means more different types of writing; words and music together, in a codex, aggressively assert the technology of writing. In the mid-twelfth century, single songs may have been transmitted on a *breu*, a small scroll or parchment leaf. Music, if included, probably would have resembled the notation of the Aquitanian *versus* found in P-BnF f. lat. 3719, fols. 33^r–44^v (see figure 1.1).

Small dashes spread out over the words of the first stanza; vertical stacks of dashes convey descending melismas.[68] Imaginary horizontal lines (possibly etched into the parchment by a drypoint pen), designated F and occasionally C at the left, offer a guide for the pitch content. The notes, however, seem to float on their own, not always clearly aligned with a text syllable or pitch line. In reading Bernart's song fresh, the lady would have encountered melodic ambiguities as well as possible verbal ambiguities. Perhaps she would have worked out a tune as cued from the notes, one that fit a song she already knew or one that fit her own sense of how a tune should go. If, following Spearing, the subject of Bernart's song manifests as text (words and music) on parchment, left open to

---

66. Bloch, *Medieval Misogyny*, 147.

67. Kendrick, *The Game of Love*, 24–52, esp. 36–39 on evidence that troubadours wrote their songs; on p. 42 she summarizes: "The aesthetic of early Provençal lyric is one of complexity and richness of sound and sense, not of simplicity and clarity." On the oral nature of medieval reading see Gehl, "*Competens silentium*," 140–41. Reading often included *meditatio*, which Gehl describes: "Texts of all sorts were 'meditated,' that is, read slowly, period by period, and repeated in the *murmur* with an eye toward memorizing them." On the oral reading habits of lay society see Saenger, *Space between Words*, 265–72. Saenger comments: "Word separation in vernacular books at the end of the Middle Ages continued to lag behind the norms of Latin codices" (266). This confusion over word separation forms an important component of Kendrick's argument.

68. Another source for Aquitanian monophony and polyphony, P-BnF f. lat. 1139, contains the earliest songs partially or wholly written in Occitan—one *versus* in Occitan (*O Maria, Deu marie*, fol. 49), and a second alternating Latin strophes with Occitan strophes (*In hoc anni circulo*, fol. 48). For a discussion of these pieces see Switten, "*Versus* and Troubadours around 1100," 94 and 94n7, 99.

interpretation, then the interpretation of that subject includes the lady's own subjective performance. Perhaps this is the ultimate consummation between lover and beloved—the merging of their voices in the act of reading, for in reading the lyric, Bernart's lady becomes the troubadour: she both composes and sings his song.

FROM RETURNS TO REFRAINS

Thus far we have seen how the *tornada*, especially the *tornada*-reprise, may send us on an endless loop, specifying and refracting the troubadour as subject in the multiple performances, vocal proxies, filiations of self, scribal inscriptions, and in the transformation of subjective words into subjectless proverbs. In the trouvère repertory, we do not find the repetition of phrases as in the early

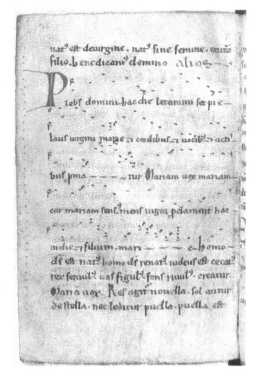

FIGURE 1.1 Twelfth-century Aquitanian *versus*, P-BnF lat. 3719, fol. 39ᵛ (Bibliothèque nationale de France, Paris)

tornada-reprises, though *envois* are occasionally called a *reprise*, as is the melody.[69] For the rest of this chapter I will consider the *envois* of Thibaut de Champagne (1201–53), a mid-thirteenth-century trouvère whose songs represent "the classic formulation of the northern French *chanson d'amour*."[70] A typology of the thirty-five *envois* culled from his thirty-six *chansons d'amour* (see table 1.7) reveals that most *envois* use one of two opening formulas: "*Chanson, va*" (Song, go now), and what I will call the "*Dame-envoi*."

Only nine of these thirty-five specify proper names or places—surprisingly few compared to twenty-five *tornadas* for the "classic" troubadour Bernart de Ventadorn (see table 1.8). We can also see from the comparison of formulas how the occasional, perhaps exceptional, use of a generic address to the song, messenger, or Domna with Bernart becomes the norm with Thibaut. Thus the *envoi*, by and large, loses its particularizing function, which gives a real-world context for the poet, as well as its proverbializing function, which frames the poet's words as transcendent of time, place, and person. What, then, do these formulaic *envois* say about subjectivity?

---

69. See Dragonetti, *La Technique poétique des trouvères*, 304–306, 572; see also Mölk, "Deux remarques sur la tornada," 4–7.

70. Brahney, Introduction to *Thibaut*, xviii.

TABLE 1.7

Typology of the *envois* of Thibaut de Champagne (ed. Brahney; 36 songs total)

Envoi type	Song number
Dame, . . . (18)	3, 6, 7, 8, 15, 18, 19, 20, 22†, 23, 25, 26, 27, 30, 31, 33†, 34, 35
Chanson, va t'en (10)	2, 9 (with refrain), 11, 12 (with refrain), 13, 14 (*chanson, di li*), 16 (*chanson, di li*), 21 (*chanson, . . . corez*), 22†, 33†
Names, code-names, and places (9)	9, 12, 22†, 23, 24, 27, 31, 32, 33
Continuation of poetic theme (6)	1, 4, 10 (with refrain), 17, 28, 29
Proverbial	5
No *envoi*	36

† Double formula.

TABLE 1.8

Typology of the *tornadas* of Bernart de Ventadorn (ed. Appel; 38 songs total)

Tornada type	Song number
Names, self-naming, code-names, and places (25)	1, 4, 5, 6†, 7, 8†, 10†, 12, 13, 15, 16†, 19, 21, 22†, 23, 26, 28, 29†, 31, 33, 35, 36, 41, 42†, 45
Messatgers, vai (6)	10†, 18, 22†, 39, 42†, 44
Continuation of poetic theme (6)	9, 17, 27, 30, 37, 40
Domna, . . . (3)	6†, 20, 25
Tristans, . . . (3)	29†, 42†, 43
Chanso, vai (2)	8†, 16†
No *tornada*	3, 24, [38]; *tensos:* 2, 14, [32]

† Double or triple formula.
[ ] Indicates uncertain authorship.

Despite their predominantly formulaic rhetoric, the *envois* of Thibaut de Champagne have a strong attachment to their lyrics: for any one song, more sources preserve the *envois* than not. This is due in part to the fact that a number of sources (trouv. *K, Mt, O, T, V, X*) transmit a comprehensive collection of his songs, and that ideal of comprehensiveness included the *envois*. Trouv. *Mt*, for example, preserves thirty-five songs, all with one or more *envois*; trouv. *O*, though not primarily arranged by author,[71] also preserves

---

71. Trouv. *O* has a primary alphabetical arrangement of songs, which resembles trouv. *C*, and the motet collection of *W*2. Within each letter group, there is a secondary and more common arrangement by author's social

thirty-five songs but is missing one *envoi*; trouv. *T* is missing three songs from the core thirty-five, but all of its songs have *envois*. The exceptional manuscript is trouv. *K*: of its thirty-five songs, only nine have their *envois*. Although the sources *KNPX* form a group of manuscripts related by song order and melodies, they diverge significantly in their transmission of Thibaut's *chansons d'amour*, as indicated below.[72] The total number of songs attributed to Thibaut in these sources, including pastourelles, *jeux-partis*, crusade songs, songs to the Virgin, is given in parentheses:

K: 35 *chansons*, 9 with *envois* (59)
N: 18 *chansons*, 11 with *envois* (28)
P: 5 *chansons*, 1 with *envoi* (7)
X: 35 *chansons*, 31 with *envois* (59)

Of this group, only trouv. *K* and *X* appear to be comprehensive in the collection of Thibaut's songs, preserving the same number in nearly the same order; however, only trouv. *X* consistently transmits the *envois*. Furthermore, trouv. *KNV* open their collections with Thibaut's songs, which are accompanied by the only illustration that appears in these *chansonniers*. Thus the illustration stands for Thibaut's particular songs, as well as for the whole genre of songs that follow. The *KNV* group shows a vielle player performing for an aristocratic couple, thus stressing the songs as performed entertainment; trouv. *X*, which uses additional miniatures to introduce other genres of songs, opens the collection of Thibaut's songs with what Sylvia Huot describes as "a crowned man gesturing toward a lady, who places her hand on her heart."[73] This depiction of noble lovers, who are the noble subjects within the fiction of the lyrics rather than the noble audience listening to the songs, corresponds with the source that preserves the *envois*. Given that the *envois* addressed an intended audience, we might have expected the illustration in trouv. *X* to have depicted them as well (in accordance with *KNV*). Yet just as the illustration in trouv. *X* clearly derives from a stock pictorial motif that origi-

---

status or fame. But none of the songs was given an author attribution. Thus each alphabetical group begins with songs by Thibaut de Champagne, who was also known as the *roi de Navarre*. See chapter 3 for further discussion.

72. Trouv. *K* and *N* are so close in their codicological details (wording of rubrics, decorated initials) that Mark Everist considers the two manuscripts to be the product of the same scribe; see his discussion of these sources in *Polyphonic Music*, 187–97. See also Huot's discussion of this group and their differences in *From Song to Book*, 47–52. See also the inventory of these manuscripts in Raynaud, *Bibliographie des chansonniers français*, vol. 1.

73. Huot, *From Song to Book*, 54. The illustration at the head of Thibaut's songs in trouv. *M* has been cut from the manuscript, but it probably would have shown a knight on horseback as the other illustrations of noble authors do, and as trouv. *T* does at the beginning of Thibaut's songs.

nates from the lyric scenario, Thibaut's formulaic *envois* themselves frequently remain within the lyric scenario, adding only subtle references to the change of address or voice that characterized the *tornadas* of the troubadours.

Thibaut's song *Les douces dolors* is a case in point; the song survives with one *envoi* addressing the Dame. In most sources the *envoi* follows a fifth stanza that also begins with *Dame*; both are given below.

V

Dame, j'ai tout mis,	Lady, I have devoted everything,
et cuer et penser,	both heart and mind,
en vous, et assis	to you, and have been steadfast
sanz ja remuër.	without ever wavering.
Se je voloie aconter	If I wanted to enumerate
vostre biauté, vostre pris,	your beauty and your worth,
j'avroie trop anemis;	I would have too many enemies;
por ce ne m'en os parler.	thus I dare not speak of them.

VI

Dame, je n'i puis durer,	Lady, I can last no longer,
que tot m'ira adès pis,	for my situation will grow ever worse,
tant que vos dïez: "Amis,	until you say: "Friend,
je vos vueil m'amor doner."	I want to give you my love."[74]

This *envoi*, like most of the *Dame-envois*, hardly sounds distinct in tone or theme from the stanza, especially given that Thibaut often opens stanzas with the word *Dame*.[75] Musically, however, the *envoi* returns to the midpoint, and importantly to the high C of the song, which resolves the tension of the Lydian F–B tetrachord in the *pedes* phrases (see example 1.5 ◉ OXFORD WEB MUSIC). This distinctively dramatic musical phrase of line 5, with the emphasis on C, the reach up to the high D, and the stepwise, syllabic descent, recurs at the end of the melody as well. Its immediate repetition for the *envoi* newly inflects this last appeal to the Dame with vocal if not also emotional intensity. In the context of the *envoi*, the final line is the imagined speech of the lady—a marked intrusion of voice, but also a fantastical alignment of lover and beloved.

---

74. RS 2032. Text and translation from *Thibaut*, 106–109.

75. Songs 6, 15, 18, 19, 23, 25, 26, 31, 35 (ed. Brahney) use the *Dame-envoi* after an earlier use of *"Dame"* to open a stanza.

EXAMPLE 1.5 Thibaut de Champagne, *Les douces dolors*, final stanza and *envoi* from trouv. *M*, fol. 67/BX

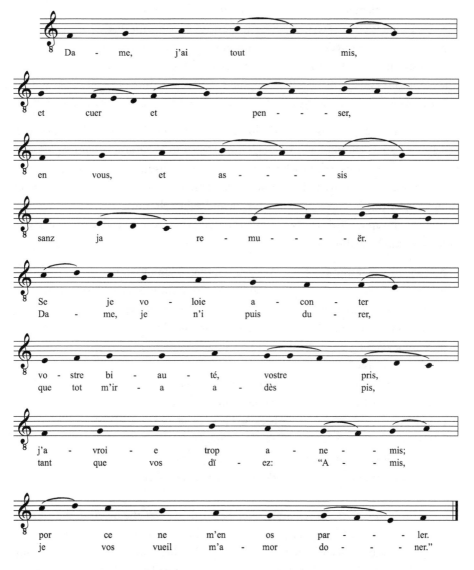

Da - me,   j'ai   tout   mis,

et   cuer   et   pen - - - ser,

en   vous,   et   as - - - - sis

sanz   ja   re - mu - - - - ër.

Se   je   vo - loie   a - con - ter
Da - me,   je   n'i   puis   du - rer,

vo - stre   bi - au - té,   vostre   pris,
que   tot   m'ir - a   a - dès   pis,

j'a - vroi - e   trop   a - ne - - mis;
tant   que   vos   dï - ez: "A - - mis,

por   ce   ne   m'en   os   par - - - ler.
je   vos   vueil   m'a - mor   do - - - ner."

In many motets and songs in northern France, when a line of verse introduces speech or song, that reported voice comes in the form of a quoted refrain—a courtly aphorism assumed to be circulating freely in the public domain much like proverbs. In *Quant je voi l'erbe amatir*, attributed to Perrin d'Angicourt, every stanza ends with a distinct refrain; the last stanza is given here:

IV

Mort m'a sanz point d'acheson   Slain me without the slightest grounds
cele en qui j'ai atorné   she has, in whom I have turned

mon sens et m'entencion	my mind and my attention,
pour fere sa volenté.	in order to do her will.
S'or le daignoit prendre en gré,	If she deigned to accept that,
pour tout autre guerredon	for more than any other reward
mis m'avroit fors de friçon,	it would relieve me of anxiety,
si diroie sanz esmai:	thus I would say without trouble:
"Bone amor que j'ai mi tient gai."	*"The good love that I have keeps me happy."*[76]

Here the imagined speech is that of the lover, who expresses his imagined happiness in a widely-circulated little phrase.[77] Although there is no formal "return" to a prior phrase of music (indeed, we assume that each refrain carries its own distinct music), the lover's own turn of mind to the beloved, the merging of his action and her will, results in this final complex voice that is both a private sentiment and public chorus.

Refrains also appear frequently without introductory lines at the end of motet parts, as in this motetus from *Mo*:

Au comencement d'esté	At the beginning of summertime
que naist la flor ou vert pré,	when the flowers in the green meadow burgeon,
Amors qui m'ont en baillie	Love who has me in his power
m'ont si doucement navré	wounded me so sweetly
qu'or muir a mon gré	that now I want only to die
se la bele renvoisie	if the gay, fair one
qui est ma joie et ma vie	who is my joy and life
ne m'a pardouné	has not pardoned me
ce qu'en s'amour ai torné	because I have turned to love
tout mon pensé.	all of my thoughts.
Je voz ai tout mon cuer douné	*I have given my entire heart to you*
Bele, tres douce amie.	*Beautiful, very sweet beloved.*[78]

The refrain in this motetus resembles the imagined voice of the beloved in Thibaut's *envoi*, who says "Friend, I want to give you my love." Both *envoi* and refrain are terse statements of devotion, couched in terms of giving. Furthermore, these ending refrains function like *tornada*-reprises: they are quoted or quotable phrases that bring the lyric to a close with a subtle shift from an individual to a public voice.

Scholars once thought that all such refrains originated as the refrains of *rondet de carole* and later *rondeaux*, that is, the structurally repeating words and music in a popular song (see chapters 4 and 5). Yet the number of anonymous aphorisms circulating in non-repeating contexts, such as motets, verse narratives, or *chansons* with changing refrains,

---

76. RS 1390. Text and translation (modified) from *Songs*, 328.

77. B-ref 289, and its close variants 935, and 1247.

78. Gen 118. Text and translation (modified) Tischler, *The Montpellier Codex*, 4:35. For other citations of the refrain see B-ref 1155 and its variants 668, 962, 1310.

far surpasses those surviving in *rondeaux*. This evidence suggests that refrains originated not from a particular popular genre, but rather from a general compositional practice among trouvères and their clerical contemporaries—namely, the practice of quoting commonplace phrases, or producing phrases that were self-consciously generic and could themselves circulate anonymously. In this sense, quoted refrains can be considered cultural refrains—the obsessive repetition of particular phrases and ideas on the macro-level of literary production. As imagined speech or song within a song, refrains add an element of irony in the attribution of public words to a private source. Here again medieval cultural practice resonates with modern theory: refrains function as elemental a priori linguistic structures setting the terms for individual expression.

Ardis Butterfield, writing about the *rondet de carole*, notes that while refrains suggest communal voices, it is in fact the non-repeating verses that are the most formulaic and likely to be readily recognizable by their audience.[79] Such ambiguity and tension between individual and communal or generic voice is writ large at the end of Thibaut's song *Li rosignox chante tant*, which survives in four sources with three *envois*.[80] The final stanza and three *envois* are given here:

V

Je ne cuit pas que serpent	I do not think that the serpent
n'autre beste poigne plus	or any other animal strikes
que fet Amors au desus;	as fiercely as does Love;
trop par sont li coup pesant.	her blows are exceedingly heavy.
Plus tret souvent que Turs ne Arrabiz,	She strikes me more steadily than a Turk or an Arab,
n'onques oncor Salemons ne Daviz,	and not even Solomon or David,
ne s'i tindrent ne q'uns fox d'Alemaigne.	or a madman from Germany, could withstand the assault.

VI

N'est merveille se je sui esbahiz,	It is no wonder that I am dismayed,
que li conforz m'en vient si a enviz	for comfort is so difficult to win
que je dout mult que toz biens ne sosfraigne.	that I fear greatly that I shall lack all goods.

VII

Dame, de vos ne puis estre partiz,	Lady, I cannot be parted from you,

---

79. Butterfield, *Poetry and Music*, 46–49. In stressing the "clausal interruption, change in voice, change of theme" of refrains, Butterfield argues that refrains are "a disjunctive element" in *rondets*, but also that musically refrains are "the primary generating element of the dance-song" (49). Her main point is that refrains are "autonomous" from other genres, "not simply fragments of *rondets de carole*" nor "fragmentary citations in a romance either" (50).

80. RS 360. All three *envois* appear in trouv. *Mt*, *T*, *O*, and *V*. In *O* (fol. 71) and *V* (fol. 12), the scribes ran the first and second *envoi* together as if they were two halves of the same stanza despite the repetition of rhymes, which conform to the last three lines of the preceding stanzas. In *Mt* and *T* (9) all three *envois* are marked with decorated capitals. No music survives for the song in *T*.

si vos en jur les grez et les merciz	thus I declare to you the pleasures and mercies
que je atant qu'ancor de vos me viegne.	I still wait for you to grant me.

VIII

Mainz durz assaux m'avra Amors bastiz.	Love will have struck me many harsh blows.
Chançon, va tost et non pas a enviz	Song, go quickly and not reluctantly
et salue nostre gent de Champaigne.	And greet our people of Champagne.[81]

The first *envoi* is rhetorically indistinguishable from the stanzas, signaled only by the musical return to the midpoint of the melody; the second and third *envois* use the verbal *Dame* and *Chanson, va* formulas respectively. While many lyrics survive with two *tornadas* or *envois*, three is exceptional. They could represent performance options, but on closer look, a progression of subjects emerges in this series, from the lyric "I" to the Dame, to the song, and finally with the last line to "the people of Champagne," who take their place in an international lineup of Turks, Arabs, and Germans.

In performance, the fourfold iteration of the second half of the melody (lines 5–7) creates the sonic effect of a "broken record"—the seemingly indefinite repetition of the same melodic segment (see example 1.6 ◉ OXFORD WEB MUSIC). The medieval audience may have associated such repetition and formulas with sacred Litanies—musically repetitive invocations and petitions. This feel of invocation is intensified by shared motifs among the last three lines: the first four notes of lines 5 and 7 are the same (F–E–F–G), and all three lines end with the same cadential formula of a descending third from B to G.

Each turn back to the midpoint of the melody paradoxically spirals outward from the register of specific and personal to the register of generic and public, ending with a collective that perfectly reconciles the two. Thibaut's serial *envois*, their strangely redundant signaling of the end with a looping melodic fragment, verbal formulas, and the final salute to the *gent de Champaigne* mimetically interpellate the audience with musical and poetic returns. Like refrains, these shifting but formulaic *envois* present the semblance of an autonomous voice that is, however, irreducibly socially configured.

While there may not be direct links between *tornadas* or *envois* and refrains, they do seem to share a profile as refined musical-poetic turning points in medieval lyric, where questions of subjectivity and expression are brought to the fore and answered with a twist. Far from assertions of autonomy and agency, *tornadas*, *envois*, and refrains corrupt the first-person voice with vocal proxies and constructed kinships,

---

81. Text and translation from *Thibaut*, 89–91.

EXAMPLE 1.6 Thibaut de Champagne, *Li rosignox chante tant*, final stanza and three *envois*, melody from trouv. *O*, fol. 70ᵛ

aphorisms and proverbs, imagined speech, implied chorus, and recognizable formulas. In all of these we find the "trope of the turn"—the conundrum of agency and subordination that Butler describes as "irreducibly mimetic and performative"— a condition of subjectivity that is outside of language, perhaps, but codified in music.

2

Delinquent *Descorts* and Medieval Lateness

THE WORD "DELINQUENT" means being late, being past due; it also refers to someone who regularly violates the law. The word "*descort*," according to medieval music treatises and present-day dictionaries of Old French and Occitan, means "discord"; it also refers to a song that expresses discord in thematic, poetic, and melodic construction.[1] I begin with a detail from the *descort Qui la ve en ditz*, excerpted in example 2.1 ◉ OXFORD WEB MUSIC: a pair of phrases opens the second strophe, each containing a single-syllable trailing rhyme.[2] In the second of these phrases (line 2), the sound of the word *Fatz* points backward, while the sense of word "Fool" points forward. Although the isolated note punctuates the end of a phrase, the singer must also think of it as an anacrusis to the next one. The music amplifies this friction with melodic leaps that disturb the tonal focus. With that word *Fatz* we are precariously poised between past and future, between poetic sound and linguistic sense. The moment is full of delinquency.

Anc de nulla gen	Never was there of any people
non fon atrobatz	a man found
natz	born

---

1. S.v. "Descort," *Old French–English Dictionary*; and "descort," in *PDP*.
2. PC 10-45. The term "echo rime" is used by the lyric's editors, in *Aimeric*, 216; "trailing rhyme," which I find a more accurate description, was supplied to me by Gary Moulsdale, who learned and recorded these pieces for an earlier incarnation of this project.

que tan finamen	who loved so nobly,
ames desamatz.	though not loved.
Fatz	Fool
suy, car non laten	I am, for neither do I expect
joy, ni no·m n'es datz	joy, nor am I given any
gratz.	favors.

EXAMPLE 2.1 *Qui la ve en ditz*, strophe II excerpt from trouv. *M*, fol. 185ᵛ/B170ᵛ

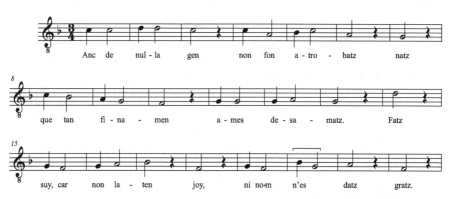

We have about forty Occitan poems that can be identified as *descorts* (four survive with music), and ten Old French poems (nine with music).[3] Occitan *descort* lyrics first appear around the year 1200, with the third-generation troubadour Raimbaut de Vaqueiras (fl. 1180–1205).[4] Scholars count five generations of troubadours, spanning over two centuries, from around 1100 to 1300, and so the arrival of the *descort* marks roughly the midpoint of the tradition and culture of the troubadours.[5] As most *descorts* name themselves as such, they also bear witness to the emerging genre system—perhaps still embryonic— that treatise writers and manuscript compilers would help to crystallize by the middle of

---

3. See Aubrey, "The Dialectic between Occitania and France," 35. Aubrey counts "about thirty-eight in Occitan (three of which survive with music) and ten in French (all surviving with music)"; Maillard, *Évolution et esthétique du lai lyrique*, indexes eleven titles for French *descorts* and forty-two titles of Occitan songs as *descorts* (rejecting eleven), 119–27.

4. See Aubrey, *The Music of the Troubadours*, 5–25, esp. 9.

5. The five generations of troubadours are as follows (listing prominent troubadours): the first flourished between 1100 and 1150 (Guilhem de Peitieu [Guilhem IX], Jaufre Rudel, Marcabru); the second flourished between 1140 and 1175 (Bernart de Ventadorn, Peire d'Alvernha, Raimbaut d'Aurenga); the third flourished between 1160 and 1210 (Giraut de Bornelh, Arnaut de Maruelh, Gaucelm Faidit, Bertran de Born, Raimon Jordan, Folquet de Marselha, Arnaut Daniel, Raimbaut de Vaqueiras, Peire Vidal, Comtessa de Dia, Gui d'Ussel); the fourth flourished between 1180 and 1240 (the Monk of Montaudon, Peire Raimon de Tolosa, Peirol, Aimeric de Peguilhan, Raimon de Miraval, Albertet, Cadenet, Guilhem Augier [Novella], Uc de Saint Circ); the fifth flourished between 1230 and 1300 (Sordello, Guilhem de Montanhagol, Peire Cardenal, Guiraut d'Espanha, Guiraut Riquier).

the thirteenth century.[6] Northern examples of *descorts*, which also frequently name themselves, emerged sometime between 1200 and 1236, during the second or third generation of trouvères.[7]

As the name suggests, *descorts* express discord generically, though what this means is not entirely clear.[8] *Descort*, and its antonym *acort* (harmony, agreement), have two possible Latin roots that may have mingled in later derivations: (1) *chorda* (Occitan, *corda*), meaning cord or rope (to bind things) or the string of a musical instrument; and (2) *cors, cordis* (Occitan *cor*) meaning heart, which, as previously noted, was believed to be the organ of love and other emotions, and to have something to do with memory (as in our word re*cord*, and the idiom "to learn by heart").[9] Many troubadour lyrics engage a

---

6. Prior to about 1170, troubadour lyrics were called *vers* (song). William Paden cites an Occitan poem dated from the 1170s (*Escotatz, mas no say que s'es* by Raimbaut d'Aurenga; PC 389–28) that lists discrete genres (*vers, estribot, sirventes*), though he cautions that even if the idea of lyric genres was "in the air" that early, "to be in the air, however, is far from having crystallized as the genres would do many years later in the arts of poetry." See Paden, "The System of Genres in Troubadour Lyric," 37; see also 29–36 for a discussion of the crystallization of genres in later treatises. Van Vleck comments: "With the second generation, the basic framework of troubadour poetry is in place. Even before the terms come into use, a central division between the love song (*canso*) and the invective (*sirventes*) takes shape, and poets tend to specialize in one or the other." See Van Vleck, "The Lyric Texts," 28. The earliest treatise to name lyric genres is Raimon Vidal's *Razos de trobar* (ca. 1190–1213), which lists several: *romanz, pasturellas, vers, cansons,* and *serventes*. See Marshall, ed., *The* Razos de trobar *of Raimon Vidal,* 6.

7. The generations of trouvères span 1160–1300, or from Chrétien de Troyes (fl. 1160–90) to Adam de la Halle (ca. 1240–88 or after 1306). Although not often clustered into discrete generations in the literature, the flourishing dates of the most prominent trouvères fall into roughly five compact, overlapping groups: the first flourished between 1160 and 1215 (Chrétien de Troyes, Chastelain de Couci, Blondel de Nesle, and Gace Brulé); the second flourished between 1180 and 1220 (Conon de Béthune, Gontier de Soignies); the third flourished between 1200 and 1236 (Guiot de Dijon, Audefroi le Bastart, Gautier de Dargies, Gautier de Coincy); the fourth flourished between the 1230s and 1260s (including Guillaume le Vinier, Thibaut de Champagne, Colin Muset, Perrin d'Angicourt, Jehan Erart, and Richard de Fournival); the fifth flourished between the 1240s and 1300 (including Gautier D'Espinal, Jehan Bretel, and Adam de la Halle).

8. For a list of at least four possible interpretations of how *descorts* express discord, see Köhler, "Deliberations," 3. I will consider this question in detail below.

9. There is some debate about the etymology for *acordar* and related words in modern and medieval Spanish, French, and Occitan. See Singleton, "Spanish *acordar* and Related Words," and Davis, "Acordar(se): One Verb, or Two?" While Singleton argues for the primacy of *cor* over *chorda*, Davis argues that *chorda* contributed equally in the formation of the Latin *accordare* and its derivatives, and that the two roots mingled through popular use and coalesced into one word. Most scholars of Occitan literature cite the Latin *chorda* or the late Latin *acchodare*. Linguists cite two possible Latin roots that may have become confused: *cor, cordis* (heart), *chorda* (cord, string). *LR* lists *acort, descort* and all related forms as derivatives of *corda* from the Latin *chorda*; see also Paden, *An Introduction to Old Occitan,* 356; *Songs of the Women Troubadours,* 170; *Anthology of the Provençal Troubadours,* 2: 108. However, the *Dictionnaire de l'occitan médiéval* states that Latin *accordare* was primarily formed from *concordare,* and that *chorda* is of secondary influence (1:122). For a discussion of the heart's involvement in memory, see Carruthers, *The Book of Memory,* 48–49. For a good summary and bibliography of medieval "pectoral psychology," see Jager, "The Book of the Heart," 2–4. See also Wack, *Lovesickness in the Middle Ages,* 78–79, 94–95. Julie E. Cumming offers an excellent discussion of the concepts of concord and discord in ancient music theory, their transmission in medieval music theory, and their metaphorical use to describe the state; see her "Concord out of Discord," 3–71.

notion of harmony and agreement—between the lover and beloved, or between any warring factions or antithetical concepts—that may stem from the idea of strings being in or out of tune with one another, but which also (as might be expected) speak to affairs of the heart. In this stanza from an early thirteenth-century *tenso* (debate poem) between the trobairitz Na Lombarda and the troubadour Bernart d'Armagnac (d. 1226), the antithesis of seeing and not seeing the beloved (referred to as a mirror) is combined with a dense wordplay on *acord* and *descorda*, and *desacorda*. The voice is Na Lombarda's:[10]

Car lo mirailz e no veser descorda	For the mirror and its absence from view disrupts
tan mon acord, c'ab pauc no·l desacorda	so my harmony, that it is almost de-tuned.[11]

Within the common poetic topos of song composition itself, *acort* and *acordar* describe the ideal linking of sound and sentiment—*chorda* and *cor*—as the following excerpts illustrate.

Giraut de Bornelh (fl. 1160–1200):

mas voill qe·l cors s'acord al chan	but I want my heart to be in tune with my song[12]

---

10. The stanza is Na Lombarda's response to Bernart, who first calls her *Mirail de pres* ("mirror of worth"), after comparing her to two other women. Evincing some doubt as to his sincerity (for he leaves without seeing her), she asks him in the previous stanza to say "in which mirror are you gazing?" (*e·l mirail on miraz*), that is, which woman does he refer to by his epithet. Bernart de Ventadorn's famous *Can vei la lauzeta mover* contains a paradigmatic reference to the beloved as a mirror quoted below; text and translation (modified) from *Bernart*, 166–68.

Anc non agui de me poder,	Never have I been in control of myself
ni no fui meus de l'or'en sai	or even belonged to myself from the hour
que·m laisset en sos olhs vezer:	she let me gaze into her eyes,
en un miralh que mout me plai.	into a mirror which pleases me much.
Miralhs, pus me mirei en te,	Mirror, since I mirror myself in you
m'an mort li sospir de prëon,	sighs from deep down have slain me,
c'aissi·m perdei com perdet se	and thus I have lost myself, as was lost
lo bel Narcisus en la fon.	the fair Narcisus in the pool.

11. *Lombartz volgr' eu esser per na Lombarda* (PC 54-1 and 288-1); for the text see *Songs of the Women Troubadours*, 72–73, lines 29–30. Following Köhler, "Deliberations" (6) and others, I have changed "c'ab pauc vo·l descorda" to "c'ab pauc no·l descorda." These lines have been translated in many different ways; my translation is a modification of Köhler's literal one: "For the mirror and the absence of view trouble my *acord* in such way that they almost discord it."

12. *Alegrar mi volgr'en chantan* (PC 242-5); see Giraut de Bornelh, *The Cansos and Sirventes*, ed. Sharman, song 17, line 17; 115 (text), 118 (translation).

Arnaut Daniel (fl. 1180–1200):

…amors mi asauta,	it is Love that delights me
qui·ls motz ab lo son acorda	and harmonizes words and music[13]

Peirol (1180–1225):

e pens d'un vers cossi·l fass' e l'acort,	and I think how I may compose a *vers*, and arrange it suitably [harmonize it]
tal que sia bos e valens e fis	so that it shall be good, of worth, and perfect[14]

Aimeric de Belenois (1216–1242):

Per so non puesc motz ni sos acordar	Therefore, I cannot harmonize words nor tune
qu'om, quan plora, no pot ges be chantar.	for a man who cries cannot sing well.[15]

One late treatise on grammar and verse writing takes up this notion of *acort* as the defining feature of the troubadour's art. *La Doctrina d'Acort* (the Science of Harmony), written in Occitan rhyming couplets by Terramagnino da Pisa after 1282, even names itself as an *acort*, thus bringing into alignment the content of the disquisition with a generic poetic designation. Once again, sound aligns with sense and sentiment.[16]

In chapter 1 I argued that *tornadas*, along with *envois* (their more formulaic northern counterparts) express the paradox of the interpellative turn from the self (prior to language) to the subject (formed by language). The tension between the agency of the turn and the subjugation of a priori language finds verbal expression in the *tornada's* shiftiness between the individual voice of the author and the collective voice of the public. But the music, as much as words, announces this ambiguity of voices: in most cases this musical expression takes a mimetic form—a willful breaking of the *canso's* strophic pattern with a turn to the middle of the stanza. This emphatic repetition is simultaneously specifying and stylizing—a musical gesture that has functional affinities with repeated and quoted

---

13. *Autet e bas entre·ls prims foils* (PC 29-5); for text and translation see Paterson, *Troubadours and Eloquence*, 188 (song 8, lines 8–9).

14. *Si be·m sui loing et entre gent estraigna* (PC 366-31); see *Peirol*, ed. Aston, song 22, lines 3–4; 121 (text), 124 (translation; the bracketed suggestion is mine).

15. *Ailas! Per que viu lonjamen ni dura* (PC 9-1); see Aimeric de Belenoi, *Poésies*, ed. Dumitrescu, song 12, lines 7–8; 114 (text; translation my own).

16. For a critical edition of this treatise, see Marshall, ed., *The Razos de trobar of Raimon Vidal*, 27–53. A few late songs name themselves as *acorts* as opposed to being a *descort*; these will be discussed below.

refrains. Thus the strophic *canso*—the emblem of individual expression—formally encodes the paradox and density of the subjective voice in the *tornada*, shedding light on the submissive and resistant operations of music and words.

In this chapter I trace the encoding of self-expression on the level of genre. The emergence of *descorts* around 1200 signals the moment when composition—the *art de trobar*—begins to undo itself conceptually, if not also formally and performatively. In other words, with the *descort*, composers intended to disrupt the *canso*'s *acort* of sound and sense, the raison d'être (or *razo* in troubadour-speak) of song itself.

Only thirteen *descorts* survive with music; twelve of these appear in a single manuscript, trouv. *M*. The *descorts* in this manuscript represent both Old French (eight) and Occitan (four) composition, as well as several chronological layers of scribal activity, spanning the second half of the thirteenth century. While most discussions of *descorts* either concentrate on one language or the other, or focus on the *descort*'s relationship to the northern *lai* and the southern *canso*, little attention has been paid to how *descorts* function as a force of discord and disruption across regional affiliation, or to the challenge they present to the main interpreters of the genre: music composers, scribes, and performers. By looking at the situation of the *descorts* in this single source, then, my intent is to understand better what it meant to cultivate songs of discord, and to show how and why that discord touched other songs and, indeed, the manuscript as a whole. I will argue that the *descorts* in this source offer us early examples of musical composition that seem to be not only self-consciously unharmonious, but also—and relatedly—self-consciously belated, long before the presumed "autumn" of the Middle Ages or the "decline" of chivalric culture.

EARLY THOUGHTS ON LATENESS

In a posthumously published book entitled *On Late Style*, Edward Said, echoing Theodor Adorno's thoughts on late Beethoven, concisely summarizes the two prevailing views of artistic endpoints.

> Each of us can readily supply evidence of how it is that late works crown a lifetime of aesthetic endeavor. Rembrandt and Matisse, Bach and Wagner. But what of artistic lateness not as harmony and resolution but as intransigence, difficulty, and unresolved contradiction? ... It is this second type of lateness as a factor of style that I find deeply interesting. I'd like to explore the experience of late style that involves a nonharmonious, nonserene tension, and above all, a sort of deliberately unproductive productiveness going *against*."[17]

---

17. Said, *On Late Style*, 7. For Adorno's thoughts on late Beethoven, see his "Late Style in Beethoven," and "Alienated Masterpiece: The *Missa Solemnis*"; and the collection of essays and fragmentary writing on Beethoven collected in Adorno, *Beethoven: The Philosophy of Music*, esp. 123–61.

One possible endpoint of an individual artist's stylistic trajectory is synthesis, resolution, harmony (*acort*); the other endpoint is contradiction, tension, the nonharmonious (*descort*). For Adorno, Beethoven's late pieces expose the idealism represented by his middle-period pieces—specifically, the seeming Hegelian synthesis of the dialectic between subjective freedom and objective constraints as signified by the developing variation of motifs and themes through-large scale form.[18] By contrast, Beethoven's late pieces refuse this organicism and coherence with "anachronism and anomaly" (to quote Said),[19] with empty "irascible" gestures that expose musical conventions for what they are.[20] The inscrutable surface of the late works effectively hides Beethoven's subjectivity behind arbitrary, unmediated conventions that disrupt an ideal harmony between the composer and his musical self-expression. Paradoxically—and romantically—we come to feel the presence of Beethoven more acutely for his seeming absence; and we come to understand this absenting of self as transcendence. Adorno writes:

> [V]ery late Beethoven is called both subjective and objective. Objective is the fractured landscape, subjective the light in which—alone—it glows into life. He does not bring about their harmonious synthesis. As the power of dissociation, he tears them apart in time, in order, perhaps, to preserve them for the eternal. In the history of art late works are the catastrophes.

Late art, then, is the prophetic realization—in sound or image—of the catastrophic impossibility of synthesis, the unavoidable dissolution of subject and object back into "negative dialectics"—irresolvable contradictions.

It is not surprising that the organic stages of human life, from youth to maturity to old age, serve as the model for understanding both individual artistic development and historical or cultural eras. The late period of an artist's production, when presumably the artist contemplates death and the totality of his or her career, gives way to "late style" that in turn, for philosophically-minded cultural critics, gives way to "lateness" or belatedness—the quality of being out of step (perhaps heroically so) with the general culture, as Adorno believed late Beethoven to be,[21] or of being haunted by precursors, as Harold Bloom believes all poets to be.[22]

---

18. See Subotnik, *Developing Variations*, 15–41, esp. 20, and the commentary by Leppert, *Essays on Music*, 513–28.

19. See Wood, introduction to *On Late Style*, xiii.

20. In "Late Style in Beethoven," Adorno writes: "The power of subjectivity in the late works of art is the irascible gesture with which it takes leave of the works themselves. It breaks their bonds, not in order to express itself, but in order, expressionless, to cast off the appearance of art.... Thus in the very late Beethoven the conventions find expression as the naked representation of themselves. This is the function of the often-remarked-upon abbreviation of his style" (566).

21. For Adorno, late Beethoven, and Adorno's own anachronistic sensibilities, were heroic struggles against the morally and intellectually bankrupt "present"—the failure of the French Revolution and the ensuing Napoleonic regime for Beethoven, and the horror of the World Wars and mass-produced culture for Adorno. See Leppert, commentary to *Essays on Music*, 513–16; see also Said, "Adorno as Lateness Itself" [reworked as chapter 1 in *On Late Style*)]; Subotnik, *Developing Variations*, 18–19.

22. Bloom argues that post-Enlightenment poetry manifests a sublimated rivalrous relationship between the poet/ephebe and his precursors. The poem itself is a result of the melancholy of the "latecomer-poet" who, despite

The correlation of historical periods with life stages dates back to classical writers such as Cicero, Livy, and Seneca, appearing again with Augustine.[23] "Lateness" in this context can also refer to the ends of historical eras or periods—the old age of a civilization—and bear the meaning of decline.[24] This conception of "late style" as a marker of historical "lateness" gained prominence in German intellectual circles through the highly influential art historian Johann Joachim Winckelmann (1717–68), who enumerated several periodizing schemes, all with a clear organic arc: three stages of art (necessity, beauty, superfluity), four stages of Greek cultural development with corresponding poetic genres (childhood/epic, youth/lyric, manhood/dramatic, old age/elegiac), five epochs of Greek art analogous to the narrative trajectory of five dramatic acts (beginning, progress, state of rest, decrease, and end).[25] It was Johann Wolfgang von Goethe (1749–1832) who rescued old age from mere decline with a notion of transcendence—notably, a transcendence that is also "the gradual withdrawal from appearance."[26] This disappearing act of old age is an idea that Adorno echoed in his understanding of late Beethoven.[27]

Yet the unidirectional thrust of a human life cannot account for the continuation of historical time, and so historians have turned to another model—that of the cycle of seasons. This offers the perfect fusion of the biographical arc with the necessity of regeneration. The philosopher G. W. F. Hegel (1770–1831), greatly influenced by Winckelmann and Goethe, viewed world history as a complex combination of these two models: the ongoing development of the world spirit's self-consciousness occurs through the life-courses of successive civilizations—from their embryonic stage and blossoming to their decline and fall—whose principles naturally dominate the historical epoch.[28] The route of the spirit, then, while abstractly linear, nevertheless zigzags from one location to another. This geo-temporal warping of historical epochs was perhaps most evident in the complex border constructed between the Middle Ages and the Renaissance. In 1860 the

various defense mechanisms, always comprehends on some level "his lack of priority." See Bloom, *Anxiety of Influence*, esp. xxv, 55, 77–92, 96, 106, and Said, "Adorno as Lateness Itself," 272. For an application of Bloom's idea of belatedness, see also Wilson, *The Challenge of Belatedness*.

23. See Breisach, *Historiography*, 85–86; see also Barone, "Richard Wagner's 'Parsifal' and the Theory of Late Style," 40n12. For remarks about the confusion of the personal or individual time with the aesthetic progress or general time see Said, "Adorno as Lateness Itself," 267; see *On Late Style*, 3–7 for an extended rumination on personal and general time.

24. The following discussion of "lateness" owes much to the excellent survey and discussion in Barone, "Richard Wagner's 'Parsifal' and the Theory of Late Style" see also Painter, "On Creativity and Lateness." German scholars in the 1960s pursued the idea of historical lateness; see Painter 4–5 and 11n16.

25. For these periodizing schemes see Winckelmann, *History of Ancient Art*, 29. These passages are quoted and discussed in Barone, "Richard Wagner's 'Parsifal' and the Theory of Late Style," 40–41.

26. Quoted in Barone, "Richard Wagner's 'Parsifal' and the Theory of Late Style," 43–44.

27. Barone notes the connection between Goethe and Adorno, and the dialectic between subject and object; see ibid., 50, 53–54.

28. See paragraph 347 and the accompanying remark in *Elements of the Philosophy of Right*, 374.

Swiss historian Jacob Burckhardt published *Die Kultur der Renaissance in Italien*, which proposed the widely accepted argument that the Italian Quattrocento marks a radical break with prior "medieval" institutions and modes of thought, initiating the *modern* era of Europe. This Renaissance in Italy, Burckhardt argued, saw the replacement of corporate feudal identities with conscious individualism, static universalist histories with dynamic local histories, and impersonal symbolism with humanistic realism in the arts.[29] Johan Huizinga, in his influential and controversial book, *Herfstij der Middeleeuwen* (1919)—first translated as *The Waning of the Middle Ages* (1924), and retranslated as *The Autumn of the Middle Ages* (1996)—challenged the hegemony of Burckhardt's burgeoning "*early* Modern" conception of this historical epoch with the contrasting idea of the declining *late* Middle Ages. Specifically, Huizinga argued that older cultural forms persisted in fourteenth- and fifteenth-century France and Netherlands in contrast to the newer principles of thought emerging contemporaneously in Italy.[30] Late medieval life was marked by passionate extremes—brutal hardships, greed, vengeance, and pessimism on one hand; chivalric idealism, courtly games, and artistic grandeur on the other. But these antinomies—squalor and splendor—did not promise a dialectical resolution.[31] Rather, Huizinga saw the cultural forms of such lateness as "empty convention," with escapist rather than critical intentions.[32]

Huizinga's portrait of medieval lateness as derivative and formalistic had a lasting impact on historians and musicologists alike.[33] The tremendous success of the first English translation spawned a long-lived academic rhetoric of cultural "waning"; as recently (or as late) as the year 2000, even the vaunted Italian Renaissance was diagnosed as "waning"—its freedom and optimism giving way to "doubt and anxiety."[34] Perhaps the

---

29. In the opening paragraph of "Part II: The Development of the Individual" of *Die Kultur der Renaissance in Italien*, Burckhardt makes his bold statement that the Renaissance Italian "was the first-born among the sons of modern Europe." For a discussion of Burckhardt's thought and method see Weintraub, *Visions of Culture*, 115–60. For a challenge to Burckhardt's Italo-centrism, see Durand, "Tradition and Innovation in Fifteenth Century Italy"; for a defense of Burckhardt's earmarks of Renaissance and modern thought, see Baron, "Towards a More Positive Evaluation of the Fifteenth-Century Renaissance."

30. For a contrast of Italian with the Franco-Burgundian developments, see Huizinga, *Autumn of the Middle Ages*, 17, 30, 32, 39, 38, 319–21. Huizinga occasionally argues that the line between Italy and the other countries cannot be clearly drawn; see 42, 73–74, 382–86.

31. For discussion of Huizinga's antinomies, see Kossmann, postscript to *Johan Huizinga (1872–1972)*, 225–26; and Weintraub, *Visions of Culture*, 208–46.

32. Huizinga, *The Autumn of the Middle Ages*, 304; Huizinga does not have much to say about music; see 314 and 322–23.

33. Huizinga expresses some embarrassment about his title in the preface to the German translation; see *The Autumn of the Middle Ages*, xxi–xxii, and Weintraub, *Visions of Culture*, 231n102. Christopher Page has surveyed and critiqued the uses of Huizinga by musicologists in *Discarding Images*, 140–88. Page's footnotes offer many references to uses and critiques of Huizinga in other disciplines. His influence is especially clear in Kilgour, *The Decline of Chivalry*.

34. See Bouwsma, *The Waning of the Renaissance*; Bouwsma traces the ways in which "the characteristic Renaissance sense of creative freedom was constantly shadowed by doubt and anxiety," vii.

most widely influential writer in this vein is Fredric Jameson, with his pessimistic conception of postmodernism and "late captialism." Jameson's description of postmodern theory, art, literature, and architecture in *Postmodernism or, The Cultural Logic of Late Capitalism* owes much to the legacy of Huizinga: "the waning of affect" (10, 11, 15) "the waning of historicity" (21), the "waning of content" (25)—all amount to the waning ("death") of the subject in aesthetic and intellectual endeavors (15), which, Jameson argues, reveals the "cultural logic" of late capitalism. Late capitalism is not waning capitalism, however; it is, rather, a "pure" and "all-pervasive" stage of capitalism (3, 36). In the vast new global network of production and consumption, enabled and signified by technology, spatial thinking replaces historical thinking, erasing legacies of human thought and labor.[35]

The disappearance of the subject in the opacity of surfaces, the fascination with conventions and forms to the seeming neglect of content, spatial or cosmopolitan imagination cut loose from historical memory—these markers of "lateness" will pertain to the belated *descorts* under consideration here. But in the medieval concept of history, everything that was "now" was already "late."

MEDIEVAL GENRES OF TIME

Medieval historical thinking was inextricable from the biblical "universal" time line of Creation, Incarnation, and Last Judgment. Thus "history" encompassed an idea of the end of history, marked by the Second Coming of Christ and leading to an afterward of timelessness. Three competing (but often mingled) historiographic schemes provided a deep structure to ecclesiastical and worldly historical writing.[36] The first scheme, transmitted to the Middle Ages by the writings of St. Jerome (ca. 340–420), enumerated Four Empires of the world (Assyrian, Persian, Greek, Roman) and a fifth heavenly empire.[37]

---

35. Jameson, *Postmodernism*, 1; on late capitalism and spatial thinking see xviii–xxi, 5–6, 48–49, 154–80, 364–76; on late capitalism as pure, see 3, 36; on labor, class struggle, and technology see xix, 3, 35–36.

36. Several genres of historical writing existed in the Middle Ages, loosely following late classical models described by Isidore of Seville (d. 636) in his *Etymologies*. Ernst Breisach summarizes these: "histories—full and somewhat artful narrations of more recent events; chronicles—brief accounts centering on dates proposed by Eusebius and Jerome; annals—year-by-year accounts of long periods; *calendaria*—month-by-month accounts; and *ephemerida*—day-by-day accounts." See Breisach, *Historiography*, 95–96; see also Deliyannis, introduction to *Historiography in the Middle Ages*, 3–7.

37. The concept of the Four Empires of the world is popularly traced to interpretations of the book of Daniel (2:31–45 and 7:1–14) but has roots in classical pagan thought. See Swain, "The Theory of the Four Monarchies," 19–20 for a discussion of St. Jerome. The designation of the empires preceding Rome were a matter of some dispute or confusion; Jerome himself offers two different versions: an earlier (ca. 380) listing of Assyrians, Persians, Greeks, and Romans in his translation and expansion of portions of Eusebius' *Chronicles*, and a later (ca. 418) listing of Babylonians, Median-Persians, Greeks, Romans in his *Commentary on Daniel*. Paulus Orosius (ca. 418) listed Assyria, Macedonia, Carthage, and Rome, with a fifth empire after the birth of Christ replacing the fourth. Eusebius of Caesarea (240–309) was a pioneering writer of both world chronicles and ecclesiastical history; given that, as an advisor to Constantine, he witnessed and participated in the takeover of the Roman Empire by a Christian ruling class, his histories are the first in which the political history of

This view entwined the fate of an ongoing final (Holy) Roman Empire with Christendom and became especially important to biographers and chroniclers of Carolingian and Ottonian "emperors," who argued for the transfer of imperial power (*translatio imperii* or *translatio regni*) from antiquity to their present day.[38] A second scheme, transmitted to the Middle Ages by Augustine, derived Six Ages of the world from the six days of creation. The Seventh Age is the Sabbath—the age of rest and the close of history—to be followed by an Eighth Age (though not worldly) of eternity. Augustine's time (and our time) is the Sixth Age, which is a penultimate moment of indeterminate length; he occasionally likened this Sixth Age to old age.[39] Although Augustine argued vigorously against attempts to predict the end of the world, he advanced the idea of its imminence as a motivation for moral behavior: "now" was closer to the end than the beginning, at least psychologically.[40] From the twelfth century on, continuing political upheavals, scholastic debates, and heretical movements pushed medieval historical writers to grapple with the "awareness of *change* as a factor in human experience, which seems at odds with the timeless realities of Faith."[41] A third, Trinitarian periodization of history emerged that reconciled dynamic local history with the static universal history of the church. History became not simply waiting out God's predetermined plan of worldly disintegration; rather, history marked man's progress and education toward God and worldly completion.

Rome plays a central role in sacred history. His *Ecclesiastical History* (ca. 325, the year of the Council of Nicaea), translated by Rufinus (ca. 410), remained an authoritative text throughout the Middle Ages. On Eusebius, see Breisach, *Historiography*, 81–83; Momigliano, *The Classical Foundations of Modern Historiography*, 138–42, 146–51. On the role of the books of Daniel and Genesis to "the Christian organization of time," see Breisach, *Historiography*, 83–84. For an overview of early universal histories, see also Allen, "Universal History 300–1000."

38. See Breisach, *Historiography* 97–98, 103–106, 143–44; see also McKitterick, *Perceptions of the Past*, esp. 35–89, for a discussion of the interweaving of Frankish and Roman history. Charlemagne was crowned emperor by the Pope in 800 (marking the beginning of the "Holy Roman Empire"); his grandsons later split the realm in 843, losing the eastern half to German dukes in 911, and the western half to Hugh Capet in 987. In the eastern half, Otto I had himself crowned emperor in Rome in 962, a title held by the monarchs of Austro-Germanic and central European lands until 1806. Otto of Freising, writing ca. 1145, famously utilized the notion of *translatio imperii* to organize his history; see Goetz, "The Concept of Time," 148n39 and 153–65.

39. Though most associated with Augustine, the analogy between days of creation and world ages was a traditional Christian scheme. Each age is marked by a biblical figure or a generation (Adam, Noah, Abraham, David, the period of captivity and exile, Christ). Augustine famously enumerates these ages in the very last paragraph of *The City of God* (20.30); see Augustine, *The City of God*, 867. In his earlier commentary on Genesis against the Manichees, and elsewhere, Augustine correlates historical periods and life stages (infancy, childhood, adolescence, young adulthood, mature adulthood, old age). For further discussion of Augustine's historical periodization see Breisach, *Historiography*, 84–87; Fredriksen, "Apocalypse and Redemption in Early Christianity," esp. 163–68 and 180n68.

40. McGinn, "The End of the World and the Beginning of Christendom," 63.

41. Reeves, "The Originality and Influence of Joachim of Fiore," 277. See also Breisach, *Historiography*, 138–43. For a discussion of how medieval historians integrated sacred and secular events, see Goetz, "The Concept of Time.".

Three periods of time—*ante legem* (before the law; the age of the Father), *sub lege* (under the law; the age of the Son), and *sub gratia* (under Grace; the age of the Spirit)—lead progressively to the Last Judgment.[42] While Hugh of St. Victor (d. 1141) believed "now" to be *sub gratia*, when sacramental union with God could be achieved, Joachim of Fiore (d. 1202) believed "now" to be on the cusp between the *sub lege* (the stage or *status* of the Son under New Testament laws) and *sub gratia*, when a fuller illumination of the Spirit would be achieved *in history*. This period of peace would begin after the church's trial under the Antichrist, and signified essentially a second post-Incarnation climax of history (still to be followed by a more perfect age of eternity).[43] Joachim's ideas influenced a wave of eschatological writings and scholastic debates in the thirteenth and fourteenth centuries about predicting the events that would signal the Last Age.[44]

Although historians during the age of the troubadours and trouvères positioned their "now" as a late period of history, they looked ever forward, tying the particularities of a historical epoch to the overarching idea of continuity in the history of human salvation. Thus *mutabilitas mundi*, the changeability of the world, also became *mutatis mutandi*—the same condition with due alterations. This engendered typological thinking in which the rise and fall of kings, regents, and bishops became topoi, and real persons became timeless figures, such that chroniclers (and propagandists) could anachronistically relate Augustus with Charlemagne, and Charlemagne with Philip IV of France (r. 1285–1314). Even the developmental history of Joachim of Fiore yielded prophetic character types—the Antichrist, the Last World Emperor (a messianic *translatio imperii*), and the Angelic Pope—potentially manifested in tyrannical or benevolent leaders who might lead the world into its final stage.[45] In this way, medieval histories acquired a literariness that functioned within a genre system alongside literary genres that had historical themes, such as epic poems, biographies (*vitae*), crusade songs, the *gesta* (recounting of deeds), and its

---

42. In *De Trinitate*, Augustine also describes this three-period scheme that correlated historical time with individual spiritual progress; see Breisach, *Historiography*, 85, and Fredriksen, "Apocalypse and Redemption in Early Christianity," 164. The twelfth-century Trinitarian periodizations incorporated Augustine's Six Ages.

43. Joachim placed Augustine's Seventh Age within time, which stems from earlier beliefs held by some (Hildegard of Bingen, for example) that there would be a period of peace after the death of the Antichrist and before the Last Judgment. Augustine and others placed the period of peace before the coming of the Antichrist. Joachim's ideas of history are far more fluid and mystical than this summary suggests. For an account of the complexity and historical context of Joachim's Trinitarian views see Reeves, "The Originality and Influence of Joachim of Fiore," 269–97.

44. For a discussion of Joachism in later medieval periods, see Reeves, "The Originality and Influence of Joachim of Fiore," 297–316, and ead., "Pattern and Purpose in History"; for an extensive discussion of the association of prophetic characters with historical persons, see Reeves, *Joachim of Fiore*, esp. 27–82.

45. For a discussion of temporal ambiguities and anachronisms in medieval histories, see Goetz, "The Concept of Time," 153–65; for a discussion of Philip IV as the "second Charlemagne" and Joachism, see Reeves, "Pattern and Purpose," 97, and ead., *Joachim of Fiore*, 67.

musical vernacular relative, the French *chanson de geste*.[46] The *descort* appears at roughly the same time that the writings of Joachim of Fiore attracted the attention of the Pope, and, as I will argue here, the *descort*, too, inscribes reflections on time and history.

The quality of lateness traced and felt by modern scholars such as Huizinga and Adorno, and postmodern scholars such as Jameson, stems not from a forward-looking standpoint characteristic of medieval historiography, but rather from a primary relationship to the past. A latecomer is marked by the time prior, not the time ahead or even the present. This sense of belatedness emerges in the writings of Petrarch (1304–74), who famously prepared the Renaissance (and the demarcation of the "Middle Ages") with his nostalgic look back to a prior "Golden Age" of Roman history.[47] Petrarch believed that the stretch of time between the fall of Rome in the fifth century up to his own present was an era of "darkness" and decline (especially apparent with the Avignon papacy, from 1309 to 1377), though he occasionally showed optimism for a rhetorical and political revival. In his writings on history, and importantly on art, Petrarch deployed classical rhetorical strategies and commonplaces, one of which was a critical distinction between "then" and "now" or between "ancients" and "moderns."[48]

The comparison of *antiqui* and *moderni* formed a standard topos within the rhetoric of praise and blame deployed in numerous genres (panegyrics, dialogues, diatribes, histories, sermons, scholastic debates and treatises) from late antiquity to the eighteenth century.[49] Depending on the point of view of the writer or the topic at hand, either historical position could be defended or disparaged. Students and historians of medieval music know this rhetoric from Oliver Strunk's anthologized excerpt of the Seventh Book of the *Speculum musicae* (ca. 1325) by Jacques de Liège, in which Jacques defends the

---

46. The concept of historical writing as a literary genre can be traced to Isidore of Seville. See Goetz, "The Concept of Time," 142–45; Breisach, *Historiography*, 95–97, 100–103. Deliyannis notes that history "was usually classified as a branch of grammar or rhetoric"; see the introduction to *Historiography in the Middle Ages*, 1. For a discussion of the vernacular literary genres that treat past events, see Ainsworth, "Legendary History," 387–416.

47. Marjorie Reeves observes that in some fifteenth- and sixteenth-century writing "medieval concepts of the Sabbath Age and [Joachimist] Third *Status* became fused with the cyclical pattern of the returning Golden Age belonging to the classical tradition;" see "Pattern and Purpose," 100. The earliest instance of the concept of the "Middle Ages" (the age between antiquity and the revival of classical learning) appears in 1469 (*media tempestas*), though it was not widely used until the early seventeenth century; see Robinson, "Medieval, the Middle Ages," 748; and Gordon, "*Medium Aevum* and the Middle Age."

48. See Mommsen, "Petrarch's Conception of the 'Dark Ages'"; Mazzotta, "Antiquity and the New Arts in Petrarch" Baxandall, *Giotto and the Orators*, 51–66; Panofsky, *Renaissance and Renascences in Western Art*, 1–41. Petrarch did not see a "rebirth" of classical aesthetics in the art he describes (even Giotto) so much as use the art as a topic for his revival of classical rhetoric. His student Boccaccio applied Petrarch's revived classical rhetoric to an aesthetic evaluation of Giotto, extending the concept of revival itself to the visual arts, and drawing a parallel between Petrarch and Giotto.

49. See Black, "Ancients and Moderns in the Renaissance," esp. 3–8. For a survey of this topos in medieval and Renaissance writing see Gössmann, *Antiqui und Moderni im Mittelalter*; Courtenay, "*Antiqui* and *Moderni* in Late Medieval Thought."

music of the *ars antiqua* against the music of the *ars nova*. For Jacques, the noble ancients are represented by Franco of Cologne and Magister Lambertus, whose treatises—both written between 1260 and 1280—describe a performance and notation practice based on perfect (triple) divisions of the long and breve.[50] This "ancient" mensural practice (not more than sixty years in the past) elaborated the earlier modal system in which music flows in a pattern of long and short values. Franconian notation allows for breaking the underlying modal pattern, which could produce a dramatic effect (see example 2.6 below); but it does not allow for imperfect (duple) divisions of longs and breves, nor for subdivisions of the semibreve into smaller values (minims). The new art, Jacques complains, is dominated by imperfect values, the proliferation of metrical and notational complexities, and, above all, the loss of certain repertories (old-style motets, organum purum, measured organa, conductus), banished by modern singers. Furthermore, the teachers of the new art are not in agreement, and this "discord" belies an instability that threatens the very nature of the music itself. Jacques writes:

> Moreover, measured music seeks concord and shuns discord. It does not seek discordant teachers to attain these ends; indeed, all things accord together unto good. Would that it pleased the modern singers that the ancient music and the ancient manner of singing were again brought into use!...Have not the moderns rendered music lascivious beyond measure, when originally it was discreet, seemly, simple, masculine, and chaste?[51]

For commentator F. Joseph Smith, Jacques is a belated and even tragic figure, "standing in the midst of the new musical practice of the Ars Nova with his magnificent tomes on the Ars Antiqua," hoping to secure the traditional metaphysical concepts of music against the new performance and composition practices that seem to disregard speculative principles of numerical *concordia* and Trinitarian perfection.[52] The *Speculum musicae* is notable among medieval discussions of the measurement of time in music for its hint of contemporaneous eschatological concerns. Using biblical allusions, Jacques finds an ironic twist to the old and the new: he argues that the perfection of the *ars antiqua* compares to New Testament law (freer, plainer, fewer precepts) while the complexity of the *ars nova* compares to Old

---

50. Franco's *Ars cantus mensurabilis* is dated between 1260 and 1280, and Lambertus's *Tractatus de musica* is dated ca. 1270. See Hughes, "Franco of Cologne," and Baltzer, "Lambertus, Magister." Manuscripts from the thirteenth century show the possibility of an ad hoc reading of two successive semibreves as equal (suggesting a duple division of the breve) or unequal (as Franco describes).

51. "Musica insuper mensurabilis concordiam requirit et discordiam refugit. Ideo, quantum ad hoc, doctores discordes non appetit; vero etiam et bono omnia consonant. Utinam placeat modernis cantoribus ut ars antiqua, cantus antiqui modusque cantandi ad usum revocentur!...Nonne Moderni musicam, quae in suo exordio fuit prudens, honesta, simplex et mascula et bene morata, lascivam nimium reddiderunt?" For the Latin text, see Jacobus Leodiensis, *Speculum Musicae, Liber Septimus (VII)*, ed. Bragard, 94; trans. Strunk, rev. McKinnon in *Source Readings in Music History*, 277.

52. Smith, *Jacobi Leodiensis*, 2:xiv (quotation); see also 2:xi–xvi, 8–14; and 3:18–27, 60–64.

Testament law (diverse moral, judicial, and ceremonial precepts).[53] Thus the new practice represents a spiritual regression, a move backward from liberty to servitude. Such inversion and regression potentially signal the End Times—an apocalyptic vision shared by the authors and compilers of the interpolated *Roman de Fauvel*, which features *ars nova* motets.[54]

THE (LATE) WORLD TURNED UPSIDE DOWN

Like the quarrel between ancients and moderns, topsy-turvy inversion, or the "world upside down," is a rhetorical motif with a long history going back to Virgil; many times the two motifs were combined, as in Jacques' diatribe, to critique modern times for the inversion of past values. Preachers in the twelfth and thirteenth centuries found prophetic biblical sources for eschatological images of worldly inversions.[55] Troubadours employed the motif of sensory inversion (as a symptom of love)[56] and worldly inversion (as a symptom of declining morality).[57] Although they never spoke specifically of "ancients" and "moderns," the comparison of new and old ways of behaving and composing

---

53. See *Source Readings in Music History*, 275.

54. For a discussion of apocalyptic themes and figures in *Fauvel* and its predecessor *Renart le nouvel*, see Haines, *Satire in the Songs of* Renart le nouvel, 181–225.

55. For a discussion of the "world upside down" topos in ancient and medieval literature, see Curtius, *European Literature*, 94–98. Curtius also links the "world upside down" topos to the quarrel between ancients and moderns. The biblical sources are Isaiah 3:5 and 24:1–2. For a discussion, see Owst, *Literature and the Pulpit*; and *Marcabru*, 424 commentary to lines 37–40. Bernard of Clairvaux used inversion and reversal of values found in the New Testament (1 Cor. 1:20) in order to preach anti-materialism to the laity. See Bynum, *Jesus as Mother*, 127–28; and Léglu, *Between Sequence and Sirventes*, 98.

56. Raimbaut d'Aurenga wrote an entire song, *Ar s'espan la flors enversa* (PC 389-16), that not only plays with images of sensory inversion, but also forms of the verb *enversar*. Lines 1–5 from stanza II offer a good example (text and translation from *Anthology*, 106–107):

Quar enaissi m'o enverse	For in such manner do I invert all this
que bel plan mi semblon tertre,	that hills seem to me fair plains,
e tenc per flor lo conglapi,	and I take the frost for blossom,
e·l cautz m'es vis que·l freit trenque,	and the warmth, it seems to me, cuts the cold,
e·l tro mi son chant e siscle.	and thunderclaps are to me songs and whistles.

57. Marcabru, in *Lo vers comens cant vei del fau* (PC 293-33), employs the "world upside down" motif to describe the decline of *pretz* (worth, value) and *jovens* (youthful generosity)—key components of courtliness. Stanza VII proclaims:

Cel prophetizet ben e mau	He prophesied well and ill
qe diz c'on iri' en becill	who says that man would go to wrack and ruin
—seignor ser et ser seignorau—	—peasant like lords and lordly peasant—
e si sunt ill,	and indeed they are (going to wrack and ruin)
que·i an fait li buzat d'Anjau	for in this respect the buzzards of Anjou
cal d'esmerill.	have demonstrated a merlin's fighting spirit.

Text and translation (modified) from *Marcabru*, 420–21. For an example of this motif in Old French literature, see Shirt, "'Le Chevalier de la Charrete': A World Upside Down?"

provided fodder for *sirventes*, one of the earliest lyric genres to be distinguished by name.[58] The rhetoric of praise and blame was fundamental to troubadour *cansos*. The noble ladies of these songs, or Love itself, receive both in nearly equal measure; competing troubadours, courtiers, and sometimes jongleurs get their fair share of blame, and the poet often heaps boastful praise upon his own poem.[59] *Sirventes* were set apart by their especially critical or satirical tone and references to current political events. Full of moralistic invectives against court culture, clerics, and noblemen, *sirventes* became a favorite genre of the later generations of troubadours, many of whom migrated to Italy and Spain due to regional warfare in the last decades of the twelfth century, and a rapid cultural decline of the Midi in the aftermath of the Albigensian Crusade (1209–29) and the conquest of southern lands by northern nobility.[60] In the *sirventes Ja mais non er hom en est mon grazitz* by Guiraut Riquier (fl. 1254–92), this "last" troubadour seems highly conscious of his belatedness; here the loss of a discerning audience for his compositions is couched in terms of topsy-turvy judgments:

Ja mais non er hom en est mon grazitz	Never more will a man in this world be thanked
per ben trobar belhs digz e plazens sos,	for well composing fair words and pleasing melodies,
ni per esser de bon grat enveyos,	nor for being eager for esteem,
tant es lo muns avengutz deschauzitz.	so much is the world come to its decline.
Quar so que sol dar pretz, grat, e lauzor,	For that which used to inspire merit, approval, and praise,
Aug repenre per folhïa major;	I hear blamed as the utmost folly;

---

58. An early example is Raimbaut d'Aurenga poem *Escotatz, mas no say que s'es*, dated from the 1170s, which lists discrete genres (*vers, estribot, sirventes*) (see note 6 above), though satirical and moralizing *vers* emerged alongside courtly ones in the earliest generations of troubadours. The first reference to "*sirventes*" appears in a poem by Marcoat (ca. 1150) with reference to the death of Marcabru, though the latter did not use the word *sirventes*. See Léglu, "Moral and Satirical Poetry," esp. 47–48.

59. Later treatises on troubadour song would sometimes use praise and blame to describe generic differences. See Dagenais, "Genre and Demonstrative Rhetoric."

60. For a charting of the increased percentage of *sirventes* composition in the later generations of troubadours see Paden, "The System of Genres in Troubadour Lyric," 24–27. In the biographical information on Sordello (fl. 1220–69) Alan R. Press remarks that *sirventes* were "increasingly cultivated"; see *Anthology*, 239. For a discussion of troubadours in Italy see Keller, "Italian Troubadours"; Gallo, *Music in the Castle*, 11–46. See also Cabré, "Italian and Catalan Troubadours." Cabré notes that the courts of northern Italy and the Crown of Aragon "became the main focus of late troubadour culture" (127), noting that "after the Albigensian Crusade, the male line of the dynasties of Toulouse and Provence died out, and were replaced by two French princes in 1246 and 1249 respectively" (129). The Battle of Muret in 1213 marked the turning point in the crusade, leading to "the decline of the culture that nourished the troubadours." See Smith, "Rhetoric," 403.

| e so qu'om sol repenre e blasmar | and that which one used to criticize and blame, |
| vey mantener, et aug per tot lauzar. | I see upheld, and hear it praised by all.[61] |

Some *sirventes* lyrics, and later descriptions of *sirventes*, make a point of saying that their melodies (*son*) are "old" or "borrowed" or "well known," and scholars have indeed noted the copying of poetic schemes to be a common feature of this genre, especially after Bertran de Born (1160–96), who systematically composed *sirventes* as *contrafacta*.[62] Bertran mentions his model song *S'ie·us quier conseill, bell'ami'Alamanda* (PC 242-69), a *tenso* (debate poem) in which the troubadour Giraut de Bornelh seeks the advice of his lady's chambermaid, in the *sirventes D'un sirventes no·m cal far loignor ganda*, which scolds the sons of Henry I—here Richard ("the Lionhearted," then duke of Aquitaine):

Conseill vuoill dar el son de n'Alamanda	I want to give advice to the tune of n'Alamanda
lai a·n Richart, si tot no lo·m demanda:	there to Richard, though he hasn't asked me for it:
ja per son frair mais sos homes non blanda.	never should he flatter his men because of his brother.[63]

While this borrowing can be understood as an aspect of the genre's intertextual parody (evident in the shared theme of advice-giving and seeking), the reuse of music and poetic schemes can also be understood as part of the historicity of the *sirventes*. Just as the lyrics record historical events, particular moments in time, or a temporal relation between old and new, the recycled melody and poetic form also become a historical record—the sonic/musical event "retold" and, perhaps, parodied.

Troubadours used a wide range of models for their *sirventes*, from *cansos*, *tensos*, and other *sirventes* to sacred songs. Catherine Léglu discusses a cluster of nearly thirty *sirventes* and other moralizing and boastful lyrics (from Marcabru to Peire Cardenal) that share a poetic construction related to the para-liturgical sequence—specifically, the *versus*

---

61. PC 248-45. Text and translation from *Anthology*, 314–15. For an earlier lyric lamenting the indifference of the younger crowd to the troubadour's art see *Per solatz revelhar* by Giraut de Bornelh (PC 242-55) in *Anthology*, 144–49, esp. stanza VI.

62. On imitation and *contrafacta* see Aubrey, *The Music of the Troubadours*, 109–23; Chambers, "Imitation of Form in Provençal Lyric" Gennrich, *Die Kontrafaktur im Liedschaffen des Mittelalters*, esp. 11–47 for a discussion of troubadour compositions. On the meaning of *son* as "sound," "melody," or "tune," and its specificity to Occitan lyric see Aubrey, "References to Music in Old Occitan Literature," 111–13; Paden, "Old Occitan as a Lyric Language," 38–39, 42; Page, *Voices and Instruments*, 31.

63. PC 80-13 stanza IV, lines 25–27; for text, translation (modified), and critical notes see Bertran de Born, *The Poems*, ed. Paden, Sankovitch, and Stäblein, 188–89; for a discussion of imitation in Bertran's poems, see the introduction, 44–56.

tripertitus caudatus (aab ccb; 448 448) and similar patterns (aab aab; 887′ 887′), where parallel three-line versicles linked by a "tail-rhyme" form a larger, rhyming couplet. Few *cansos* were written in this type of parallel versicle form, and thus Léglu argues that the form correlates with the content in that both "display a trend away from the *canso*." In other words, these *sirventes* differ from *cansos* in both sound (poetic form) and sense (non-love themes).[64] The sound of this subset of *sirventes* intersects with *descorts*, which are similarly composed in groups of parallel versicles. But the *sirventes*, like the *canso*, is an isometric strophic form (called "isostrophic"); that is, the rhyme scheme and syllable count of the initial large couplet repeat with each strophic unit. In the majority of *descorts*, the metrical construction and rhyme scheme change from one set of parallel versicles to the next, forming heterometric strophes (called "heterostrophic"). In terms of sense, the *sirventes* and the *descort* would seem to part company, since *descort* lyrics are not satirical or political: they are about unrequited love.[65] Yet the border between *descorts* and *sirventes* was somewhat permeable: two *descorts* provided models for two later *sirventes*; Guilhem Augier Novella wrote a hybrid *Sirventes avols e descortz* (PC 205-6; only the first few lines survive); and the lyric catalogues of Alfred Pillet and István Frank disagree on the generic designation of a handful of songs, one seeing *descorts* where the other sees *sirventes*.[66] How, then, does the love-lorn *descort* link to the moralizing *sirventes*? Perhaps the answer lies in the "world upside down" motif, a local, rhetorical exaggeration in the *sirventes*, writ large and formally encoded in the *descort*, whereby a song of love that should be *acort* becomes *descort*, and the relatively "new" genre becomes "late"—delinquent and declining.

The two *descorts* that provided the *son* for later *sirventes* are important to our story here: one is *Qui la ve en ditz*, composed by Aimeric de Peguilhan while at the court of Este in Italy sometime after 1210.[67] This song stands close to the earliest examples of the genre by Raimbaut de Vaqueiras, also written in Italy, at the court of Montferrato between 1197 and 1201.[68] One of these, Raimbaut's polylingual *Eras quan vei verdejar* (PC 392-4), served as the model for a later polylingual *sirventes* by Bonifaci Calvo, *Un nou*

---

64. See Léglu, *Between Sequence and Sirventes*, 34–62, esp. 48–50. Léglu looks at two of the rhyme schemes tabulated by István Frank: no. 193 (aab ccb) and no. 91 (aab aab). To her list, I would add three songs (a *gap* [boasting song], a religious song, and a *sirventes*) listed under no. 83 (aaab cccb). Elizabeth Aubrey mentions seven troubadour strophic *cansos* with surviving melodies that use a double versicle construction. See Aubrey, "Issues in the Musical Analysis of Troubadour *Descorts* and *Lays*," 72.

65. Léglu calls attention to this distinction, while at the same time noting instances of the *versus tripertitus caudatus* in some *descorts*; see *Between Sequence and Sirventes*, 49.

66. Where Pillet sees *descorts* (PC 335-63; PC 461-195a), Frank sees *sirventes*, and where Pillet sees a *sirventes* and a religious song (PC 101-2; PC 434a-17), Frank sees *descorts*. These scholarly disputes revolve around the dichotomy of form versus content in the determination of genre; Frank adheres to a strict formal identification, purging all isostrophic forms from his list of *descorts*, while Pillet seems to consider rhetoric, yielding such identifications as "sirventes in the form of a descort."

67. The *sirventes* modeled on *Qui la ve en ditz* is *Maint baro ses lei* (PC 335-36), composed by Peire Cardenal.

68. See *Aimeric*, 13; and *Raimbaut*, 21–22.

sirventes ses tardar (PC 101-17), as well as Dante's direct imitation, *Ai! Fals ris. Qui la ve en ditz* similarly generated other imitations in addition to the *sirventes*: a *tenso* (PC 229-1) and a religious *canso* (PC 266-8). Neither *Qui la ve en ditz* nor *Eras quan vei verdejar* is strictly heterostrophic; both lyrics cleverly combine low-level sequential (i.e., parallel versicle) and high-level isostrophic construction (see table 2.2 and discussion below). Thus as the borrowed *son* for the *sirventes*, these particular *descorts* allowed the isostrophic principle generic to *sirventes* composition to be kept intact. Yet these *sons* also sounded the history of formal and conceptual discord that was generic to the *descort*.

STOP MAKING SENSE: INVENTING THE *DESCORT*

Known for his formal inventiveness and aptitude with languages, Raimbaut de Vaqueiras is likely to have composed the first *descorts*, along with the earliest *estampida* lyric, during his productive third visit to Italy following travels to Provence and a military expedition in Sicily.[69] Manuscripts attribute two *descorts* to Raimbaut, one of which is uniquely polylingual.[70] This poem, *Eras quan vei verdejar*, contains five isometric strophes, each in a different language—Occitan, Italian, French, Gascon, and Galician-Portuguese. The other *descort* attributed to Raimbaut, *Engles, un novel descort* (PC 392-16), is a heterostrophic Occitan poem in which each of the six strophes contains a different number of lines, syllables per line, and rhyme scheme. Both songs name themselves as "*descorts*" in their first strophes, although they present two contrasting poetic realizations of "discord." *Eras quan vei verdejar* offers a textbook definition of the *descort*, including an almost pedantic explanation of the metaphorical nature of *descort* as form and *descort* as content. Note that the strophe can be divided into two halves or parallel versicles (lines 1–4, 5–8), each with the same metrical and rhyme scheme (abab abab; 77′77′ 77′77′).[71]

---

69. For biographic details see *Raimbaut*, 3–22. Linskill also remarks: "the principle characteristic of Raimbaut's poetry is a striving after originality of form" (52; see also 53–54). For the identification of Raimbaut de Vaqueiras as one of the earliest *descort* composers, see Bec, *La lyrique française*, 1:195n20 and 205; see also Köhler, "Deliberations," 8. Köhler also notes that along with Raimbaut's *descorts*, the anonymous *descort En aquest son gai e leugier* (PC 461-104) "can be established with some certainty as having been extant before 1200." The vida of Garin d'Apchier states that he composed the first *descort*, and quotes two lines from a lost poem, "Quan foill' e flors reverdezis / Et aug lo chan del rossignol" (When the leaf and the flower bud / and I hear the song of the nightingale; PC 162-6). Margarita Egan lists Garin among troubadours of the mid-thirteenth century. See Egan, trans., *The Vidas of the Troubadours*, 36 and 117. Garin wrote perhaps as many as seven *sirventes* criticizing another troubadour, Torcafol, who responded in kind with at least three *sirventes*. See Latella, *I Sirventesi di Garin d'Apchier e di Torcafol*.

70. One manuscript also identifies Raimbaut's *estampida Kalenda maia* as a *descort*; see *Raimbaut*, 188n1.

71. For a discussion of the metrics, see Billy, "*Lai* et *descort*," esp. 101–102; also discussed in Aubrey, "The Dialectic between Occitania and France," 36; see also Marshall, "The Isostrophic *descort*," 140–41. Marshall follows Friedrich Gennrich in seeing the parallel versicle construction as derived from a musical construction modeled on the Latin sequence; elsewhere in the article, he sees the *descort* as evolving away from this form toward "greater unity" on the model of the *canso* (see his remarks on 143, 155–57).

Eras quan vey verdeyar	Now when I see the meadows
pratz e vergiers e boscatges,	and orchards and woods turn green,
vuelh un descort comensar	I would begin a *descort*
d'amor, per qu'ieu vauc aratges;	on love, on whose account I am distraught;
q'una dona·m sol amar,	for a certain lady was wont to love me
mas camjatz l'es sos coratges,	but her heart has changed
per qu'ieu fauc dezacordar	and so I produce discordance
los motz e·ls sos e·ls lenguatges.	in the rhymes, melodies and languages.[72]

Raimbaut's second *descort*, *Engles, un novel descort*, can easily be read as a follow-up effort, one that needs no explanation about the metaphorical connection between sound and sense. I quote only the first half (or first versicle) of the first strophe below.

Engles, un novel descort	Engles, a new *descort*
fauc per remembransa	I compose, in memory
de vos, en cui me conort	of you, in whom I find comfort
de ma greu malenansa	from my dire straits,
qu'atressi·m nafr' amors fort	for love wounds me
cum vos de sa lansa,	as it does you, with its lance,
estiers que gaug e deport	save that you have joy and pleasure from it,
n'avetz et ieu pezansa.	and I tribulation.[73]

The metrical patterns of the versicles are given below for each strophe. Note that the lyric repeats a rhyme sound only once, linking the first and second strophes, and that the third and sixth strophes are nearly parallel in metrical construction. Otherwise, the syllable counts and lines per versicle vary widely.

I.	abab abab; 75′76′ 75′76′	-ort, -ansa
II.	aab aab; 3′3′5′ 3′3′5	-ansa, -endre
III.	aaa; 666	-es
IV.	aab aab; 4′5′5 4′5′5	-enher, -iers
V.	ab ab; 5′6 5′6	-enha, -ai
VI.	aaa; 7′7′7′	-aita

While the trick of *Eras quan vei verdejar* lies in making the various discordant languages conform to a metrical and rhyme scheme (though the rhyme sounds change with each

---

72. Text and translation in *Raimbaut*, 194 and 201 respectively. I retain the word "descort" where Linskill writes "discord."

73. PC 392-16. Text and translation (modified) from *Raimbaut*, 199 and 203 respectively.

strophe), the trick of *Engles, un novel descort* lies in maximizing metrical and sonic discord among strophes in the same language.

Despite his apparent interest in new forms, Raimbaut was not averse to borrowing metrical and rhyme schemes for his *sirventes*, or recycling ideas from himself. His political *sirventes Leus sonetz* (PC 392-22), which refers to the conflict between the houses of Toulouse and Barcelona just prior to 1190, adopts the metrical pattern and nearly half of the rhyme words from a *canso-sirventes* by Giraut de Bornelh, *Los aplegz*. This unique *son* bears a striking resemblance to double-versicle constructions: the seventeen lines in each strophe fall into low-level rhyming couplets (ab cc dd ee ff gg hh hh).[74] Shortly after *Leus sonetz*, Raimbaut composed a bilingual isometric *tenso*, *Domna, tant vos ai preiada* (PC 392-7) between himself and a no-nonsense Genoese lady. Raimbaut's Occitan stanzas are full of standard courtly entreaties to the married noble woman, who answers him with insults in her northern Italian dialect. This discord between Raimbaut and the lady is replicated in their exclusive languages, and the exclusive rhyme sounds given to their strophes—a fitting precursor to *Eras quan vei verdejar*.[75]

Although scholars believe Raimbaut composed both *descorts* in Italy, only *Engles, un novel descort* appears in an Italian manuscript close in time and place to its author (troub. *D*, dated 1254). *Eras quan vei verdejar*, although more widely represented in medieval anthologies of troubadour lyrics, first appears in fourteenth-century sources from Italy, southern France, and Catalonia. Neither *descort* survives with music.[76] From the twenty or so *descorts* attributed to specific troubadours, we can glean that the genre was cultivated alongside the *sirventes* in the southeastern-most stretches of Occitanian culture—primarily Lombardia, Provence, Languedoc, Catalonia, and the southeastern area of Auvergne.[77]

---

74. Frank 828:3. Only three lyrics use this metrical scheme, all direct imitations of Giraut de Bornelh's *sirventes* (PC 242–47). See *Raimbaut*, 89–97.

75. See *Raimbaut*, 98–107; Köhler "Deliberations," 5; and Gaunt, "Sexual Difference and the Metaphor of Language in a Troubadour Poem."

76. On the dating and provenance of troubadour anthologies see Aubrey, "Sources, MS, §III, Secular monophony, Occitan," and the registry of troubadour sources in "Appendix 4: The *Chansonniers*," in *TI*, 303–305. Both songs' lyrics appear in troub. *C* and *R*, fourteenth-century collections from southern France, and in troub. *a¹*., an Italian manuscript dated 1589. The famous *estampida Kalenda maja* (PC 392-9) appears in *C* right before *Eras quan vei verdejar*; *Engles un novel descort* follows four songs later. All three songs are placed in the middle of a group of Raimbaut's lyrics.

77. The following troubadours have *descorts* attributed to them: Aimeric de Belenois, Aimeric de Peguilhan, Albertet de Sestaro, Bonifaci Calvo, Cerverí de Girona, Elias Cairel, Elias de Barjols, Garin d'Apchier, Guilhem Augier Novella, Guilhem de Salinhac, Guilhem de la Tor, Guiraut de Calanson, Guiraut Riquier, Peire Raimon de Tolosa, Pons de Capduelh, Raimbaut de Vaqueiras. For biographical information, see Diez, *Leben und Werke der Troubadours*; Egan, *The Vidas of the Troubadours*; Gaunt and Kay, "Appendix I: Major Troubadours," in *TI*. See also Maillard, *Évolution et esthétique du lai lyrique*, who notes that "[d]u Nord de l'Italie au Nord de l'Espagne, en passant par la Vallée du Rhône, l'Auvergne, le Limousin et la Gironde, toute l'ancienne Provincia a vu naître des auteurs de descorts" (145). Maillard goes on to observe that these troubadours migrated along longitudinal rather than lateral lines.

Gautier de Dargies (ca. 1165–1236) is credited as the first trouvère to compose *descorts*, three of which survive in two *chansonniers*: trouv. *M* (dated between 1253 and 1277), and trouv. *T* (dated sometime in the 1270s or 1280s). Both Gautier and the sources that preserve his *descorts* have ties to the regions of Picardy and Artois, and perhaps more specifically with the musical culture of Arras.[78] All three of Gautier's *descorts* name themselves as such, though not in the initial strophes as in Raimbaut's lyrics; rather, the genre is first signaled by discordant sounds—the heterostrophic structure of the poetry—and confirmed later by name within the lyric.[79] Music does survive for all three of Gautier's *descorts* in both trouv. *M* and trouv. *T*, and although the two manuscript readings of the notes often diverge, the melodies are similarly constructed in parallel versicles that divide the poetic strophes into two, three, and even four repeated segments of music.

Given that the flourishing dates of Raimbaut and Gautier overlap significantly, and the sources place the *descort* in Italy and northern France at roughly the same time,[80] literature and music scholars have long puzzled over the origin of the *descort* and its relationship to two other lyric genres, namely the northern *lai* and the southern *canso*. Here, too, the *descort* presents a discord between sound and sense, for scholars' opinions fall into two principal camps: those who prioritize form and emphasize the connection between the *descort* and other genres with parallel-versicle construction such as the *lai* or the Latin sequence,[81] and those who prioritize poetic content and emphasize the connection

---

The coincidental cultivation of the *sirventes* (a major genre) and the *descort* (a minor genre) can be traced in the charts and graphs of genres in Paden, "The System of Genres in Troubadour Lyric," 24–28.

78. On the dating and provenance of these two *chansonniers*, see Everist, *Polyphonic Music*, 171–87; Aubrey, "Sources, MS, §III, Secular monophony, French" and Haines, "The Transformation of the *Manuscrit du roi*," 16–19. See also Cyrus, "Musical Distinctions between Descorts and Lais," 12.

79. For an edition of the *descort* lyrics see Gautier de Dargies, *Chansons et Descorts*, ed. Huet. The three *descorts* are *De celi me plaing qui me fait languir* (RS 1421), *J'ai maintes foiz chanté* (RS 416) and *La douce pensée* (RS 539). See also Bec, *La Lyrique française*, 1:198.

80. Bec stresses this point; see *La Lyrique française* 1:195n20 and 204–205. The encroachment of northern Capetian rulers into the south from the early thirteenth century on, and the mingling of noble entourages during the Third Crusade (1188–92) and the Fourth Crusade (1202–1204), brought rapid cultural exchanges between southern and northern poets and musicians. One notable meeting took place in Constantinople in 1204: there Raimbaut de Vaqueiras and the trouvère Conon de Béthune (ca. 1150–1220) met and composed a bilingual *partimen* (a debate poem that poses a specific problem). Conon was born in the region of Artois and became an important diplomat for the Counts of Flanders, eventually settling in Constantinople with Baldwin I, elected the first Latin Emperor of Constantinople in May 1204, defeating Raimbaut's patron Boniface of Monferrato. For an edition of the *partimen Seigner Coine, jois e pretz et amors* (PC 392-29) see *Raimbaut*, 236–40; for a discussion of the musical exchanges between troubadours and trouvères, see Aubrey, "The Dialectic between Occitania and France," esp. 1–8.

81. See Wolf, *Über die Lais, Sequenzen und Leiche*; Jeanroy, Brandin, and Aubry, *Lais et descorts*, xi–xvii. This view was shared by Karl Bartsch, Hans Spanke, and Friedrich Gennrich in various publications; see Baum, "Le Descort ou l'anti-chanson," 82–91, for a summary of their opinions, including the opposing view of Carl Appel (cited below). Within this camp there is a further division between those who believe the *lai* to have Celtic origins in narrative *lais* (Jeanroy et al.) and those who believe the lyric *lai* to have developed from the liturgical sequence (Wolf, Gennrich, Spanke). For a review of the scholarship on the *lai* and a discussion of the many meanings of the word "lai" found in troubadour poetry see Baum, "Les Troubadours et les lais."

between the *descort* and the courtly themes, rhetoric, as well as formal aesthetic of the
southern *canso*.[82] For the scholars in the latter camp, it is not the parallel-versicle
construction that is important so much as the "heterostrophic" result, which stands
(self-consciously) in stark contrast to the "isostrophic" *canso*; thus form becomes an
aspect of the *descort*'s content—an idea that is summed up in the title of Richard Baum's
oft-cited article: "Le Descort ou l'anti-chanson."[83] As I have suggested above, following
Léglu, the genealogy of the *descort* may also include the *sirventes*, with its critical stance,
topsy-turvy rhetoric, musical intertextuality, and links to parallel-versicle constructions.

Pierre Bec, *La lyrique française*, vol. 1, argues that the *descort* and the *lai* are regional variations of the same
form (for which he coins the term "*lai-descort*" to refer to the genre's heterostrophic form) where the mostly
southern *descort* contains interference from the *canso* (202) and the mostly northern *lai*, many of which have
pious rather than courtly lyrics, integrates with genres in a religious register (205; Bec does not specify the
Latin sequence, however). Bec gives priority to the southern form, though his reasoning is convoluted. He
argues that the term *lai*, which is less specific, is attested in Occitan (with Marcabru) earlier than in French
(with the *Roman de Brut*), and earlier than the more specific term *descort* in the south (with Raimbaut de
Vaqueiras; 206). Bec is relying here on presumed dates of authorship rather than dates of extant manuscript
sources. He goes on to argue that the "*lai-descort*" genre in French is first called *lai* and later sometimes called
descort; the choice of one term over the other, according to Bec, is tied to "the greater or lesser distance of the
poet in relation to *la mode troubadouresque*" ("le choix d'une désignation ou de l'autre paraissant essentielle-
ment lié à la plus ou moins grande distanciation du poète par rapport à la mode troubadouresque," 205).
Furthermore, he says that the term *lai* "by a type of backlash" (*par une sorte de choc en retour*) is rarely used in
the troubadour repertory in the technical sense of *descort* (that is, to refer to heterostrophic songs) (206).

82. See Appel, "Vom Descort"; Baum, "Le Descort ou l'anti-chanson," 97–98, argues that "the opposition of the
categories regular/irregular is the generating principle of the descort" ("L'opposition des catégories régulier/
irrégulier est le principe générateur du *descort*," 97). Baum's suggestion is echoed by Köhler, "Deliberations,"
1–13. Jean Maillard takes the position that although the *descort* is a distant "offshoot" of the *lai*, it diverged
significantly to the point of becoming a discrete genre that has more in common with the troubadour *canso*
and the trouvère *grande chanson* (including poetic themes, melodic profile, the use of *tornadas* and *envois*, and
disposition in the manuscripts); see his *Évolution et esthétique du lai lyrique*, 128–33, 379. See also Marshall,
"The *Descort* of Albertet." Marshall argues that two criteria distinguish the *descort* and the *lai*: (1) *lais* repeat
all or part of the melodic material of the first strophe for the last strophe; (2) "*descorts* were exclusively courtly
and secular in substance, whereas a *lai* often had a religious text" (302). In a later article, Marshall sees the
descort in a primary relation with the strophic *canso* as the genre develops over time; see his "The Isostrophic
Descort," 130–57.

See also Billy "Le Descort occitan." Billy, taking into account Marshall's work, concludes his study with the
suggestion that the *descort* positions itself as an "alter ego" of the *canso* rather than an "anti-chanson," inte-
grating foreign models, notably the parallel versicle procedures from the para-liturgical sequence, into the
"ideological and formal framework of the Occitan courtly lyric" ("le cadre idéologique et formel de la lyrique
courtoise occitane," 18).

83. Baum, "Le Descort ou l'anti-chanson." This is the title of Baum's historiographic survey of scholarship on the
descort. Dominique Billy also provides a brief but instructive historiographic survey of scholarship in his "*Lai
et descort*," 100–101. Billy also sees the scholarship falling into two camps: (1) those who consider the *lai* and
the *descort* to be fundamentally the same genre on the basis of "le principe du *Versikel*"; and (2) those who
consider the *lai* and the *descort* to be autonomous genres on the basis of fifteen criteria including theme, form,
production, music, intertextual references, diffusion, and reception (101–108). He also makes a keen observa-
tion about a scholarly tendency that results in the continued confusion between the *lai* and the *descort*,
namely the emphasis placed on form in the definition of genres to the neglect of historical, cultural, functional
aspects as well as production and reception (110–11).

Elizabeth Aubrey points out, however, that as far as the extant notated *descorts* are concerned, only northern sources show heterostrophic, "anti-*chanson*" melodies; the one melody preserved in an Occitanian source (from the fourteenth century) is recorded in the manner of a strophic *canso*, with music written for only the first strophe (in fact, it is a second melody for *Qui la ve en ditz*, unrelated to that recorded in trouv. *M*). Given the similarly dubious southern origin of notated Occitan *lais*, Aubrey concludes that "extended heterostrophic paired-versicle musical structure was not indigenous to the south."[84]

With only thirteen notated *descorts* surviving for both Occitan and French lyrics, the projection of a formal paradigm onto all *descorts*, especially backward onto the troubadour repertory, quickly leads to dead ends. This leaves open the question of a conceptual paradigm.

Medieval treatises on troubadour poetics do not describe a parallel-versicle structure for the *descort*; rather, they couch their explanation almost entirely in conceptual terms, implicitly mobilizing the semantic dichotomy between *acort* and *descort*. The *Donatz Proensals* ("Provençal Donatus," written by Uc Faidit in northern Italy, ca. 1225–45) puts it succinctly: the *descort* is a song having "*sonos diversos*"—different sounds that produce a babble emblematic of "discord."[85] The late thirteenth-century Catalan treatise *Doctrina de compondre dictats* (probably written by Jofre de Foixà ca. 1290) distinguishes various lyric genres firstly by poetic theme (*razo*), and secondly by poetic form and melodic construction. In many cases Jofre's descriptions are too neat, betraying idealized concepts rather than accurate portraits of the repertory. He first separates the *descort* from the *canso* in terms of the rhetorical categories of praise and blame.[86] To compose a *descort* lyric, he instructs that "you must speak of love, such as a man who is separated from it or a man who cannot have pleasure from his lady and is tormented" (deus parlar d'amor com a hom qui n'es desemparat e com a hom qui no pot haver plaser de sa dona e viu turmentatz); whereas the *canso* "must speak pleasingly of love, and you can put in your poem examples of other themes, but without speaking evil, and praising nothing but love" (deu parlar d'amor plazenment, e potz metre en ton parlar eximpli d'altra rayso, e ses mal dir e ses lauzor de re sino d'amor).[87] As previously mentioned, many *cansos* rail against the beloved Domna if not also Love itself.[88] So in fact the *descort* may not be unusually

---

84. Aubrey, "The Dialectic between Occitania and France," 39; see also 34–40.

85. See Aubrey, *The Music of the Troubadours*, 106; and Marshall, ed., *The Donatz Proensals of Uc Faidit*, 230.

86. See Dagenais, "Genre and Demonstrative Rhetoric," esp. 245–47. Jofre de Foixà, a Catalan monk and diplomat, is without question the author of the *Regles de trobar* written between 1286 and 1291 at the behest of King Jacme II of Sicily. For a discussion of Jofre de Foixà and his possible authorship of the *Doctrina de compondre dictats* see Marshall, ed., *The Razos de trobar of Raimon Vidal*, lxxii–lxxviii, and Aubrey, *The Music of the Troubadours*, 73.

87. For text and translation see Aubrey, *The Music of the Troubadours*, 105–106 (*descort*) and 86 (*canso*), respectively.

88. Bernart de Ventadorn's famous *canso Can vei la lauzeta mover* disparages the beloved and women in general; in his *Lo rossinhols s'esbaudeya*, lines 13–14, he disparages Love: "For Love hardly wants one so honest and true as

discordant in its subject matter or *razo* in comparison to *cansos*. Jofre goes on to say that
the *coblas* or strophes of *descorts* can include "one or two more words in one *cobla* than in
another, because this would be much more discordant" (E potz metre un o dos motz mes
en una cobla que en altra, per ço que mils sia discordant). Here Jofre describes the het-
erostrophic construction of *descort* lyrics (but not necessarily parallel versicles); more
importantly, he calls attention to the way in which the *descort* is *not* like the *canso* because
of its lack of accord among strophes. Turning to melody and performance, Jofre writes
"when it is sung, wherever the tune ought to rise, it is low; and it does the opposite of all
other songs" (E que en lo cantar, lla hon lo so deuria muntar, que·l baxes; e fe lo contrari
de tot l'altre cantar). In other words, the melodies of *descorts* should violate the rules of
good behavior; they should be delinquent.[89]

The fourteenth-century treatise *Las Leys d'Amors* (ca. 1330) was compiled in Toulouse
by Guilhem Molinier for a literary society calling itself the Consistori de la subregaya
companhia del Gai Saber (Consistory of the Exceedingly Merry Company of the Joyous
Knowledge), which endeavored to revive regional poetry and codify its language,
grammar, and rules for composition. *Las Leys d'Amors* corroborates and amplifies the
description of the *descort* found in the earlier *Doctrina*: "these stanzas must be unique,
discordant and different in rhyme, melody, and language" (las quals coblas devon esser
singulars, dezacordablas e variablas en acort, en so, et en lengatges).[90] The author prob-
ably has in mind Raimbaut de Vaqueiras's *Eras quan vei verdejar*, and perhaps also his
earlier bilingual *tenso*, and his later bilingual *partimen* with the trouvère Conon de
Béthune, for *Las Leys d'Amors* goes on to link the polyglot *descorts* to poems that feature
multiple points of view:

Also you should know that in those poems that are made by different persons or in
those that involve different persons, one can use different languages as in the
descort. And such poems are tensos, partimens, pastorelas, vergieras, ortolanas,
monias, vaqueiras, and many other types of poems.[91]

I am" (C'a penas vol Amors celui / qu'es francs e fis si cum eu sui). Text and translation from *Bernart*, 125 and
127, respectively.

89. See Aubrey, "Musical Analysis," 71.

90. Text and translation ibid., 71; see also Fleischman, "The Non-Lyric Texts," 179–80; Smith, "Rhetoric," 404–
405; and Kendrick, "The *Consistori Del Gay Saber* of Toulouse (1323–circa 1484)." The Consistori was
founded in 1323 and engaged Guilhem Molinier to compile the treatise between 1330 and 1332. The treatise
exists in several redactions: the earliest is a prose version (version A) surviving in two manuscripts from ca.
1340; it was then versified somewhat later (version B) and revised in ca. 1355 (version C). Aubrey quotes from
version A. For an edition and translation into modern French see Gatien-Arnoult, ed., *Las Leys d'Amors*,
1:343–47 and 358–59 for the passages on the *descort*. For an edition and discussion of version C, see Anglade,
ed., *Las Leys d'Amors*, 2:177–78 for the passage on the *descort*.

91. "Encaras devetz saber que en aytals dictatz que·s fan per diversas personas, oz en los quals hom fenh que sian
diversas personas, pot hom uzar de diverses lengatges, coma en descort. E d'aytals dictatz son tensos, partimens,
pastorelas, vergieras, ortolanas, monias, vaqueiras, et enayssi de trops autres dictatz." Text and translation from

For the compilers of this treatise, looking back nostalgically on the troubadour repertory and the particular dialect of Toulouse, the *descort* presents a complexly heterogeneous *son* that goes beyond divergent meters, rhymes, and melodies to encompass multiple languages; these, in turn, imply diverse persons, authors, and a plethora of genres, some fancifully named after non-noble personages (*vergieras* and *ortolanas* [gardeners], *monias* [monks], *vaqueiras* [cattlemen]), such that the *art de trobar* seems to disperse among a chattering riffraff of discordant voices. One version of this treatise follows its discussion of the *descort*'s many languages with a general statement about foreign languages and dialects and their place (or rather lack of place) in the *Leys*. Only those dialects that use "oc" fall within the purview of the *Leys*; the other languages—"Frances, Norman, Picart, Breto, Flamenc, Engles, Lombart, Navarr, Espanhol, Alaman"—"are not subjected to our Laws" (*A nostras Leys non es sosmes*).[92] They dwell outside, in a state of lawlessness that had already laid waste to Languedoc and *langue d'oc*.

PERFORMING DISCORD

My intention thus far has not been to find the "origin" of *descorts*, but rather to trace their genealogy—more specifically, the etymologies, rhetoric, forms, genres, languages, voices, and idealized concepts that converge with the *descort* melodies preserved in trouv. *M*. This genealogy left the genre open to interpretations from the very beginning: Raimbaut de Vaqueiras himself provided two interpretations of *descort*—one linguistic, the other formal and metrical. In the hindsight of *Las Leys d'Amors*, a treatise marked by the clear belatedness of its prescriptions and protectionism, the *descort* is in turn marked by a worrisome heterogeneity—an opposition to standardization, a porousness to foreign language, and a reach beyond a single voice and a single genre. It may not be surprising, then, that the Occitan *descort* lyric offered the composers and scribes coming late to trouv. *M* a chance to turn the world upside down with new melodies and notations for pre-existing songs, setting the stage for a certain unruliness that fanned out across genres as still later scribes added to the collection.

The *chansonnier* trouv. *M* bears witness in a particularly revealing way to this mixture of ongoing practice and the impetus to record a waning tradition. Full of diverse languages and genres, it is the only *chansonnier* to include by design both troubadours and trouvères, as well as polyphonic motets, vernacular Marian pieces, and *lais*. The compilation of this manuscript will be discussed in greater detail in the following two chapters. Here it is important to note that the original compilers sometimes left blank spaces at the ends of gatherings in order to maintain discrete sections. Many later hands added

---

Aubrey, "Musical Analysis," 71; I have retained the word "poem" for *dictatz* where Aubrey uses "song" at the opening of the second sentence.

92. From version C; see Anglade, ed., *Las Leys d'Amors*, 2:177–79, quotation from 178.

instrumental pieces, Latin devotional songs, and a wide array of vernacular songs in both Occitan and French to these blank spaces, thus expanding an already cosmopolitan anthology.[93]

Recording a song in the Middle Ages was not always a routine act of copying from an exemplar, and the songs, if well known, were not necessarily treated as museum pieces. Indeed, in a number of cases in trouv. *M*, as we shall see here and in the next chapter, scribes dismantled and refashioned the forms and melodies of old musical chestnuts, and made creative use of mensural notation to offer their own interpretations and commentaries on the past.[94] We cannot know, of course, whether the scribe and composer of the song were one and the same; what we can surmise is that this manuscript remained unbound and accessible within an obviously musically active environment to possibly itinerant scribes over several decades.

Three Occitan *descorts* were recorded by the same hand in mensural notation to trouv. *M* after the bulk of the *chansonnier* had been produced.[95] Among the over forty songs and instrumental pieces added to this collection, the formal Gothic script and the two-column format of the *descorts* most resembles the original corpus of songs, thus suggesting their early entry into the collection, perhaps between 1265 and 1285.[96] Two of the three added *descorts* survive in other sources with attributions, while the third is anonymous and unique to trouv. *M* (see table 2.1).

According to the Pillet-Carstens register of troubadour lyrics, the fifty-three poems attributed to Aimeric de Peguilhan enjoyed wide distribution and obvious popularity. By contrast, the seven lyrics attributed to Guilhem Augier Novella appear in few sources,

---

93. See Haines, "The Transformation of the *Manuscrit du Roi*," 19–21.

94. See Peraino, "Re-Placing Medieval Music" and chapters 3 and 4; see also Haines, *Eight Centuries of Troubadours and Trouvères*, 7–13, 27–30. Haines notes that even the first scribes recording troubadour and trouvère *chansons* should be understood as "not just mechanically copying the music…[but] interpreting it, refashioning it to fit the book being copied" (7).

95. Elizabeth Aubrey identifies one of these songs, *Bella domna cara* (the manuscript actually reads *Bella donna cara*, which betrays a French influence), as an Occitan *lai*, while István Frank lists the song as a *descort* in his *Répertoire métrique* (1:191, descort 23). Aubrey notes that two *lais* recorded in the earliest layer of trouv. *M* are written in a hybrid Franco-Occitan. These *lais* are given individual rubrics: the *Lai Markiol* (fol. 212/B206) and the *Lai Nompar* (fol. 213ᵛ/B207), and they have a clear double-versicle musical construction whereas the later *Bella donna cara* is through composed. See her discussion of the notated Franco-Occitan *lais* and Occitan *descorts* in "The Dialectic between Occitania and France," 34–40.

96. This range of dates reflects the mention of *"reys Karles"* (Charles d'Anjou, crowned king of Sicily in 1265, d. 1285) in the *dansa Ben volgra s'esser poges* entered by the same hand as the Occitan *descorts*. The dating of these additions will be discussed in greater detail in chapter 3. For fuller descriptions of the scripts and disposition of the late additions to trouv. *M* see Peraino, "New Music, Notions of Genre," 92–136, and Haines, "Musicography," 162–67. For a facsimile and discussion of trouv. *M* see Beck, *Le Manuscrit du roi*. The Occitan *descorts* are described in vol. 2:170–72; see also Spanke, "Der Chansonnier du Roi." The facsimile presents the folios in a reconstructed order according to the medieval index, which has been criticized by various generations of scholars (Spanke, Haines). Folio numbers with a B in front of the number refer to the Becks' facsimile; otherwise folio numbers reflect the order as currently bound.

TABLE 2.1

Sources for the three *descorts* added to trouv. *M*

Incipit	Attributions	Sources (troub. MSS; ♪ indicates with music)
Qui la ve en ditz, PC 10-45	Aimeric de Peguilhan	C, D, E, I, K, Q, R♪, a¹
	Anonymous	M, N, W♪ (trouv. *M*)
Sens alegrage, PC 205-5	Guilhem Augier Novella	C*, D, I, K, R
	Peire Raimon de Toloza	S, c
	Anonymous	M, N, W♪
Bella donna cara, PC 461-37	Anonymous	W♪

* The alphabetical song register names Guiraut de Calanson as author.

often with differing attributions; thus the wide distribution and relatively stable attribution of his *Sens alegrage* is a notable exception. The table above shows that *Qui la ve en ditz* and *Sens alegrage* often traveled together in the same manuscripts; in troub. *M* they even appear close to one another in a small grouping of *descorts*. In trouv. *W* (troub. *M*) the two *descorts* are separated by an anonymous Occitan *dansa, Ben volgra s'esser poges*, entered by the same hand. Formally, the *dansa* looks forward to the fourteenth-century *virelai*, with the typical structure of Abba [A]; three more *dansas* or Occitan *virelais* were added to the collection by different hands (see chapter 5), but all using the same form. In contrast, the musical forms of the three *descorts*, added by the same hand, have little in common with one another, though they are connected by other melodic and rhythmic details, which I will discuss below.

The poetic form of *Qui la ve en ditz* has a large-scale isostrophic structure that is camouflaged by small-scale versicle constructions—a strophic form hidden by surface details analogous, in a way, to Goethe's and Adorno's hidden belated subject. Table 2.2 gives an analysis of this structure; the large-scale strophes (Roman numerals) contain three double versicles (Arabic numeral), each versicle (A1, B1, C1) contains four poetic lines.[97] The version in trouv. *M* replaces the third strophe with a new one, and adds a fourth strophe and a new *tornada*. Both newly composed strophes replicate the large-scale poetic construction of the other strophes, with a few metrical infelicities within the fourth strophe (the B1 versicle is missing its twin, and the new *tornada*

---

97. For a thorough discussion of this structure see Marshall, "The Isostrophic *Descort*," 146–57. According to Marshall, only five distinct Occitan *descorts* show this type of large-scale, isostrophic construction; three more are *contrafacta* of *Qui la ve en ditz*. Marshall considers the trailing rhymes as part of the preceding poetic line.

TABLE 2.2

Isostrophic analysis of *Qui la ve en ditz* in troub. *R* and trouv. *M*

I	1 (A1, A2)	2 (B1, B2)	3 (C1, C2)
II	4 (A1, A2)	5 (B1, B2)	6 (C1, C2)
III	7 (A1, A2)	8 (B1, B2)	9 (C1, C2)
Tornada			10 (C3; full versicle)
added strophe in trouv. M			
IV	10 (A1, A2)	11 (B1)	12 (C1, C2)
Tornada			(C3; half versicle)

forms a truncated C3 versicle; the complete lyric with translation appears on the companion website).

As previously mentioned, in recording *Qui la ve en ditz* the scribe in troub. *R* followed the paradigm of a *canso*, that is, he wrote the melody for only the first of the three large strophes of the text. The melody itself, however, is comprised of repeated versicles with minimal variations.[98]

Example 2.2 ◐ OXFORD WEB MUSIC presents the second full strophe of *Qui la ve en ditz* as added to trouv. *M*. Perhaps the most striking feature of this song is the extensive melodic invention and the absence of structuring melodic repetition over the course of four long strophes (each nearly 100 measures). Frequent motion by thirds, large leaps between lines, and a determined avoidance of the final at the ends of lines further challenge both performer and listener with tonal uncertainty. The melody does not always match the versicle structures of the lyric; in measure 18 the poetic structure has been overridden by the composer's interest in creating a non-rhyming trailing rhyme within a local pattern of four-measure phrases (yielding a musical rhyme of the two isolated Fs in mm. 18 and 22, respectively). This is a point of high friction between poetry and music—a moment of musical delinquency that carves its own sonic pattern across that of the words. Indeed, this whole strophe is rife with emblems of discord: six forward-looking trailing rhymes create enjambments on multiple structural levels, between lines (mm. 42, 53, 57), versicles (mm. 14, 77), and double-versicle units (m. 29). In two notable instances (mm. 15 and 54) the ensuing syntactic resolution is musically evaded by the mode 2 rhythmic pattern.[99] There is even a chromatic note setting, perhaps ironically, the word "peace" (m. 29).

---

98. For a discussion of the melodic structure of this version see Aubrey, *The Music of the Troubadours*, 63, and Aubrey, "Musical Analysis," 74–75 (diplomatic transcription, 84). The melody from troub. *R* is also transcribed in Fernández de la Cuesta and Lafont, *Las cançons dels trobadors*, 406–407.

99. The isolated "joy" in m. 18 actually "corrects" the enjambment of the poetic line and allows for an expressive setting of "car non laten joy" (for neither do I expect joy). István Frank reports that enjambment of stanzas does not occur in the troubadour *canso*, but it does occur between strophes and versicles in the Occitan *descorts*. See

EXAMPLE 2.2 *Qui la ve en ditz,* strophe II from trouv. *M,* fol 185ᵛ/B170ᵛ

The other preexisting song, *Sens alegrage,* uses a melodic option that might be considered "standard" in light of the *descort* melody preserved in troub. *R* and those that survive for trouvère *descorts.* A double-versicle melody matches the poetic couplets in each strophe, splitting each strophe into symmetrical halves;[100] furthermore, repeated or closely related stepwise cadential gestures, all ending on D, create tonal and melodic

Frank 1:xli. Marcabru's *Pus la fuelha revirola,* quoted in chapter 1, contains an enjambment between stanzas VIII and IX.

100. For a transcription and discussion of the poetics of *Sens alegrage,* see Marshall, "The Isostrophic *Descort,*" 137–43. Marshall's edition includes the three *tornadas,* which participate in the *coblas capfinidas* pattern. See also Frank 1:186 (*descort* 11).

EXAMPLE 2.2 Continued

coherence throughout. The three *tornadas* are set to three distinct melodies and do not use any of the recurring cadential gestures—not even at the conclusion of the piece, which ends with a downward leap from A to D. Nor do these *tornadas* repeat the rhyme scheme of the previous versicle, as does the *tornada* for *Qui la ve en ditz*. Instead, each *tornada* presents new rhymes, though all three echo the metrics of prior lines at various points in the whole lyric. Thus the *tornadas* do not make an obvious "turn" back to the music or poetic structure of the previous semi-strophe; rather, they stand in a discordant relation both to the song itself and to the generic expectation of the *tornada* as well. (See the website for a complete transcription ⊙ OXFORD WEB MUSIC.)

The third Occitan *descort*, *Bella donna cara*, in an oppositional way, identifies itself as an *acort* rather than a *descort*.[101] Frank parses the lyric into six strophes with double versicles of different lengths, finishing with a two-line *tornada*; however, his chart regularizes what is a rather poetically confusing piece, containing enjambments, dense internal rhymes, and the odd extra syllable or line—all of which obscure the double-versicle

---

101. PC 461-37. See also Frank 2:72 (*descort* 23). For a discussion of this piece as an *acort* see Köhler, "Deliberations," 5–6.

EXAMPLE 2.3 *Bella donna cara*, strophe I from trouv. *M*, fol. 117/B109

structure. As with *Qui la ve en ditz*, the song is through-composed, though, unlike *Qui la ve en ditz*, the music reflects the double-versicle structure through generally symmetrical divisions within the strophes. Moreover, this "anti-anti-*canso*" is far more tonally and melodically coherent than *Qui la ve en ditz*, with closed-sounding cadences on D at the end of most versicles, thus resembling *Sens alegrage* in this way (see example 2.3 ⬤ OXFORD WEB MUSIC).[102]

---

102. The first strophe, with the rhymes –ara –ar, can be subdivided into four parallel versicles, two of which roughly equal the length of the other versicles and those in *Sens alegrage*.

But despite this semblance of order, the music occasionally sets up conflicting dispositions of the poetic lines such that rhyme scheme, syllable count, and syntax become jumbled. This is most evident in strophe 5 (marked as E in the example), which is also the most tonally unstable section of the song. The lyric divides into two four-line versicles, alternating seven and three syllable lines; enjambment connects the two versicles syntactically:

V

So qu'als autres fins aymantz	7	What to the other true lovers
es afantz,	3	is a hardship,
es a mi gautz e dousors,	7	is to me a joy and sweetness,
car Amors	3	for Love
vol qu'ieu am sens totz engantz	7	wants me to love without any deceit
totz mos antz	3	all my life
tals [tal] que sobre las gensors	7	a one who is higher than the most noble
m'es ausors.	3	in my opinion.

Yet the melody—full of stops and starts—lurches through these lines, chopping the longer ones into smaller segments, and pausing on the non-rhyming words *gautz* and *sens* (see example 2.4 ⊙ OXFORD WEB MUSIC). Symmetry is nevertheless maintained: each versicle contains the same number of measures or perfect longs.

The final sixth strophe of *Bella donna cara* ends the *descort* with a complete breakdown of symmetry: an initial four-line versicle is paired with a six-line versicle (and no distinguishable *tornada*), shot through with word games and internal rhymes.

EXAMPLE 2.4 *Bella donna cara*, strophe V from trouv. *M*, fol. 117ᵛ/B109ᵛ

Ironically, the lyric subject renounces discord here at the lyric's most metrically confounding strophe:

VI

Amors ben es mos acortz	7	Love, well is my pledge
que "acortz"	3	that my song is called "acortz"
s'apel mos cantz totz tems mays	7	from now on
entrels fins aymans verays	7	among true, pure lovers
cuy plas solatz e deportz,	7	to whom amusement and entertainment are pleasing,
que descortz	3	for "descorts"
non deu far qui non s'irays,	7	must not be composed by him who is not angry,
per qu'ieu lays		for which reason I abandon
descortz	5	descorts (discord)
per far acortz gays	5	in order to make merry acorts (pledges)
entre·ls gays.	3	among the merry.

Despite the metrical variety and games observable in the lyrics of these three *descorts*, their music never strays from simple modal rhythmic patterns: *Qui la ve en ditz* proceeds in mode 2 (breve–long), *Bella donna cara* and *Sens alegrage* in mode 1 (long–breve). The scribe used Franconian mensural notation, however, which can provide far more rhythmic variety than offered in these songs.[103] Breves and longs carry the syllables in strict, monotonous alternation; only rarely are breves subdivided into melismatic semibreves. There are only two outstanding moments where the notation indicates a change of rhythmic mode—in the final versicle of *Bella donna cara*, and in the eighth strophe of *Sens alegrage* (see example 2.5, mm. 8–11 and 29 🎵 OXFORD WEB MUSIC).

In both instances the sudden switch from mode 1 to mode 2 highlights an important statement in the lyric, such as the moment of self-naming in *Bella donna cara* and a pointed description in *Sens alegrage* (discussed below). Overall, however, these *descorts* show a low-level rhythmic conservatism, which is surprising given their large-scale expansiveness and freedom of melody. Is this retention of modal rhythmic patterns a sign of archaism? Or avant-gardism, given that non-mensural notation is standard for recording monophonic songs? In the last decade of the thirteenth century scribes, no doubt responding to musical practice, began to inflate note values so that the semibreve could carry syllables, and breves could be broken into as many as seven unmarked semibreves, as in the motets of Petrus de Cruce in the seventh fascicle of *Mo*. Alongside these changes, syllables began

---

103. Views differ as to the date of the *Ars cantus mensurabilis* attributed to Franco of Cologne; scholars have proposed either 1260–65 or ca. 1280. Other treatises that describe mensural notation by Lambertus and the St. Emmeram anonymous are dated ca. 1279. See Hughes, "Franco of Cologne."

EXAMPLE 2.5 *Sens alegrage*, strophe VIII from trouv. *M*, fol. 187/B170ᵗᵉʳ

to stretch across ever longer melismas. The three Occitan *descorts* may have been recorded before the spread of these innovations, or perhaps in isolation of them. In any case, the composer intended to write *descorts* that directly challenged the performer to merge what was probably a rhythmically free, expressive tradition of monophonic *cansos* with the rhythmically regular system of modal rhythm developed in the context of polyphony. Indeed, these three mensural *descorts* seem to probe the expressive possibilities—and limits—of modal rhythm. Recall that Jacques de Liège, writing in 1325, championed the older, controlled rhythmic practices and genres tied to the perfect long over and against the "discordant" and libertine practices of the moderns who introduced imperfect values. With these *descorts*, the rhythm of the *ars antiqua* is made to sound excessive and hackneyed, breaching the musical decorum that Jacques attributed to it. In other words, this late modal rhythm appears as a convention emptied of meaning—or rather, whose meaning resides in calling attention to its own failure.

Perhaps the most striking aspect of these late Occitan *descorts* is the trailing rhymes that break the melodic line in a way that resembles an extracted part from a polyphonic hocket. *Qui le ve en ditz* is saturated with the gimmick. The setting in troub. *R* mitigates the jarring effect of the isolated syllables with short melismas or a stepwise cadential motion, while the version in trouv. *M* plays up the potential for melodic discord with wide leaps to unexpected pitches.[104] In *Bella donna cara* trailing rhymes and melodic hockets appear only in two strophes, first as an expressive exclamation "ay!" in the third strophe (m. 12), and then, as if unleashed, in a sudden torrent in the fourth strophe, where they end every line except the last (see example 2.6 ⊙ OXFORD WEB MUSIC). The perfectly regular phrase lengths in this fourth strophe call attention to the melodic gaps, and suggest the possibility of an improvised second part to fill them.[105]

EXAMPLE 2.6 *Bella donna cara*, strophes III and IV from trouv. *M*, fol. 117/B109

---

104. Aubrey makes this point as well. See "Musical Analysis," 76.

105. William E. Dalglish argues that the technique of hocket emerged from improvisational singing practices. See Dalglish, "The Hocket in Medieval Polyphony" and "The Origin of the Hocket." For a counter-argument that the hocket emerged from codified modal practices, see Sanders, "The Medieval Hocket in Practice and Theory."

EXAMPLE 2.6 Continued

By way of contrast to the virtuosic flourish of disrupted music in *Bella donna cara, Sens alegrage* contains only a few isolated trailing rhymes scattered throughout. In the last full strophe, however, melodic hockets appear gratuitously, independent of the rhyme (see example 2.5 above, mm. 6–7 and 20–21). Here the disassociation of words and music also signals a shift of rhythmic mode, which enjoins us to listen to the words that address or

describe the beloved. Though described as the fount of beauty, she is, of course, also the fount of discord.

Monosyllabic trailing rhymes are not common in the Occitan *descort* repertory; I count only four distinct pieces that use them—the three considered here, and one other, *Amors sousors mi assaia*, which also appears uniquely in trouv. *M* (without music) as the only *descort* recorded in the original troubadour section by the first compilers.[106] Such trailing rhymes are non-existent in French *descorts* and lais. Thus it seems that these three late *descorts* were chosen in part for this poetic and melodic device, as particularly emblematic of discord, perhaps inspired by the example recorded by the first compilers.[107] Hockets, or hocket-like fracturing of melody, became the focus of twelfth- and thirteenth-century churchmen, who heard worrisome transgression in disrupted musical sound. The celebrated Cistercian abbot Aelred of Rievaulx, in his *Speculum caritatis* (ca. 1143), complains:

> At one time the voice is strained, at another broken off. Now it is jerked out emphatically, and then again it is lengthened out in a dying fall.... You may see a man with his mouth wide open, not singing but rather breathing forth his pent-up breath, and with ridiculous interceptions of his voice, now threatening silence, and then imitating the agonies of the dying or of men in ecstasies.[108]

The Franciscan monk David of Augsburg, in his *De exterioris et interioris hominis compositione* (ca. 1235), warns "nor should you break up the voice in a courtly way when singing, for, if you ask how to please God in singing, then, the more simply you sing, the more you will please him."[109] Hocketing became associated with rowdy drunkenness in secular music: the triplum of the motet *Entre Adan et Hanikel/Chief bien seantz*/APTATUR

---

106. *Amors sousors mi assaia* (PC 461-17; Frank, 1:188, *descort* 16; fol. 199/B191) is a *descort* comprised of six isostrophes. Frank lists this piece under "*Principe ternaire pur*" (Frank, 2:71); each strophe contains three versicles. I have counted *Qui la ve en ditz* as a *descort*, although Frank lists it among the *chansons* (1:101, *chanson* 528). In the 885 songs (excluding *descorts*) surveyed by Frank, only twelve use single-word rhymes: nos. 22, 39, 68 (*estampida*), 82, 109, 119, 151b, 191, 529 (perhaps a *contrafactum* of *Qui la ve en ditz*?), 659 (*sirventescanso*), 840, 841. Most of these are attributed to late troubadours such as Cerverí de Girona (22, 68, 659, 840) and Peire Cardenal (529). Three strophic songs with monosyllable trailing rhymes are included among the songs of the much-belated troubadours Raimon de Cornet and Peire de Ladils from the Toulousian *Consistori de gay saber* (fl. 1324–40); Frank accounts for only one (151b). See Noulet and Chabaneau, *Deux Manuscrits provençaux du XIVe siècle*, 99–104.

107. Aubrey, "Issues in the Music Analysis of Troubadour *Descorts* and *Lays*," 76, connects these single-word lines to the notion of discord.

108. *Speculum caritatis* bk. 2.23; excerpted and translated in Hayburn, *Papal Legislation on Sacred Music*, 19.

109. "Nec vocem curialiter frangas in cantando, quia si quaeris Deo placere in cantando, tunc, quanto plus cantaveris simpliciter, tanto magis ei placebis." Text and translation (modified) in Dalglish, "The Origin of the Hocket," 8.

(Gen 725, attributed to Adam de la Halle) describes Adam and his buddies boisterously singing hockets, clapping louder than pipes, and performing drunken antics. In 1320, the Cistercian Order explicitly forbade hockets "simply because such things better serve dissoluteness than devotion."[110]

The mensural *descorts* in trouv. *M*, with their abundant and often gratuitous melodic hockets that indeed "break up the voice in a courtly way," seem devilishly designed with this long-standing controversy in mind: they are decadent melodies, pointedly discordant with the conservative musical tastes of churchmen, who equate moral integrity with melodic integrity. Indeed, these *descorts* bring the principle of discord into the body of the singer with their minefields of melodic leaps and hockets, monotonous modal rhythm with the odd momentary modal shifts, and poetic enjambments that run across lines, versicles, and strophes. But above all, these *descorts* confound with a paradox the fundamental activity of performance itself, which is to "make sense" of, and bring to *accord*, the form and meaning of words with their notated musical expression in order to fashion a persuasive interpretation of song. What does a performer do, then, with a song that is by definition and design about the nonsensical and unharmonious union of words and music? How does a singer give meaning to words and notes that have been evacuated of meaning by interruption and isolation? How literally should the performer read the rests surrounding the trailing rhymes, and how rigidly should they be articulated? What gets priority in conflicts between the syntax of the words and the flow of the melodic phrase? In sum, how discordant or harmonious a performance should the singer strive for? It is precisely in the struggle to reconcile words and music that the discord in these *descorts* comes about: they call attention to the juncture of words and music that is performance by posing a direct challenge to the performer to make sense out of sound.

I argued in chapter 1 that the melodic turning points of the *tornadas* and *envois* push the voice and body of the performer to the fore, not in a mimesis of the author's subjectivity, as Sarah Kay asserts, but in a mimesis of the agency and subordination that is the paradox of the self becoming a subject. Both agency and subordination, as well as individual and social expression, are embodied in performer and performed with the voice. The melodies of these late Occitan *descorts* similarly showcase the performer as the nexus of subjectivity; they subject the performer to a musical language that is seemingly not a priori—not overly stylized by standard repetition patterns, although highly contrived to the point of banality nonetheless. In this way, these late *descorts* bring self-consciousness and spontaneity—two antithetical possibilities for self-expression—into *acort*, a synthesis realized in the drama of the voice in discord.

I have spent considerable time discussing these three songs in order to describe what Occitan *descorts* had become by the end of the troubadour and trouvère tradition. In sum, they present studies in performative disruption, housed in musical forms that range from through-composed, free melodies to straight-forward double versicles. Twenty or so

---

110. Quoted ibid., 9; see also 4–10 for other complaints about hockets and fractured melodies.

years earlier, the first compilers of trouv. *M* planned for eight French *descorts*. These were all placed at the ends of author collections or gatherings.[111] Thus *descorts* seem to have a function within the manuscript of marking closures and transitions with stark difference—songs that represent structural disruption.[112] Following the pattern set by the first compilers, the three mensural Occitan *descorts* were added to the ends of author groups: *Bella donna cara* appears with French *descorts* attributed to Willaumes li Viniers, while *Qui le ve en ditz* and *Sens alegrage* form their own cluster, along with a *dansa*, to end songs by Carasaus (see table 2.3; the late Occitan *descorts* and the *dansa* are given in bold).[113]

TABLE 2.3

Descorts as clustered in trouv. *M*

Mon Signeur Gautier d'Argies (Gautier de Dargies) [gatherings 13–14]

De celi me plaig qui me fait languir (89ᵛ/B79ᵛ)

La doce pensée (90/B80)

J'ai maintes fois chanté (91/B81)

Maistre Willaumes li Viniers [gathering 17]

Espris d'ire et d'amour (115/B107)

Se chans ne descors ne lais (116/B108)

Bella donna cara (117/B109)

Maistre Gilles li Viniers [gathering 20]

A ce m'acort (136ᵛ/B118ᵛ)

Sire Adans de Gievenci [gathering 22]

Trop est coustumiere Amors (157/B141)

La douce acordance (158ᵛ/B142ᵛ)

Carasaus [gathering 25]

Qui la ve en ditz (185/B170)

[*dansa* **Ben volgra s'esser poges** (186/170bis)]

Sens alegrage (186ᵛ/B170bisᵛ)

---

111. The anonymous Occitan *descort Amors sousors mi assaia* does not seem to mark any particular juncture in the troubadour collection.

112. In the related *chansonnier* trouv. *T*, the disposition of the *descorts* is similar. The same three *descorts* that appear in the middle of a collection by Gautiers d'Argies (Gautier de Dargies) in trouv. *M*, but which end a gathering, also appear at the end of his songs in trouv. *T*. In troub. *R Qui le ve en ditz* does not end the collection of songs by Aimeric de Peguilhan.

113. The scribe seemed rather keen on writing down these three pieces in a row for he (or someone before him) added a bifolio ruled from top to bottom, seemingly in preparation for long, heterostrophic pieces. Beck signals this with "bis" and "ter" added to his folio number.

According to the medieval table of contents, the songs of Carasaus—part of a collection of poets from Lille and Dijon—were intended to precede a gathering devoted to Artesian *pastourelles*, which would conclude the section of northern poets, to be followed by southern poets.[114] In the current state of the manuscript, however, the suite of mensural Occitan additions, including two *descorts*, appears just before the beginning of the troubadour section—a seemingly appropriate place that suggests the gathering's proximity to the troubadour section at the time of their addition. (A pre-ruled bifolio was added at the end of the gathering to provide more space for these songs.) The three grand Occitan additions thus enhance the division between northern and southern repertories with striking examples of virtuosic troubadour composition, and they further mark this division with their direct formal and generic contrast to the strophic love songs that surround them.

In her study of *lais* and *descorts*, Cynthia Cyrus plots the melodies on a continuum from systematic to freely through-composed.[115] Of the seven French *descorts* in the earliest notated layer of trouv. *M* (left column of table 2.4) three can be called systematic, with exact or near exact repetition of long musical phrases; four can be called unsystematic, with varied repetition of phrases and motivic migration across strophes. For the eighth French *descort*, *La douce acordance*, a through-composed, mensural melody was added to existing staves some time after the first compilation of songs, but before the addition of the Occitan *descorts*.[116] In the life of this manuscript, then, we can see that *descorts* marked physical and performative junctures with musical properties that contrast with the *chanson*, namely heterostrophic lyrics and unsystematic melodies, that, over time, tended to be through-composed and mensural.

Like all delinquents, the *descort* had a disruptive influence on other songs. This is evident in the mensural *chansons* and *lais* added after the three Occitan *descorts*. These late additions can be plotted on the same melodic continuum as the *descorts* (see right column of table 2.4.)

The first song to come under the influence of the *descort* was a Latin song to the Virgin. *Iam mundus ornatur* uses the same melody as that added for the French *descort*, *La douce acordance*.[117] *Iam mundus ornatur* is part of a suite of five relatively short Latin songs whose lyrics follow liturgical order; together they could be thought of as

---

114. For a discussion of the various medieval and modern orderings of the manuscript see Haines, "The Transformation of the *Manuscrit du roi*," 21–29, and chapter 3. The medieval table of contents indicates a third song for Carasaus, which was not recorded. It is possible that the space in which *Qui le ve en ditz* was recorded was intended for this third song.

115. See Cyrus, "Musical Distinctions between *Descorts* and *Lais*," esp.7–12. Cyrus does not include *Bella donna cara*.

116. This same notator added music to perhaps as many as twenty-eight empty staves, including a total of five using Franconian note shapes. See Haines, "Musicography," 154–55.

117. Haines, "Musicography," 164, notes that the same hand added a total of five Latin pieces to this collection.

TABLE 2.4

Melodic continuum for *descorts* and late additions to trouv. *M*

Bold = late Occitan additions; <u>underline</u> = mensural notation

SYSTEMATIC HETEROSTROPHIC MELODIES

(regular, exact repetition of phrases and motifs within strophes)

Descorts:	*Other late additions*
A ce m'acort	<u>Quant je voi plus felons rire</u> (RS 1503)
Espris d'ire et d'amor	(AAB, CCD, EEF, etc.)
Trop est coustumiere Amors	<u>Ki de bons est, souef flaire</u>
Sens alegrage	(AAB, CCD, EEF, etc.)

UNSYSTEMATIC

(irregular, inexact repetition of phrases and motifs)

De celi me plaig	<u>A mon pooir ai servi</u> (RS 1081)
La doce pensée	(AxB, AyB, AzB, etc.)
J'ai maintes fois chanté	
Se chans ne descors ne lais	

THROUGH-COMPOSED

<u>La douce acordance</u> (added to existing staves)	= IAM MUNDUS ORNATUR (+ four songs/strophes?)
Qui la ve en ditz	<u>Se j'ai chanté sans guerredon avoir</u> (RS 1789)
Bella donna cara	<u>La plus noble emprise</u>

through-composed strophes in a longer, pious *descort*.[118] The same hand contributed a mensural recomposition of the trouvère *chanson A mon pooir ai servi*;[119] two more such songs were added, each by different hands: these are *Quant je voi plus felons rire* and *Se j'ai chanté sans guerredon avoir*. All three additions provide unique heterostrophic realizations of preexisting, strophic trouvère *chansons*. Along with these recomposed *chansons*, two more mensural songs, both anonymous *lais*, were recorded by yet another hand: these are *La plus noble emprise*, which is through-composed, and

---

118. These additions appear in a collection of songs attributed to Thibaut de Champagne (King of Navarre) that was itself added to the main anthology sometime in the late thirteenth century. See Haines, "The Transformation of the *Manuscrit du roi*," 8.

119. Haines, "Musicography," 174–75. This scribe also added to the monophonic motets, discussed in ch. 4. See Peraino, "New Music, Notions of Genre," 95, 112–18; and Beck, *Le Manuscrit du roi*, 2:175.

Ki de bons est, in which each contrasting strophe is set to a different *pedes-cauda* (or AAB) melody (similar to *Quant je voi plus felons rire*). There is an experimental impetus behind all these unusual song forms, which I will discuss further chapter 3. For now, I simply want to point out that in trouv. *M* these experiments began with the Occitan *descorts*.

The mensural Occitan *descorts* in trouv. *M*, like many of the trailing rhymes within them, point both forward and backward—forward to fourteenth-century mensural melodies, foreshadowing the "anachronism and anomaly" of Machaut's *lais* (discussed in chapter 5), and backward to thirteenth-century notation, rhythmic procedures, and lyrics. Here, too, they mark a juncture with discord; they seem to prepare the later musical experiments with trouvère *chansons* and *lais*, experiments that spotlight the belatedness of strophic courtly songs. As a genre, the *descort* provided the conceptual space for thinking "outside the *chanson*," but still in relation to it. Within trouv. *M*, composers applied the free conceptual space to the free physical space. There they mixed the *chanson* form with elements from motets and dance songs, and created *chansons* and *lais* warped nearly beyond recognition—genre delinquents all.

To bring us back to the subject of self-expression, let us take one final look at *Qui la ve en ditz*. The composer of the original lyric, Aimeric de Peguilhan (fl. 1190–1225), was a fourth-generation troubadour who grew up in Toulouse but left during the troubled years of the Albigensian crusades. Commenting on Aimeric's lyrics, his modern-day editors say "the mass of his work provides abundant evidence of the monotony and triteness of Provençal poetry."[120] Despite, or because of, his apparent conventionality, he enjoyed the patronage of the King of Aragon in Spain and various nobles in Italy. *Qui la ve en ditz* (a highly unconventional lyric), as previously noted, was probably written in Italy at some point after 1210, while he was at the court of Este, for the first strophe mentions a Lady Beatrice—identified by scholars as the daughter of the Marquis. Close to this time Aimeric also wrote a crusade poem, perhaps in the spring of 1213, after Pope Innocent III began to agitate for the Fifth Crusade to regain the Holy Sepulcher (which the Fourth Crusade had failed to do). In this poem Aimeric urges his first Italian patron, the Marquis of Monferrato William IV, to take the cross.

Ara parra qual seran enveyos	Now it will be evident who desires
d'aver lo pretz del mon e·l pretz de Dieu,	to have praise from the world and from God,
que bel poiran guazanhar ambedos	for they can win both loyally
selh que seran adreitamen romieu	those who will soon be pilgrims in order to
al sepulcre cobrar. Las! Qual dolor	regain the Sepulcher. Alas! How grievous it is

120. *Aimeric*, 3.

que Turc aian forsat nostre senhor!	that the Turks have done violence to our Lord!
Pensem el cor la dezonor mortal	Let ponder in our hearts that deadly dishonor
e de la crotz prendam lo sanh senhal	and then let us take the holy sign of the cross
e passem lai, que·l ferms e·l conoissens	and pass overseas, for the good Pope Innocent,
nos guizara, lo bos pap'Innocens.	the strong and wise, will guide us.[121]

Example 2.7 🅢 OXFORD WEB MUSIC presents the final strophe and the *tornada* from *Qui la ve en ditz* as preserved in trouv. *M*. Recall that this strophe is not original to Aimeric de Peguilhan; it is, rather, the work of an anonymous poet who mimicked the metrical structure of Aimeric's lyric and grafted on his own ending. And the anonymous poet had his own critical agenda, for the lyrics of this grafted fourth strophe open with a response to Aimeric's crusade poem:

Donc dic a la gen	Hence I say to the people
que mandon crosar	who are summoning us to take the Cross
ar,	now,
qu'ieu non ay talen	that I have neither the desire
ni cor de passar	nor the heart to cross
mar,	the sea,
neys s'il monimen	even if the Holy Sepulchre
sabia cobrar,	I could regain,
car	for
sella m'o defen!	she forbids me!
De prez non a par,	As for her worth, she has no equal,
car…	for…

As Aimeric was himself one of those people who recruited for the cross, this sequel lyric presents a deliciously sacrilegious inversion of Aimeric's sentiments—a rejection of the cross in the name of love. Such a stance places our anonymous poet squarely on the other side of the mostly failed crusades, which finally ended in 1270. In the hands of the younger anonymous *descort* writer, then, Aimeric himself becomes delinquent, refusing to turn at the sound of his own hailing.

We cannot determine definitively that this anonymous poet also composed the music for the entire *descort*. In contrast to the newly-composed words, the newly-composed

---

121. PC 10-10. Text and translation from *Aimeric*, 85 and 87, respectively.

EXAMPLE 2.7 *Qui la ve en ditz*, strophe IV and *tornada* from trouv. *M*, fol. 186/B170^{bis}

music in no way follows the large-scale poetic structure, which might lead us to believe that poet and composer had two different objectives—one to mimic the large-scale poetic structure, the other to dismantle it into short, atomized phrases. The constantly changing surface hides the large-scale strophic structure—and therefore Aimeric's distinctive voice—perhaps allowing for a seamless graft between the original poem and its later continuation. The music of this fourth strophe becomes particularly difficult: angular melodic lines hover in the upper tessitura of a melodic range that spans a major

EXAMPLE 2.7 Continued

ninth from a low G to a high A. By this time, both listener and performer have had it with the relentless modal rhythm and the gimmick of trailing rhymes. Yet there are some stunning moments of tunefulness and even lyricism when a sentimental expressiveness breaks through the low-level distortion. The strophe's opening versicle (A1), telling of the subject's lack of desire to travel across the sea, builds a large musical period (mm. 1–14) with a series of paired smaller phrases (mm. 1–7 and 8–14) and complementary pitch sets. The tonal focus of this period shifts from a G–C tetrachord, ending with the open cadence on G in measure 7, to the upper C–G pentachord with a closed cadence and dramatic climax on F on the word *mar* (m. 14). But the real climax of this pointed lyric comes in the middle of the next versicle (A2), where the poet claims that he is forbidden to take the cross by his beloved. After two recitational phrases that bring a hushed calm to the line "even if the Holy Sepulcher I could regain" (mm. 15–21), the melody ramps up to the climax with the forward-looking trailing rhyme *car* (for), then explodes to the highest point in the whole song with the words *sella m'o defen!* (she forbids me!), and an emphatic cadence once again on the high F. The *tornada* is especially haunting with the address to Blanc' Elena set within a Lydian tetrachord and a smooth descent—minus the melodic hocket—to the final echoing rhymes and a firmly closed cadence on G.

Such attention to the sense of the words, in the fourth strophe no less, is exactly what the isostrophic melodies of *cansos* cannot do. And though the double-versicle construction of *descorts* has greater expressive flexibility, the content profile of the A1 and A2 versicles places their dramatic high points at different poetic lines. Although I have been describing these *descorts* as collisions of sound and sense, the extraordinary concern with expression in this final strophe and *tornada* suggests that the composer of the new text was indeed the composer of the music. But we must remember that this composer not only devised new music for *Qui la ve en ditz*, but also for *Sens alegrage* and *Bella donna cara* as well. This might suggest the opposite conclusion: the composer chose specific pre-existing lyrics to set in his own particular style. Regardless, the consistency of musical style across all three Occitan *descorts*, including the musical motif of the trailing rhymes and the modal rhythm, brings the composer's musical, subjective voice to the fore, superimposing his own sound and sense onto the genre of the *descort*.

In his essay "Adorno as Lateness Itself," Edward Said describes Adorno's construction of late Beethoven as the forecaster of the modernist paradox, the self-alienating future orientation of artists who seem to have the end squarely in mind, whose avant-gardism both drives and is driven by a sense of accelerated time and the catastrophic final moment. Said on Adorno on Beethoven describes a "formal law" of the "late style" born of what Said calls "a queer amalgam of subjectivity and convention."[122] In Beethoven it is revealed in his highly idiosyncratic, episodic, discontinuous, and fragmentary music that recasts or rejects conventions altogether.

The temptation here is to posit an abstract "late style" that comes about regularly in a natural cycle of art—a spiral or, better, a double helix of subjectivity and convention folding in on itself time and again. It is a temptation that I will yield to for now, saying "the *descort* made me do it!" *Qui la ve en ditz* is indeed a strange amalgam of a threefold composite subjectivity—Aimeric (a conventional poet writing an unconventional *descort*), the later anonymous poet (following Aimeric's pattern), and perhaps a third separate music composer (who distorts both poets with his "late style" music)—that spirals through nearly a century. The melodic and poetic revisions in this and the other *descorts* that I have examined here are indisputably, and I believe also self-consciously, late: they seem to fulfill the genre-troubling endgame of the *descort*, undoing the pretense of subjective interiority in the love song by means of itself, that is, by truly subjective music that renders itself banal, that calls attention to the external agent of the performer and to the concept of a love that is so interior as to be the abnegation of self, and hence, in the end, purely a convention, like the turn of the subject who hears a hail.

---

122. Said, "Adorno as Lateness Itself," 269.

3

Changing the Subject of the *Chanson d'amour*

"TIME MAY CHANGE me, but I can't trace time." So sings David Bowie in "Changes" (1971), a song about the mutable identities of youth and Bowie himself. The phrase points to a paradox: while change over time is predictable, the nature of those changes is unpredictable. Bernart de Ventadorn offers his own meditation on time:

Lo tems vai e ven e vire	Time comes and goes and turns
per jorns, per mes, e per ans;	through days, through months, through years;
et eu, las, no·n sai que dire,	and I, alas, know not what to say about that,
c'ades es us mos talans.	for my desire is always one.
Ades es us e no·s muda,	It is ever one, and does not change,
c'una·n volh e·n ai volguda,	for I want and have wanted one
don anc non aic jauzimen.	from whom I have never had joy.[1]

Bernart claims that through the turn of days and seasons his desire remains steadfast. This is a twist on the springtime opening, where the change of season itself generates desire and song. For Bernart, the change of seasons provokes not song but silence—a loss of words because change is itself incomprehensible according to his desire. But Bernart does change his "one" desire from the masculine *us* referring to his own *talans*, to the feminine *una*, referring to the female love object. As the opening lines imply, this play with the

---

1. PC 70-30. Text and translation (modified) from *Bernart*, 129 and 130–31, respectively.

morphology and referent—from *us* to *una*, from self to other—has something to do with time. The shifty pronoun belies the stability it is meant to express, while at the same time deftly uniting self and other in the tautology of the troubadour's desire. That desire is both subject (*es us mos talans*) and object (*c'una·n volh*), and both subjective (personal) and objective (empirical). Thus over time this "one"—the universal, the generic subject—bifurcates, and becomes (at least) two.

In chapter 1 we saw how the subjective voice, with its attendant paradoxes and pluralities, emerges in the highly stylized musical form of the strophic *canso* and *chanson*. I argued that self-consciousness was musically expressed precisely in *tornadas*, *envois*, and refrains—interpellative turns that effectively call the subject into an irreducible plurality. Chapter 2 examined the undoing of the *canso* by the *descort*, first in heterostrophic, double-versicle structures, and later interpreted in freely through-composed melodies that seem both spontaneously generated and yet full of artifice. The self-consciousness of the *descorts* reflects their particular historical emergence within the genre system of love lyrics, concomitant with the emergence of a characteristic belatedness. Yet, if we take Goethe's and Adorno's understanding of lateness as a withdrawal or hiding of the subject, then the *descorts* hide the troubadour as they allow the later composer/scribe, and potentially the performer as well, to come into view.

Chapter 2 dealt with a key concept in medieval historiography, namely the thematics of the impending Last Age of earthly time, reflected in the "world upside down" motif, the increasingly popular satirical genre of the *sirventes*, and divisions between "ancient" and "modern" thought and practice. The genre of the *descort* emerged within that topsy-turvy, endgame discourse around 1200, maintaining the sense of the *canso*'s themes of love while turning its sound from *acort* into *descort*. The present chapter will focus on a particular historical moment, from the midpoint of the thirteenth century, when the songs of the troubadours and trouvères were first written down, to the years around 1300, when some of those *chansonniers* began to show signs of a collision between the nostalgic enterprise of recording those songs and new assertions of a "here and now" in the form of unique and unusual melodic realizations.

In the middle of this collision is the status of the individual, or rather the individuality of the "I"—a seemingly empty construct that is generic to the lyric, and that becomes robust in the production of the song anthologies, in their illustration, organization, rubrication, and in the glosses on songs by the *vidas* and *razos*. Medieval manuscripts transmit a clear fascination with names, though perhaps not a clear veneration of "the author" or reverence for a sacred tie that binds "the author" to his or her artistic expression. Yet we can see a project of creating "individuals" in the manuscripts for troubadours and trouvères. The *vidas* and *razos* of the troubadour manuscripts (mostly Italian and mostly fourteenth century) work to tie the abstract language of love lyrics to a particular personage, providing back stories and fleshing out the identity of the author with biographical information. Even if fanciful and derivative of the lyrics themselves, these prose narratives in effect invent authorial identity and secure the songs as self-expression.

William Burgwinkle remarks that the inclusion of *vidas* and *razos* bespeaks the songs' "cultural capital," and that the compilers of the *chansonniers* saw these anthologies as "complex and encyclopedic, documenting not just the lyrics but also the lives of the poets, the development of the genres, and the courts which supported the practice and practitioners of song." At the same time, the critical tone of some of the *vidas* ties them to the tradition of commentary, while some *razos* spin such lengthy stories that they become independent narratives.[2]

In *The Death of the Troubadour: Late Medieval Resistance to the Renaissance*, Gregory B. Stone argues that one can read a dialectic between the anonymous subject and the autonomous subject embedded in medieval texts beginning in the mid-thirteenth century—in other words, a dialectic between the generic, indefinite "I" of love lyrics that interpellates "everyone and no one," and the specific, named "I," historicized and localized in the *vidas* and *razos* and later verse and prose narratives. Stone sees the persistent generalizing of the subject in certain medieval texts as reactionary to the encroachment of what later historians will consider the "birth of the individual" in the Renaissance—a resistance, in other words, to the "death of the troubadours" and their corporate, lyric "I."[3] Stone's focus on the retention of a generic subject jibes with Sarah Kay's recent investigation of universality and "monologism" in texts from 1270 through the fourteenth century in *The Place of Thought: The Complexity of One in Late Medieval French Didactic Poetry*. Kay finds that didactic poems routinely ask readers to imagine themselves in certain common places (by a fountain, in a garden, on a path, in a castle), and that these locations serve as devices to "unify both expression and reception" of thought—in other words, to delimit or corral potential dialogism between text and reader into a monologism.[4] Yet, as per Bernart de Ventadorn's bifurcated *us/una*, what Kay calls medieval "oneness" and its "complexities" can be read in two ways: as a universal that absorbs and neutralizes autonomy, or as a plurality bound together under a singular sign (such as the lyric "I"), blurred by tensions between anonymity and autonomy.

Debate genres, such as the *tenso* and *partimen* in which troubadours name one another, and instances of "signatures" in other stanzas or the *tornada*, may seem to contradict the notion that the lyric "I" was always or uncomplicatedly generalized. These are, to some extent, "exceptions that prove the rule," however, in that the effect of names is always striking, always overdetermined as a gateway leading outside the lyric fiction. This is especially true of the *tenso Ara·m platz, Guiraut de Borneill*, where Raimbaut d'Aurenga and

---

2. See Burgwinkle, "The *Chansonniers* as Books," 247 and 250–51; see also Poe, *From Poetry to Prose*, esp. 35–65. Poe writes, "*Vidas* and *razos* open up poems as a way of preserving, and, indeed, celebrating the lyric universe. Paradoxically, though, they help to destroy the very thing which they work to preserve, for, by increasing the means of access to the lyric composition, they break down the integrity of the lyric world. Much that was unique to *fin'amors*—secrecy, exclusiveness, ambiguity, unattainability—gets lost when exposed and clarified in *vidas* and *razos*" (65).

3. Stone, *The Death of the Troubadour*, 1–12.

4. Kay, *The Place of Thought*, esp. 8–16.

Guiraut de Bornehl argue over the *trobar clus* style and whether the merit of a song is measured by its accessibility or by inherent artistry. Through direct address and style debates, the lyric sentiment is exposed as artifice and conceit.[5]

The question remains, then, to what extent the autonomous individual is a product of manuscript culture—indeed, the *invention* of anonymous scribes. Michel Zink and Sylvia Huot both see the emergence of self-conscious autonomy in the rise of Old French narratives and the move of "literature" from predominantly oral to predominantly written in conception and transmission (thus mapping the binary generic/specific onto other binaries such as lyric/narrative, and oral/written). Zink proposes that "French literature," including troubadour and trouvère lyrics, owes "its sustenance from the book."[6] He writes:

> The troubadour and trouvère songbooks…reflect a belated reception of pieces dating from the previous generation or century. Through the intervention of the *vidas* and the *razos*, those of the troubadours—often copied in Italy, thus adding a cultural gap to the time gap—invited anecdotal and biographical readings no longer corresponding to the aesthetics of courtly lyricism. Their usual indifference to melody confirms this separation. The trouvère songbooks seem more respectful of this aesthetics.… But it was also in langue d'oïl that the literature of their time developed a poetics of the anecdotal expression of the self that, adopting new forms, made it unnecessary to graft it onto traditional lyricism.[7]

Huot similarly argues that the careful ordering, rubrication, and illustrations in trouvère *chansonniers* "is a first step toward the codification and establishment of an Old French lyric canon, which can be studied as such."[8] More specifically, she traces a tension between the aristocratic lyric subject (read: generic) and a clerical narrative one (read: specific) in the visual and organizational program of *chansonniers*. The author portraits with details of heraldry (for nobility) or occupation (for clerics) function in comparable ways to the *vidas* and *razos*: they have a "particularizing quality in spite of their formal similarity" that "points to an actual historic existence for these persons, grounding the lyric 'I' in an extratextual reality."[9] But Huot believes the concern with author identity "is also indicative of the self-reflexive quality of the lyric," its concern with "the event of its own making."[10] This concern with "the event of its own making" becomes a principal theme in later, clerical compositions that convey a poetics of writing in their self-conscious preoccupation with the activities of literary production (composing, writing,

---

5. PC 389-10a. See *Anthology*, 114–17 for text and translation.

6. Zink, *The Invention of Literary Subjectivity*, 12.

7. Ibid., 39.

8. Huot, *From Song to Book*, 53.

9. Ibid., 57.

10. Ibid., 48.

and compilation), and which give equal measure to the author as lover-protagonist and as poet-narrator.[11]

In what follows I investigate the ways in which anonymous scribes and compilers made robust the named voices of the love lyric while paving the way for the emergence of self-consciously autonomous but still anonymous musical compositions. Most medieval song collections, whether they stand alone (such as trouv. *M*) or form part of a larger miscellany of texts (such as the "collected works" of Adam de la Halle in trouv. *W*), give the impression of an intended compilation plan that has been subjected to revision and supplementation over time. In some cases the original plan was not fully executed, and later hands made attempts to complete the work of prior scribes by "filling in the blanks"— be they empty staves, lacunae of authors and genres, or the physically blank folio space left at the ends of gatherings. The impetus to complete and supplement a collection over time had the twin effects of preserving and dismantling tradition. The first part of this chapter looks at the preserving of tradition in the addition of discrete *libelli* of songs by Thibaut de Champagne and Adam de la Halle in trouv. *T*. It is here that we can also see something of an "invention" of the individual in northern sources, and an implied narrative, as a result of compilation over time, regarding the inheritance of the lyric voice. The second part of this chapter looks at the dismantling effects of continued compilation by examining the late additions to trouv. *M*, specifically focusing on three songs that take strophic lyrics by named trouvères and set these to unique non-strophic melodies. Without pushing the point of a detectable "writerliness," I want to suggest that the additions to trouv. *M*—especially the recomposed *chansons*—are a musical reflection on "the event of their own making." In other words, it is the anonymous "new" music, not the lyrics or the names associated with them, that stands for the subjective voice, the self-conscious expression of an autonomous subject.

BOOKENDS: THIBAUT DE CHAMPAGNE, ADAM DE LA HALLE,
AND THE PLACE OF SONG

Sarah Kay's notion of thought unified by a metaphorical place has analogs in the *chansonniers*. The collections physically and figuratively construct a "place" for the songs that have both geographical and social meaning. The identity of a person was inextricably bound with a geographical place in the Middle Ages, evident in common naming practices such as Bernart de Ventadorn and Guiot de Dijon. Strategic marriages and the acquisition of land by force or reward produced a constant traffic of people for the control of principalities and patrilineal inheritance. "Place" can also mean place in society; here, too, naming practices offer evidence of such placing: Willaumes li Viniers, Cholars

---

11. In addition to Huot, *From Song to Book*, see Uitti, "From *Clerc* to *Poète*", and Brownlee, "The Poetic Oeuvre of Guillaume de Machaut."

li Boutelliers, Hues li Chastelains d'Arras, Willammes d'Amiens li Paignieres. *Chansonniers* organize their songs in a variety of ways—by social status of author, by genre, alphabetically by the first letter of the lyric—and each compilation scheme provides a map for the reader that places song in a unified field of signification. Geography, social status, and the temporality of inheritance play important roles in all of these schemes, which I will trace in the handling of the works of Thibaut de Champagne, the king of Navarre, and Adam de la Halle, a cleric from Arras.

The songs of both Thibaut and Adam were disseminated in separate "collected works" booklets (*libelli*) that foreground the author as both the creative agent and lyric subject of the songs. One version of the *Grandes Chroniques de France* (from ca. 1380) suggests that Thibaut had a hand in compiling his songs: "And he had them written down in his hall in Provins and in the one in Troyes, and they are called *The Songs by the King of Navarre.*"[12] No such attestation survives for Adam's supervision of his song collections; however, his temporal and geographical proximity to the sources for his compositions, coupled with his compositional expansion into polyphonic and narrative forms, increases the possibility of his input.[13] But these two figures—one a mid-century aristocrat, the other a late-century bourgeois cleric—represent quite distinct types of authors and, by extension, ideologies of authorship and projections of subjectivity.

Paul Zumthor claims that if there is any "subjectivity" to be found in the trouvère *chansons* it is a collective one—namely, that of a social class, and most abundantly the aristocracy.[14] What, then, is the subjectivity of the nobility in the thirteenth century? During the reign of French king Philip II (Philip Augustus, r. 1179–1223), the power of the aristocracy declined in the face of a newly strengthened monarchy. The decisive turn of fate for the landed nobility was Philip Augustus's victory in the Battle of Bouvines in 1214, where he defeated, among others, Ferrand (or Ferdinand), Count of Flanders, as well as John, King of England, who held the duchies of Brittany and Normandy.[15] At the height of the struggles during the years 1201–13, a new genre of literature, vernacular prose histories, emerged as an attempt to buttress the culture and ideology of the weakening aristocracy. Gabrielle Spiegel has documented that the patrons of this new type of writing "held lands and tenures in or dependent on the contested region of Artois."[16] These historical accounts of Charlemagne and Roland, and ancient figures such as Julius

12. "Et les fist escripre en sa sale à Provins et en celle de Troyes, et sont appellées *Les Chançons au Roy de Navarre.*" See Huot, *From Song to Book*, 64.

13. Ibid., 66–74.

14. See Zumthor, *Towards a Medieval Poetics*, 41–45.

15. For an excellent history of the strife between Philip Augustus and the aristocracy of Flanders and Artois see Spiegel, *Romancing the Past*, 11–54; see also Baldwin, *The Government of Philip Augustus*, 191–219.

16. Spiegel, *Romancing the Past*, 53.

Caesar, Alexander the Great, and Aeneas, celebrated aristocratic and chivalric values of prowess, honor, and valor, thus affirming the place of the nobility in the social hierarchy. At the same time, by recounting the civil wars of the ancient past, these histories "displace to linguistic mediation the conflict between king and nobility."[17] The new prose form added truth-value, for it had no exigencies to conform to rhyme or meter and therefore had no artifice to cast doubt upon the story conveyed.

In the years leading up to 1250—the approximate date of the first *chansonniers* in both northern and southern regions—royal *baillis* (salaried officers) and mercenary armies had largely replaced established feudal vassals and knights as the principal administrators of monarchal power. A revived money economy enabled non-noble merchant and clerical classes to prosper while the cash-poor nobles increasingly sold off their lands and seigneurial rights.[18] None of the northern *chansonniers* was produced in Paris, the site of the royal government; all come from regions that once boasted powerful aristocracies— especially Picardy and Artois, but also Lorraine and Burgundy.[19] Furthermore, many of the song collections give noble authors pride of place at the front. Thus at the time of their compilation these anthologies monumentalized a socio-economic world no longer operative. As the aristocracy continued to promote their status in cultural forms such as songs, verse narratives, prose histories, and tournaments, so too did the middle class aspire to imitate the aristocracy.[20] Yet conservative imitations also accompanied liberal innovations. Non-noble authors, many coming from the prosperous trade and banking town of Arras, composed courtly *chansons* in the high style of the troubadours and early trouvères as well as hybrid and new forms that joined lofty love rhetoric, filled with dichotomies of agency and submission, with the pithier emotional statements found in refrains. Table 3.1 lists genres composed by five prominent trouvères in successive generations, illustrating the shift from noble to non-noble authors correlated to the expansion of genres.[21]

As the above table indicates, earlier noble trouvères, such as Gace Brulé and Gautier de Dargies, stuck close to the principal troubadour genres of the *canso*, the *descort*, and

17. Ibid., 118; see also 54–57, 77–89, 114–15.

18. See Baldwin, *The Government of Philip Augustus*, 101–75, and Spiegel, *Romancing the Past*, 16–23.

19. Aubrey, "Sources, MS, §III: Secular monophony, 4. French" see also the list of sources in the front matter.

20. See the remarks of Huot, *From Song to Book*, 60–63; see also 53–64 for a discussion of the organization of *chansonnier* content by class. See also Räkel, *Die musikalische Erscheinungsform der Trouvèrepoesie*, 259–61.

21. See the entries for these trouvères in Linker, *A Bibliography of Old French Lyrics*. For Thibaut de Champagne see also *Thibaut* (I have added RS 1516 to the thirty-six found in *Thibaut*); for Adam de la Halle see *Adam*. For the *jeux-partis* I have included all those in which the given trouvère participated as a respondent, even though the trouvère who proposed the exchange is presumed to have composed the melody. Nelson and other scholars identify one of Adam de la Halle's *chansons* as a *chanson de femme* (RS 658) because of its highly repetitive music and popular "tone"; only the version found in trouv. *W* uses a masculine pronoun to refer to the beloved (see *Adam*, 188).

some ancillary genres such as the *pastourelle* and the *aube*, both of which have antecedents in the troubadour repertory. The *jeu-parti* (also called *partures*) emerged as a significant genre with Thibaut de Champagne, who was one of the earliest contributors in *langue d'oïl*. The genre stemmed from the troubadour *joc partit* or *partimen*—an exchange between two persons on a proposed topic or dilemma (usually of love) as a

TABLE 3.1

The compositions of five prominent trouvères

Gace Brulé (knight from Champagne, fl. 1180–1213)

79 chansons d'amour (8 with repeating refrain)

1 pastourelle

1 jeu-parti

1 aube (with refrain)

Gautier de Dargies (knight from Picardy and Artois, fl. 1195–1236)

17 chansons d'amour (none using refrains)

3 descorts

2 débats or tensos

1 chanson de Croisade

1 motet voice or monophonic motet

Thibaut IV (count of Champagne, and king of Navarre, fl. 1225–53)

37 chansons d'amour (4 with a repeating refrain; 1 with changing refrains)

2 pastourelles

9 jeux-partis

5 débats or tensos

3 chansons de Croisade

1 serventois

4 chansons à la Vierge

1 lai religieux

Willaume li Viniers (cleric from Arras, fl. 1225–45)

15 chansons d'amour (3 with repeating refrain)

1 "balade" (with refrain)

5 pastourelles (2 with repeating refrain; 1 with changing refrains)

2 descorts

7 jeux-partis

3 chansons à la Vierge

Adam de la Halle (cleric from Arras, fl. 1270– ca. 1288)

33 chansons d'amour (1 with repeating refrain)

1 chanson de femme

18 jeux-partis

2 chansons à la Vierge

16 polyphonic rondeaux

5 motets

1 pastourelle play with musical interpolations (*Le jeu de Robin et Marion*)

1 satiric play (*Le jeu d'Adam ou de la feuillée*, including 1 refrain)

1 *Congé* (non-musical poem)

1 incomplete *chanson de geste* (*Chanson du roi de Sezile*)

game (*joc, jeu*), where the questioner gives the respondent a choice between two sides of the argument. This style of debate lyric differs from the earlier troubadour *tenso* (trouvère *débat* or *tençon*), in which the questioner challenges the respondent's held position. (In other words, the first stanza of the *jeu-parti* asks "Which is better?" while the first stanza of the *tençon* asks "Why do you think X is better?").[22] Guilhem Molinier, in *Las Leys d'Amors*, recognized the two debate frameworks as separate, though the manuscripts and sometimes the songs themselves do not; one of Thibaut's *jeux-partis* opens with the lines "Sire, help me make a choice in this *jeu*," but concludes with the statement "Raoul, I would rather end our *tençon* in a courteous manner."[23] As with the *descorts*, these quasi-scholastic debates arose in the generation of troubadours composing between 1180 and 1220, a significant period that saw not only the ascendancy of the northern Capetian monarchy and the decline of the southern nobility, but also the formation of the Universities of Paris and Montepellier among others, in which the scholastic genres of debate—the *questio, disputatio,* and *quodlibetica*—were developed and disseminated.[24] With mid-thirteenth-century trouvères, debate poems occasionally took on the satirical tone of *sirventes*, as in the *jeu-parti* between Thibaut and a cleric, *Bons rois*

---

22. For a discussion of the form and chronology of *jeux-partis* see Långfors, *Recueil général des jeux-partis français*, 1:v–xxiii.

23. *Sire, loëz moi a choisir* (RS 1393); see *Thibaut*, 180–83.

24. For the rise of the *descort* see the chart in Paden, "The System of Genres Troubadour Lyric," 27. See Verger, "Patterns," 41–55. Verger remarks on the prevalence of this scholastic pedagogical method, which was inherited from the earlier twelfth-century schools of logic and theology (Paris), law (Bologna), and medicine (Salerno) (43). He also notes that the universities of Oxford, Bologna, Paris, and Montpellier "seemed to have

Thiebaut, sire, conseilliez moi, in which Thibaut characterizes the cleric as lustful and uncourtly.[25]

Among the trouvères, the increased cultivation of this explicitly multi-voiced genre also coincides with the increased percentage of *chansons* with repeating or changing refrains, which, as argued in chapter 1, also present a multiplication of voices within a single song. Adam de la Halle may seem an exception, for all but one of his *chansons d'amour* are without refrains. The conservatism of his monophonic *chanson* style is balanced, however, by his progressive sixteen polyphonic *rondeaux*—a song form based entirely on the music of the refrain. Taking Adam's compositions altogether, the thirty-four *chansons d'amour* are in fact outnumbered by his other lyric and non-lyric genres, and thus effectively consigned to a secondary position, as nostalgic emblems of the past—not the future—of songcraft. As argued in chapter 2, such belatedness is itself emblematic of self-consciousness, especially when conjoined with innovations that create a tension between "ancient" and "modern" practices. In the *descorts* we observed such conjunction occurring within single compositions, where tradition-subverting free-form melodies and hocket-like gimmicks flow in the modal rhythms of the *ars antiqua*. By way of contrast, Adam de la Halle chose to segregate his "ancient" and "modern" practices, thus staging this temporal debate, as it were, on the level of genre. Within Adam's oeuvre, then, the *chansons d'amour* clearly become museum pieces, a display of his own mastery of a venerable and aristocratic genre, while his polyphonic motets and *rondeaux*, as well as his interpolated *jeux*, figure by comparison as cutting edge or even avant-garde.

The reception and meaning attached to genres, forms, and authors depends entirely on the intervention and creativity of the compilers and scribes who put together the song anthologies. As a "book," the *chansonnier* held significance beyond its content, with its assembly of multiple systems of signification—graphic, linguistic, and, of course, musical. Jesse M. Gellrich argues that the "idea of the Book" in the Middle Ages functioned as a part of the medieval episteme, an understanding of the world as a dense network of resemblances, relating microcosm to macrocosm. All books resembled, in a conceptual way at least, the Bible, which was itself the ultimate sign of a totality, and of unified meaning, inscribed by a divine hand. Learned medieval treatises often bore the name *summa* (sum, totality) or *speculum* (mirror), which insinuated a connection between the particulars of a specific topic and the grand cosmic order.[26] Gellrich links the idea of

---

become genuine universities between 1200 and 1215" (45). For descriptions of the scholastic debates see Le Goff, *Intellectuals in the Middle Ages*, 89–92. For discussions of the resonance of scholastic methods in vernacular poetry, see Neumeister, *Das Spiel mit der höfischen Liebe*, 51–69; Bec, *La Joute poétique*, 11–28; and Grande Quejigio and Moreno, "The Love Debate Tradition," 103–26.

25. RS 1666; see *Thibaut*, 174–79, and comments on xxiv.

26. Gellrich, *The Idea of the Book*, 1–50. Foucault defines an episteme as part of a non-verbal experience of order, an "epistemological field" through which a sense of order is conveyed. See *The Order of Things*, xxi–xxii; for Foucault's discussion of the medieval episteme of resemblance, see 17–45.

the Book—its "encyclopedic and totalizing structure"—to the retention of pagan mythological thinking in which the replication of forms, as opposed to deviation from them, serves to reproduce the sacred spaces, works, and texts of the gods (or God, as the case may be).[27] Yet as Jacques Derrida (to whom Gellrich is indebted) formulates it, there is "a good writing and a bad writing: the good and natural is the divine inscription in the heart and soul; the perverse and artful is technique, exiled in the exteriority of the body." Thus the "idea of the Book" was also, ironically, the "protection against the disruption of [bad] writing, against its aphoristic energies" that threatened to dismantle the conceptual unity into material plurality.[28] But sometimes not even the Bible could protect itself: Roger Bacon, writing in 1267 about his student days in Paris, complained of corrupt versions of sacred texts, and scribes who "added further changes on top of the corruption."[29] As we shall see, the *chansonniers* under consideration in this chapter manifest both the unifying idea of the Book, and the disruptive, aphoristic energies of writing.

Bonaventure, in his prologue to Peter of Lombard's *Libri sententiarum* (ca. 1250s), offered a typology of writing, in order of degrees of creative input on the part of the writer:

> There are four ways of making a book. For someone writes out the words of others, without adding or changing anything; he is called the scribe (*scriptor*) pure and simple. Someone else writes the words of others, adding material but not his own, and he is called the compiler (*compilator*). Someone else writes both words of others and his own, but with those of others constituting the principal part while his own are annexed to clarify the argument, and he is called the commentator (*commentator*), not the author. Someone else writes both the words of others and his own, but with his own constituting the principal part and those of others being

---

27. Gellrich writes: "the dominance of the schematic in this order rests upon the same sense of sacred space that is evident in formulaic artistic styles of the middle ages. The sacrality of spatial arrangement controls how thinking proceeds; thought is the speculum of sacred order." See *The Idea of the Book*, 68; see also 94–96.

28. Derrida, *Of Grammatology*, 17 and 18, respectively; see also Gellrich, *The Idea of the Book*, 31–32. In *Of Grammatology*, Derrida expands the notion of "writing" from the act of inscribing with graphemes to include the very potentiality of signification—"all that gives rise to an inscription in general, whether it is literal or not and even if what it distributes in space is alien to the order of the voice: cinematography, choreography, of course, but also pictorial, musical, sculptural 'writing'" (9). The concept of the linguistic sign, even with its partition into the signifier and the signified, historically privileges speech as immediate and interior, and writing as secondary, exterior, and supplemental. This cultural "phonocentrism" or "logocentrism" posits an "absolute proximity of voice and being, of voice and the meaning of being, of voice and the ideality of meaning" (11–12). Derrida asserts, on the contrary, that "[t]he exteriority of the signifier is the exteriority of writing in general . . . there is no linguistic sign before writing. Without exteriority, the very idea of the sign falls into decay" (14). For Derrida, the overarching theory of the linguistic sign as "writing," with its insistence on exteriority, finally rids the sign of its metaphysical attributes and pretense to unity and naturalism.

29. Quoted in Rouse and Rouse, *Manuscripts and their Makers*, 1:32.

annexed merely by way of confirmation, and such a person should be called the author (*auctor*).[30]

Elizabeth Poe cites the above passage in the prologue to her study of the *chansonnier* troub. *H*, a northern Italian source from the last quarter of the thirteenth century that contains discrete sections of material including: (1) prose commentaries to songs (*vidas* and *razos*); (2) glossed *cansos* by various troubadours (notably a block by Arnaut Daniel); (3) a section of *coblas* (one or two free-standing stanzas) further organized into clusters showing a variety of schemes—by author (such as a block by *trobairitz* or by Uc de Saint Circ), by subgenre (such as *coblas tensonadas* or exchanged *coblas*), and by shared metrical patterns. Poe sees the traces of *compilatio* here—the careful selection and ordering (*ordinatio*) of smaller independent collections to make a whole. The coherence of this whole may not be readily apparent, or may be "superficial"; as Poe observes, it is a "coherence resulting from compilation as opposed to that residing in composition."[31]

Yet the activities of compilers and scribes making books in the thirteenth century—especially books with notation—intersected with the activities of authors composing words and music. In their exhaustive study of commercial book producers in Paris between 1200 and 1500, Richard and Mary Rouse stress that the requirement of "speed of completion and quantity" in commercial production precluded anything more than standard designs and stock illuminations. The Rouses examined only one manuscript with music: *Fauvel*, long thought to be the work of professional book-makers. Yet the Rouses remark: "musical notation is a strong indicator of 'owner-production,' since notating always required the efforts of a specialist, even for ordinary service books." Furthermore, the chancery book hands, and the careful program of contents and inserted folios, indicate "a close physical proximity and an immediate connection between the author or authors of the text and the copyists."[32]

---

30. "Quadruplex est modus faciendi librum. Aliquis enim scribit aliena, nihil addendo vel mutando; et iste mere dicitur scriptor. Aliquis scribit aliena addendo, sed non de suo; et iste compilator dicitur. Aliquis scribit et aliena et sua, sed aliena tamquam principalia, et sua tamquam annexa ad evidentiam; et iste dicitur commentator non auctor. Aliquis scribit et sua et aliena, sed sua tamquam principalia, aliena tamquam annexa ad confirmationem et debet dici auctor." See Poe, *Compilatio*, 17–18.

31. Poe, *Compilatio*, 32; see also 13–42.

32. Rouse and Rouse, *Manuscripts and their Makers*, 1:231. The Rouses focus on the figure of the *libraire*, who was "a combination book-seller and book-contractor." Wealthy patrons, possibly through an intermediary agent, commissioned a book with specified content from a *libraire*, who then obtained parchment, found exemplars, hired illuminators and scribes (and sometimes acted as a scribe to save money) (1:14). These were clerics in minor orders who operated independently of the university, though enjoyed some of its protections (1:33). The question of who was responsible for the *compilatio* and *ordinatio* of the book—patron or *libraire*—remains unanswered in the Rouses' study; though they mostly credit the patron with decisions of content and design, in one case study from 1318 they admit that the *libraire* may have had "a more than ordinary editorial manipulation of the text...assembling disparate parts into a reasonably well-integrated whole" (1:181).

Extrapolating from the Rouses' discussion of *Fauvel*, we can better imagine the circumstances of *chansonnier* production. While some trouvère *chansonniers* display a consistency of style and content that bespeaks a measure of commercial production (the *KNPX* group), others (*M, R, T, U, V, a*) show informalities of production, idiosyncrasies of content, and revisions (*remaniement*) reflecting the changing taste of patrons, or possibly changing patrons or recipients of the book as a gift, all of which suggests "owner-production" and not commercial production. "Owner-production" for the *chansonniers*, then, would mean the proximity of the scribes and illuminators, hired ad hoc or on retainer within a court, to whomever had the creative task of designing and compiling the contents of the manuscript. Such a non-commercial *compilator* may have been a figure within the court of the aristocratic patron, and thus able to consult the patron about a list of named composers and perhaps even specific songs and genres. Thus with regard to *chansonniers* it becomes especially difficult to know where compilation ends and commentary begins, or where commentary ends and authorship begins.[33]

In Bonaventure's typology, compilers do not add material of their own, but the Book that results from their "writing" may produce its own unified, readable text. Medieval compilers often organized narrative anthologies in a way that created a metanarrative of *translatio studii* or *translatio imperii*—the transmission of learning and authority from antiquity to the medieval present.[34] We can also see such a metanarrative of *translatio—translatio vocis*—at work in the *chansonnier* trouv. *T*, which preserves discrete *libelli* for both Thibaut de Champagne and Adam de la Halle, placed at either end of the primary collection. The articulation of a book's contents into chapters emerged in the thirteenth century with the rediscovery of Aristotelian logic and the new impetus to define and structure various fields of human knowledge. The concern with *ordinatio* within books resulted in a new visual aid for study—tables of contents with a hierarchical scheme of

33. Emma Dillon argues this point in her study of *Fauvel*; with its extensive musical interpolations and narrative expansions, the creative energies of the anonymous scribes who designed, wrote, and decorated the elaborate manuscript are on a par with those of the named "authors" Gervais du Bus, Chaillou de Pesstain, Philippe de Vitry, etc.; see Dillon, *Medieval Music-Making*, 147; see also 146–72. Dillon's argument is not contradicted by the Rouses in *Manuscripts and their Makers*. John Haines also makes the point that the medieval scribes who created the troubadour and trouvère *chansonniers* were "interpreting it [the music], refashioning it to fit the book being compiled." See his *Eight Centuries of Troubadours and Trouvères*, 7. In *Manuscripts and their Makers*, however, the Rouses cast doubt on any commentary or interpretation attributable to jobbing scribes and illuminators hired by the *libraire*, likening them more to "seal-cutters and poultry sellers…than to the poets and translators and adaptors whose works they disseminated" (1:227). Yet they include two compelling pieces of evidence to contradict their depiction of scribes and illuminators as unthinking cogs in the machinery of book production. The first is Roger Bacon's complaint that scribes willfully changed sacred texts (quoted above); the second is two *bas-de-page* self-portraits of a husband and wife team of book-makers (see 1:239–40; see also their figures 22 and 23). While not exactly responding to the content of the words, the marginal self-portraits effectively write the book-makers themselves into text: they are assertive expressions of self and craft that comment on the materiality and exteriority of the written words, on the event of their making.

34. See the discussion in Huot, *From Song to Book*, 11–45, and Freeman, *The Poetics of* Translatio Studii *and* Conjointure.

headings and subheadings (in red and black repetitively).[35] Eight *chansonniers* contain medieval tables of contents, created shortly before or after the execution of the collection, that structure the field of song primarily by author (in order of prestige) and secondarily by genre.[36] Although trouv. *T* does not contain a contemporaneous table of contents, a thoughtful *compilatio* is nonetheless apparent, as table 3.2 reveals:

TABLE 3.2

A schematic inventory of trouv. *T*

I. 3 gatherings

1ʳ–20ʳ	"Li Roi de Navare fist ces chançons. cz. liiii." (55 songs, 4 with melodies)
20ᵛ–22ᵛ	blank

II. 20 gatherings

23ʳ–61ᵛ	30 poets
62ʳ–75ᵛ	13 lais (with separate rubrics, including 2 in Occitan)
76ᵛ–170ʳ	51 poets (plus scattered anonymous songs)
170ᵛ–172ʳ	6 anonymous songs
172ᵛ–176ᵛ	11 songs by Jehan de Renti (separate scribe)
177ʳ–178ᵛ	blank

III. 7 gatherings

179–197ʳ	91 motets (none by Adam de la Halle)
197ᵛ–199ʳ	4 lyric songs of Artois
199ᵛ–216ʳ	24 dits from Artois
216ᵛ–217ᵛ	blank
218ʳ–221ᵛ	*Vers de la mort* by Robert le Clerc
222ʳ–223ᵛ	blank

IV. 2 gatherings

224–233ᵛ	"Les chançons Adam li Boçus" (33 songs, 12 with melodies)

35. On *compilatio* and *ordinatio* see Parkes, "The Influence of the Concepts of *Ordinatio* and *Compilatio*," 115–41, esp. 119–23; on *remaniement* ("rehandling"), see Gaunt and Kay, *Medieval French Literature*, 6. See also Dillon, *Medieval Music-Making*, 41–44.

36. Those song collections with contemporaneous tables of contents include trouv. *K, M, I, W, R, U, a,* and troub. *R*. The alphabetical ordering of trouv. *O* and *C* also betray the influence of scholastic schemes of *ordinatio*. See also the remarks of Haines, *Eight Centuries of Troubadours and Trouvères*, 14–15.

the manuscript brings together four separate collections physically set apart from one another by blank folios.[37]

Although the *libellus* of songs by Thibaut de Champagne appears to have been produced separately from the central song collection of the *chansonnier* (judging by the sparse notation, different scribe, and discrepancies in ruling), certain features suggest that it was part of the original plan, for the single-column format, size of the letters and the written block, and the pattern of decorations (large *champie* initials mark the beginning of songs, small colored capitals with pen-flourishes mark each subsequent stanza) conform to the look of the central collection of songs in section II of the *chansonnier*.[38] Furthermore, Thibaut is conspicuously absent in section II, and, perhaps to distinguish him from the other authors, the rubricator announced "Li Roi de Navare fist ces chançons. *cz* [*ez*] *liiii*" (The King of Navarre made these chansons. There are 54), advertising (or boasting) the quantity and quality of the Thibaut anthology (though one more appears).[39] In this "collected works" of Thibaut, genres are mixed together without distinction, except by way of format, where songs such as the pious *lai Comencerai a fair un lai* required that staves were ruled for every strophe. A scan through the manuscript quickly reveals to the eye a change of genre with this dramatic change in the look of the page, where words and notes fill the space of writing in equal measure.

As with Thibaut, Adam's songs do not appear elsewhere in trouv. *T*, and the *libellus* that ends the *chansonnier* contains only his monophonic strophic *chansons d'amour*—none of his *jeux-partis*. This select group of songs points to a determined conservatism, as well as a clear sense of genre; Adam's *chansons d'amour* have been bracketed and isolated, seemingly by design, from his newer, more popular, and, importantly, more particularizing forms that traffic in names. And they have been isolated by design more literally: unlike the Thibaut *libellus*, which attempted to match the look of the central song collection, the Adam *libellus* contains notable discrepancies. While the single-column format is maintained—perhaps most important for a visual uniformity across all the different song collections—the large initials that begin each song are decorated with pen-flourishes (not *champie*), and the small colored capitals that mark the internal stanzas have no

37. For descriptions of the handwriting and contents of trouv. *T* (compared to trouv. *M*) see Schwan, *Die Altfranzösischen Liederhandschriften*, 19–38; Everist, *Polyphonic Music*, 175–81; Aubrey, "Sources, MS, §III: Secular Monophony," and Berger, *Littérature et société arrageoises*, 17–19. An inventory of the monophonic songs appears in Raynaud, *Bibliographie des chansonniers français*, 1:153–72.

38. *Champie* initials are usually gold leaf on a two-color rectilinear ground and further decorated with filigree. See Rouse and Rouse, *Manuscripts and their Makers*, 2:359.

39. This clear division of the *libellus* of Thibaut's songs from the collections of other authors contrasts with the design of trouv. *M*, which includes four songs by Thibaut within the original collection of authors. During one of many revisions of this *chansonnier*, the medieval compiler(s) grafted a collection of sixty songs, including duplicates of the original four. See Haines, "The Transformation of the *Manuscrit du Roi*," 26–28. The Thibaut *libellus* in trouv. *T* was certainly part of the anthology by the fifteenth century, and probably much earlier; the blank folios separating the first three sections have been filled by a verse written in a fifteenth-century script.

calligraphic decoration. These codicological details suggest that the Adam *libellus* was prepared ca. 1300, perhaps as an independent anthology.[40] But another such detail links Adam's songs to the other gatherings: the abbreviation for *nota* (No[a]) has been written in a consistent hand sporadically in the margins throughout the Thibaut *libellus*, the collection of songs in fols. 23–176, and most abundantly in the Adam collection; in all cases it appears to indicate lines where decorated capitals were called for (and perhaps overlooked in the illuminator's first pass through the folios). It is possible that the medieval revision of the manuscript that resulted in the addition of the Adam *libellus* also included corrections or touch-ups in other sections, or that the same project manager oversaw various stages of the manuscript's creation.[41]

We do not know with certainty when the two bookend author *libelli* were united with the central collection; nevertheless, the *compilatio* of trouv. *T* seems to be telling its own history through an implicit commentary on authorship and genre: at first the noble identity of the author advertised the song's value, and the distinction between *chansons*, *lais*, and *jeux-partis* was not paramount. Over time, however, and with the influx of non-noble authors, a diversity of genres became significant in the profile of the author—a demonstration of a new type of (literary) prowess. Given the strong presence of Artois and Arras in the contents of this manuscript, and the variety of genres it contains, the collection of Adam's songs suggests a conscious choice to concentrate on this single, traditional "noble" genre among the many that form Adam's oeuvre. This makes more sense if we read the collection of Adam's songs in relation to that of Thibaut.

The bookend collections represent not only specific authors, but also specific geographical places—Champagne and Artois—with their particular temporal positions in the chronology of the love song. These regions manifestly come together with the many *chansonniers* that have ties to Picardy and Artois, but which give primacy to Thibaut de Champagne's songs, referring to him only by his title "*li rois de navare*."[42] What might this codicological

40. See Everist, *Polyphonic Music*, 178–79. Everist argues that the existence of a similar *libellus* of Adam's monophonic songs, now bound with trouv. *W* but originally independent, strongly suggests that the *libellus* added to trouv. *T* was not prepared specifically for the *chansonnier*.

41. See Cappelli, *Dizionario di abbreviature*, 237. In most of the instances in sections I and II, one sign appears to mark only one line in the margin, and usually an internal stanza (except for fol. 175[v], where it marks a large initial with pen-flourishes), while in the Adam *libellus* the sign often appears more than once to mark multiple lines. Despite the same cue for decoration, the capitals in the Adam *libellus* are distinct from those in the other sections. The *No*[a] abbreviation does not appear in the margins of other *chansonniers*, though the word *Nota* marks the spot for a historiated initial in trouv. *M* (fol. 40/B47) that was never produced.

42. These include trouv. *K, M, N, P, R, T, V*, and *a* (we can add to this the alphabetical divisions of the Burgundian *O*). For a discussion of the disposition of Thibaut's songs in these manuscripts see Baumgartner, "Présentation des chansons de Thibaut de Champagne dans les manuscrits de Paris." Despite the title of this essay, Baumgartner does not argue for a Parisian provenance for these manuscripts. Among these nine *chansonniers*, Adam de la Halle's songs appear in the main collections of trouv. *R* (twenty-five songs but unattributed), *V* (seven songs; all songs in this manuscript are unattributed), and *a* (nearly twenty songs attributed to "Adan li Boçus"); his songs do not appear in the main collections of *K, M, N, P*, and *T* (though trouv. *P* contains a *libellus* of Adam's songs appended to the end).

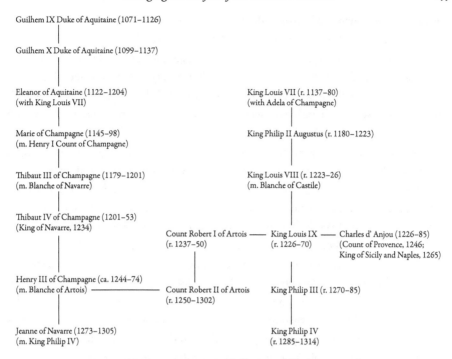

FIGURE 3.1 Marriage ties between the houses of Champagne and Artois

alliance between Champagne and Artois signify? The bulk of these *chansonniers* were compiled between 1270 and 1280, twenty or so years after Thibaut's death in 1253 (forty or more years after he inherited the title "king of Navarre" in 1234), and at a time when the principalities of Artois and Champagne were linked through the marriage (ca. 1269) of Thibaut's son Henry III, Count of Champagne (r. 1270–74) to Blanche of Artois, sister of Robert II, Count of Artois (r. 1250–1302), and niece of King Louis IX (see figure 3.1). With the death of Henry III, Blanche of Artois inherited the counties of Champagne, Brie, Troyes, and Meaux, as well as the kingdom of Navarre, all of which she ruled until 1284, when her daughter and sole heir, Jeanne of Navarre, married the future king Philip IV "the Fair" (r. 1285–1314), and Champagne thus lost its independence (as well as Navarre).[43]

Unlike Champagne, the region of Artois had long been part of the royal domain, having been annexed in 1191 from Flanders. Prior to this, however, there existed a division between the episcopal *city* of Arras, under the lordship of the French king, and the *town*, which had its own representative government but was under the lordship of the abbey of Saint-Vaast and geopolitically part of the independent county of Flanders.[44] In 1237, King Louis VIII established and bequeathed the county of Artois to his second son Robert

---

43. Arbois de Jubainville, *Histoire des ducs et des comtes de Champagne*, 429–56. Other feudal ties between the two regions include the trouvère Huon III d'Oisy (fl. 1189), who held two offices—castellan of Cambrai and viscount of Meaux. See Benton, 'The Court of Champagne as a Literary Center,' 577.

44. Symes, *A Common Stage*, 31.

(previously the province of Artois did not have the title of "county" but was called "La terre d'Atrébatie").[45] The county then passed to Robert II in 1250 (d. 1302), patron of Adam de la Halle, who frequently left to fight for the King against the barons of Guyenne and Flanders, as well as for his uncle Charles d'Anjou in Italy. Although Robert II granted a new charter to the town of Arras in 1269 and expanded the power of elected officials (*échevins*), he reserved the right to select the mayor, which began a "cold war" between the commune of the town and their lord.[46]

Artois and Champagne were both centers of high literary patronage and production. Champagne boasted a lineage to the troubadour Guilhem IX through his great granddaughter Marie de Champagne (1145–98), daughter of Eleanor of Aquitaine and King Louis VII, and grandmother of Thibaut de Champagne. Many poetic and scholastic luminaries of the late twelfth century addressed their literary works to Marie or her husband Henry I ("the Liberal"), including vernacular romance writers Chrétien de Troyes and Gautier d'Arras, the trouvère Gace Brulé, and the churchmen Andreas Capellanus, Pierre de Celle, Guido de Bazoches, and John of Salisbury.[47] Arras's literary scene began with the establishment of the confraternity of jongleurs (Carité de Notre Dame des Ardents) chartered by the cathedral ca. 1175. Despite royal annexation in 1191, tensions and rivalries remained between the ecclesiastical city and the mercantile town and became thematic in the Artesian plays, such as the earliest *Jeu de saint Nicolas* by Jehan Bodel (d. 1210) and the foundational miracle story of the Carité, which implicitly criticizes the abbey's spiritual care of the town. By the middle of the thirteenth century, as Carol Symes notes, "the competing claims of clerical factions were reconciled through the agency of the jongleurs who claimed the bishop of Arras as their patron and gradually made alliances with the monks of Saint-Vaast and the mendicants."[48] Artesian literature increased dramatically in second half of the thirteenth century, created by the abundance of educated clerics from the cathedral school of the city and the monastery school of the town, and by some members of the patrician class. At one time Arras boasted some 200 trouvères (professional and amateur) in a population of 20,000, and perhaps a second patrician literary academy or *puy* (documented only in a few song lyrics).[49]

---

45. Lecesne, *Histoire d'Arras*, 1:125–26.

46. Gruy, *Histoire d'Arras*, 83, 86.

47. See Benton, "The Court of Champagne as Literary Center," 551–91; McCash, "Marie de Champagne and Eleanor of Aquitaine."

48. Symes, *A Common Stage*, 92; see 80–87 for a discussion of the politics of the Carité's founding miracle. See also Berger, *Littérature et société arrageoises*, 25–115 for a detailed study of Arras society in the thirteenth century.

49. Gruy, *Histoire d'Arras*, 72. For details about the history of the confraternity, see Symes, *A Common Stage*, 84–85, 98–120. Symes rejects the idea that there was a separate patrician literary academy or *puy*, citing the lack of documentary evidence (216–17); see also 41–49 for a discussion of the relationship between the city and the town of Arras. For arguments regarding the existence of the *puy* see Ungureanu, *La Bourgeoisie naissante*, and Richardson, "The *Confrérie des jongleurs*."

The proliferation of trouvères within the burgher class contrasts with the seemingly rarified song production of trouvères within the upper nobility. Among counts and dukes, viscounts (*châtelains*) and vidames (viscounts to the Bishop), only Thibaut de Champagne produced a substantial oeuvre comparable to the two most prolific trouvères, Gace Brulé and Adam de la Halle. The *chansonniers* always identify Thibaut as the *li rois de Navare* rather than the *conte* or *cuens de Champagne*, though some of his partners in the *jeux-partis* address him as *cuens*. It is presumed, then, that these *jeux-partis* were composed prior to 1234, the date Thibaut inherited the kingdom of Navarre after the death of his uncle King Sancho VII.[50] Nevertheless, Thibaut appears as the only consistently titled "king" in the *chansonniers*,[51] though the trouvère Charles d'Anjou (brother to the king of France, "Saint" Louis IX, and Robert I, Count of Artois) could have been identified as a king as well, for in addition to being the Count of Anjou and Maine in the north (by royal apanage in 1246), and Provence and Forcalquier in the south (by marriage in 1246), he achieved the status of King of Sicily and Naples by papal investiture in 1265 and by conquest in 1266, and also became King of Jerusalem by purchase after 1277 (he was expelled from Sicily in 1282, but retained the kingdom of Naples). In the main corpus of trouv. *M*, Charles d'Anjou is referred to as *li cuens d'Angou* (the count of Anjou) by the rubricators; neither his title nor the heraldry shown on the shield of the illumination reflects his status as a king. This evidence suggests the *chansonnier* was planned and mostly put together before 1265. Yet the title *li cuens d'Anjou* appears in three *chansonniers* from Artois, trouv. *PNX*, all dated between 1270 and 1280—after Charles gained his royal title. (They include a single song, *Trop est destroiz qui est desconforté*, RS 423). Despite Charles's partial success at building a grand Mediterranean kingdom, and his patronage of many trouvères and some troubadours, in the *chansonniers* his title remains "count." Some scholars believe this reflects not the time of compilation of a given manuscript, but the time of the songs' composition.[52] Yet freezing Charles's title as if it were his pen name would be a pointedly nostalgic gesture, and at odds with the flattery of nobility that is part of the design of these manuscripts—

---

50. Långfors, *Recueil général des jeux-partis français*, 1:xix–xxiii.

51. Trouv. *C* attributes *Ja nus hons pris ne dirois sa raison* (RS 1891) to *Li rois Richar* (King Richard I "the Lionhearted" of England); the song appears anonymously in trouv. *K*, *N*, *O*, *U*, and *X*. In trouv. *M*, the medieval table of contents lists "Roi Jehans" whereas the rubric in the manuscript records "Jehans de Braine." Jehan de Brienne (also Jehan de Constantinople) was the Latin emperor of Constantinople from 1231 to 1237. Jongleurs or clerical trouvères were occasionally given the title "king" or depicted with a crown to signify their status as "king of the minstrels." See the discussion of Adenet le Roi, who worked in the court of Flanders and in the royal court in the last quarter of the thirteenth century, in Rouse and Rouse, *Manuscripts and their Makers*, 100–103, and the depiction of Pierrekin de la Coupele in trouv. *M*, fol. 163/B148 (discussed below).

52. See Dyggve, "Personages historiques." See Everist, *Polyphonic Music*, 184–85 (Everist must be discussing Charles I, though he identifies the Count as Robert); see also Prinet, "L'Illustration héraldique du chansonnier du Roi."

unless the intended noble audience held little stake in the fortunes of Charles d'Anjou.[53] This may have been the case for the intended audience of trouv. *PNX*, and perhaps also trouv. *T* and the other *chansonniers* that do not include songs by Charles; but it is not the case, in fact, for trouv. *M*, as will be discussed below. Thibaut and Charles ascended to royalty by dramatically different means: as the dynastic heir to Navarre, Thibaut came by the title "king" honestly, so to speak, legitimated by the belief in the natural order (and divinely ordained) lineage rights; Charles, on the other hand, fought or bought his way to kingship. The usurpation of a kingdom often required another means of legitimization, frequently the manufacture of hereditary rights or, by the mid thirteenth century, crowning by the Pope.[54] Charles used both of these strategies; moreover, Adam de la Halle's unfinished *chanson de geste*, the *Chanson du roi de Sezile* (ca. 1285), reads as a propagandistic panegyric to Charles, extolling his virtues as "*le seignor des seignours*," shortly after losing one of his kingdoms to a popular uprising.[55]

As count of Champagne, Thibaut may have been particularly emblematic of the nobility's conflicts with the crown in the thirteenth century (and in a way that Charles d'Anjou, brother to the king, could not be). Legendary for his lackluster commitment to King

---

53. Charles was overbearing, ambitious, and ruthless, often battling with those subject to his rule, especially in Provence and Sicily. See the remarks by Cadier, *Essai sur l'administration du royaume de Sicile*, 1–5. A number of troubadours wrote *sirventes* critical of his governance and campaigns. See Dunbabin, *Charles I of Anjou*, 205–206. In his extension of the *Roman de la rose* (ca. 1268–85), Jean de Meun provides a laudatory yet vivid account (with chess metaphors) of "king" Charles's takeover of Sicily, the execution of his adversaries, and the suppression of an uprising in Marseilles (lines 6631–741). Jean also mentions that it was customary to call Charles *conte* (count), which he rhymes with *conte* (to recount), and thus poetic license may be at work, although this custom is reflected in the *chansonniers* (lines 6723–4).

   Charles had a warm relationship with Robert II, Count of Artois, and was an ally of Margaret II, Countess of Flanders (his aunt) during the struggle for succession between her two sons throughout the 1250s (and he briefly held the county of Hainaut). John Haines has convincingly argued that the interpolated narrative *Renart le nouvel*, composed in Lille between 1288 and 1292 and circulated also in the Picardy-Artois region, is a satirical animal allegory of French and Flemish conflicts in the regions of Artois and Flanders, and that Charles d'Anjou is portrayed as a lecherous leopard. See Haines, *Satire in the Songs of* Renart le nouvel, esp. 111–49 and 175–77. In the *Roman du comte d'Anjou*, by the royal administrator Jean Maillart (ca. 1316), Charles is portrayed as militarily impotent (losing at chess in a reversal of the *Roman de la Rose* description) and sexually depraved with incestuous desires for his daughter. See Black, "The Politics of Romance."

54. Jacques Le Goff notes that even the Capetians had to legitimate their claim to kingship by claiming a lineage to Charlemagne, and that Charles d'Anjou did have the Pope crown him King of Sicily in 1266 (given his eventual expulsion, this coronation may not have been effective); see "Le Roi dans l'Occident médiéval," esp. 8–11.

55. See the account of Adam de la Halle as propagandist in Symes, *A Common Stage*, 261–65; and Maillard, *Roi-trouvère*, 30. Charles d'Anjou is always referred to as a count in song lyrics by other trouvères: he serves as a judge in four *jeux-partis* (RS 491, 940, 664, 1514) and is named as a count in all of them. He also appears as the respondent in a *jeu-parti* with Perrin d'Angicourt (*Quens d'Anjou, prenés*, RS 938), an in the *envoi* to another of Perrin's songs (*Quant partis sui de Provence*, RS 625), and as an authority on song in *E, cuens d'Anjou, on dit par felonie* (RS 1154), attributed to Raoul de Soissons in trouv. *C* (the first strophe of this song appears in trouv. *O* with the opening line *Aucune gent ont dit par felonie*). Besides Adam de la Halle's *chanson de geste*, only Rutebeuf refers to Charles d'Anjou as "*roi de Sezile*" in his *Dit de Pouille* (1265). See Maillard, *Roi-trouvère*, 11–36.

Louis VIII (r. 1223–26), his rumored love affair with Queen Blanche of Castile, and clashes with her son King Louis IX (r. 1226–70),[56] Thibaut and his songs represent a final heroic assertion of independent noble identity and culture before its obsolescence. Indeed, Marie-Noëlle Toury argues that Thibaut "affirms his independence" from literary tradition as well, with images that run directly contrary to received motifs, themes, and symbols inherited from the troubadours and earlier trouvères.[57] His lyrics often take a combative tone; they are filled with irresolvable antitheses and negations that portray the song as an outburst from the strain of warring forces. One song begins with this stanza:

Chanter m'estuet, car ne m'en puis tenir,	I must sing, for I cannot keep from it,
et si n'ai je fors ennui et pesance;	and yet I have nothing but vexation and grief;
mès tout adès se fet bon resjoïr	but it is always good to rejoice
qu'en fere duel nus del mont ne s'avance.	for no one gets ahead by mourning.
Je ne chant pas com hons qui soit amez,	I sing not like a man who is loved,
mès com destroiz, pensis, et esgarez;	but like one who is distressed, pensive, and abandoned;
que je n'ai mès de bien nule esperance,	since I no longer have hope of anything good,
ainz sui toz jorz par parole menez.	I am always led along by words.

Full of contradictions and about-face turns, agency is held open to question; the words themselves lead the hopeless Thibaut to his destiny, as if to corroborate Zumthor's observation that "the poet is situated in his language, not the other way around."[58] In the fifth stanza we see (or rather, hear) again how words burst forth without reason to rescue the *amour* from the *dolour* that threatens to silence the song itself:

Resons me dit que g'en ost ma pensee,	Reason tells me to take my thought away,
mès j'ai un cuer, ainz tex ne fu trouvez;	but I have a heart like no other;
touz jorz me dit: "Amez, amez, amez!"	Constantly it tells me: "Love, love, love!"[59]

---

56. Thibaut had to enlist the aid of the crown to defend his territories against invasion by his rival barons from 1229 to 1234. See Brahney, Introduction to *Thibaut*, xiii–xvii; Thibaut de Champagne, *Les Chansons*, ed. Wallensköld, xii–xxvii; and Sidney Painter, "The Historical Setting of *Robert veez de Perron*." For comprehensive historical accounts of Thibaut de Champagne, see Arbois de Jubainville, *Histoire des ducs et des comtes de Champagne*.

57. Toury, "Les Chansons de Thibaut de Champagne," 45–55 (quotation).

58. Zumthor, *Towards a Medieval Poetics*, 44.

59. RS 1476. Text and translation (modified) from *Thibaut*, 84–87, lines 1–8 and 36–38. This song appears on fol. 9 of trouv. *T* without notation. The conflict presented in stanza V recalls the head-versus-heart split of Folquet de Marselha's *En chantan m'aven a membrar* quoted in the introduction.

The repeated imperative "Amez, amez, amez!" seems a concentrated presentation of the entire song, if not also the genre of the *chanson d'amour*, in which every stanza can be reduced to the imperative "Amez!"[60] The personified figure of Love, often merging with the lady, appears in Thibaut's lyrics as an overlord from whom Thibaut seeks recompense for his service. While such feudal metaphors are common in both troubadour and trouvère lyrics, Thibaut's compositions offer sharp-edged, oxymoronic accusations ("Love hates me") that turn Love into an antagonist. Indeed, Thibaut debates Love directly in *L'autre nuit en mon dormant*—a dream-poem in which Love chides Thibaut for his inconsistency and Thibaut accuses Love of falseness.[61]

As a king, Thibaut represents the highest social and ethical achievement for the lyric aspirant: the noble subject who is subject only to Love's command. Thibaut, as *rois de Navare*, was without a doubt an icon of the inherent nobility of trouvères and their connoisseurs. This is made more evident by the annex of his songs to trouv. *T* and *M* (this *libellus* is identified separately as trouv. *Mt*). Thus it seems that by the 1270s, Thibaut came to symbolize, in a belated way, both resistance and traditionalism, and his prominence in the *chansonniers* promoted the emblematic nature of the anthologies themselves. They express an ideology—namely that the practice of love, self, and song that so ennobles the lyric "I" derives from the actual nobility of star practitioners. In trouv. *T*, the named and anonymous authors who follow Thibaut are majestically led to song like an army to battle; Thibaut's songs in trouv. *T* receive the only historiated initial in the collection, depicting a knight on horseback.

Adam's songs, introduced by an abstractly ornamented initial, bring up the rearguard to Thibaut's forward charge. If Thibaut bestows heroism and sovereignty on the lyric subject, Adam bestows craftsmanship, learnedness, and even pedantry, which heralds the end of the love song as an artifact of noble *amateurs* and advertises the new voice of the professional cleric. Yet while Thibaut was honored with the title *roi* in the *chansonniers*, Adam was frequently referred to as *li bossu*, meaning "crippled" or "awkward"—an epithet contrary to Thibaut's, one denoting an unrefined subject, either himself disfigured, or one who disfigures language.[62] Modern editors confess a lack of originality in Adam's strophic love songs, but their distinction from those of Thibaut is striking. The combative tone, antagonism toward Love, and quick-witted reversals are replaced by humility, a deference to Love, melancholic or joyous resignation to suffering, and, above all, a self-consciousness about tradition, social rank, and the source of his poetic voice.[63] In the third stanza of *Il ne vient pas de sens chelui ki plaint* ("There is no sense in a man's

---

60. I thank Monica Roundy for this interpretation.

61. The phrase "qu'Amors me het" quoted from *Chanter m'estuet, car ne m'en puis tenir* (line 18); for text and translation of *L'autre nuit en mon dormant* (RS 339) see *Thibaut*, 202–205. See also Ménard, "Le Dieu d'Amour."

62. See Nelson, introduction to *Adam*, xv. Trouv. *T* calls Adam *li boçu*.

63. See Huot, "Transformations of Lyric Voice," esp. 149–53 on his monophonic songs.

bewailing") Adam positions himself within a "custom" (*l'usage*) dictated and protected by Love:

Voirs est ch'Amours toute valour ataint	It is true that Love attains complete worth
et par li sont furni tout vaselage;	and that through it all qualities of a vassal are furnished;
les siens garnist, toute crualté vaint;	it provides for its own, vanquishing all cruelty;
dont sacent tout k[e] j'ere en son siervage.	thus may all know that I labor in its service.
De bien amer voeil maintenir l'usage;	I want to maintain the custom of loving well;
plus doucement ne quier mon tans user,	I do not seek to spend my time more sweetly,
car jou vailg mix del saverous pensser	for I am worth more for the delicious thought
et du joli espoir ki m'asouhaige.	and for the pleasant hope that comforts me.[64]

Though Adam constructs himself as a humble custodian of Love, the customs or traditions that he hopes to maintain sometimes appear only as hints; common topoi such as the springtime exordium are implied in keywords (*renouveler*), and even the lady becomes a secondary character to the overbearing figure of Love. In *Jou senc en moy l'amor renouveler*, Adam insists on the renewal of his own love and song, yet Love takes over in the end:

Jou senc en moy l'amor renouveler,	I feel in myself a rebirth of love,
ki autre fois m'a fait le doc mal traire	which formerly made me bear the sweet suffering
dont je soloie en desirant chanter,	about which I used to sing from desire,
par koy mes chans renouviele et repaire.	and because of which my song returns and renews.
C'est bons maus ki cuer esclaire,	It is a good suffering that lightens the heart,
mais Amors m'a le ju trop mal parti,	but Love has set the odds too heavily against me,
car j'espoir et pens par li	for I hope and think, because of Love,
trop haut; s'est drois k'il me paire.	too highly; it is just that he [Love] places me on the same level.[65]

---

64. RS 152. Text and translation (modified) from *Adam*, 14 and 15, respectively.

65. RS 888. Text and translation (modified) from *Adam*, 30 and 31, respectively.

Here, rebirth and renewal pair with nostalgia for the past, the *autre fois* of singing *en desirant*. We can also read another hint at changes wrought by time—the shift from the twin activities of loving and singing found in the tradition of earlier troubadours and trouvères, to the commands of allegorical Love in the later tradition of clerical authors.

If we can distinguish between a noble and a clerical lyric subject in the words of love songs, then can we do the same with their melodies? Hans-Herbert Räkel argues that among the collectors and amateurs of poetry at the end of the thirteenth century, Thibaut figured as "a king of song" and that he exerted a regal prowess over melody, "neutralizing" with a carefully controlled repetition of key melodic motifs and phrases a rising tide of refrain forms coming from the burgher class.[66] Yet Thibaut did compose at least five *chansons d'amour* with refrains, while Adam seemingly avoided them (composing only one *chanson* with a refrain), which indicates that while refrains need not implicate the social class of the author, they do color the voice of the song with a tint of the popular. Table 3.3 summarizes the melodic designs of Adam's *chansons d'amour* from the *libellus* attached to trouv. *P*, and those of Thibaut from the *libellus* that forms trouv. *Mt*.[67]

TABLE 3.3

Melodic designs in the *chansons d'amour* of Adam de la Halle and Thibaut de Champagne		
Melodic Form	Adam (31)	Thibaut (33)
oda continua		
ABCD EFGH…	1	4
pedes-cauda		
ABAB CDEF…(or ABA′B etc)	19	14
CDEF/GH[I] = changing refrains		1
CD/E = refrain		1
CDE/FG = refrain		1
non-standard pedes		
ABCA′ DEFGH	1	
ABAC DEF…	3	3
ABAC DEF/GH = refrain	1	

66. Räkel writes: "A un moment où la tendance artistique va s'acheminer vers des formes poétiques fixes, des montages de refrains, des rythmes de danse autonomes, le roi Thibaut neutralise les répétitions de ses mélodies structurées et dans les formes sans schéma déclaré, il cache des allusions répétitives pour dérouter l'auditeur" ("Le Chant du roi, le roi du chant," 64).

67. In *Mt* a few of Thibaut's songs were partially completed by the original scribe and either left blank (see the songs on fols. 68, 72ᵛ–73, 74; B XI, XVᵛ–XVI) or completed later by another hands (fol. 72ᵛ/BXVᵛ). I have not counted these in my tabulations.

Melodic Form	Adam (31)	Thibaut (33)
repetition in cauda		
ABAB A´CDE		1
B´CDEF		1
CDEA		1
CDEB		1
CDEE´CDE´		1
CDEA´FG		1
CDEC		1
CDECFG	1	
non-standard melodic designs		
ABCB DBEDF	1	
ABB´CD ABB´CD	1	
AAAB CDE/F = refrain		1
AA´AA´ BCD/EF = refrain		1
AA´AA´ BCDA´	2	
AA´AA´ CDEFGHI	1	

The table corroborates Räkel's observations: more than half of Thibaut's songs use non-standard designs, including *oda continua* as well as diverse patterns of repetition within the *cauda* (see the melodic rounding in *Les douces dolors* in example 1.5 above). By contrast, two-thirds of Adam's songs have a *pedes-cauda* design, and these by and large show no structural repetition within the *cauda*.[68] Furthermore, as Räkel observed, quite a few of Thibaut's songs contain phrases linked by their opening melodic gestures or recurring melodic cells. Often two phrases begin in the same manner but diverge at their midpoints.[69] In *Chanter m'estuet, car ne m'en puis tenir*, for example, every phrase in the *pedes* begins with the same stepwise ascent from G to C or D in a forthright syllabic line, and two phrases in the *cauda* also begin in this manner (see example 3.1 ⊘ OXFORD WEB MUSIC). The musical effect is chant-like, resembling the repetitive phrases of a Litany, answered

---

68. O'Neill supplies a chart of the metrical structure and large-scale melodic repetition of Adam's *chansons* in *Courtly Love Songs*, 187–90.

69. Thus *Li rosignox chante tant* could be describes as an *oda continua* (ABCDEFG), yet phrases C, E, and F all open with the same four notes. Similarly, *Dame, li vostre fins amis* (RS 1516) could be a modified *pedes-cauda* (ABA´C DEF), though the F phrase is clearly related to the A´ phrase, suggesting melodic rounding; see also

EXAMPLE 3.1 Thibaut de Champagne, *Chanter m'estuet, que ne m'en puis tenir*, stanza I from trouv. *M*, fol. 65/BVIII

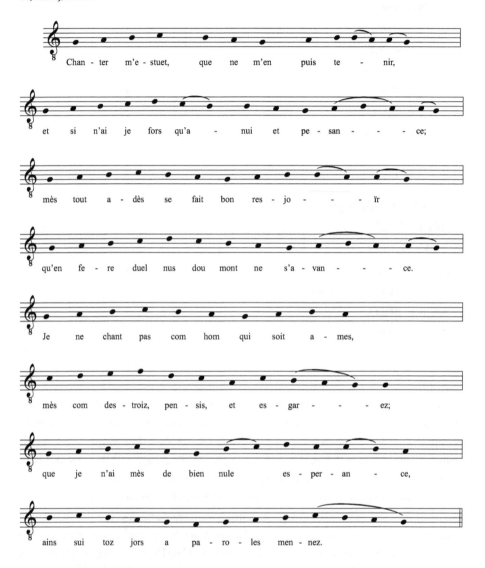

in the second half of the phrases by modest expressive gestures and penultimate melismas. The placement of the last melisma on the final rather than penultimate syllable seems particularly expressive, especially for the first stanza, leading ("menez") the singer by notes as Thibaut is led by words.

Qui plus aime plus endure (RS 2095; ABAB B′CDEF or ABAB B′CDD′E); *Chanter m'estuet, car ne m'en puis tenir* (ABAB A′CDE or ABAB A′CA′′D). The famous song *Ausi conme unicorne sui* (RS 2075), though an *oda continua*, connects phrases through a dense network of three-note melodic cells derived from the opening line. I thank Katherine Walker for her melodic analysis of the song.

This linkage of phrases via opening melodic gestures may have been a salient feature of Thibaut's style. Two melodies preserved in trouv. *T* show more linked phrases than their concordances in trouv. *Mt*.[70] If such melodic links are what the medieval audience came to expect in a Thibaut song, then scribal intervention in trouv. *T* may have worked toward further particularizing Thibaut's melodies.

The clerkish modesty of Adam's lyrics is matched, some believe, by the less innovative quality of his melodies. Hendrik van der Werf, having edited all versions of his mono-phonic *chansons*, notes their clear formal structures (only one of his melodies can be iden-tified as an *oda continua*, the vast majority being in *pedes-cauda* form; see table 3.3 above) and average level of ornateness (as opposed to Gautier de Dargies, whose songs stand out as particularly melismatic). But van der Werf also writes "[a]lthough the melodic style of Adam's *chansons* is not unusual among trouvère melodies in general, one can justify the conclusion that Adam de la Halle was one of several trouvères to have had his own melodic style."[71]

While the majority (25/37) of Thibaut's *chansons d'amour* stanzas are isometric (if one includes in this count lyrics that mix oxytonic and paroxytonic rhymes),[72] nearly all of Adam's lyrics are heterometric, that is the stanzas contain lines of differing lengths beyond the "extra" syllable in paroxytonic (feminine) rhyme words.[73] As a result, Adam's songs have less predictable phrasing, especially in their *caudae*. The melody for *Jou senc en moy l'amor renouveler* is a case in point (see example 3.2 from trouv. *P* 🔊 OXFORD WEB MUSIC): the flow

---

70. The melodies preserved for *Je ne voi mès nului qui gieut ne chant* (RS 315) and *De bone amor vient seance et biauté* (RS 407) in trouv. *Mt* are typical *pedes-cauda* structures (ABAB CDEF) while the versions preserved in trouv. *T* show linked phrases (ABAB CDEE′ and ABAB CDED′ respectively). There are some other quirks to these two melodies in trouv. *T*: the second *pes* in both songs was copied a step below where it should be. Of the six sources (*K, Mt, O, T, V, a*) that transmit roughly the same melody for *Je ne voi mès nului qui gieut ne chant*, only trouv. *a* corroborates the melodic repetitions found in *T*; of the ten sources that transmit the melody for *De bone amor vient seance et biauté* (*B, K, M, Mt, O, R, T, V, Z, a*), only the melody in trouv. *M* matches that of trouv. *T*).

71. Van der Werf, Musical Introduction to *Adam*, xxx. He also comments: "in his chansons, Adam does not seem to have been an innovator." For the synoptic transcription of his melodies, see van der Werf, *Trouvères-Melodien*, 558–61. For other studies of Adam de la Halle's song style see Barth-Wehrenhalp, *Studien zu Adan de le Hale*, esp. 70–83, and Maillard, *Adam de La Halle*. Maillard (27) tabulated the melodic designs of Adam's *chansons d'amours* though he does not specify the source or sources that he used for his melodic schemes. See also O'Neill, *Courtly Love Songs*, 186, and 191–96; O'Neill notes the "higher instances of an overall chanson (AAB) form in Adam de la Halle's chansons than, for instance, in Dargies's chansons" (186).

72. Twenty-four out of the thirty-six *chansons d'amour* listed in *Thibaut* are isometric; Brahney does not include *Dame, li vostre fins amis* in her collection. A few that are heterometric, such as *Les douces dolors*, contain *caudae* phrases that are more long-winded than those of the *pedes*, thus facilitating melodic linkage.

73. See table III in Maillard, *Adam de la Halle*, 30–31; and table 2.6 in O'Neill, *Courtly Love Songs*, 185. O'Neill also observes that "Adam shows a decided preference for heterometric structures: only five of his songs are isometric," for which she call Adam "adventurous" (she also notes Dargies's preference for heterometric struc-tures). Adam's songs are also *unissonans* in their rhyme scheme, while Thibaut's songs most often show a *coblas doublas* rhyme scheme.

EXAMPLE 3.2 Adam de la Halle, *Jou senc en moy l'amor renouveler*, stanza I from trouv. *P*, fol. 214

of repeated longer lines in the *pedes* comes to a sudden end with the first line of the *cauda*, where the dramatically shorter phrase is further emphasized by a syllabic setting and fresh cadential pitch. In performance the flexible rhythmic pacing may suggest spontaneous expression. Indeed, the melody of *Jou senc en moy l'amor renouveler* has a general restlessness about it; the chains of plicated notes and two- or three-note ligatures that constantly change direction keep the ear floating unmoored in the pitch space. This decorative style is common among Adam's melodies, and those in trouv. *P* use more plicated notes than do other sources, as if to amplify the particularities of his style. The double-plicated gesture even becomes its own melodic motif, linking all but two of the phrases.[74] Recall that in Thibaut's *Chanter m'estuet, car ne m'en puis tenir* the repeated opening gesture also linked all but two of the phrases in the stanza. Though the contrast between Adam's ornate, meandering melody and Thibaut's syllabic, direct melody is striking on the surface, both display the basic compositional techniques of thrift and varied repetition across phrases and formal schemes.[75]

Preferences for certain finals also differentiates the songs of these two trouvères, as table 3.4 indicates. Although more of Adam's songs create tonal continuity between the *pedes* and the *cauda* sections by using the same cadence pitch, the melismas and ornamentation and the often long, melodically inventive *cauda* sections undercut the force of the final as a tonal center (*Jou senc en moy l'amor renouveler* is a case in point). And by the same token, the predominantly syllabic settings of Thibaut's songs often clarify local and long-range pitch centers.[76]

What distinguishes one trouvère's melodic style from another is an important but fraught question given the minimal information that survives in the sources—strophic, monophonic, diatonic songs lacking clear indications of rhythm and no indications for instrumental accompaniment. Tendencies toward either ornamented or syllabic settings combine with melodic and metrical designs to give us some means of describing an individual musical

TABLE 3.4

Finals for the *chansons d'amour* of Thibaut de Champagne and Adam de la Halle

Thibaut de Champagne in *Mt* (33)	Adam de la Halle in *P* (31)
G = 10	F = 11
D = 9	C = 10
C = 6	G = 6
F = 4	D = 3
A = 4	A = 1
second *pes* cadence on the final = 17	second *pes* cadence on the final = 21

---

74. This melody is not preserved in trouv. *T*, although those that are preserved in trouv. *T* are in lockstep with those in trouv. *P*; the only difference in "house style" seems to be that the melodies in trouv. *T* are slightly less ornamented, showing single plicated notes where trouv. *P* often has double plicated notes. This could be less an issue of melody and performance than a question of how to notate the ornament itself.

75. One exception among Thibaut's songs seems to "prove the rule" about his more straightforward style: *Tout autresi con fraint nois et yvers* (RS 906) stands out for being exceedingly melismatic right from the first word. See van der Werf, *Trouvères-Melodien*, 133–36.

76. See Maillard, *Adam de la Halle*, 26–33 for general remarks about Adam's melodies, and 33–64 for treatment of specific songs. For a discussion of the modal properties of troubadour and trouvère songs see Parker, "Troubadour and Trouvère Songs," 20–37.

style.[77] But these are relatively generic variables within the limited parameters of trouvère song. While serving to differentiate two trouvères when their songs are placed side by side, such variables quickly lose their particularizing aspect among the hundreds of preserved melodies. Thus an "individual" style does not mean an "original" style.

In addition, we must also consider a given scribe's notational habits or musical sensibilities. Preferences or "house styles" are manifest in melodies from certain *chansonniers*; for example, the notator of troub. *R* regularized melodic repetitions, using literal, note-for-note repeats where other sources show slight variations.[78] Similarly, the notator of trouv. *O* wrote an unusual amount of accidentals as well as rudimentary mensural notation for melodies that are otherwise not divergent from other sources.[79] Trouv. *V* contains lyrics whose readings are close to the *KNPX* group, but whose melodies are unrelated (except those by Thibaut de Champagne) though they show their own stylistic unity. The same is true for trouv. *R*, which contains many melodies that are unrelated to those found in the *KNPX* and *AMTa* groups.[80] Mary O'Neill argues that the melodies in the later trouvère *chansonniers*, especially trouv. *R* and *V*, reveal a decided change in musical taste. Many of the variant melodies are syllabic and more "tonally oriented"—a simpler and more direct style that O'Neill believes stems from the rising influence of popular songs.[81]

Thibaut's and Adam's songs are among the most stable in the trouvère repertory and thus scribal intervention seems to have been minimal, even in trouv. *R*. Yet just as scribes could distinguish one author from another in their creative *compilatio*, as in trouv. *T*, scribes could also confuse and obscure authorial identity despite the stability of melodies, paying no heed to melodic or poetic style. In trouv. *R*, the voices of Thibaut and Adam collide and jumble at the end of the collection, where they dominate the last fascicle of forty-one anonymous songs. Although anonymous, nearly all the songs have attested attributions elsewhere, and they are recorded in an orderly fashion: first comes a block of five songs (four by Perrin d'Angicourt), then close by follow two large clusters of thirteen songs by Adam and Thibaut, respectively, separated by two songs of other composers. (Two songs embedded within the Thibaut sequence are in fact by Adam de la Halle.)[82] It

---

77. Mary O'Neill reports repetition patterns in the songs of Gautier Dargies that are comparable to those in the songs of Thibaut, but Gautier's melodies are far more melismatic than Thibaut's. See *Courtly Love Songs*, 101–105.

78. See the remarks of Treitler, "Troubadours Singing their Poems," 25, who calls the scribe "pendantic" and suggests such regularization is "the consequence of a more literate mentality"; Switten, "Music and Versification," 151, suggests this "normalization" "obscures what we must imagine as the medieval reality." See also Aubrey, *The Music of the Troubadours*, 48.

79. Trouv. *O* records nearly the same melody for Thibaut's *Les douces dolors* (example 1.5) as does trouv. *Mt*, but trouv. *O* flats many of the Bs, thus changing the Lydian tritone of the *pedes* to a Mixolydian perfect fourth.

80. See Karp, "The Trouvère Tradition"; Karp notes the stylistic unity of songs in *V*: they are syllabic, have smaller ranges, fewer skips, less repetition, less clearly established tonal centers (27–28).

81. O'Neill, *Courtly Love Songs*, 154–59.

82. For a scholarly study of this manuscript see Schubert, *Die Handschrift Paris, Bibl. Nat. Fr. 1591*, 149–77 for a discussion of the final fifth fascicle.

seems ironic that these two iconic authors are most represented among the anonymous songs in *R*, and that the scribes and compilers leveled the playing field between the *roi* and the *boçus*, eradicating their names and social distinctions. Yet the clusters of songs suggest that the scribes worked from discrete collections, though apparently the names of these particular authors were not attached to those exemplars. Here, initially at least, two of the biggest names in trouvère song are lost, and the autonomy of their subjective voices enveloped by the corporate, anonymous "I." A later medieval hand did add rubrics identifying several of Thibaut's songs, and a final statement at the end of the manuscript (perhaps by the same or a later hand) proclaims: "Explicit les chançons au roy de navarre et as autres princes" (Here end the songs by the king of Navarre and by other princes). Curiously, although the manuscript stems from the region of Arras in the early years of the fourteenth century and contains a large number of Adam's songs (twenty-four in total), Thibaut's name is recuperated, while Adam's songs remain among the anonymous.[83]

The *compilatio* of trouv. *R* seems an undoing of the *compilatio* in trouv. *T*, where the bookend *libelli* of Thibaut and Adam added to a central collection of songs, motets, and *dits* reveal the efforts of compilers and scribes over time to build an anthology of songs with chapters that offer the expressive gamut of lyric authorship. We might also read a quasi-narrative arc from the ennobling aristocratic past of Thibaut to the ennobled clerical present of Adam. In trouv. *T*, Adam becomes Thibaut's rightful heir to the noble lyric voice, and Arras becomes the new Champagne, the new center for literary production, the one bound to the other through feudal and codicological ties. The collection in trouv. *T* shows Adam at his most generic, most conservative, for only with the *chanson d'amour* can the late, great son of Arras prove his mettle against Thibaut de Champagne.

Yet between the main song collection and Adam's *libellus* there intervene the motets and *dits*, which disperse the aristocratic lyric voice with a specifically "Arrageoise" spin.[84] Joseph A. Dane understands the *dits*, many of which poke fun at the "bourgeois dilettante of Arras," as a jovial ribbing among these nouveau-riche trouvères. Dane argues that the *dits* should not be read as *ad hominem* attacks on the named social figures, but rather as attacks on literary forms—sermons, epics, and lyrics—through parody. Parody has a subversive force; Dane writes, "once language and literature itself are exposed as purely conventional entities, their relation to society is no longer meaningful. When parody attacks a set of conventions, it challenges the validity of those conventions, by demonstrating that the message they bear can be trivial or nonsensical."[85] The parodies in the *dits* feature the oxymoronic figure of the "noble merchant," and thus they "attack the very

---

83. Seven of Adam's songs are clustered in fascicle 3 (fols. 100–105), and two more appear in succession in fascicle 4 (152–153). Schubert notes that the appearance of authors and songs associated with Arras, as well as details of spelling that reflect the Picard dialect, provide indirect evidence that the manuscript stemmed from that general region. See Schubert, *Die Handschrift Paris, Bibl. Nat. Fr. 1591*, 29–32.

84. See Dane, "Parody and Satire," parts I and II. See Berger, *Littérature et société arrageoises*, 119–58 for a critical edition and discussion of all twenty-four *dits*.

85. Dane, "Parody and Satire" Part I, 12.

language by which the rich Arras merchant defined himself as a member of the new thirteenth-century aristocracy—the language of the courtly lyric." In this way, according to Dane, the literate classes addressed their "uneasiness with the new social structure" by destabilizing the language of the traditional nobility, which in turn called into question the traditional class divisions themselves.[86] Read in light of the *dits*, the songs of Adam de la Halle take on the hue of parody: they represent a complete transformation of the ennobling love song into a trivial literary exercise, divested of an expression of class, let alone an expression of self. Here, then, is the last chapter in the memoir of the lyric "I."

In trouv. *T* Adam's monophonic songs seem to conclude the trouvère tradition with suspect imitation, while in his "collected works" manuscript (trouv. *W*) the same songs seem to initiate, with (mock?) solemnity, a display of diverse musical and narrative genres: these include (in order) thirty-four monophonic songs, sixteen *jeux-partis*, sixteen three-voice *rondeaux*, four three-voice motets, one two-voice motet, *Le jeu du pelerin*, *Le jeu de Robin et Marion*, *Le jeu de la feuillée*, *Roy de Sezile*, *Vers d'amour*, *Congé d'Adam*. The rubrics in the table of contents alert the reader to this plethora of genres that belong to Adam: *ses partures, ses roundiaus, ses motes* (*his* partures, *his* rondeaux, *his* motets).[87] The singularity of authorship and the plurality of genres advertise Adam's particular mastery of all musical and literary forms, old and new, aristocratic, clerical, and lay. His subjective voice becomes a generic one—that is, an expression of the singular self by way of multiple genres.

SELF-EXPRESSIONS IN A *CHANSONNIER*

The orderly *compilatio* of trouv. *T* over time—particularly the addition of the discrete *libelli* of two authors on either temporal and social end of the trouvère tradition—contrasts markedly with the nearly eighty anonymous additions scattered throughout the folios of trouv. *M*. Within trouv. *T* we can ascertain a metanarrative on the large-scale of the compendium; the bookend additions, which generally conform in design and script to the central song anthology, form introductory and concluding chapters in a Book that charts the autonomous lyric voice, linking the noble Thibaut de Champagne to the cleric Adam de la Halle. The multiple layers of additions to trouv. *M*, on the other hand, constitute a different story from the one in *T*—perhaps its sequel. Recorded on both pre-existing and newly ruled staves, in single- and double-column formats, and in non-mensural and mensural notation, these additions assert a shift in our metanarrative's protagonists from the venerated named authors of the lyric to the unnamed practitioners of song who uphold tradition as well as dismantle it.

---

86. Ibid., Part II, 137–43; quotations on 137 and 140 respectively.

87. Contrast this wording with the list of genres in trouv. *a*, which begins with *cançons* by various named authors (headed by *le roi de navare*) followed by the rubrics: *Ce sont pastoureles, ce sont motet et roondel, ce sont chançons de notre dame,* and *ce sont partures.*

As noted in chapter 2, the first compilers of trouv. *M* designed the *chansonnier* as a *summa* of thirteenth-century vernacular music, bringing together trouvère and troubadour songs, polyphonic motets, *lais*, and vernacular songs to the Virgin. The medieval table of contents, constructed prior to production, lists authors by status and region, as well as two genres ("*Les motes*," and individually named *lais*). This served more as a "wish list" than an index, however, for the original compilers put together a collection that differs in many respects, especially in the trouvère gatherings. Despite the scrambling and substitution of some authors, which disturbed the intended design, the program of illuminations maintains the distinction of status such that songs by noble trouvères are depicted with a knight on horseback and non-noble trouvères are depicted in clerical garb with scrolls or instruments.[88] Further details of *compilatio* suggest that it was commissioned by or destined for the court of Guillaume de Villehardouin—the Champagnois prince of the Morea (a Latin territory on the Greek Peloponnesus) who ruled from 1246 to 1278.[89] The collection is inaugurated by songs to the Virgin, after which follow two songs by *li prince de le mouree*, and one song by his powerful ally *li cuens d'Angou*, for the two were fellow crusaders during the campaign in which the Morea was acquired.[90] Guillaume nominally handed the principality over to Charles d'Anjou in 1267—an occasion possibly reflected in the *chansonnier*. Two more references to Charles appear in the mensural additions (discussed below), both with lyrics that are unique to this manuscript, suggesting their composition, and their recording in the *chansonnier*, after 1265 and before his death in 1285.

While the original corpus of trouv. *M* was planned and constructed prior to 1265, the manuscript remained unbound and open to revisions and additions for many decades. Three stages and types of medieval additions occurred within the manuscript: the earliest was the annex of the separate Thibaut de Champagne *libellus*, which brought the anthology in line with other *chansonniers* (including its relative, trouv. *T*) but which also strengthened the collection's ties to Champagne.[91] Table 3.5 shows the intended order of gatherings after this stage of *compilatio*, following John Haines's careful reconstruction; the gathering order in Jean and Louise Beck's facsimile edition roughly reflects the order in the medieval table of contents. Most trouvères hail from regions east of Paris (Champagne and Burgundy [Dijon]),

---

88. For illustrations of non-noble authors see fols. B144 (Robert de le Pierre) and B148 (Pierrekin de la Coupele); the picture on fol. B120ᵛ (for Colars li Boutellier) depicts a lyrical scene of supplication instead of an author portrait. See also Prinet, "L'Illustration héraldique du chansonnier du roi."

89. The title "prince," from Latin *princeps*, meaning "first citizen" in the context of the Roman Empire, was used to designate high magnates of the state who had sovereignty over their principalities; Latin conquerors in the East frequently took the title "prince." S.v. "Princeps," Du Cange, *Glossarium*; Jean Longnon has written extensively on the principality of the Morea; see his *L'Empire latin de Constantinople*.

90. The campaign was the Fourth Crusade, 1198–1204, in which Western forces captured Constantinople, annexing portions of the Byzantine Empire, including the Morea. On the commission of trouv. *M* see Haines, "The Transformations of the *Manuscrit du Roi*," 11–18. Haines corroborates the theory first proposed by Longnon in "Le Prince de Morée chansonnier."

91. See Beck, *Le manuscrit du roi*, vol. 2 for a discussion of their reconstruction; for a diagram of the gathering structure and more on the intended ordering see Haines, "Musicography," 48–77. Prior to Haines's

and north of Paris (Artois, Picardy [Somme, Lille], and Cambrai), which argues for either Champagne or Artois as the provenance for the *chansonnier*'s initial compilation.[92]

In a second stage, non-mensural music was added to twenty-seven preexisting staves left blank by the initial scribes, and seven more songs were similarly completed with

TABLE 3.5

Reconstructed *compilatio* for trouv. *M*

	Intended order	Current gathering	Beck
1	Marion Songs, Prince of Morea, Charles d'Anjou	1–2	1–2
	and nobles from Champagne	(ending with Thibaut)	
2	Thibaut de Champagne	10–12	*Mt*
3	Gace Brulé (Champagne)	5–6	3–4
4	mostly Artesian and Picard nobles	7–9	5–7
5	non-Artesian nobles (mostly from Champagne)	3–4	8–9
6	non-Artesian poets plus Gautier de Dargies (Artois)	13–14	10–11
7	mostly Artesian poets; poets from Somme and Dijon	21–23	16–19
8	Blondel de Nesles (Somme)	20	12
9	Audefrois le Bastart and mostly Artesian poets	21–23	17–19
10	various poets; several from Lille, plus Guiot de Dijon	24–25	20–21
11	Artesian pastourelles	15	22
12	Artesian poets	16–19	13–16
13	motets	28	25
14	southern poets	26–7	23–24
15	lais	29	26

examination of the manuscript, most scholars considered the Thibaut *libellus* to be a separate collection not intended as a graft to the original corpus as the overlap in songs and the inferior grade of parchment suggest (hence the separate sigla *Mt*). The graft is made seamless, however, by an overlap in hands whereby the scribe for the *libellus* also filled the space left blank at the end of gathering 2 with songs by Thibaut that are not duplicated in the *libellus*.

92. Everist (*Polyphonic Music*, 186) has suggested Artois, based mostly on the similarities in the motet collection with trouv. *T*, and Haines has suggested Champagne or perhaps even the Morea, based on the trouvère

mensural notation. All but one of these transmit unique melodies.[93] The third stage of medieval additions took place over the course of several decades, from after 1265 to perhaps the first decade of the fourteenth century: thirty-three monophonic songs and eleven instrumental pieces were added to the columns and folios left empty by the original compilers. All but one of these additions were written in mensural notation (the exception being the Occitan *cobla Ben volgra quem venques*). Jean and Louise Beck proposed that these additions represented "autographs"—songs entered directly into the manuscript by the trouvères, since five lyrics (two *descorts* and three *chansons*) have attributions in other sources (the Becks then parceled out many of the remaining additions to these and other authors). While few scholars have accepted the Becks' attributions, their idea of direct entry by a composer-scribe may not be too far-fetched.[94]

Most of the additions betray an anomaly in scribal procedures in that the folios were ruled first (evident in leftover staves), before the entry of words. Other features, such as five-line staves common to motet codices, single- rather than double-column format, larger sizes of notes, letters, and written block, and calligraphic styles of decorated capitals, visually contrast with the anthology's original design (including its *champie* initials). Yet some additions—presumably early entries—approximate the design of the original corpus with multichrome initials, red four-line staves, and compact formal Gothic bookhands (notably the Occitan *descorts* and two French *lais, La plus noble emprise* and *Ki de bons est*). Others—presumably later entries, and notably the four *rondeaux*—show less formality and more hastiness in their cursive scripts, brown staves (some hand-drawn), and simple monochrome calligraphic initials (see figure 4.4 below for a variety of hands on a single folio; all the staves are pre-ruled in red ink, with the exception of the bottom staff hand-drawn in brown ink.[95])

---

collection ("Transformations of the *Manuscrit du Roi*, 13–23 and 37, and, "Musicography," 48–57). It is noteworthy that the troubadour, motet, and *lai* gatherings correspond exactly with the medieval table of contents. Jean and Louise Beck argued for the court of Charles d'Anjou between 1254 and 1270, which could be in Provence, northern France, or Naples, as the provenance for the *chansonnier* (*Manuscrit du roi*, 2:18–20). This idea has found recent support by Butterfield (*Poetry and Music in Medieval France*, 163–64), who suggests the Francophone court of Charles in Naples. Charles's court included Occitan and French poets (quite a few from Artois) and government officials, though Dunbabin remarks that manuscript production at the Regno was primarily utilitarian (see *Charles I of Anjou*, 209). The poor state of the troubadour section of trouv. *M* (corrupt Occitan, missing stanzas, misattributions, and blank staves) suggests that Occitan exemplars and experts were not readily available during its first stage of compilation. Surprisingly, the Occitan of the mensural additions is more accurate than the Occitan found in the original corpus, which may indicate that the manuscript traveled, perhaps to Provence and Naples, and then back to Artois with the entourage of Robert II, who returned to the region from Italy ca. 1290, bringing with them the plays of Adam de la Halle among other compositions. See Symes, *A Common Stage*, 266.

93. For a discussion of the hands and some of the melodies for this layer of additions see Haines, "Musicography," 154–61. Haines song 32, *Quant voi partir* (RS 553), has a melodic concordance in trouv. *T*.

94. See Beck, *Le Manuscrit du roi*, 2:160–77; and Spanke, "Der Chansonnier du Roi," 92–102, who dismisses the "autograph" idea.

95. A single scribe could have several vocabularies of scripts ranging from a formal bookhand to a functional, more practical cursive. Some of the additions had more planning behind them, as evident from the formal

No later scribe added a complete composition by Adam de la Halle, despite his association with Charles d'Anjou in his court at Naples after 1282, though one monophonic *motet enté*, *Bone amourete m'a souspris* (discussed in chapter 4), uses the words and melody of a refrain from one of his *rondeaux*. While the absence of Adam de la Halle in this manuscript's many layers suggests that it remained or was detained in a region other than Artois or Naples, the mensural additions to trouv. *M* effect an expansion of genres comparable to Adam de la Halle's output as preserved in trouv. *W*, filling out the original *summa* of song with "new" and unique monophonic examples—*rondeaux*, *dansas* (or *virelais*), various heterostrophic songs, *motets entés* (or monophonic motets), and instrumental dances. Some of these genres (heterostrophic songs and monophonic motets) point to characteristic Artesian invention, if not also authorship. Table 3.6 and 3.7 list these additions and their genres in two orders: table 3.6 offers a hypothetical chronology of their entries, and table 3.7 gives their placement within the gatherings.

The earliest mensural additions appear to be the Occitan *descorts*, probably entered before 1285, but sometime later than the original corpus, as evident in the use of the round "s" in final position.[96] As discussed in chapter 2, these long heterostrophic songs prepared the way for the riot of melodic forms that followed, most immediately two French *lais* and a series of Occitan *dansas* added to the ends of gatherings and to the copious blank parchment left in the first gathering. (These *dansas*, which have the same form as French *virelais*, will be discussed further in chapter 5.) Although distinct in their language, the mensural contributions of the first two scribes are linked in three significant ways. First, they share details of production, with similarly decorated initials, formal Gothic scripts, and two-column formats. Second, both scribes embedded a homage to Charles d'Anjou and his compositional skill in their lyrics. The *dansa Ben volgra s'esser poges*, which intervenes between two *descorts*, concludes with the following *tornada*:

Dansa, car ieu ay apres	Dansa, since I have learned
qu'el reys Karles fay gent chan,	that King Charles composes fine song,
per aquo a sel ti man,	I send you to him,
car de fin pres es apres.	for he is learned in what constitutes fine merit.

script, multichrome or cued initials, or other marginal marks; other additions appear to be more opportunistic than planned, as evident in hand-drawn staves or cramped entries. For these opportunistic additions, the scribes may not have felt compelled to use their "best" handwriting. For more detailed discussion of the hands adding to trouv. *M*, see Peraino, "New Music, Notions of Genre," 92–136; and Haines, "Musicography," 162–67. I am here revising my earlier assessment of these hands in part based on the work of Haines, and on further consideration.

96. The scribe of the *descorts* is inconsistent in his use of a long or rounded "s" at the ends of words, whereas the scribe for the original corpus consistently used a long "s." The rounded "s" indicates a later date. I thank James J. Johns for his help in paleographic matters.

TABLE 3.6

The mensural additions grouped by scripts and scribal hand

Scribe	B fol.	Current fol.	Incipits	Genre
Formal Gothic Textura Scripts				
1	109	117	Bella donna cara	descort
	170	185*	Qui la ve en ditz	descort
	170bis	186*	Ben volgra s'esser poges	dansa (virelai)
	170bis	186^{v}*	Sens alegrage	descort
2	41	44*	La plus noble emprise	lai
	209	215*	Ki de bons est	lai
3	XXI^{v}	78^{v}*	Tant es gay et avinentz	dansa (virelai)
4	XXI^{v}	78^{v}*	Ben volgra quem venques	cobla
5	3^{v}	1^{v}	Donna pos vos ay chausida	dansa (virelai)
6	3^{v}	1^{v}	Pos qu'ieu vey la fualla	dansa (virelai)
7	170^{terv}	187^{v}*	Amors m'art con fuoc am flama	dansa (virelai)
8	176^{v}	103^{v}*	four estampies "royal"	instrumental dances
9	4^{v}	2^{v}	J'aim bele dame et de no[m]	motet enté
	4^{v}	2^{v}	[Dorme cuers ou n'a nul bien]	motet enté
	5	3	Hé, très douce amouretes	motet enté
	5	3	L'autrier lés une fontaine	pastourelle stanza
10	204^{v}	211^{v}*	Jolietement m'en vois	motet enté
11	204^{v}	211^{v}*	J'aim loiaument en espoir	motet enté
12	5^{v}	3^{v}	Bone amourete m'a souspris	motet enté
	145^{v}	161^{v}*	Se j'ai chanté sans guerredon (Robert de Castel, RS 1789)	heterostrophic song
13	143^{v}	159^{v}	Se j'ai chanté sanz guerredon (Robert de Castel, RS 1789)	heterostrophic song
Gothic Cursive Scripts				
14	5^{v}	3^{v}	Vous le defoidés l'amer	motet enté
15	7	5	two "danses"	instrumental dances
16	203	210*	A mon pooir ai servi (Pierrekin de la Coupele, RS 1081)	heterostrophic song
	XX	77*	five Latin songs	single strophes
17	7^{v}	5^{v}	Joliement du cuer, du cuer	motet enté

continued

TABLE 3.6

(continued)

Scribe	B fol.	Current fol.	Incipits	Genre
18	6ᵛ	4ᵛ	J'ai un chapelet d'argent	motet enté
	6ᵛ	4ᵛ	Trop ai esté lonc tans mus	rondeau
19	129	135*	Quant je voi plus felons rire (Guiot de Dijon, RS 1503)	heterostrophic song
20	7ᵛ	5ᵛ	J'ai bele dame amée	rondeau
	177ᵛ	104ᵛ*	four estampies "real"	instrumental dances
	177ᵛ	104ᵛ	"dansse real"	instrumental dance
21	3	1	U despit des envieus	rondeau
	7ᵛ	5ᵛ	Se je chant et sui envoisiés	rondeau

*Denotes a position at the end of a gathering.

TABLE 3.7

The mensural additions in folio order

Scribe	Folios	Beck #	Incipits	Genre
Gathering 1				
21	1	1	U despit des envieus	rondeau
5	1ᵛ	2	Donna pos vos ay chausida	dansa (virelai)
6	1ᵛ	3	Pos qu'ieu vey la fualla	dansa (virelai)
9	2ᵛ	4	J'aim bele dame et de no[m]	motet enté
9	2ᵛ	5	[Dorme cuers ou n'a nul bien]	motet enté
9	3	6	Hé, très douce amouretes	motet enté
9	3	7	L'autrier lés une fontaine	pastourelle stanza
12	3ᵛ	8	Bone amourete m'a souspris	motet enté
14	3ᵛ	9	Vous le defoidés l'amer	motet enté
18	4ᵛ	10	J'ai un chapelet d'argent	motet enté
18	4ᵛ	11	Trop ai esté lonc tans mus	rondeau
15	5	12a–b	two danses	instrumental dances
17	5ᵛ	13	Joliement du cuer, du cuer	motet enté
20	5ᵛ	14	J'ai bele dame amée	rondeau
21	5ᵛ	15	Se je chant et sui envoisiés	rondeau

Scribe	Folios	Beck #	Incipits	Genre
	Ends Gathering 7 (mostly Andrieu Contredit d'Arras; after Pierres de Moilns [Champagne])
2	44^{r-v}	16	La plus noble emprise	lai
	Ends Gathering 12 (Thibaut *libellus*)
16	77–8	29–33	five Latin songs	single strophes
3	78^v	34	Tant es gay et avinentz	dansa (virelai)
4	78^v	35	Ben volgra quem venques	cobla
	Ends Gathering 15 (Artesian poets)
8	103^v–104	24a–d	four estampies "royal"	instrumental dances
20	104^v	24e–i	four estampies and dansse real	instrumental dances
	Midpoint in Gathering 17 (with French *descorts* attributed to Willaumes li Viniers)
1	117^{r-v}	17	Bella donna cara	descort
	Ends Gathering 19 (Artesian poets)
19	135^{r-v}	18	Quant je voi plus felons rire	heterostrophic song
	Ends Gathering 22 (mostly Artesian poets; after Robert de le Pierre)
13	159^v	19	Se j'ai chanté sanz	heterostrophic song
12	161^v	19bis	Se j'ai chanté sans	heterostrophic song
	Ends Gathering 25 (mostly Lille and Dijon poets; after Carasaus)
1	185–86	20	Qui la ve en ditz	descort
1	186	21	Ben volgra s'esser poges	dansa (virelai)
1	186^v–187^v	22	Sens alegrage	descort
7	187^v	23	Amors m'art con fuoc am flama	dansa (virelai)
	Ends Gathering 28 (motet section)
16	210–11	25	A mon pooir ai servi	heterostrophic song
10	211^v	26	Jolietement m'en vois	motet enté
11	211^v	27	J'aim loiaument en espoir	motet enté
	Ends Gathering 29 after 2 Occitan *lais*
2	215^{r-v}	28	Ki de bons est	lai

Ki de bons est ends with this *envoi*:

Car nouvel chant trouver,	For he wishes so noble a lord
i veut si noble seignour,	as the prince of the *Terre de Labour*
	[= Naples]
com li prinches de Terre de Labour.	to compose a new melody.

The unusual flattery of Charles as both trouvère and king or sovereign prince suggests that these unique songs (one in Occitan and the other in French) were written as occasional pieces by composers in his entourage and reflect Charles's patronage of troubadours as well as trouvères.[97] Third, the French *lai La plus noble emprise* musically resembles the Occitan *descorts*, especially *Qui la ve en ditz* and *Bella donna cara*, with its continuous melodic invention, angular and unpredictable contours, shifting line lengths, and few repeated melodic ideas, though, as with *Bella donna cara*, every strophe ends on D.

Ki de bons est appears to have been recorded in two separate stages: while the words were written by the same hand as *La plus noble emprise*, plans for a decorated initial were never realized, and the musical notation displays features of a later era. As Theodore Karp first observed, the five strophes and the *envoi* each use a different rhythmic mode as described in the treatises of Magister Lambertus (ca. 1270) and Franco of Cologne (ca. 1260 or 1280), progressing in an orderly fashion through long–breve patterns to a final strophe of breves and semibreves, and an *envoi* full of ligatures. No other mensural addition contains syllabic semi-breves, which are characteristic of fourteenth-century practices, and the numerous erasures in the final strophe indicate that the scribe was not very familiar with them.[98] Nevertheless, *Ki de bons est* is a monophonic *tour de force*—an appropriately grand and learned melody to end a grand and learned anthology. The lyric identifies itself as a *lai* though, as noted in chapter 2, its ingenious melodic construction

97. Haines, following Longnon, believes the *chansonnier* switched focus, so to speak, from Guillaume de Villehardouin to Charles d'Anjou after 1267, to "honor the book's new owner." See Haines, "The Transformations of the *Manuscrit du Roi*," 12–16 (quotation). Most of the instrumental pieces bear the title *royal* or *real*, perhaps also with reference to Charles's royal title, though their scripts appear to be later than the *dansa* and *lai* that reference him. The *chansonnier*, even after Charles's death in 1285, remained a repository for musical compositions for well over a decade. For a discussion of Charles's appearance in *chansons* see Dyggve, "Personages historiques"; Maillard, *Roi-trouvère*, 31–32; and Chambers, *Proper Names*, 92.

98. For a discussion and transcription of *Ki de bons est* and *La plus noble emprise* see Karp, "Three Trouvère Chansons in Mensural Notation." In consultation with paleographers, Karp suggests that *Ki de bons est* "was written out a decade or so before 1300, not too long after the main body of the Ms had been compiled. Under these circumstances, it would appear that the melody was entered into the Ms within three decades of its composition, and there is an excellent chance that the melody is the original one" (477).

is modeled on another mensural addition, *Quant je voi plus felons rire*—one of three pieces that feature newly-composed heterostrophic music for strophic lyrics attributed to named thirteenth-century trouvères.

I will spend the rest of this chapter looking at these three songs, for with these songs we can see and hear a density of subjectivities in the convergence of autonomous and anonymous voices with the known authors of the lyrics and the unknown composers of the melodies. We can also see playfulness and parody at work in the musical settings, as well as an open-ended musical debate or *jeu-parti* about the continued relevance of the traditional strophic *chanson d'amour.*

The practice of making *contrafacta*—composing new lyrics to preexisting melodies or metrical patterns—has a long tradition in the troubadour and trouvère repertory; indeed, part of the ethos of the genre system was the understanding that certain lyrics (such as the *canso*) received new melodies, while others (such as the *sirventes*) could use borrowed tunes.[99] The borrowed tune or metrical scheme (and sometimes wording) allowed for an expanded, intertextual reading of the new lyrics. This is most evident in the Marian songs of Gautier de Coinci, many of which are *contrafacta* of secular love songs by well-known trouvères such as Blondel de Nesle, thus affecting a self-conscious *translatio* of love from the profane to the sacred.[100] There is a remarkable *contrafactum* within the mensural additions: as mentioned in chapter 2, each strophe of the French *descort La douce accordance* serves as a separate little song in a carefully ordered series of Latin devotional compositions. The inverse situation—composing a new melody for preexisting lyrics—has no clear tradition as a self-conscious "practice." To be sure, the study of troubadour and trouvère songs is vexed by alternate melodies, but the bulk of these maintain the traditional strophic form and melodic schemes.[101] By contrast, the three mensural melodies examined here seem to be radically counterposed to the tradition of strophic song to which the lyrics are tied,

99. For a description of this ethos in theory treatises see Aubrey, "Genre as a Determinant of Melody." Many songs announce their "newness" within the lyric, for example *Farai chansoneta nueva* (I will compose a new little song; PC 183-6), attributed to Guilhem IX, or the anonymous trouvère song *Chanter voil un novel son* (I want to sing a new tune; RS 1900). See also Gennrich, *Die Kontrafaktur*; for a discussion of the distinction between *contrafacta*, melodic borrowing, and chance formulaic similarities see Karp, "Borrowed Material in Trouvère Music."

100. See Falck, "Gautier de Coincy"; Butterfield, *Poetry and Music*, 103–15; Duys, "Minstrel's Mantel and Monk's Hood"; and Hunt, *Miraculous Rhymes*, 75–121. For a general study of *contrafacta* in the trouvère repertory see Räkel, *Die musikalische Erscheinungsform der Trouvèrepoesie*; see also the collection of transcriptions in Tischler, *Conductus and Contrafacta.*

101. Werner Bittinger coined the term "contraposita" for alternate melodies, and Karp has proposed the term "peripheral melodies"; see Karp, "The Trouvère MS Tradition," 26. For a typology of melodic variants in the trouvère repertory see O'Neill, *Courtly Love Songs*, 53–92.

thus reinventing the role of melody by replacing the constancy of strophic procedures with the variability of heterostrophic ones.

Se j'ai chanté sans guerredon avoir, attributed to Robert de Castel of Arras (or Robert du Chastel), was the first of the mensural trouvère songs added to trouv. *M*. The words are written in a thick rounded Gothic script that developed in Bologna, but spread to southern France and even to the scriptorium in Arras via Tuscan exiles (notably Brunetto Latini) who found a safe haven there under Robert II.[102] Both *Se j'ai chanté sans guerredon avoir* and the second piece added by the same scribe, *Bone amourete m'a souspris*, have strong ties to Arras. A high-toned courtly *chanson d'amour*, *Se j'ai chanté sans guerredon avoir* enjoyed wide circulation (twelve sources) and stability of both melody and authorship.[103] The melody also served as the basis for a vernacular religious *contrafactum*, *La volontés dont mes cuers est ravis* (RS 1607). *Se j'ai chanté sans guerredon avoir*, however, was not included in the original corpus of trouv. *M*; in fact, Robert de Castel is not represented there at all. We know from titles attached to his name that he was a cleric and a member of the patrician class. Although not a prolific composer, with only six *chansons* to his name, Robert was nevertheless held in high regard among the trouvères in Arras, for he appears in a *jeu-parti* with Jehan Bretel (d. 1272), as a judge for another between Jehan Bretel and Jehan de Grieviler, in a *Congé* by Baude Fastoul composed in 1272, and as the named recipient of an anonymous song *Bien s'est en mon cuer reprise* (RS 1639). Thus Robert de Castel's active years as a trouvère must have been in the 1260s, though, surprisingly, his songs do not appear in trouv. *T*, despite its strong ties to Arras.[104]

The complete lyric for *Se j'ai chanté sans guerredon avoir* consists of five stanzas divided by rhyme sounds into an initial group of three stanzas followed by a group of two stanzas. The well-known strophic melody (see example 3.3 ⊘OXFORD WEB MUSIC) has a clear *pedes-cauda* organization and, in typical fashion, defines a pitch-space in two complementary parts: the *pedes* begin with a narrow melodic range, outlining the lower D–A pentachord (occasionally touching the lower C as a neighbor note to D), and the *cauda*

---

102. Symes notes that the scriptorium at Arras was "partly staffed by local clerics which turned out vernacular manuscripts written by Italian scribes and illustrated by Picard artists into the early part of the fourteenth century" (*A Common Stage*, 259). The scribe for the two additions in *littera bononiensis* may be from southern France, as indicated by the crossed Tironian *et*, which Italian scribes did not use (I thank James J. Johns for this observation); it is also possible that Italian scribes working in Arras fused Italian and French traits. For a more detailed description of this hand see Peraino, "New Music, Notions of Genre," 106–11. Haines believes the melody of *Bone amourete m'a souspris* was written by a different music scribe than *Se j'ai chanté sans guerredon avoir*; see his "Musicography," 165–67. For a thorough discussion of the "Littera Bononiensis" see Pagnin, "La 'littera bononiensis'", and Morison, *Politics and Script*, 228.

103. Five of the twelve sources (*C, K, N, X, a*) attribute the song to Robert de Castel; the song is anonymous in the remaining sources (*M, O, R, S, V, U, Z*), though *O, V*, and *Z* do not contain any author attributions.

104. See Melander, "Les Poésies de Robert de Castel."

EXAMPLE 3.3 *Se j'ai chanté sanz guierredon avoir*, stanzas I and II from trouv. *O*, fol. 130ᵛ

widens the melodic range, exploring the sixth from F to the high D (phrase 5), and the C octave (phrase 6), finally returning to the "home" D–A pentachord with the last phrase.

In contrast to this logical melodic flow, the first stanza of the lyric is remarkable for conflicts between sound and sense on a par with the *descorts* discussed in chapter 2.

I

Se j'ai chanté sanz guierredon avoir
tout mon vivant, por ce ne doi je mie
mon chant laissier, ainz doi en bon
   espoir

If I have sung without recompense
all my life, for that I should never
leave my song (stop singing), instead
   I ought in good hope

amors servir, car la mieuz enseignie | to serve love, for the best educated woman
qui soit ou mont de sen, de cortoisie, | in the world with respect to wisdom,
    and courtliness,

me fait Amors si de fin cuer amer | Love causes me to love with such a true
    heart

que tuit mi mal me sont douz sanz | that all that hurts me is sweet to me
  amer. | without bitterness.

II

Si doucement me fait amors doloir | So sweetly does love cause me pain
q'il m'est avis c'il ment par tricherie, | that it seems to me that he lies by deceit,
qui dit qu'amors li fait mort recevoir; | whoever says that love kills him;
car bone amours est parmenauble vie. | for good love is everlasting life.
Qui bien aimme, il ne li grieve mie, | Whoever loves well, he is not upset at all,
s'il a travail de veillier, de penser. | if he has suffering from lying awake,
    from being pensive.

C'est fins desduis d'amie desirer. | Desiring one's lady love is true pleasure.

The first five poetic lines in stanza I are linked by enjambments that push through both rhyme sound and musical cadence. Yet the mid-line caesuras set up by these enjambments fall uncomfortably in the melodic contour, especially for lines 2 and 4, where the descending gesture ends on the other side of the syntactic break. Given the enjambment between lines 4 and 5 in the first stanza, the *pedes-cauda* scheme of ABAB CDE marks no particular syntactic division; rather the disjunction between sound and sense calls attention to the abstract musical design itself. The second stanza of this song corrects all these conflicts of sound and sense, coordinating musical phrase and syntactic unit on the level of the line and the mid-strophe division between *pedes* and *cauda*.

Could it be that the later contributor to trouv. *M*, who would pen his own melody to this lyric, chose this lyric precisely for its resemblance to the expressive discord of the *descorts*? Only the first two stanzas of *Se j'ai chanté sans guerredon avoir* were recorded on a blank folio at the end of a group of songs by Robert de le Pierre, another patrician trouvère of Arras, who also appears in a *jeu-parti* with Jehan Bretel. This placement strongly suggests the conscious filling of a perceived gap in the original collection of Artesian authors. Yet, save for the words, the song was made unrecognizable. The scribe wrote the initial two stanzas of words first, in a two-column format, providing space for staves over each stanza, thus planning for a melody that would resemble *descorts* or *lais*—rather than *chansons*—in its heterostrophic design (see figure 3.2).[105]

---

105. If the three recomposed *chansons* were not written directly into trouv. *M* by the anonymous composers themselves, then, as the Rouses surmise about *Fauvel*, it is likely that the scribes who recorded the words and notes worked closely with those composers, who directed them to write strophic *chansons* in the format of a *descort* or *lai*.

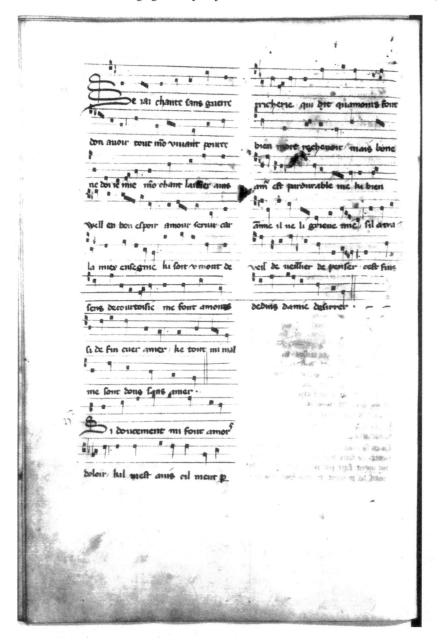

FIGURE 3.2 *Se j'ai chanté sans guerredon avoir* from trouv. *M*, fol. 161ᵛ (Bibliothèque nationale de France, Paris)

Distinct music was then provided for both stanzas, neither of which makes use of a *pedes-cauda* melodic design. Though free of any exact repetition of phrases, the melodies of both stanzas are tonally anchored to the F final (supported with a B♭ signature), and together form large-scale melodic complements: the first stanza stays mostly in the lower F–C pentachord, while the second stanza moves immediately and dramatically up to the

high F, and remains mostly in the upper C–F tetrachord (see example 3.4 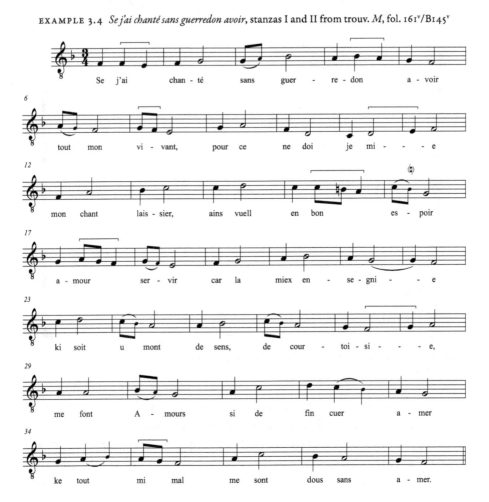OXFORD WEB MUSIC).
Thus it seems the composer of this melody sought to retain the tonal principle of the
pedes-cauda construction—the complementary exploration of lower and upper registers
within a specific pitch-space—but stretched this process over two stanzas of continuous
melodic invention.

Further details of melodic construction reveal this composition to be extraordinarily
well crafted. The composer preserved a semblance of strophic construction by using the
same phrase schemes for both stanzas (ten-syllable oxytonic lines disposed in phrases of
five perfect longs; ten-syllable paroxytonic lines disposed in phrases of six perfect longs)
and the same five-note cadential formula (a stepwise descent from C to F). On a lower
level, the stanzas are connected by a pervasive rhythmic motif—two ligated semibreves
followed by an imperfect long (see mm. 3, 6, 7, 16, etc.). Within each stanza, melodic
echoes offer brief moments of familiarity and subtle schematic organization. In the first
stanza, the composer alludes to a parallel *pedes* construction by beginning the first and

EXAMPLE 3.4 *Se j'ai chanté sans guerredon avoir*, stanzas I and II from trouv. *M*, fol. 161ᵛ/B145ᵛ

EXAMPLE 3.4 Continued

third lines on F and the second and fourth lines with similar descending melodic gestures that pause on a low E (see mm. 6–7 and mm. 17–18), and articulate the poetic caesura. (Also in this stanza, a signed B♮ highlights the words *bon espoir*). In the second stanza, a melodic echo cuts across the would-be *pedes* structure by linking lines 2 and 3 (see mm. 6–8 and 12–14), creating the effect of a double versicle with *ouvert* and *clos* endings. In sum, the composer took pains to invoke and destabilize the listener's anticipation and perception of melodic pattern, both within and across stanzas.

The cohesive yet free melody of *Se j'ai chanté sans guerredon avoir* matches Dante's description of the *oda continua*: "For some are accompanied by an uninterrupted melody (*oda continua*), in an ordered progression from beginning to end—that is, without any repetition of musical phrases."[106] This melody type is not uncommon in the troubadour

---

106. "Quia quedam sunt sub una oda continua usque ad ultimum progressive, hoc est sine iteratione modulationis…"; *De vulgari eloquentia*, 74–75.

repertory, though it is frequently linked to the *trobar clus* poetic style, characterized by obscure words and meaning.[107] Melodies without repetition schemes are rarer in the trou-vère repertory, though many melodies stray from the *pedes-cauda* design (see table 3.3 above). What is unique about *Se j'ai chanté sans guerredon avoir* is the "writing large" of the *oda continua* across two stanzas: its extensive melodic invention literally overwrites the traditional verbal boundaries and principle of strophic repetition, musically obscuring its generic identity. We can see exactly this effect in the second entry of the lyric in trouv. *M*.

The expressive inventiveness of this recomposed *chanson d'amour* captured the imagi-nation of another scribe, who entered the words of the same two stanzas of *Se j'ai chanté sans guerredon avoir* two folios before the fully notated entry (See figure 3.3). This second copy was spaced but never ruled for music, and the script is considerably more casual—smaller in dimension and lighter in hue than any of the other additions; in other words, it appears to be a rough draft made by a different scribe. Furthermore, this scribe seems to have been unfamiliar with the piece, as made evident by several corrected mistakes. For the first stanza the scribe maintained a left-hand margin with the exception of the penul-timate word; he originally wrote "*sont douz amour*" rather than "*sont douz sanz amour*" and then corrected his error by adding "*sanz*" in the margin. He then proceeded to write the first line of the second stanza, thus failing to distinguish the second stanza from the first. Having realized his error, he crossed out the words and rewrote the opening line of the second stanza on a new line. Later in the second stanza, the scribe erased nearly the entire penultimate line of verse (leaving only the first word of the line, "*grieve*" and the last syllable "*pen-*" of *penser*; see the first line of the right-hand column in figure 3.3), and seems to have given up on his endeavor before filling in the blank line.

Owing to a shared grammatical error—the mistaking of *amors* for a plural, leading to the verb *font* rather than *fait*—both entries can be dated to the last decades of the thir-teenth century or the early fourteenth century; other details of orthography suggest that the rough draft came later than the notated version.[108] Thus it seems the rough draft was the work of a scribe who hoped to write yet a third version of the *chanson* that responded not to the "authoritative" strophic version, but to the new heterostrophic

---

107. Haines, "Vers une distinction *leu/clus*."

108. On the mistaking of *amors* for plural, see Frappier, *Amour courtois et Table Ronde*, 118–21; the grammatical error also appears in the version preserved in trouv. *Z*, dated as late thirteenth to early fourteenth century. Two details of orthography suggest that the addition on fol. 159ᵛ/B143ᵛ might be later: the use of "ou" instead of "u" (modern day *au*) in stanza I, and "ou" in *douloir* instead of *doloir* in stanza II. In a couple of instances, the scribe of the rough draft used more grammatically correct forms, such as *tuit* for the nominative plural of *tout* at the end of stanza I, and the pronoun *me* for *mi* at the beginning of stanza II. The first scribe (figure 3.2) betrays some Picard influence in the word *rechevoir* (stanza II)—written as *recevoir* by the second scribe (figure 3.3)—and in the preference for "k" over "q" (*qui/ki; qu'il/k'il*), also common to Anglo-Norman orthography. Picardisms mixed with Francien became common in medieval literary manuscripts, probably on account of the prominence of Arras authors, and thus do not necessarily indicate the scribes' particular dialect. I thank Alice Colby-Hall for her assistance in these matters.

FIGURE 3.3 *Se j'ai chanté sanz guerredon avoir* from trouv. *M*, fol. 159ᵛ, reproduced from fol. 143ᵛ, Jean and Louise Beck, *Les Chansonniers des troubadours et des trouvères*. Reprinted with permission from the University of Pennsylvania Press and Broude Brothers

version, whose unusual format he was trying to copy. One thing is certain: the confusion over the division of the two stanzas in the rough draft implies that this scribe was attempting to record a piece for which he had no models; in other words, a visually and conceptually "new" genre. The written conflation of the stanzas paradoxically erased the only remaining marker of the *chanson*'s traditional strophic construction, given the apparent plan for a non-strophic melody. The subsequent correction of the mistake then rein-scribed that modicum of tradition, thus averting a total formal collapse of an already shaky edifice. Two later composers, however, found musical solutions that clarify this game of generic reinvention.

Both *A mon pooir ai servi* (attributed to Pierrekin de la Coupele, fl. 1250–60) and *Quant je voi plus felons rire* (attributed to Guiot de Dijon, fl. 1215–25) were included in the original corpus of strophic songs, but left unnotated within their respective author-groups. Rather than "filling in the blanks" of these empty staves, the later scribes wrote out lengthy het-erostrophic versions, each with a unique and clever melodic scheme stretched over five stanzas (plus an *envoi* in the case of *A mon pooir ai servi*). Both these added songs appear at some distance from their authors' names—*A mon pooir ai servi* at the end of the motet collection, and *Quant je voi plus felons rire* at the end of a gathering dedicated to Artesian poets, following a group of songs by Gillebert de Berneville, who was active in Arras.[109] In contrast to the rounded Gothic hand of *Se j'ai chanté sans guerredon avoir*, these two songs were recorded in French cursive scripts—a faster style of writing characterized by ligated letters, exaggerated ascenders, and extravagant loops that developed in chanceries charged with preparing legal and diplomatic documents. Such cursive and semi-cursive scripts appear in northern and southern regions from the mid-thirteenth century, entering schools by the late thirteenth century; they became acceptable bookhands in the fourteenth century, especially in collections of vernacular literature.[110]

Although little is known about Pierrekin de la Coupele, he received a grand illustration in trouv. *M* (fol. 163/B148): he is depicted as a crowned vielle player, thus signaling an alternative royalty—among the professional musicians—to those noble authors that head the collec-tion.[111] His name implies that he hailed from the region of Flanders (now the Pas-de-Calais), and he appears among the Artesian composers in trouv. *M*. The scarcity of sources for his six extant songs—five are transmitted in trouv. *M* and *T*, with two in *C*—suggests that he had only a regional reputation.[112] Thus we can surmise that the anonymous composer who sin-gled out his *chanson à refrain* lyric *A mon pooir ai servi* as a vehicle for new composition had an affiliation or familiarity with the poets of Artois and Flanders.[113]

---

109. See Dyggve, *Onomastique des Trouvères*, 114–15. Gillebert addresses Charles d'Anjou in an *envoi* for *Onques d'amours n'oi nule si grief paine* (RS 138), though the song does not appear in trouv. *M*.

110. Bischoff, *Latin Paleography*, 140; see also 136–45. For points of comparison see Thomson, *Latin Bookhands of the Later Middle Ages*, plate 13 (dated 1289); *Recueil de paléographie normande*, Document no. 6a (dated 1301); and Prou, *Manuel de paléographie*, plates 4 (1295) and 5 (Marseille, 1302). The loops and flourishes on ascenders and descenders, the forked "r," and the excess ink on the long "s" and "f" (due to a mannerism of bearing down on the quill) are among the distinctive French traits. See also Nesbitt, *The History and Technique of Lettering*, 48.

111. See the comments of Huot, *From Song to Book*, 60.

112. See Långfors, "Mélange de poésie lyrique français VII." *A mon pooir ai servi* has a concordance in trouv. *T* (without music).

113. The orthography of the words, however, is close to the Francien of the main collection.

A mon pooir ai servi consists of five stanzas plus an *envoi*, each of which ends with the same three-line melodic and textual refrain (the refrain begins in figure 3.4 at the capital D).[114] For the version in trouv. *M*, however, the scribe also wrote a stable phrase of music that sets the first line of each stanza. Together these two stable melodic phrases frame new, non-repeating melodic material. A schematic formula for this piece would look something like axB, ayB, azB, etc., where "a" stands for new words with repeating melody, the middle term stands for complete variability from stanza to stanza, and "B" stands for the refrain.

While the composer of this song had a certain genius for formal experimentation, and despite the great expanse of this setting (filling a total of three folios), the new melody shows no obvious motivic play or phrase pairings within the bodies of the stanzas; and though many hover around C—the final of both melodic refrains—there is no discernable systematic exploration of the lower or upper tetrachords surrounding this apparently central pitch, as a *pedes-cauda* melody would do (see example 3.5 OXFORD WEB MUSIC).[115]

FIGURE 3.4 *A mon pooir ai servi* from trouv. *M*, fol. 210^{r-v} (Bibliothèque nationale de France, Paris)

---

114. The refrain (B-ref 558) has no other concordance.

115. The composition also exhibits some infelicities of word setting. See stanza I, mm. 36–38 (*guarrai* stretched over three notes), and stanza II, m. 26 (the last two syllables of *traveillié* are given one note.) The notation of this piece is without much ambiguity; however, the scribe inconsistently writes simple, double, and even triple longs at the ends of stanzas. Thus I have modified the last double long of stanza II to conform to the simple long of stanza I.

Like the mensural Occitan *descorts* discussed in chapter 2, the monotonous mode 2 breve–long pattern is seldom varied. What we do clearly hear through the heterostrophic din, however, are those musical aspects that remain the same from strophe to strophe—the framing musical material, which the composer took pains to highlight: every stanza begins with a dramatic leap of a fifth from F to C, and the refrain

EXAMPLE 3.5 *A mon pooir ai servi*, stanzas I and II from trouv. *M*, fol. 210^r/B203^r

EXAMPLE 3.5 Continued

begins with an expansive rhythm and sweeping melody that offer a much-needed contrast to the relentless modal rhythm.

Thus in *A mon pooir ai servi* we have a combination of musical and verbal refrains grafted onto the body of a courtly *chanson*. In his *De musica* (ca. 1300), Johannes de Grocheio describes such a hybrid song: "There is also another kind of *cantilena* which they call 'ornamented song' (*cantus insertus*) or 'grafted song' (*cantilenam entatam*). It begins in the manner of a *cantilena* and ends or comes to a close in their fashion."[116] According to Grocheio's typology of monophonic vocal genres, a *cantilena* is a song-type that uses a structurally repeating refrain, whereas the *cantus* song-type does not. Thus a *cantilena entata* could refer to the splitting and grafting of a refrain from a *cantilena* on to either end of a *cantus*; or, as *cantus insertus* leads us to think, a *cantus* could be adorned with a repeating refrain-like element. The two distinct styles of *cantilena* (refrain song) and *cantus* (strophic courtly chanson) bear a resemblance of formal repetition (refrains repeat, as do strophic melodies); the opening melodic repetition thus references the strophic repetition of the *cantus*, while the final melodic and verbal repetition references the refrains of the *cantilena*. It is the contrast of the heterostrophic internal material in *A mon pooir ai servi*, however, that calls our attention to these interstylistic similarities, and constitutes the implication of *cantilena* and *cantus* by parading an alternative type of melodic construction.

In the secondary literature, songs showing a similar "grafting" of musical segments of both the words and music of preexisting refrains have been identified as *motets entés*—a medieval term thought to be the vernacular translation for Grocheio's Latin *cantilena entata*.[117] All of the monophonic pieces that have heretofore been identified as *motets entés* consist of a single strophe of words (about the length of a motet) set to music: ten such pieces were added to trouv. *M* (see chapter 4). *A mon pooir ai servi*, however, is a multi-stanza example of this type of grafted song, and the only example to engage an entire preexisting courtly lyric with a named author. Indeed, this recomposed *A mon pooir ai servi* retained the *envoi*, which names Pierrekin as the composer:

Pierrekins a tous amans	To all lovers Pierrekin
sa chançon vuelt envoier	wants to send his chanson
et sa dame, qui lonc tans	and to his lady, who for a long time
l'a tenu en son dangier	has held him in her power,
et tendra: "Si l'amerai."	and he continues to maintain: "and I will love her."
Dieus, que ferai,	*God, what will I do*
se l'amour n'ai	*if I don't have love*
de la bele ou mon cuer	*from the beautiful one to whom I have given*
mis ai?	*my heart?*

---

116. "Est etiam alius modus cantilenarum, quem *cantum insertum* vel *cantilenam entatam* vocant, qui ad modum cantilenarum incipit et earum fine clauditur vel finitur." Text and translation from Page, "Johannes de Grocheio on Secular Music," 27.

117. See Page, "Grocheio, Johannes de." Page believes that *cantilena entata* encompasses "various song-forms that modern scholars call *chanson avec des refrains* and *chanson à refrain*"—that is, *chansons* with changing and unchanging refrains. In his earlier article, "Johannes de Grocheio on Secular Music," Page equates *cantilena entata* with *motet enté* (27).

As discussed in chapter 1, the turn to the middle of the stanza with the *envoi* usually coincides with a shift in voice, from generic lyric "I" to a specific, autonomous "I"; the familiar yet fresh presentation of music spotlights the ambiguities of subjectivity and expression inherent in medieval love songs. Given the hybrid melodic design of *A mon pooir ai servi*, its combination of strophic and heterostrophic procedures, there is no discernable place for the *envoi*—the autonomous "I"—to turn. Pierrekin's supposed assertion of self begins and ends like every stanza, with the same framing melodic material. The *envoi* stands as an undistinguished, compressed coda that ironically monumentalizes an author who has lost control of his composition.

The anonymous composer of *A mon pooir ai servi* set himself the challenge of grafting together abstract musical properties culled from various genres and styles—free melodic invention of *oda continua* and motets, repeating refrains of dance songs, and multi-stanza lyrics of the *chanson d'amour*—in a play of stable and changing musical elements over a large-scale form. We can also discern a comparable play of authorship in the use of Pierrekin's song and name as a vehicle through which another unnamed (but idiosyncratic) voice can be heard—in other words, the grafting of one subjective voice onto another. Placed at the end of the two-voice motet collection, *A mon pooir ai servi* offers a linear exposition of the preceding polyphony's density of voices and subjectivities.

Both *Se j'ai chanté sanz guerredon avoir* and *A mon pooir ai servi* maintain a tentative link to the identity of the purported author—the former in its logical position among Artesian authors, and the latter with the retention of the *envoi*. By transforming an attributed song with generic features into an anonymous song with unique features, *Se j'ai chanté sanz guerredon avoir* and *A mon pooir ai servi* comment on the problematics of individual expression within the stylized musical vocabulary of the strophic *chanson*. The third recomposed *chanson*, *Quant je voi plus felons rire*, makes another point: the gratuitous proliferation of *pedes-cauda* melodies attests to the form as classic yet routine, and therefore impersonal.

Quant je voi plus felons rire is a *chanson* with changing refrains (*chanson avec des refrains*) that has four other concordances, most importantly one in the original corpus of trouv. *M* (with the staves left empty), and another in trouv. *T* with an unrelated, through-composed, strophic melody (the only other extant melody for this lyric). In both these earlier versions, the *chanson* is attributed to Guiot de Dijon (fl. 1215–25), a native of Burgundy, though in trouv. *C* the song is attributed to Amauri de Craon, an aristocratic trouvère from the region of Anjou.[118] Many of Guiot's songs have a conflicting attribution from source to source. The loose grip of his name on songs may explain why the later composer chose this lyric to "make his own" rather than filling the empty staves in the original corpus.

What type of composition did the scribe record? Visually, this addition is one of the most impressive; it is brazenly spread out in a single column across the width of the folio,

---

118. See Karp, "Guiot de Dijon"; and Prinet, "L'Illustration héraldique du chansonnier du roi," 528–30.

with oblique ligatures cutting diagonals across the staves, matched by a script full of decorative calligraphic loops and flourishes (see figure 3.5). The hand-drawn staff at the end of the composition suggests an unusual order of events, namely, that the words and music were added to pre-ruled staves (in this case, ruled in brown ink). It also suggests that the word and music scribe were possibly the same (and possibly the composer)

FIGURE 3.5 *Quant je voi plus felons rire* from trouv. *M*, fol. 135 (Bibliothèque nationale de France, Paris)

because no provision was made for ruling a staff above the last line of words before the notes were entered.

Musically, the composition shows a similar assertiveness. The genre of the *chanson avec des refrains* combines strophic and non-strophic elements: while the main body of the lyric is set to the same music as with a *chanson*, each refrain introduces a new musical ending. (Trouv. *M* and *T* are the only sources that provide separate staves for each refrain in such compositions). Despite the popular element of the changing refrains, *Quant je voi plus felons rire* is a bitter complaint about the trials of love; the first two stanzas give an idea of its relentlessly dour tone:

I

Quant je voi plus felons rire	When I see more villains laughing
et envoisier et chanter,	and making merry and singing,
et voi que chascuns souspire	and I see that each sighs
faussement, pour miex guiler,	falsely, for better trickery,
lors me fait desconforter	then I am distressed by
Amours, qui mes maus empire,	Love, who worsens my suffering,
et ma dame tel martire,	and my lady who makes me suffer such martyrdom,
qui sans morir me fait doloir.	without dying.
Amours font de moi lor voloir;	*Loves have their way with me;*
j'endur les maus pour miex valoir.	*I endure the suffering in order to be more worthy.*

II

Mout par est crueus li sire	Very very cruel is the lord
c'om sert de cuer de fausser	whom one serves with one's heart
qui se courouche et aïre	who out of duplicity becomes angry and violent
quant li doit guerredouner;	when he ought reward one;
mais toustans fait a blasmer	however, my lady deserves to be blamed,
ma dame, ou mes cuers se mire,	she on whom my heart fixes its attention,
la mieudre c'om puist eslire,	the best lady that could select,
la plus vaillans des meillours.	the most worthy of the best.
Se je l'aim, ne me blasmes mie;	*If I love her, don't blame me at all;*
mes fins cuers ne pense allours	*my true heart thinks of no one else.*

Note that the refrains are grafted to the stanza with a transitional line whose final word rhymes only with one or both of the refrain lines. This suggests that the refrains were locked in at the point of composition of the entire lyric.

For this mensural version of *Quant je voi plus felons rire* (see example 3.6 🅢 OXFORD WEB MUSIC), the scribe wrote new music for all five stanzas, and, in direct contrast to the strophic but

EXAMPLE 3.6 *Quant je voi plus felons rire*, stanzas I and II from trouv. *M*, fol. 135/B129

through-composed melody preserved in trouv. *T*, each strophe uses the classic *pedes-cauda* construction (thus AAB, CCD, EEF, etc.). Neither phrase nor motif is shared among the five stanzas, and the background modal patterns often change from one stanza to the next.[119] Yet the piece maintains large-scale coherence through cadences: every

119. For another treatment of this song see Tischler, "A Unique and Remarkable Trouvère Song." Tischler believes this song offers evidence that trouvère songs were "metric-rhythmic in concept" (112); his transcription

EXAMPLE 3.6 Continued

stanza ends on D, every pair of *pedes* ends on F, with the exception of first stanza, which
ends on D. Within each stanza the melodies follow the general melodic tendency of stro-
phic *chansons*, setting up a registral or tonal contrast between the *pedes* and the *cauda*
sections. Furthermore, the gimmick of the changing refrains is here made nearly invisible,

---

shifts between 6/8 and 9/8. In transcribing this and the other two additions, I have given the modal pattern
priority when conflicts arise between the pattern and the conventional reading of the ligature.

absorbed into the *pedes-cauda* formula with only the wink of a capital letter to distinguish them from the stanza proper. This composition has thus transformed one strophic courtly *chanson* into a suite of five distinct miniature *chansons*, related only by a tonal scheme and a preexisting association of the poetic stanzas; it is a medieval "song cycle," akin to the five Latin pieces added to trouv. *Mt*, which use the five stanzas of the French descort *La douce acordance* for their melodies.

The reiteration of the *pedes-cauda* structure in changing melodic garb highlights the difference between the background context of the strophic *chanson d'amour* and the foreground text of this ever-mutable song. In this new context, the *pedes-cauda* form, which is indeed repeated with every stanza, is abstracted, and thus defamiliarized in light of its changing surface. Linda Hutcheon defines "parody" as imitation of a form or text that creates an ironic inversion of foregrounded image and backgrounded context, prompting a critical reevaluation of both.[120] In *Quant je voi plus felons rire*, what would have been in strophic versions a local point of playful musical tension between the "canonical" courtly, stable stanzas and the "lesser" courtly, unstable refrains here becomes a full-blown musical inversion, whereby the courtly stanzas take on the changing aspect of the popular refrains, and the refrains become absorbed within the normative *pedes-cauda* form. This parodic monumentalizing of trouvère melodic form makes for a curious setting of a courtly complaint. The surprise of successively new melodies and the jauntiness of their mensural rhythm play against the bitterness and resignation of the words, offering a musical illustration of the merry-making and singing, and perhaps even the trickery, that the lyric reproaches.

As with *Se j'ai chanté sanz guerredon avoir*, where two scribes attempted to realize a heterostrophic melody for the same strophic lyric, the unique design of *Quant je voi plus felons rire* inspired a second scribe to try his hand at writing a chain of *pedes-cauda* melodies, but this time for the heterostrophic lyric of *Ki de bons est*, which proclaims itself a *lai* in the first strophe, though the poetry is not organized into double versicles.[121] If we consider that the words of *Ki de bons est* were probably entered before *Quant je voi plus felons rire*, then the direction of influence may have been from the hybrid *chanson-lai* lyric of *Ki de bons est* to the experimental musical setting of *Quant je voi plus felons rire*, which transformed the already hybrid *chansons avec des refrains* into another new genre. The later melodist for *Ki de bons est* continued these musical experiments by adding another abstract dimension—the systematic exposition of mensural notation. This "purely academic" melody has its own expressive force, though not one we can associate with the content of the words or the assertion of an individual voice. Rather, *Ki de bons est* expresses a corporate scholastic view and hints at the episteme of the *summa* still functioning in the

---

120. Hutcheon, *A Theory of Parody*, 6–7; see also 32–37. She points out that the Greek noun *parodia* combines *odos* meaning "song," and *para* meaning either "counter" but also "beside," suggesting a tension between accord and contrast (32).

121. See Karp, "Three Trouvère Chansons in Mensural Notation," 477.

compilatio of the mensural additions. The clusters of melody types among these late thir-teenth- and early fourteenth-century entries suggest a select community of composers who not only independently engaged the traditional genres with musical glosses and cri-tiques, but also directly engaged each other's song experiments, responding with yet more musical commentary.[122]

What, then, does this commentary say? Earlier in this chapter I referred to Joseph Dane's work on parody and the Artesian *dits* in trouv. *T*. It is relevant here to revisit his ideas, which pertain to the three heterostrophic *chansons* discussed above. He writes: "parody can be subversive by calling attention to the artificiality of poetic language and by questioning the ordinary responses of an audience" and further, "by exposing a deca-dence in a preceding genre, parody encourages either the creation of new genres or a revitalization of old genres."[123] The heterostrophic recomposed *chansons* all augment tra-ditional formal types: *Se j'ai chanté sanz guerredon* extends the *oda continua*, *A mon pooir ai servi* explores both repeating refrains and the *entata* or grafting technique, and *Quant je voi plus felons* meditates on strophic and non-strophic procedures in its ever-changing *pedes-cauda* designs. Yet this attempted revitalization of old genres with new music marks the point of exhaustion for the classic trouvère *chanson d'amour*, as the anonymous com-posers uncoil the strophic form and disperse its expressive possibilities over abstracted formal procedures and relentless melodic invention. In this way they are all parodies, exposing the artifice of that musical and poetic language, and, by extension, the artifice of the author's name. Like the oxymoronic character of the "noble merchant" in the Artesian *dits*—an uncomfortable fusion of two distinct social identities—these songs are similarly oxymoronic in their combination of strophic and non-strophic musical identities, and named and unnamed voices. The subversive quality of these songs lies in their inverse relationship of words to music in that music—once stable and transparent to the chang-ing words—becomes the principal changing element from stanza to stanza. Indeed, changing the predictable to the unpredictable seems to be the game of these recomposed *chansons*, and this returns us to the comment made at the very beginning of this chapter: while change over time is predictable, the nature of those changes is unpredictable.

Why did later composers revisit and reinvent the thirteenth-century strophic *chanson d'amour* in trouv. *M*? The answer may lie in the *compilatio* of *chansonniers*, through which both the songs and their authors become historical texts for (musical) commentary. Compilation begins with a keen awareness of the patron, and the need to reflect his or her political ties; in the case of trouv. *M*, the *chansonnier* initially reflected the Champagnois Prince of the Morea and his association with Charles d'Anjou, who had ties to Artois as well as Provence. Later, it seems, this *chansonnier* became purely an

---

122. Karp argues that *Ki de bons est* points to trouvères with training in the Liberal Arts and modal theory; see ibid., 487. I pursue the argument of the mensural chansons as analogous to a marginal gloss on the courtly *chanson* in "Re-placing Medieval Music."

123. Dane, "Parody and Satire," Part I, 10.

archive of compositional activity. This marks a shift in the purpose of the Book, the reorientation from the politics of patrons to the creativity and self-assertion of composers-scribes. The metanarratives of the lyric voice brought out in trouv. *T* and trouv. *M* reveal a subtle movement toward ever more self-conscious musical composition, from the formal variety of Thibaut, to the formal purity of Adam, to the formal parodies in trouv. *M*. In this *translatio vocis*, musical ingenuity became emblematic of self-expression. But if there is a transmission of voice still sounding in the recomposed *chansons* in trouv. *M*, it is a voice pointedly distorted by the "aphoristic energies" of "writing" as Derrida understands it—namely, the fracturing of the apparent metaphysical unity between words and voice, and, by extension, between the song and its named author and presumed subject. This "writing," exposed in the music of these songs, disturbs the self-evident meaning of words as it displaces the self-evident subject who sings them.

The history of visual art provides another lens through which we can view the recomposed *chansons* in trouv. *M*; they resemble conceptually the reworkings, variations, and parodies of past masters by younger generations, especially by self-consciously "modern" artists such as Picasso and Mondrian. These artists looked at the paintings of Cézanne and van Gogh and saw through the objects they depicted to abstractions of lines, planes, and shapes, attributing to Cézanne and van Gogh new ways of seeing that allowed for their own later radical break with representation.[124] Visual quotations of shapes and designs depict a lineage of seeing—or better, an inheritance of "voice."[125] This refashioning of a past artwork is compatible with the medieval tradition of scholastic commentary and the metanarrative derived from *compilatio*, for commentary is embedded in the new visual composition. Just as Mondrian's horizontal and vertical lines gloss Cézanne's schematic pine tree branches, revealing another meaning of the image, so too did the later composers adding to trouv. *M* hear in the song designs of the past the possibility for new ways of organizing melody. While the model songs do not perhaps represent "masterpieces" of the thirteenth century, nor do the later composers quote from the models, each lyric had some property of design that offered a point of departure for abstraction and parody: Robert de Castel's *Se j'ai chanté sans guerredon avoir* offered the basic strophic *chanson d'amour* with a *pedes-cauda* melody and no refrain; Pierrekin de la Coupele's *A mon pooir ai servi* offered a song with a repeating refrain; and Guirot de Dijon's *Quant je voi plus felons rire* offered a song with changing refrains. In the hands of the younger artists, these song designs were reduced to their basic materials—repeating and non-repeating elements—which were then used to paint abstract melodies on the canvas of the parchment folio, retaining only a few key references to the original "object" of the strophic *chanson*.

I believe that the scribes who recomposed these three trouvère *chansons* understood the old forms to be essentially moribund. That all these songs have names attached to

---

124. See the essays in *Cézanne and Beyond*, and Galassi, *Picasso's Variations of the Masters*.
125. For a discussion of the idea of "voice" in music and painting, see Karol Berger, "*Diegesis* and *Mimesis*."

them is part of the "vision" and lineage that is under scrutiny. Neither Robert de Castel, nor Pierrekin de la Coupele, nor Guirot de Dijon figures as avant-garde for the later composers; rather, their "Cézanne" appears among the earlier anonymous mensural addition—the composer of the Occitan *descorts*. The *descorts*' radical break with strophic form and traditional melodic behavior allowed for the other anonymous composers to produce their own experiments in form and genre. Thus, alongside a metanarrative context, we can also determine a metalyrical one: it is the staging of a grand *jeu-parti* about the continued relevance of past genres, forms, styles, and identities. This debate can be found in the lyric and narrative collections in trouv. *T* and continues with the recomposed *chansons* and the many other marginal genres that fill out the *chansonnier* trouv. *M*. Each unique melody poses the questions: Which makes the better love song, strophic or non-strophic forms? Ancient or modern practices? Named authors or anonymous scribes? It is through these songs that we *can* trace time and its changes to the conception and expression of the self.

4

The Hybrid Voice of Monophonic Motets

SELF-EXPRESSION REQUIRES THE differentiation of one's voice from the crowd that renders language collective and formulaic. Troubadours frequently embed self-consciousness about the differentiation of voice and the act of composition within their lyrics, often couching these in terms of craftsmanship and manufacture. Thus Guilhem IX writes "of a song that is of good color, that I have brought forth from my workshop," where "good color" refers to the quality of metal in smelting and tempering as well as to the rhetorical term for figures of speech (*colores rhetoricae*);[1] similarly, Arnaut Daniel boasts "I create words, and cut (or scrape) and shape them, and they will be exact and certain, when I've passed the file over them."[2] Peire d'Auvernha (fl. 1149–68) pokes fun at

---

1. "D'un vers, si es de bona color / qu'ieu ai trait de mon obrador," lines 2–3 from *Ben vueill que sapchon li pluzor* (PC 183-2). Text and translation from *William*, 24–25. See also Nichols, "The Early Troubadours," 74–75, for a connection of *bona color* to tempering; and Ferrante, "The Craft of the Early Troubadours," 98 and 113–14, for a connection of *color* to rhetoric. Ferrante occasionally notes the craftsmanship metaphors of the early troubadours but does not discuss the conceptual implications of those metaphors except to call attention to the self-consciousness of technique. James J. Murphy notes that "it was a common medieval practice after the eleventh century to refer to any figure as *color* (often by analogy to the verb *coloro*)"; Murphy, *Rhetoric in the Middle Ages*, 20n38; see also 39n102 and 171 for an example of the term in Geoffrey of Vinsauf's *Poetria Nova* (ca. 1208–16).

2. "Fauc motz, e capuig e doli, / que serant verai e cert / qan n'aurai passat la lima," lines 2–4 from *En cest sonet coind'e leri* (PC 29-10). In the next line Arnaut goes on to say that Love "smooths and gilds" his singing ("qu'Amors me deplan'e daura / mon chanter..."). Text and translation from Arnaut Daniel, *The Poetry*, ed. Wilhelm, 40–41. I have modified his translation of lines 2–4 using alternative meanings for *doli* and *capuig* found in his glossary.

the craftsman metaphor: "I deploy both skill and craft, and in it there's no false word to grow rusty, nor one planed down too smooth."[3] "Too smooth" here suggests the slender difference between refinement and over-wrought affectation.

Differentiation of voice works through a delicate balance of formula and invention, of public and private language. This polarity of language fueled the "style wars" among the third generation of troubadours (ca. 1160–1210), which replaced metaphors of craftsmanship with a debate about the function and merit of songs as public entertainment or private expression. Giraut de Bornelh offers a sustained explanation of his choice between accessible (*leu*) and inaccessible (*clus*) styles in the first three stanzas of *A penas sai comenssar*.[4]

I

A penas sai comenssar
un vers que vuoill far leugier,
e si n'ai pensat des hier
qe·l fezes de tal razo
que l'entenda tota gens
e que·l fassa leu chantar;
q'ieu·l fauc per plan deportar.

I hardly know how to begin
a "vers" which I want to make light and easy,
and so I have been thinking since yesterday
how to compose it on a theme
which would be easy for everyone to understand
and easy to sing,
since I am composing it just to give pleasure.

II

Be·l saubra plus cubert far,
mas non a chans pretz entire
qan tuich no·n sunt parsonier.
Qui qe·is n'azir, mi sap bo
qand auch dire per contens
mon sonet rauqet e clar,
e l'auch a la fon portar.

I could certainly make it less explicit,
but a song does not have perfect merit
unless everyone can enjoy it.
Whoever else this may annoy, I am glad
when I hear hoarse and clear voices
vying for one another to sing my song,
and when I hear it being taken to the well.

III

Ia, pois volrai clus trobar,

non cuich aver maint parier,
ab son que ben ai mestier
a far una leu chansso;
q'ieu cuig q'atretant grans sens
es, qui sap razon gardar,
cum es motz entrebescar.

Never, should I want to compose in the
      closed style,
do I think I would have many equals,
given that I serve well
to make an easy song;
for I think that it takes as much great wit
to know how to keep to the theme
as to cleverly weave words together.

---

3. "Detorz e l'art e l'aparelh, / e no·i a motz fals que rovelh, / ni sobredolat d'astehla," lines 62–65 from *Bel m'es qu'eu fass' oimais un vers* (PC 323-9); for text and translation see *Anthology*, 96–97. See also Van Vleck, *Memory and Re-Creation*, 167–73 for a discussion of metaphors of "rust" and "splinters."

4. PC 242-11. For text and translation of this lyric see Giraut de Bornelh, *The Cansos and Sirventes*, ed. Sharman, 196–97; I have modified the translation of stanzas III and IV (below).

These stanzas are remarkable for their explicit concern with singing—the public context, the quality of voices, the ease of memorability and performance. Giraut de Bornelh, it seems, wants to compose what we would call a "pop song," one that appeals to the widest possible audience—including women, who are implied in the domestic task of going to the well.[5] The four stanzas that follow these introductory ones provide exactly that—a highly conventional love song that deploys courtly clichés with ironic banality, as the fourth stanza below illustrates:

IV

D'al m'aven a cossirar;	But my thoughts are elsewhere;
q'ieu am tal cui non enqier	for I love a lady I do not woo,
per so car del cossirier	because by merely thinking of her
sai ben q'ieu fatz mespreiso.	I know too well I am doing wrong.
Que farai? Q'us ardimens	What am I to do? For boldness tells
mi ven que l'an razonar,	me that I should go speak to her,
e paors fai m'o laissar.	and fear makes me hold back.

The lyric, then, presents a grafting of two "voices": one is artful and individual, self-consciously concerned with the principles of composition; the other is artless and generic, reciting the well-worn principles of love. Giraut hints at this graft with the phrase *motz entrebescar*—to weave or entangle words.

Giraut calls his poem a *un vers* (line 1) but also *una leu chansso* (line 18), and he may have been among the first troubadours to distinguish between the two.[6] For Giraut, a *vers* connotes an older genre marked by poetic complexity, moralizing, or satire, while a *chansso* or *canso* connotes the straightforward sentimental love songs of the previous generation, including those of Bernart de Ventadorn. Ruth Sharman argues that with *A penas sai comenssar*, Giraut created "something poetically new," namely, "a *vers* that is *leugier*."[7] This "easy *vers*" is not only new, it is oxymoronic—a generic hybrid made from the graft of the newer-style *canso* to the older-style *vers*. In this way Giraut cleverly constructs the complexity of meaning the lyric superficially denounces and calls attention to the sterility of the *canso*'s language.

---

5. See the editorial remarks in Giraut de Bornelh, *The Cansos and Sirventes*, ed. Sharman, 41. See also Piponnier, "The World of Women," 334.

6. The earliest troubadours used the term *vers* to refer to the song as a whole (words and music) while often reserving *chant* or *canso* with reference to bird songs or to emphasize the song as melody. Elizabeth Poe makes the connection of *chan* to birdsong in "*Segon lo vers del novel chan.*" For a discussion of *chan* as initially music and later as replacing *vers* see Ferrante, "The Craft of the Early Troubadours," 95, 101–105, 110. See Giraut de Bornelh, *The Cansos and Sirventes*, ed. Sharman, 42; and chap. 2, n. 6.

7. Sharman goes on to conclude that "it is possibly this ambiguity of intention, the composition of an easy poem which is at the same time a parody of such poetry, which leads Giraut to call *A penas sai comenssar* a *vers* in imitation of the early troubadours." See, ibid., 42.

With the compositions of the trouvères, the lyrics of medieval song reference the act of composing less frequently, while the music becomes more self-referential. Late monophony in particular often reveals a tension between "ancient" and "modern" practices that accentuates its foundational belatedness—a monophony tricked out with polyphonic melodic styles and notation. The three recomposed *chansons* considered in the previous chapter provide obvious examples of this musical self-consciousness: their heterostrophic, mensural melodies and their unusual formal solutions comment on songcraft itself; in other words, the music is about the composition of music.

This chapter concerns the song-type that medieval scribes called *motet enté*, a term that signals musical grafts and resulting hybrids that trouble notions of genre, form, and voice in ways that spotlight techniques and concepts of songcraft. They present musical analogs to the troubadours' explicit remarks about filing and planing, but here related not to woodworking or metallurgy, but rather to another important technology of production—horticultural grafting. Grafting procedures abound in medieval music. Giraut's grafted *vers-canso* resembles the sudden shift of voice affected by many *tornadas*, as discussed in chapter 1. At their most disjunctive, *tornadas* may appear as the graft of real-world concerns onto the courtly fiction of the stanzas; and those *tornadas* or *envois* that blur into refrain-like repetition or courtly formulas resemble all the more the weaving or grafting of refrains to the stanzas of *chansons* via rhyme.[8] Chapter 3 examined several types of grafting, on the level of *compilatio* with the *libelli* of Thibaut de Champagne and Adam de la Halle, and on the level of composition, especially with *A mon pooir ai servir* and its musical grafting of *cantilena*, *cantus*, and motet features.

The compositions discussed in this chapter differ from the mensural *chansons* added to trouv. *M* in several important ways: they operate on a larger temporal and geographic scale, appearing in many manuscripts, over a longer period of time, and they resemble extracted voice parts of polyphonic motets rather than trouvère *chansons*. They are, in other words, monophonic motets. Table 4.1 offers a preliminary list of such melodies from a survey of the major *chansonniers* and motet collections.[9]

---

8. In the fourteenth-century treatise *L'Art de dictier*, Eustache Deschamps describes the attachment of the *envois* to the final stanza of a *chanson royale* as being "entez par eux aux rimes de la chancon" (themselves grafted to the rhymes of the chansons). Quoted and translated in Butterfield, "*Enté*: A Survey and Reassessment," 95.

9. Incipits whose text is also part of an attested refrain are in italics. I have listed Boogaard's numbers only for those refrains that have multiple sources. See Gennrich, "Trouvèrelieder und Motettenrepertoire." Unlike Gennrich, I have not included in table 4.1 motet parts that appear as multi-stanza songs in *chansonniers*, such as *Quant voi le douz tens venir* (RS 1485; Gen 235), and I have incorporated the collection of *unica* in trouv. *N* and *M*, which Gennrich does not include. I have listed a few single-stanza compositions with schematic melodic repetition, but only those clustered together with other monophonic motets in the manuscripts, such as items 5, 32, and 33 (all three items in trouv. *T* are attributed to Jehan Erars). Though not reported in the table as monophonic motets, the numerous single-stanza *chansons* in trouv. *O* provide a context within which the single monophonic motet (item 30) easily blends. Similarly, the singular monophonic motet in trouv. *X* (item 34) is one of three songs attributed to Robert de Reins (or Rains) grouped together in the manuscript. Importantly, the two associated songs (RS 1510 and 1852), both multi-stanzas compositions in trouv. *X*, appear

TABLE 4.1

Monophonic motets in major sources

No.	Folio	Incipit	Bibliographies		
			RS	Gen	B-ref

Trouv. _M_ (Beck's reconstructed order)

original corpus:

No.	Folio	Incipit	RS	Gen	B-ref
1	B153	_En non Dieu c'est la rage_*†	33	271	665

later additions:

No.	Folio	Incipit	RS	Gen	B-ref
2	B4	_J'aim bele dame et de no[m]_	—	1069	—
3	B4	[Dorme cuers ou n'a nul bien]	—	1070	—
4	B5	_Hé, tres douce amouretes_	—	1071	873
5	B5	L'autrier lés une fontaine	—	1072	—
6	B5ᵛ	_Bone amourete_ m'a souspris	—	1073	289
7	B5ᵛ	_Vous le defoidés l'amer_	—	1074	1859
8	B6ᵛ	_J'ai un chapelet d'argent_	—	1075	985
9	B7ᵛ	Joliement du cuer, du cuer	—	1076	—
10	B204	_Joilietement m'en vois_	—	1076a	1165
11	B204	_J'aim loiaument en espoir_	—	1076b	955

Trouv. _N_ (Everist's reconstructed order)

No.	Folio	Incipit	RS	Gen	B-ref
12	184	Douce seson d'esté que verdissent	1641	—	—
13	184	_Douce dame debonaire_†	—	1077	604
14	184ᵛ	_Hé amors, morrai je_	—	1078	796
15	184ᵛ	Tres haute amor jolie	—	1079	—
16	184ᵛ	Hé Dex, tant doucement	—	1080	—
17	190	D'amors vient et de ma dame	—	1081	—
18	190	_Mesd[isa]nz creveront_†	—	1082	1322
19	190	_Or ai ge trop demoré_	—	1083	1432
20	190ᵛ	_De vos vient li maus, amie_	—	1084	487
21	190ᵛ	Aimi, li maus que j'ai	—	1085	—
22	190ᵛ	Quant plus sui loig de ma dame	—	1086	—
23	189	Hé Dex, que ferai	—	1087	—
24	189	D'amors vient toute ma joie	—	1088	—
25	189	Hé Dex, je n'i puis durer†	—	1089	—
26	189ᵛ	_Amoreusement_ languis por joie avoir	—	1090	144

No.	Folio	Incipit	Bibliographies		
			RS	Gen	B-ref
27	189ᵛ	*[Biaus]Dex, la reverré je ja†*	—	1091	538
28	188ᵛ	D'amor nuit et jor me lo*	—	339a	—
Chansonnier de Mesmes					
29	247	El mois d'avril qu'yver*	—	318	—
Trouv. O					
30	80	Li douz chanz de l'oiseillon*	1877	1138a	—
Trouv. T					
31	131ᵛ	*Mes cuers n'est mie a moi*	1663	1137	1320
32	131ᵛ	Piécha c'on dist par mauvais öir	1801	1137a	—
33	132	L'autrier par une valée	558	1138	—
Trouv. X					
34	189	L'autrier de jouste un rivage	35	—	—
Trouv. a					
35	16ᵛ	Pour noient me reprent*	—	384	—
36	24ᵛ/133ᵛ	En espoir d'avoir merci*	1055	791	—
37	40ᵛ	Je m'estoie, mis en voie*	—	352	—
38	50ᵛ	Par main s'est levée*	—	528c	—
39	82ᵛ	Tout adés me troveres*	—	153	—
40	82ᵛ	Bele se vous ne m'amés*	—	52	—
41	104ᵛ	Je n'os a m'amier aler*	—	199	—
42	113ᵛ	Renvoisiement i vois a mon ami	—	1143a	—
43	144ᵛ	Douce dame par amors*	—	711	—
Mo					
44	268ᵛ	Onc voir par amours n'amai	—	1039	—
Fauvel					
45	26ᵛ	*Han, Diex! our pourrai je trouver*	—	895a	—

Italics indicate attested refrains.
* Indicates concordances in polyphonic motet repertory.
† Indicates concordances in trouv. *I*.

Altogether these monophonic motets present an odd assortment of pieces with numbers too large to be simply aberrations and too small to suggest a coherent "genre." Rather, the word "phenomenon" seems more appropriate for these compositions, complexly related by their musical and poetic features and various deployments in the manuscript sources. While the recomposed *chansons* considered in chapter 3 called attention to the autonomous voice of a particular scribe, the monophonic motets, or *motets entés* as the medieval scribes called them, represent a sustained collective interest in creating songs that cross-pollinate monophonic and polyphonic repertories, and, at the same time, differentiate a single voice from a polyphonic crowd.

THE POLYPHONY OF THE VOICE

En non Dieu c'est la rage will serve as our introduction to the monophonic motet (see example 4.1 ⊘ OXFORD WEB MUSIC). The words and music together survive in four sources: in two *chansonniers* as monophonic songs with attributions to "*li moine de Saint Denis*" (the monk of Saint Denis) and two polyphonic motet collections as the upper voice of a two-part motet (also attributed to "*li moine de St. Denis*" in one of these).[10] The melody and poetry look nothing like typical trouvère *chansons*, whose multiple stanzas reiterate schematic designs of syllable count, rhyme, and melodic repetition. In contrast, the whole of *En non Dieu c'est la rage* roughly equals one stanza of a modest *chanson* and presents a brief expression of emotional anguish rather than a slow unfolding of courtly appeals and complaints. Furthermore, the line lengths, rhymes, and melody do not create any definitive patterns. Rather, exclamations indicative of a popular poetic register provide a frame for the poem: the first exclamation is one of those courtly aphorisms or refrains that appears in multiple lyrical contexts, while the final exclamation seems to be a musically-

---

in other sources as voice parts in polyphonic motets. I have also generally excluded motet parts recorded as seemingly independent melodies (that is, without any tenor incipit or spatial provision for a tenor part) within a designated group of polyphonic motets (with the exception in *Mo*, to be discussed later). This occurs mostly in trouv. *T* and *a*, where the casual treatment of tenor parts conveys a sense of optionality, tantalizingly suggestive of monophonic performances, especially with regard to the *unica* motet melodies in *T* (Gen 1033, 1034, 1035, 1036). For a discussion of these, see Wolinski, "Tenors Lost and Found." While these excluded songs and motet melodies relate to the phenomenon I am tracing here by illustrating interchanges among polyphonic motet and monophonic *chanson* repertories, the songs listed in table 4.1 engage those two repertories in a qualitatively different way by maintaining certain formal and, as I will argue, possibly functional distinctions. I should also note here the parallel phenomenon in Latin repertories: four isolated and texted organa parts interrupt the second alphabetical collection of two-part motets in fascicle 7 of *W2* (fols. 167–73), and fifteen Latin single-stanza monophonic songs with ornate free melodies appear in the Las Huelgas Codex (ca. 1300); see Anderson, *Las Huelgas Manuscript*, 2:112–20.

10. The monophonic versions appear in trouv. *M*, fol. 168 (B153) and trouv. *T*, fol. 61; the polyphonic versions appear *W2*, fol. 227 and *Mo*, fol. 234, the latter of which carries the attribution. Huot briefly discusses the two-part motet in *Allegorical Play*, 172–73.

derived series of repeated words with a concluding remark that resembles a refrain but has no other attested contexts:

En non Dieu, c'est la rage	*In the name of God, lovesickness is madness*
que li maus d'amors s'il ne m'asoage!	*if I have no relief!*
Ne puis soufrir son outrage,	I cannot suffer this outrage,
mon corage en retrairai	I will withdraw my heart from it
de li partirai.	and take my leave of love.
Mais n'est pas par moi,	But it is not in me,
car quant la voi la voi la voi	for when I see her, see her, see her,
la bele la blonde a li m'otroi.	the beautiful, the blonde, I grant myself to her.

EXAMPLE 4.1 *En non Dieu c'est la rage* from trouv. *M*, fol. 168

The melody is held together not by repeating structural pillars that index a form, but by low-level motivic manipulations—a compositional aspect that characterizes both *chanson* and polyphonic motet melodies—in this case, the melodic motif of an upper neighbor-note ornament, always notated by a liquescent or a ligature incorporating the highest note of the phrase (see lines 1–3 and 5–6). The melody strongly projects G as an organizing pitch, with D as a secondary point of repose, and can be parsed into pairs of lines by melodic contour and by semblances of open and closed endings. Another striking feature of this piece is the penultimate line, which interrupts the undulating melody with a completely static phrase. Thus the entire song closes with an aural disjunction— literally a refrain recitation. In sum, this monophonic motet is a single stanza of free verse set to an unpatterned but coherent melody, traditionally called "through composed." I prefer to call it "free melody," to match the usual description of the verse. Free melody, like the rhymes of free verse, may have melodic echoes sprinkled throughout in unexpected ways; and, like the rhythmic patterns of free verse, may have line lengths that form brief or extended moments of correlation, or they may have none of these things.

Before trying to determine the number of extant monophonic motets, certain distinctions must first be made. Many strophic free melodies, though not free verses, survive in the troubadour repertory of courtly *cansos*; they are far less common, though not necessarily exceptional, among the more homogeneous courtly *chansons* of the trouvères. Some *contrafacta* of multi-stanza troubadour songs have been recorded as single-stanza free melodies in Northern *chansonniers*, and these do stand out for their less regular melodic and sometimes poetic constructions.[11] They should be kept in mind as an important background to the pieces under consideration here. Another important background is that of the *descorts* discussed in chapter 2, with their principle of large-scale free (or discordant) composition. Despite their free melodies, I believe these two originally strophic forms (or anti-strophic in the case of the *descort*) are only distant relatives of *En non Dieu c'est la rage*; rather, it belongs to the large family of single-stanza French free verses and melodies found in thirteenth-century polyphonic motets, from which it may have originated.

The impact of polyphonic motets on monophonic song composition has received little attention. Sizeable anthologies of polyphonic motets, most with vernacular lyrics derived from the trouvère tradition, were compiled alongside the *chansonniers*. The occasional inclusion of polyphony in monophonic anthologies shows these repertories to be rubbing shoulders.[12] Most scholars investigating relationships among polyphonic motets, trouvère

---

11. See, for example, *Pour longue atente de merci* (RS 1057), uniquely recorded in trouv. *O*, fol. 105 as a single-stanza free melody, which is a *contrafactum* of Bernart de Ventadorn's *Ara non vei luzir soleill* (PC 70-7) as recorded in trouv. *M*, fol. 190/B180. Trouv. *O* contains quite a few single-stanza songs, many with isosyllabic poetic lines and a *pedes-cauda* melodic design.

12. Two *chansonniers*, trouv. *M* and *T*, include polyphonic motet gatherings; trouv. *O* includes the single motet *Bien m'ont amors entre pris*/TENOR, fol. 21 (Gen 942a), ending the block of songs beginning with the letter B. The singleton monophonic motet in *Mo* is discussed below.

chansons, and other monophonic genres such as *rondeaux* and *pastourelles*, have focused on the absorption of monophonic forms and lyrics by the newer, more technologically advanced polyphonic genre.[13] Yet of all medieval musical genres, the thirteenth-century motet is the hardest to fathom. Most students of music history know the motet as crazy little contrapuntal pieces in which each voice has its own lyrics, so that the different texts all sound simultaneously. Though the contexts and aesthetics of motets remain as obscure as the words in motet performances, their origin seems sure. The motet, as the story goes, evolved from the late twelfth-century Parisian practice of amplifying liturgical chants with melodic counterpoint and distinctive rhythms systematically disposed according to the musical map of the chant. Given the extensive polyphonic liturgical repertory, musicians soon began to extrapolate certain sections—coinciding with the melismatic portions of the chant (discant clausulae)—for further development, eventually adding non-strophic words (first sacred, then secular) to the composed melodies sung over the chant melismas, and also adding third or fourth voices to the mix.[14] Theoretical treatises, beginning ca. 1240, applied the Latin term "motetus" (or the variant "motellus") to the voice part that is verbally articulated within a two-part polyphonic texture, or to the entire polyphonic composition that included one or more verbally articulated voices. This generic identification is corroborated by rubrics in the vernacular, such as *Ci commencent li motet* in trouv. *M*, which introduce collections of polyphony.

This seems a tidy history, but of course the reality is far less so. Medieval sources for the term "motet" roughly contemporaneous with the sources of polyphonic music we call motets in fact transmit a wide range of referents.[15] The majority of late thirteenth-century instances of the vernacular word "motet" occur in association with the introduction and apparent quotation of refrains appended to or embedded within a larger literary or musical context such as a verse narrative or *chanson* as table 4.2 illustrates.[16] Thus for a

---

13. See Gennrich, "Trouvèrelieder und Motettenrepertoire"; for more recent scholarship see especially Atchison, "*Bien me sui aperceuz*"; Huot, *Allegorical Play*, esp. 1–55; Everist, *French Motets*, esp. 90–125; and Page, *Discarding Images*, esp. 43–64, 93–111.

14. Mark Everist recounts this narrative of the motet and the compositional procedures that define it; see *French Motets*, 4–6.

15. For a discussion of the history, etymology, and references associated with "motet" and "motetus" and their variants, see Hofmann, "Zur Enstehungs- und Frühgeschichte des Terminus Motette" and Beiche, "Motet/motetus/mottetto/Motette." The French *motet* appears in a *chanson de geste* from the end of the twelfth century (see ibid., 1).

16. For the passages from *Renart le nouvel* see Jacquemart Gielée, *Renart le nouvel*, ed. Roussel. There are a total of five such uses of the word "motet" to introduce refrains; see also lines 2409, 6777, and the alternate versions of lines 6963 or 6967 listed in Roussel's edition. For more examples see Hofmann, "Zur Enstehungs- und Frühgeschichte des Terminus Motette," 142–44, and Beiche, "Motet/motetus/mottetto/Motette," 7–9; neither provides an exhaustive list, however. Taking account of Hofmann, Beiche, and my own findings, I count at least fifteen unambiguous references to refrains. Beiche considers separately the use of the word "motet" to introduce refrains (II.1) from its references to little songs of an unspecified type (II.2), and from *motets entés*, which he places under the category of polyphonic music (III.1).

TABLE 4.2
___

"Motet" as refrain
___

1. From *Renart le nouvel* (trouv. *W*, fol. 165ᵛ)

lines 6729–33:

Aprés che cant, li respondi	After this song, the leopardess responded
Li luparde en cantant ensi	in singing thus
Che **motet** plein de melodie:	this motet full of melody:
Vous arés le singnourie, amis de moi,	*You will have the sovereignty, my friend,*
che que mes maris n'a mie.	*that my husband doesn't have at all.*

lines 6739–42:

Et quant chius ot pardit son cant,	And when he had finished his song,
Chele recanta pié estant,	she sang again, standing on her feet,
Che **motet** plaisant et joli:	this pleasant and pretty motet:
E Diex! si tres douc non a en ami.	*Ah, God! so very sweet to be called friend.*

2. From *Quant je voi l'erbe amatir* (Perrin d'Angicourt: trouv. *N*, fol. 52)

I

Quant je voi l'erbe amatir	When I see the grass wither
et le felon tens entre	and bad weather return,
qui fet ces oiseax taisir	which makes birds fall silent
et lessier joliete,	and cease the pleasure of love,
pour ce n'ai je pas osté	for this I have not removed
mon cuer de loial desir;	my heart from its loyal desire;
mes pour mon us maintenir	but in order to maintain my service
a cest **motet** me reclaim:	I turn to this motet:
Je sui jolis por ce que	*I am happy because of the one*
J'aim.	*I love.*

II

J'aim loiaument sanz trahir,	I love loyally and without betrayal,
sanz faindre et sanz fauseté	without deceit and without falseness
cele qui me fet languir	the one who makes me languish
sanz avoir de moi pité.	without having pity for me.
Et bien set de verité	And she knows truly

que je sui seins sanz guenchir;	that I am hers without hesitation;
mes en espoir de merci	but in the hope of mercy
li ert cest **motet** chantez:	this motet will be sung to her:
Dame, merci! vos m'ociez.	*Lady, have mercy, you slay me.*

medieval audience of vernacular song, the word "motet," perhaps more often than not, signaled the quotation of a refrain rather than polyphony. This accords with the fact that *motet* is a diminutive form of *mot*, literally translated as "wordlet" or "phraselet"—a cognate of the English word "motto."[17]

As discussed in chapter 1, refrains operate much like proverbs; they are courtly aphorisms circulating freely in the public domain, representing a public voice. Early scholars presumed that all refrains originated as structurally repeating elements in dance songs, and that refrains were sung by a chorus of voices in response to the verses sung by a solo lead singer, as outlined below (see example 4.2 🎵 OXFORD WEB MUSIC).[18]

Chorus:	A	*Prendés i garde, s'on mi regarde!*	*Take care, lest someone sees me!*
	B	*S'on mi regarde, dites le moi.*	*If someone sees me, tell me.*
Solo:	a	C'est tout la jus, en cel boschaige	It's just over there, in that wood
Chorus:	A	—*prendés i garde, s'on mi regarde!*—	—*take care, lest someone sees me!*—
Solo:	a	la pastourele u gardoit vaches.	where the shepherdess kept watch over her cows.
	b	Plaisant brunete a vous m'otroi.	Sweet brunette, I offer myself to you.
Chorus:	A	*Prendés i garde, s'on mi regarde!*	*Take care, lest someone sees me!*
	B	*S'on mi regarde, dites le moi.*	*If someone sees me, tell me.*

This early *rondeau*, attributed to Willammes d'Amiens li paignieres in trouv. *a* (fol. 119ᵛ), is deceptively simple, given its economy of music and words, yet under closer scrutiny a complexity of voice and narrative emerges. Solo and chorus articulate the same subject-position, and the elliptical language gives us just enough clues to piece together a scene: the protagonist has returned to a pastoral setting to spy on a shepherdess, bringing with

---

17. See Page, *Discarding Images*, 60; and Peraino, "*E pui conmencha a canter*: Refrains, Motets and Melody," 3–4.

18. B-rond 93; see also Gennrich, *Rondeaux, Virelais und Balladen*, I:38.

EXAMPLE 4.2 *Prendés i garde* from trouv. *a*, fol. 119ᵛ

him a companion to watch for those who might spy him spying. The chain of voyeurs and spies is as circular as the song form itself, defined by the partial return of the refrain mid-strophe. The imperatives of the refrain implicate the singers/audience in the secretive, uncourtly activity, as they call to one another to be on the lookout. Yet the last line of the verse abruptly shifts tone, addressing the shepherdess with an outburst of submissive courtly devotion. The verse "C'est tout la jus" belongs to one of two common "strophic types"; one describes a pastoral scene *la gieus* (over there), the other describes the stock character Bele Aeliz. As Ardis Butterfield points out, the relationship of verse and refrain, solo and chorus, is not what we expect: it is the solo material that is formulaic, while the presumably public refrain in fact becomes the distinguishing feature of the *rondeau*.[19]

Butterfield (quoting Mikhail Bakhtin) asserts that refrains represent "the image of another's language." She explains, "since refrains are a form of common language, that this is everybody's way of speaking…[r]efrains both set up and break down barriers between different kinds of hold over speech: between mine and yours, ours and theirs, his and hers."[20] Continuing with Bakhtin's own language, we could call the *rondeau Prendés i garde* "polyphonic" in his sense of the word. Bakhtin formulated the notion of literary polyphony to describe Dostoevsky's narrative poetics—specifically his attempt to express a synchronous, non-hierarchical "plurality of independent and unmerged voices and consciousnesses." Although a given text is "single-authored," and by convention closed in some manner, it represents a "dialogue that is in principle unfinalizable."[21] Such is the case with *Prendés i garde*, where the refrain signifies a public voice (manifested in a choral performance) as well as the individual voice of the composer Willammes d'Amiens and the fictional protagonist of the song. While these voices seem merged in the refrain, the *rondeau's* form—its division of a single subject-position between solo and chorus, the interruption of the verse with the partial return of the refrain—enacts the dialogic property of the lyric.

The seeming autonomy of refrains and how they come to represent "the image of another's language" stems not only from their identifying and interruptive function in *rondeaux*, but also from their mobility from song to song and genre to genre, creating an intertextual network of pieces that participate in an larger "unfinalizable" cultural dialogue, sometimes extending well beyond their particular historical moments. Indeed, the majority of refrains cataloged by Boogaard appear in non-repeating contexts, such as motets, *chansons avec des refrains*, and verse narratives (see table 4.2 above).[22] The refrain *Prendés i garde* appears in the triplum and motetus of a three-part motet, *S'on me regarde/Prennés i garde/HÉ, MI ENFANT*, in fascicle 8 of the motet codex *Mo*, compiled at nearly the same time as the *chansonnier* that transmits the *rondeau*

---

19. Butterfield, *Poetry and Music*, 46–48. See also Everist's discussion of the two *rondeaux type-cadres* in *French Motets*, 97–101.

20. Butterfield, *Poetry and Music*, 243.

21. Morson and Emerson, *Mikhail Bakhtin: Creation of a Prosaics*, 239. For Bakhtin, polyphony describes the creative process more than the formal construction of the finished product, since the conventions of the novel dictate some sort of closure. See also Bakhtin, *Problems of Dostoevsky's Poetics*, trans. Emerson, esp. 39; and Fast, "Bakhtin and the Discourse of Late Medieval Music Theory."

22. This is made obvious by the fact that Boogaard catalogued 1,876 refrains but only 198 *rondeaux*. See also Butterfield, *Poetry and Music*, 42–49 and 75–102; Saltzstein, "Wandering Voices: Refrain Citation in Thirteenth-Century French Music and Poetry," 20–27 and 93–130; and Saltzstein, "Relocating the Thirteenth-Century Refrain," esp. 249–53.

TABLE 4.3

Parallel texts and translations for *S'on me regarde/Prennés i garde/HÉ, MI ENFANT*

TRIPLUM		MOTETUS	
S'on me regarde,	*If someone sees me,*	Prennés i garde,	*Take care*
s'on me regarde,	*if someone sees me*	s'on me regard;	*if someone sees me;*
dites le moi;	*tell me;*	trop sui gaillarde,	*I am too bold,*
trop sui gaillarde,	*I am too bold*	dites le moi,	*tell me,*
bien l'aperchoi.	*I see it well.*	pour Dieu vous proi.	*for God's sake I beg you.*
Ne puis laissier que mon	*I cannot but let my*	Car tes m'esgarde,	*For a certain one looks at me,*
regard ne s'esparde,	*eyes wonder*	dont mout me tarde,	*for which I am very impatient,*
car tes m'esgarde,	*for a certain one looks at me*	qu'il m'ait o[u] soi,	*that I am where he is*
dont mout me tarde,	*for which I am very impatient*	bien l'aperchoi;	*I see it well;*
qu'il m'ai o[u] soi,	*that I am where he is*	et tel chi voi,	*and I see that one*
qu'il a en foi	*so that he has in faith*	qui est, je croi,	*who is, I believe,*
de m'amour plan otroi.	*the full gift of my love.*	(feu d'enfer l'arde!)	*(hellfire burn him!)*
Mais tel ci voi,	*but I see that one*	jalous de moi.	*jealous of me.*
qui est, je croi,	*who is, I believe,*	Mais pour li	*But not for him*
(feu d'enfer l'arde!)	*(hellfire burn him!)*	d'amer ne recroi,	*will I renounce loving,*
jalous de moi.	*jealous of me.*	pour nient m'esgarde,	*he watches me for nothing,*
Mais pour li	*But not for him*	bien pert sa garde:	*he wastes his time:*
d'amer ne recroi,	*will I renounce loving,*	j'arai rechoi	*I will have an escape,*
car par ma foi	*for by my faith*	et de mon ami le dosnoi.	*and the wooing of my lover.*
pour nient m'esgarde,	*he watches me for nothing,*	Faire le doi!	*I must do it!*
bien per sa garde:	*he wastes his time:*	Ne serai plus couarde.	*I will no longer be cowardly.*
J'arai rechoi!	*I will have an escape.*		
TENOR: *Hé, MI ENFANT*	*(Ah, my child)*		

EXAMPLE 4.3 *S'on me regarde/Prennés i garde*/HÉ, MI ENFANT, no. 325 in *The Montpellier Codex*, Part 3: *Fascicles 6, 7, and* 8, edited by Hans Tischler, Recent Researches in the Music of the Middle Ages and Early Renaissance, vols. 6–7. Madison, WI: A-R Editions, Inc., 1978.

EXAMPLE 4.3 Continued

(see table 4.3).[23] Triplum and motetus sing the two halves of the refrain text and a close version of the *rondeau* tune simultaneously, but with their phrases reversed so that the first half (*Prennés i garde*) sounds in counterpoint to the second (*S'on me regarde*); see example 4.3.

The musical phrases of the *rondeau* tune provide key melodic ideas that reappear in identical or varied form in both voices, sometimes resembling imitative counterpoint (see mm. 10–12). Both music and text present a fantasy on the themes of the *rondeau*; as the upper voices stack, exchange, and "chase" musical motifs from the source song, the lyrics of both parts (nearly identical in content but rearranged in form) elaborate the theme of watching and being watched, changing the subject-position from the *rondeau*'s male

---

23. The *rondeau* appears in trouv. *a*, which is dated late thirteenth to early fourteenth century. *S'on me regarde/ Prennés i garde/HÉ, MI ENFANT* (Gen 908/9) is motet number 325 in *Mo*, currently beginning on fol. 373v (after the loss of two folios). See Tischler, *The Montpellier Codex*, III:199–200. The dating of the eight fascicles of *Mo* has been much debated. Most scholars agree, however, that fascicles 2–6 form a coherent group (the "old corpus") compiled over a period of time between 1270 and 1280. Fascicles 1 and 7 are usually dated in the late thirteenth century (1280s–1290s), and fascicle 8 in the early fourteenth century (ca. 1300–10). Mary Wolinski dates the compilation of fascicles 1–7 between 1260 and 1270, and includes the compositional style of the fascicle 8 motets in that period as well, though it may have been compiled somewhat later (1270s). See Wolinski, "The Compilation of the Montpellier Motet Codex"; Mark Everist, *Polyphonic Music*, 110–34; Sanders and Lefferts, "Sources, MS, §V: Early Motet." Fascicle 8 contains an assortment of *ars antiqua* motets, proto *ars nova* motets with syllabic semibreves, as well as Anglo-Norman motets. *S'on me regarde/Prennés i garde/HÉ, MI ENFANT* is an *ars antiqua* motet with some unusual features, as will be discussed here and in the conclusion. See also the discussion of this motet in Evans, "Women *Trouvères*: Just the Same Old Refrains?," 6–9.

voyeur to the female object of the gaze. But the object of the gaze in the *rondeau* becomes in the motet the subject who watches—for the spying admirer who pleases her, and the jealous one from whom she hides. Thus the "common language" of the refrain becomes, in this extended cultural dialogue, the uncommon language of a woman—the image of the Other's language.

Let us turn from this fascinating intertextual complex of words and music (which will be discussed again in the conclusion) to consider the eyes and ears of a medieval reader of this motet. Scribes recorded the many voices of polyphonic motets in parts rather than score, dividing the page into quadrants and recording each part as if its own monophonic song (see figure 4.1).

The reader focuses on one part at a time, seeing the other texts peripherally. This experience of reading, with an eye to peripheral texts, would have been familiar to students and scribes poring over central texts and their marginal glosses—sometimes two or three "voices" thick. The experience of singing a polyphonic motet replicates the relationship between central text (one's own part) and the peripheral voices that give musical and textual context. With the density of simultaneous lyrics and melodies, the full appreciation of the intertextual referencing among parts can only occur if one studies the voice parts in succession, and then, in the midst of performance, hears peripherally the unfolding of those references over time. The static score that modern scholars transcribe represents what the medieval ear would have heard as fleeting relationships of words and notes.[24]

The peripheral listening that was surely part of the appeal of motets may also have yielded an appreciation of the melody-types that combine in the polyphonic complex. The differently texted parts moving at roughly the same pace maintain their independence of lines—their differentiation of voice—to a much greater extent than the later rhythmically stratified motets or single-texted motets of later eras. From a singer's point of view, in a motet such as *S'on me regarde/Prennés i garde/HÉ, MI ENFANT* one's own melody would have an independent identity, yet maintain a tight connection to the surrounding lines by shared words or phrases, melodic motifs, and sonorous blending of tones even when syllables and vowels clash. This dual condition of autonomy and contextual dependency of motet parts also describes the condition of refrains.[25]

Ardis Butterfied argues that the thirteenth-century refrain functioned to explore and trouble the boundaries of form and genre, but also of register (implying also social status). Refrain-citation practices in thirteenth-century narratives, *chansons*, and

---

24. For other considerations of the experience of polyphonic motets in performance, see Clark, "Hearing Text and Music in a Medieval Motet"; Page, *Discarding Images*, 343–57. Huot, *Allegorical Play*, is a book-length study of the interrelationships between the texts of motets, with an occasional discussion of word sounds and musical relationships.

25. Nico Boogaard called the refrain a "genre having its own laws" but also a "parasite" living in "symbiosis" with other genres; see his *Rondeaux et Refrains*, 17. The other important study of refrains as an autonomous genre is Doss-Quinby, *Les Refrains chez les trouvères*.

FIGURE 4.1 The motet *S'on me regarde/Prennés i garde/HÉ, MI ENFANT,* Bibliothèque Universitaire de medicine de Montpellier H196, fol. 373ᵛ (IRHT-BIU Montpellier)

motets, she contends, create generic and registral hybrids, while the repeating refrain forms of dance songs create hybrids of voice. This compelling portrait of refrains suggests their autonomy in the minds of medieval composers, yet no medieval sources transmit a discrete collection of refrains, nor do medieval treatises on poetry discuss rules for their composition. A handful of polyphonic motets are made entirely of refrains; these and lengthy successions of refrains interpolated into verse narratives form the only type of collection or *florilegium* for refrains.[26] For my purposes, the conceptual complexity of voice attendant to refrains is more important than tracking citations. Hybrid genres such as the *motet enté* may allude to the voice(s) of refrains without actually quoting them. Refrains as a category of literary language function as a foil to the concept of the single-authored, single-voiced *chanson*, as do the multiple sets of lyrics in polyphonic motets. While two-voice motets (motetus and tenor) offer a polyphonic texture that is thin enough to be perceived as a melody plus patterned rhythmic accompaniment, the simultaneous melodies and lyrics in three-part and four-part motets seem a direct aural challenge to the illusion of the singular subjective voice of *chansons*. Motets (polyphony) and motets (refrains) converge in the plurality of voices they represent, whether successively as solo and chorus, or simultaneously as stacked voices; and their shared trait of brevity demands a context for interpretation or completion.

THE *MOTET ENTÉ* IN CONTEXT

Returning to the list of monophonic motets in table 4.1, the distribution of these pieces seems to have been narrow; in fact, most are local to a single manuscript. Twenty-seven have unique extant sources while thirteen (marked with an asterisk) have concordances in the polyphonic motet repertory.[27] A provocative number of these monophonic motets are transmitted in three manuscripts: eleven in trouv. *M*, seventeen in trouv. *N*, and nine in trouv. *a*. In addition to these, but not inventoried in table 4.1, sixty-three single-stanza lyrics, identified as *rondeaux* and *motets entés* in the secondary literature, survive in the early fourteenth-century manuscript trouv. *I*, a source from the northeastern Lorraine region that contains only lyrics, arranged and labeled by genre (though the section of *rondeaux* and *motets entés* is unmarked).[28] Five *motets entés* in this collection have concordances with notated monophonic versions in table 4.1 (marked with a dagger), and only fourteen have concordances in polyphonic motets.

---

26. On the "refrain-cento" motets see Everist, "The Refrain Cento", and Everist, *French Motets*, 109–25. Saltzstein, "Relocating the Thirteenth-Century Refrain," has proposed that certain refrains functioned within clerical, scholastic practices of quotation as "vernacular *auctoritas.*"

27. Items 1 and 33 in the table appear as monophonic songs in both trouv. *M* and *T*.

28. The manuscript includes a table of contents and section rubrics that identify various genres (*grans chans, estampies, ieus partis, pastorelles, ballettes, sottes chansons contre amours*). The motets are inventoried in Ludwig, *Repertorium organorum* I, I:307–13. See also Atchison, *The Chansonnier of Oxford Bodleian MS Douce 308*, esp. 36.

The collection of monophonic motets in trouv. *a* offers the best starting point for understanding the significance and perhaps derivation of this song-type, since, unlike the other three main sources for monophonic motets, most of these monophonic motets also appear as voices in a polyphonic complex.[29] The compilers of trouv. *a* organized its contents by genre (*chançons, pastoureles, motet et roundel*, and *partures*) and by composer within the main gatherings of *chansons*. Eight of the nine monophonic motets were recorded at the ends of gatherings, most of which coincide with the ends of author groups (recall the similar disposition of the added pieces to trouv. *M* discussed in chapters 2 and 3). *Renvoisiement i vois a mon ami*, exceptional both as an *unicum* and in its position in the middle of the last *chanson* gathering, nevertheless comes at the end of a group by Cuvelier, though it bears an attribution to *maistre richars*. Nearly all the *chanson* gatherings and those of the *pastourelles*, motets, and *rondeaux*, and the fifteen *chançons de Nostre Dame* by Willaumes li Viniers, close with a monophonic motet or an allied musical and poetic composition, such as a multi-stanza song with a concordance in a polyphonic motet (*Onques n'amai tant con fui amée*, RS 498, Gen 820), or a *rondeau*. This pattern suggests a programmatic significance to their placement rather than simply opportunistic filling of empty space. A number of details further strengthens the impression of calculated distribution: (1) the monophonic motets are written in the main hand (as is one of the three similarly positioned *rondeaux*), and five are listed in the table of contents along with the *chansons* in the author group; (2) *En espoir d'avoir merci* was entered twice, concluding a *chanson* gathering and in the motet section; (3) two monophonic motets (*Tout adés me troveres* and *Bele se vous ne m'amés*) are clustered at the end of a *chanson* gathering and listed in the table of contents; (4) there is leftover space, ample enough for multiple stanzas of words, after *Je n'os a m'amier aler*. The parceling out of these songs probably took place at a later stage of production than that of the central *chanson* corpus, as evidenced by the fact that of the monophonic motets only *Par main s'est levée* was notated, as was the second entry of *En espoir d'avoir merci* in the motet section.[30] Thus it seems as if the producers of this *chansonnier* made a second pass through the collection, deciding to caulk the seams between *chanson* gatherings with distinctly non-*chanson* material, even going so far as to recycle a melody already entered in the motet section.

The idea of a musical caulk brings us close to the term *motet enté*, or "grafted motet"—a term that appears in a number of medieval sources, most importantly at the end of trouv. *N*, and in the lost *Chansonnier de Mesmes*.[31] Trouv. *N* belongs to a group of four

---

29. These are inventoried and described in Ludwig, *Repertorium organorum* I, II:574–81.

30. Of all nine pieces, *Par main s'est levée* is the only one with a concordance in the motet section of the related trouv. *M*, where the same melody is similarly recorded without provision for a tenor on fol. 207ᵛ/B200ᵛ. This may account for the monophonic motet's singular notation in trouv. *a*.

31. For a discussion of this lost source, see Karp, "A Lost Medieval Chansonnier."

FIGURE 4.2 The rubric *Ci conmencent li motet ente* from trouv. *N*, fol. 184 (Bibliothèque nationale de France, Paris)

closely-related *chansonniers* (*KNPX*), but is distinguished by a final collection of anonymous single-stanza monophonic songs, *lais*, and a *note*. The rubric *Ci conmencent li motet ente* (Here begin the *motets entés*; see figure 4.2) announces this extra group of monophonic songs from the unusual position of the right-hand margin, while the *lais* and the *note* are given individual rubrics.

The total number of *motets entés* originally gathered here is unknown owing to missing folios between these and the start of the *lais*.[32] Two more related songs are appended to either end of this assembly: the first, *Douce seson d'esté que verdissent*, precedes the rubric announcing the *motets entés*, though its free verse and melody look quite similar to the following fifteen songs;[33] the second piece, *D'amor nuit et jor me lo*, comes after the *lais* to close off the manuscript, and looks more like a polyphonic motet part than any of the others, with vertical lines grouping single notes and short phrases into rhythmic patterns that all but cry out for its complementary tenor. Indeed, this song does show up elsewhere as the top voice in a two-part motet, which will be discussed later in this chapter.

The lost *Chansonnier de Mesmes*, according to a detailed sixteenth-century description, was a grand manuscript whose contents placed it squarely within the *KNPX* group. Theodore Karp observed that *Mesmes* seems closest to trouv. *K*, but the reconstructed inventory lists a collection of five separately rubricated *lais* (one with a concordance in trouv. *N*), one rubricated and texted *estampie*, and a concluding rubric *Cy commencent li motet ente*, all of which link the collection to *N* as well.[34] The inventory included only the one incipit under this last rubric (listed in table 4.1), so nothing conclusive can be advanced about the number and type of compositions that followed. Given the similarities of rubrication and content at the end of the manuscript with that of trouv. *N*, I think it safe to presume that more than one entry existed, and that these entries were also monophonic motets.

Until recently, most scholars of medieval music understood *motet enté* to indicate that a pre-existing, musically and poetically autonomous refrain (motet), was split in a syntactically logical place and "grafted" (*enté*) onto the front and back and sometimes into the middle of newly-composed melodic material.[35] In ideal examples, the words and music of a refrain have traveled together from one source to another and can be clearly identified as a quotation. Word and music ties for *chansons* are notoriously fraught with variants and alternate melodies; the same is true for refrains, complicated further by the few examples that survive with multiple concordances (only 136 of the nearly 2,000 cataloged

32. The folios in this last section have been bound out of order. Ludwig reconstructed the order of the *motets entés* and the *lais* in *Repertorium organorum* I, I:306–307.

33. Spanke, in RS, corrected Raynaud's designation of the piece as a *lai* to that of an "anscheinend Motettenteil" (apparent motet-part); see 228.

34. The *lai* that also appears in trouv. *N* is "*La lais des Hermins*" *Lonc tens m'ai teü* (RS 2060). See Espiner-Scott, *Documents concernant la vie et les oeuvres de Claude Fauchet*, 264–71 for a complete description and inventory; see also Karp, "A Lost Medieval Chansonnier," 54–56.

35. See Ludwig, *Repertorium organorum*, I, I:305, Rokseth, *Polyphonies du XIIIᵉ siècle*, 4:211–12. A later generation of scholars enlarged the number of pieces they considered to be *motets entés* to include the grafting of refrains in the middle of pieces as well. See Hoppin, *Medieval Music*, 338–40, and Yudkin, *Music in Medieval Europe*, 402–12.

refrains).[36] Among the so-labeled *motets entés* in trouv. *N*, less than half (seven) contain refrains that are corroborated in other sources, and only two of these attested refrains have indisputable corroboration for the music as well.[37] Furthermore, only four songs clearly demonstrate a splitting and grafting process with corroborated refrains. Given the tenuous or speculative identification of medieval refrains in these pieces, Mark Everist, in his book *French Motets*, attempted to find another procedural referent for the generic rubric *motet enté* in trouv. *N*—one that did not hinge on the manipulation of refrains.

Everist found that of the fifteen pieces he considered, a majority use a substantial amount of internal melodic repetition, and a subset of these repeats the opening one or

EXAMPLE 4.4 *Quant plus sui loig de ma dame* from trouv. *N*, fols. 190ᵛ and 189

36. Jennifer Saltzstein has determined that seventy-four of these 136 refrains have relatively stable melodic transmission, taking into account the usual range of melodic variants. She calls these "intertextual refrains" to stress their function as quotation; see "Relocating the Thirteenth-Century Refrain," 256–62. Only four of the refrains in the monophonic motets listed in table 4.1 (items 1, 7, 13, and 14) appear in her list of seventy-four with stable melodies (see her 256n74).

37. See Everist, *French Motets*, 82–83; Butterfield, "*Enté*: A Survey and Reassessment," 80–81. Corroborated melodies are Gen 1077 (Gen 472), and Gen 1090 (Gen 9, RS 1148, refrain I). The refrain for Gen 1078 also appears in Gen 9 and 10, with music that bears a slight resemblance to the first half of the refrain, but not to the second.

two phrases at the end of the piece for a musical rounding effect. One such song is *Quant plus sui loig de ma dame*, transcribed in example 4.4:

Quant plus sui loig de ma dame,	When I am the farthest from my lady,
plus m'i destraint fine amor.	true love holds me all the more in its grasp.
Mes tant m'en plest la dolor	But the pain of it pleases me so
qu'en ce me reconfort	that it comforts me
quant je sa valor recort,	when I recall her worth,
et je plus i pens souvent.	and I think of her more often.

This short piece shows a highly economical use of melodic material, much like *En non Dieu c'est la rage*, but, importantly, the opening phrase of music returns for the last line (compare lines 1 and 6) and also provides the chief melodic gesture beginning nearly every subsequent phrase (lines 2, 4, and 6). An internal series of monorhyme lines is framed by the contrasting end-sounds of the first and last lines, thus creating a disjunction between those rhyme words and the others in the stanza. We can imagine that the first and last poetic lines form a refrain because they fit together grammatically, and the musical repetition cues us to associate them, though the resulting little aphorism, "When I am the farthest from my lady, I think of her more often," has no surviving concordances. Nevertheless, the lyric offers a second clue that this may have been a refrain, for the opening line is referenced in the penultimate line with the repeat of *quant*, setting up an echo of the opening grammatical formula (*quant...plus*). Thus we might understand this internal reference as another example of word-grafting—one that fortifies the connection of the last line to the rest of the piece; however, no other piece in the collection demonstrates this poetic technique.

Everist argues that the term *motet enté* might best be understood as describing a "specifically musical characteristic of 'grafting' the same musical units on to the rest of the text."[38] But once again we run into problems: the degree of melodic repetition or "grafting" varies widely among the pieces in trouv. *N*, from the exact but distant repetition of music corresponding to a poetic line as in *Quant plus sui loig de ma dame*, to adjoining double or triple versicles, to the echoing of small melodic motifs, similar to *En non Dieu c'est la rage*. Given these differences, it seems prudent to consider such repetitions as compositional options used discriminately rather than generically, with one option not necessarily precluding another. But surely not all such melodic repetitions were understood as qualitatively equal. Thus, in my estimation, only seven of the fifteen pieces demonstrate a handling of melodic phrases such that I am convinced of a compositional principle taking place that might warrant a special label like "grafted"; and this puts us right back

---

38. Everist, *French Motets*, 89. See also 85–88.

where we started, with an unsatisfying number of pieces that represent *enté* as a compositional process.[39]

Butterfield, in her assessment of the *motets entés* in trouv. *N*, also believes the rubric refers to a compositional process, but she reinstates the refrain as the key element (dismissing issues of corroboration) and understands the grafting process as both textual and musical. She acknowledges, however, that the one term *motet enté* might then signal "two radically different techniques: one involves splitting textual phrases, the other repeating musical ones." This bifurcation of techniques leads to a cleavage of the refrain music from its words, and its grafting onto other words.[40] The conjoining of textual citation and musical repetition in the interpretation of "grafted" assures that all bases are covered given the inconsistencies; where musical repetition fails to convince, textual splicing will suffice. But if the two processes were indeed part of the generic feature of the *motet enté*, then we should expect to see both occurring in the songs that most resemble the *motet entés* in trouv. *N*—namely, the other monophonic motets listed in table 4.1. But the ten mensural additions to trouv. *M* offer us little clarity. Without rubrics in the manuscript, but labeled *motet enté* in most of the secondary literature, six integrate attested refrains in a manner that conforms to the textual processes described by Butterfield and earlier scholars, but only two, *Vous me le defoidés l'amer* and *Bone amourete m'a souspris*, have refrain music that can be tracked as well (both entries appear in figure 4.4 below).[41] *Vous me le defoidés l'amer* does split and graft both the musical and textual halves of the refrain to either end, but does not repeat any portion of the refrain melody within the rest of the song.[42] Only *Bone amourete m'a souspris* displays melodic grafting akin to example 4.4—that is, grafting refrain music onto different words.[43] This is an interesting piece and one to which I will return. For now, I will simply stress that verbal and melodic grafting seemed to have

---

39. The seven are Gen 1077, 1079, 1083, 1084, 1086, 1088, and 1089, all of which illustrate the musical rounding described by Everist. Butterfield, "*Enté*: A Survey and Reassessment," 78–79, examines Gen 1087, *He Dex, que ferai* as an example of melodic grafting, but I disagree. As she points out, the piece consists almost entirely of two musical ideas (ABABBB ′CDBB′AB), and this overabundance of musical repetition casts doubt upon "grafting" as the principal procedure; rather the composer may have in mind other melodic patterns, such as *pedes* of *chansons*, the repeating versicles of the *lai*, or the repetitive and rounding patterns of the *rondeau*.

   None of these pieces demonstrates the *bordos enpeutatz* or "grafted line" technique described in *Las Leys d'Amors*, which is the rhyming of the word at the caesura of a line with the end of that line, or the end of the preceding line. See Gatien-Arnoult, ed., *Las Leys d'Amors*, 1:124–17.

40. Butterfield, "*Enté*: A Survey and Reassessment," 77.

41. The text of the refrain in Gen 1071 has a concordance in Gen 180, but the music does not match. Similarly, the refrain found in Gen 1076b has a concordance in the *Renart le nouvel* MS P-BnF fr. 1593 with a different melody. Saltzstein discusses *Vous me le defoidés l'amer*, which appears most commonly as *Vous me le defendez l'amer*, as a refrain with melodic stability; see "Relocating the Thirteenth-Century Refrain," 259–60.

42. Musical concordances are Gen 880 and the *Renart le nouvel* MSS trouv. *W*, P-BnF f. fr. 1593 and fr. 372.

43. Both *Hé, tres douces amoretes* and *Jolietement m'en vois* show the repetition of the first phrase of music for the last phrase of music, suggesting that the refrain melody was a simple AA′ tune.

been a compositional option, though not definitive of this class of pieces. The songs specifically labeled *motets entés* by virtue of their seemingly various grafting procedures—the ones we can describe, and perhaps the many more we cannot—should direct our attention to a wider, rather than the narrower, range of interpretations. Thus I think a better approach is to ask a slightly different question: not "what thing is grafted?" but "what does a grafted thing mean?"

Grafting is the technique of joining the cut surfaces of two different plants from the same or similar species to produce certain desired characteristics in the fruit or flower. A stem or bud (called a scion) is bound to a parent stock (or rootstock) so that their injured surfaces fuse, and the shoot that emerges expresses genetic aspects of both plants. This technique was widely practiced in the Middle Ages, especially in the gardens and orchards of the nobility. Surviving records reveal that nobles might spend a considerable sum of money to acquire as many as 100 or more grafted fruit trees as well as expert gardeners to take care of them.[44] Gardens and orchards with grafted trees represented wealth and power through technology and artistry. In his 1305 treatise on gardening, Petrus de Crescentiis wrote of the "great beauty and pleasure to have in one's garden trees variously and marvelously grafted, and many different fruit growing on a single tree."[45]

From the twelfth century onward, grafted trees came to signify not just the cultivation of plants, but cultivation in general. Numerous medieval romances and lyrics use the image of a grafted tree to signal human refinement: Charlemagne sits beneath the shade of a grafted tree; courtly women have skin as white as a flower from a grafted tree, or they are elegant above all grafted flowers.[46] (By way of contrast, the troubadour Marcabru used the image of grafted fruit to describe the contamination of bloodlines through adulterous unions.[47]) In the Middle English story *Sir Orfeo*, musical artistry and a grafted tree (*ympe-tre*) emerge as linked images of Orfeo's noble identity, which become disassembled as the story unfolds.[48] After his beloved queen is abducted by fairies while asleep under the grafted tree, a despondent Orfeo leaves his cultivated music and gardens to wander in the unruly wilderness as a lowly

---

44. Harvey, *Medieval Gardens*, 64, 72–82.

45. Quoted in Thacker, *The History of Gardens*, 85. See also Harvey, *Medieval Gardens*, 3; and Zirkle, *The Beginnings of Plant Hybridization*, 82–83.

46. S.v. "1. ente," *Dictionnaire de l'ancienne langue française*, ed. Godefroy. I am referring to the following lines: "E vient a Carlemaigne desuz l'umbre d'une **ente**" (*Le Pèlerinage de Charlemagne*, 795); "Blanche la char, comme la flor en l'**ente**" (*Prise d'Orange*, 205); "Tres fine et noble dame gente, / sour toutes autre florie **ente**" (*Le Livre des amors du Chastellain de Coucy*, 7671). For other references see Butterfield, "*Enté*: A Survey and Reassessment," 69–72. See also Coolidge, "The Grafted Tree in Literature."

47. See Bloch, *Etymologies and Genealogies*, 109–10.

48. "Sir Orfeo," in *Medieval English Romances*, ed. Speed, 1:123–49. See also Coolidge, "The Grafted Tree in Sir Orfeo"; Lerer, "Artifice and Artistry in Sir Orfeo," 94–97. See also Butterfield, "*Enté*: A Survey and Reassessment," 71–72, who also discusses this story.

minstrel. He eventually arrives at the fairy king's court, spies the queen frozen at the moment of abduction beneath the grafted tree, and wins her back as payment for his musical performance. Just as the grafted tree represents a mixture of human technology and divine forces of nature, so too does Orfeo in minstrel's guise mix a human craft with a legendary divine musical skill, as well as base professionalism with courtly refinement.

The exalted image of a grafted tree reaches its height in the *Roman de la poire* by Tibaut (ca. 1250), which imitates the first-person narrative of the *Roman de la rose*, replacing the motif of a flower with fruit—specifically, a famously prized species of pear from a grafted tree. With elements of Adam and Eve and Tristan and Isolde, the pear generates the story by generating love: the lady picks and tastes the pear, then offers it to the narrator, who, after his first bite, becomes smitten with love for her. The *Roman de la poire* includes twenty refrains interpolated into the narrative, which reveal the names of the author and his beloved in an acrostic. Butterfield sees the splicing of refrains into the narrative as exemplifying the process of *enté* that generates the theme and form of the hybrid text, and she argues that through the acrostic of refrains, Tibaut "confects authorial identity out of quintessential commonplaces that, by their nature, resist authorial appropriation."[49]

The fusing of many voices in a unifying authorial voice, as scions to a rootstock, also describes Matfre Ermengaud's Occitan verse treatise *Breviari d'amor* (ca. 1288–92). Here, under the rubric of a grafted branch of human love to the Divine *albre d'amor* (tree of love), Matfre quotes verses from numerous troubadours in an effort to reconcile the erotic language of the *canso* with the righteous goals of marriage and procreation. Francesca Nicholson notes that, though carefully selected to suit his purposes, the citation of troubadour lyrics "suggest a dialogue between the singular and the multiple," and she further observes that the citations "are brought into Matfre's verse medium (or stock) in such a way as to make the text 'grow' and bear finer fruit than if each species had fruited in isolation....the effect of the citation is to ramify voice, to make it productive and interminable."[50] Thus in both the *Roman de la poire* and *Breviari d'amor*, grafted trees, as complex unities themselves, serve as an organizing image for literary works that self-consciously contrast a plurality of voices supplying language with a single voice that attempts to unify content. This compiling of voices, with the citation of public refrains or the verses of others, into an "interminable" dialogue once again leads us to Bakhtin's idea of polyphony. For Tibaut and Matfre, however, it is the unified, hybrid product of the graft—not the plural constituent parts of scion and stock—that indicates technical and cultural advancement.

---

49. See Butterfield, "*Enté*: A Survey and Reassessment," 72; see also Butterfield, *Poetry and Music*, 246–52 (quotation from 247); and Huot, *From Song to Book*, 174–93.

50. Nicholson, "Branches of Knowledge," 375–85 (quotations on 380 and 376, respectively). See also the companion article by Sarah Kay, "Grafting the Knowledge Community.".

MOTETS AND TECHNOLOGIES OF SAMPLING

Motets, like grafted trees, were also associated with technical skill and refinement. Johannes de Grocheio, in his treatise *De musica*, written around 1300, identified polyphonic motets with a cultured, literate audience:

> The motet is a song [*cantus*] assembled from numerous elements, having numerous poetic texts or a multifarious structure of syllables according together at every point.... This kind of music should not be set before a lay public because they are not alert to its refinement (*subtilitatem*) nor are they delighted by hearing it, but [it should only be performed] before the literati [*litteratis*] and those who look for the refinements of skills. It is the custom for motets to be sung in their holiday festivities to adorn them, just as the *cantilena* which is called 'rotundellus' [is customarily sung] in the festivities of the lay public.[51]

To understand why motets are refined, we must go to the source of Grocheio's socio-musical ideas. Elizabeth Aubrey has noted that Grocheio describes musical compositions in terms of Aristotle's four causes: matter (or material cause: words, sounds) given form through music (formal cause) by human design and manipulation (efficient cause) with some purpose (final cause).[52] For example, concerning general procedures of writing monophonic songs, he writes: "First the texts are prepared in the place of matter; but after this, the melody is introduced in the place of form in proportion to whatever text." He extends the idea of these causes into his descriptions of individual song types. Aubrey summarizes one such example: "*cantus coronatus* 'concerns delightful and difficult matter' (material cause), 'is made from all sorts of longs' (formal cause), and 'is composed by kings and nobility' (efficient cause), 'in order to move their spirits to boldness' and so forth (final cause)."[53] With regard to the motet, the multiple poems (material cause) and melodies (formal cause) furnish the composer with a surplus of matter and form, while the final cause or purpose for the motet is, in a similar vein, a supplement (adornment) to the festivities of literate and refined or cultivated persons, just as the *rotundellus* or *rondeau* adorns the festivities of lay persons (recall that in trouv. *a* motets and *rondeaux* were also associated in a designated section and "adorning" the ends of *chanson* gatherings). Faced with so much matter and

---

51. "Motetus vero est cantus ex pluribus compositus, habens plura dictamina vel multimodam discretionem syllabarum, utrobique harmonialiter consonans...Cantus autem iste non debet coram vulgaribus propinari eo quod eius subtilitatem non advertunt nec in eius auditu delectantur sed coram litteratis et illis qui subtilitates artium sunt quaerentes. Et solet in eorum festis decantari ad eorum decorationem, quemadmodum cantilena quae dicitur rotundellus in festis vulgarium laicorum." Translation adapted from Page, "Johannes de Grocheio on Secular Music," 36.

52. Aubrey, "Genre as a Determinant of Melody," 275–78.

53. Ibid., 276 (including Grocheio's Latin and translation). "Primo enim dictamina loco materiae praeparantur, postea vero cantus unicuique dictamini proportionalis loco formae introducitur."

form, the composer must coordinate words and melodies, according to Grocheio, with the device of a uniform measure and mensural rhythms, hence his designation of polyphony as "precisely measured music" (*cantum praecise mensuratum*).[54] Thus before Grocheio discusses compositional procedures for the motet and other polyphonic genres, he first offers a digest of modal rhythm and Franconian notation "since being measured and the manner of measuring together with the art of writing or notating is common to all these."[55]

Following his usual formula of describing how matter relates to form, Grocheio submits that three "figures"—a simple square (■ called a *brevis*), a square with a line ascending or descending on the right ▟ called a *longa*) and an opposite-angled shape (♦), called a *semibrevis*)—comprise the raw material for writing polyphony. He writes that "just as the grammarian can represent any utterance from a few letters by their joining together and placement…so the musician can [represent] a measured song from these three figures."[56] However, perhaps more than letters and words, musical notation around 1300 was apparently a somewhat flexible system, as Grocheio at one point indicates: "[H]ence knowing how to sing and express a song according to one method is not the same as according to another. The diversity of all these methods will appear to those looking into the various treatises of others."[57] Furthermore, music scribes in the late thirteenth century had two available technologies for recording musical rhythm: quadratic note shapes and chant ligatures that do not indicate relative rhythmic values within a metrical scheme; and modified "mensural" notation, which relies on graphically differentiated note shapes and a low-level flow of equal beats that can be grouped together for longer values, or subdivided for smaller values.[58] Monophonic *chansons* are, by and large, recorded in nonmensural notation that resembles chant, while polyphonic motets are most frequently recorded in mensural rhythmic notation, as are refrains and dance songs upon occasion.[59]

---

54. See Page, "Johannes de Grocheio on Secular Music," 35.

55. "[Q]uoniam mensurari et modus mensurandi cum arte describendi vel signandi commune est omnibus his." Translation adapted from Johannes de Grocheio, *Concerning Music*, trans. Seay, 21; Latin from Rohloff, *Die Quellenhandschriften*, 138.

56. "Et quemadmodum grammaticus ex paucis litteris earum conjunctione et situatione potest dictionem quamlibet designare…ita musicus ex tribus figuris cantum quemlibet mensuratum." See Rohloff, *Die Quellenhandschriften*, 142; translation adapted from Johannes de Grocheio, *Concerning Music*, trans. Seay, 24.

57. "Unde sciens cantare et exprimere cantum secundum quosdam, secundum alios non est sciens. Omnium autem istorum diversitas apparebit diversos tractatus aliorum intuenti." See Rohloff, *Die Quellenhanscriften*, 142; translation adapted from Johannes de Grocheio, *Concerning Music*, trans. Seay, 25.

58. Grocheio describes this equal pulse as the *tempus*, which corresponds in notation to the breve. An intermediate stage between non-mensural chant-derived notation and differentiated mensural notation would be that of modal notation, for which the performer imagines a background cycle of alternating long and short values that dictates the rhythmic reading of ligature patterns.

59. The manuscript evidence shows that sometimes a single music scribe was familiar with a variety of notations and could deploy them according to the appropriate repertory. As John Stevens has pointed out, this was precisely the case in trouv. *W*, where a single scribe uses undifferentiated note shapes for the *chansons* and mensural notation for the polyphony and the independent refrains interpolated into of *Renart le nouvel*. See Stevens, "Manuscript Presentation and Notation."

Thus it is significant that Grocheio associates the particularities of mensural notation and writing with polyphonic music, for this not only reflects the situation of the sources, but also further characterizes the polyphonic motet as materially, formally, and technologically more refined than monophonic songs.

In light of Grocheio's discussion of the motet and its components, the idea of a single complexly bountiful grafted tree yielding a plethora of fruit seems an apt analogy for a polyphonic motet yielding diverse lyrics, melodies, and rhythms through notation. Both "grafted" and "motet" arguably connote advances in technology—human manipulation of material in such a way as to achieve a concordance of disparate elements for the delight of a cultivated audience. Given this analogy, we might expect to find the label *motet enté* applied to polyphonic motets—the poly-fruited tree—as it has been by many scholars. But this is not the case in medieval sources. Instead, the known medieval applications of that label refer to pieces of monophony—those in trouv. *N*, and the presumed multiple monophonic pieces in the *Chansonnier de Mesmes*. Thus the question of why monophonic songs were labeled "grafted motets" has still to be answered.

I believe a clue to the answer can be found in the current trend in popular music known as "sampling." Sampling is the extraction through direct imitation, "scratching" (the manual manipulation of a turntable), or digitalization and filtering of a segment or isolated part of pre-recorded material for use in a new musical context. Importantly, the extracted parts, or samples, acquire an independent existence, sometimes spawning a whole lineage of songs, as was the case with the bass line from Chic's 1979 "Good Times," sampled in Sugar Hill Gang's 1979 "Rapper's Delight" and copied in Queen's 1980 "Another One Bites the Dust." Specialists in medieval music will immediately recognize a similarity between such a family of songs and the families of polyphonic motets built on the same chant tenors. Indeed, the standard history of the motet presented near the beginning of this chapter is quintessentially a story of sampling, whether the extraction of an entire discant clausula from organum for adding counterpoint and words, or the extraction and rhythmic patterning (and re-patterning) of chant melismas for the tenors of newly-composed polyphonic motets.

Though sampling often creates continuity among different styles (for example, among funk, disco, and rap; or among organa and two-, three-, and four-part motets), it may also set up a dialogue between the old and new song through the juxtaposition of contrasting styles, such as Moby's use of Alan Lomax's recordings of African-American work songs in his techno dance music, or Janet Jackson's incorporation of Joni Mitchell's high folksy soprano refrain from "Big Yellow Taxi" (1970) into her sultry R&B number "Got Til It's Gone"(1997)—which is itself a present-day *jeu–parti* between Janet and the rapper Q-Tip.[60] Samples may be almost purposefully obscure and seamlessly embedded into a thickly textured sonic background, such as Radiohead's sampling of electronic music

---

60. Janet Jackson, *The Velvet Rope* (Virgin Records America, 1997).

partway through the staff. Such strokes in the context of *chansons* demarcate the ends of musical phrases corresponding to the articulation of a rhyme and poetic line. Musicologists assume a pause in performance, but generally do not transcribe these strokes as rests. In the context of thirteenth-century polyphony, these strokes function in two ways—as demarcations of phrases, just as in the notation of *chansons*, and as precisely measured rests, the duration of which is represented by the length of the vertical line (Grocheio describes both readings of this line in his discussion of mensural notation).[62] Polyphonic motet melodies strategically utilize rests to create contrapuntal phrases of differing lengths that overlap with the regular rhythmic patterns of the tenor.

The non-mensural "analog" notation of the *motets entés* in trouv. *N* helps conceal references to refrains and polyphonic motet parts with indeterminate rhythmic relationships, creating a visually and aurally smooth free melody that blends in with the other *chansons* in the collection. One piece from trouv. *N*, however, seems to give the game away. *D'amor nuit et jor me lo*, as I mentioned earlier, retains here certain notational indications of its pre-recorded "digital" polyphonic environment, specifically the schematic isolation of one or two notes with strokes (see figure 4.3). Examples 4.5 and 4.6 present two diplomatically transcribed excerpts from *D'amor nuit et jor me lo*, the first from from *Mo*, and the second from the *chansonnier*.

Of all the melodious motet parts circulating in the repertory, the choice of this motetus to include in a collection of *chansons* is peculiar, as it is full of short two-note phrases, a halting rhythmic pattern, and monotonous sequencing of mundane melodic ideas. As the excerpts in examples 4.5 and 4.6 illustrate, the scribe of trouv. *N* attempted to translate the digital polyphonic notation into an analog *chanson* notation, with only partial success and some struggle, as the word correction in the fifth line of figure 4.3 attests. The scribe made certain "character substitutions" in adapting the *chanson* notation technology to the rhythmic requirements of this melody, writing a stroke after a square note whose parallel is a double long in *Mo* (as for the first syllable of *D'amor* and over *mes*), or marking off the short verbal phrases with *puncta* in the text. The addition of so many strokes and dots, especially at the very beginning, quite literally creates a song comprised of pulses and spaces. This piece is so stylistically and notationally distinct from the others in the manuscript, even the other *motets entés*, that it makes a strong statement—one that divulges the ideas at play in this appended collection of single-stanza songs and *lais*, namely the deliberate cross-pollination of different types of melodies.

---

62. Grocheio writes: "Our predecessors designate [this pause] by a line placed across the staff. And modern composers use it still; either it is a general pause, which they call 'end of the puncta [phrase]', or it is of one perfection or of many, or of two tempora, or of one, or any part of the larger or equal tempus." (Quam antiqui per lineam ex transverso positam designaverunt. Et adhuc ista moderni utuntur, sive pausa universalis sit, quam 'finem punctorum' appellant, sive sit unius perfectionis vel plurium, sive duorum temporum, sive unius, sive alicuius partis temporis maioris vel aequalis.) Translation adapted from Johannes de Grocheio, *Concerning Music*, trans. Seay, 23; Latin from Rohloff, *Die Quellenhandschriften*, 142.

compositions taken from a 1976 album pretentiously titled *First Recordings: The Lea₁ of Composers-ISCM International Competition Electronic Music Winners*.[61] Only afi₁ nados of electronic music would know offhand the source of these samples, and thos the know, or those who read and trace the finely printed list of credited samples in accompanying booklet, can then appreciate how the samples not only serve as cat sound bites, but also play into the theme of technological apocalypse that characte₁ Radiohead's albums.

Monophonic motets represent a similar musical-technological phenomenon: the₁ independent samples or sample-like melodies that strategically reference or engage ₁ tiple musical repertories. Furthermore, these references or samples may be obvious, as the extraction of a melody from a motet and its deployment as a *chanson*, c embedded quotation of a refrain from a lyric narrative or dance song; or they m₁ obscure, such as resemblances to melodies from motets and implied quotations of ref₁ The nine monophonic motets in trouv. *a* function as the former type of reference obvious and direct sampling of voice parts from polyphonic motets, which, along similarly contrasting material, grafted *chanson* gatherings together. These musical not only spotlight the musical and poetic style of the *chansons* that surround them more importantly, they call attention to the form and materiality of the collection by indexing the gatherings. The designated *motets entés* of trouv. *N* function as the type of reference—imitation motet parts (motet samples) grafted onto a collecti *chansons*. In these two cases we could read the rubric quite literally as "here beg₁ grafted motets," or the "graft of motets," which will yield a more desirable fruit: th₁ nologically cultivated *chansonnier*. I will come back to this point later.

Notation also pertains to the manipulation of musical references. Record produ present choose between earlier analog technology, in which the whole sound ₁ recorded as one fluid groove on a vinyl disc or as magnetized particles on tape, an₁ digital means of recording sound as a series of pulses and spaces, easily encoded an by computer. Scratching relies on analog technology, which allows a musician to ₁ ally turn the vinyl disk on the turntable, strategically revealing and concealing the n sample. Digitalization, however, provides for consistent repetition, changes of spee the isolation of particular instruments or vocals through filters. Non-mensural nc can be compared to analog technology, recording music in a rhythmically fluid n that allows for a certain flexibility in performance; mensural or Franconian notati₁ be compared to digital technology, recording music in precise rhythmic relatio organized by a sense of pulse that also codifies and incorporates equally defined mc of rests (spaces) between and within phrases. Pauses or rests were notated with vertical lines or strokes (variously called *tractus*, *tractulus*, or *linea*) drawn wh

---

61. Radiohead's song is "Idioteque," from the album *Kid A* (EMI Records, 2000). The samples are fr₁ Lansky's "Mild und Liese" and Arthur Kreiger's "Short Piece" (Columbia/Odyssey Records, 1976).

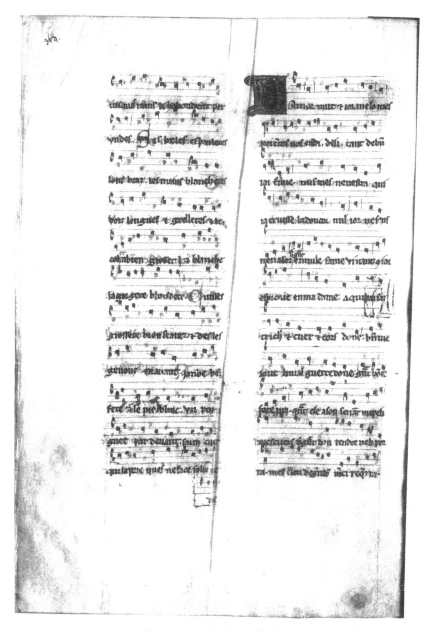

FIGURE 4.3 *D'amor nuit et jor me lo* from trouv. *N*, fol. 188ᵛ (Bibliothèque nationale de France, Paris)

Grocheio's association of notation and literacy with the polyphonic motet distinguishes it from trouvère *chansons*, and this association also fortifies the significance of monophonic motets. The one aspect most particular to monophonic motets is how they, like samples, call attention to their immediate environment, in this case the codex and its contents. *Onc voir par amours n'amai* is a case in point. This song appears as a unique piece of

EXAMPLE 4.5 *D'amors nuit et jour me lo* from *Mo*, fol. 231ᵛ

D'a-mors nuit et jour me lo.   Mes pour cer-tes vos en di: de li   tant de bien i ai

tro-vé,   nus mes ne n'e-stra   qui ja   tui-se la dou-çor   nul jor   ne sens ne va-lour

EXAMPLE 4.6 *D'amor nuit et jor me lo* from trouv. *N*, fol. 188ᵛ

D'a - mor nuit et jor me lo.   Mes   por cer-tes vos en di: de li   tant de bien

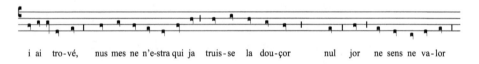

i ai tro-vé,   nus mes ne n'e-stra qui ja truis-se la dou-çor   nul jor   ne sens ne va-lor

monophony near the end of fascicle 6 of *Mo* (see example 4.7 OXFORD WEB MUSIC), its only source. In the notation, most of the vertical strokes are of the *chanson* type—that is, not indicating measured silences but demarcating poetic and melodic phrases.[63] Two rests set off the first and last phrases; otherwise, the melody flows in a continuous manner uncommon in polyphonic motet melodies. Furthermore, the expressive melodic gesture over *m'agrée* ending line 5, with its sudden drop of a fifth, is unusual in the polyphonic repertory.[64]

Onc voir par amours n'amai	I have never been truly smitten by love
hors de ma contrée	outside of my country
et sui de Paris née.	—and I am Paris-born.
Cele qu'ai tant amée	If she, whom I have loved so much,
se mieuz m'agrée	pleases me more,

---

63. See, for example, the songs in figure 4.2. This is clear from the graphic shapes of the notes on either side of the stroke. When the note shapes alternate long and short values, the stroke represents a phrase ending; when the note shapes break the pattern, the stroke represents a rest that fills the appropriate rhythmic value within the pattern.

64. I have found only two other instances of this melodic gesture in *Mo*, among the three-part motets in fascicle 4: Gen 449 and Gen 603b.

EXAMPLE 4.7 *Onc voir par amours n'amai* from *Mo*, fol. 268ᵛ

1. Onc voir par a - mours   n'a - mai   2. hors de ma con - tré - e

3. et sui   de Pa - ris né - e 4. Ce - le qu'ai tant a - mé - e,

5. se mieuz m'a - gré - e 6. l'A - mor, vo - stre   a - mis, 7. ne m'en doit blau - mer.

8. Plus loi - au - ment   de moi   9. ne   doit   nus   a - - mer.

l'Amor, vostre amis,	Love, your friend,
ne m'en doit blaumer.	mustn't blame me for it.
Plus loiaument de moi	No one could love
ne doit nus amer.	more loyally than I.

The lyric, which does not incorporate refrains or refrain-like phrases, metaphorically speaks to its own musical "outsiderness." The first line reads: "I have never been truly smitten by love outside of my country—and I am Paris-born." Presumably the monophonic motet expresses the point of view of the Parisian lover, and it would follow that the notion of a foreign beloved here might refer us to the surrounding polyphony. However, the manuscript itself is "Paris-born,"[65] and fascicle 6 transmits a core repertory of seventy-three two-part motets. Thus, in a clever self-referential twist, the lover's assertion of a central regional identity actually amplifies the foreignness of both her subject-position and her song within their presumably native land, that is, a country generally filled with compounded male voices. I use "her" because the feminine ending on *née* (born) and *amée* (loved) indicates that the lyric subject is a woman, though she later refers to her beloved with the feminine pronoun *cele*. The lyric may be corrupt, but in what way corrupt is not at all clear. The motet just prior to *Onc voir par amour n'amai* in the manuscript also conveys a female subject-position, singing happily of an amorous

---

65. See Everist, *Polyphonic Music*, 97–136.

abduction.[66] We have seen such cross-gender, cross-genre relationships before in this chapter, between Willammes d'Amiens's *rondeau Prendés i garde* and its transformation into a polyphony of female voices in the motet *S'on me regarde/Prennés i garde/HÉ, MI ENFANT. Onc voir par amour n'amai*, by comparison, isolates the female voice that had just been given polyphonic expression, and it (perhaps inadvertently) grafts subject and object by force of rhyme and musical setting of the mute -e (*contrée, née, amée, agrée*). This gender troubling of poetic and musical language befits the genre troubling of the monophonic motet, and, like the various clustering of monophonic motets in *chansonniers*, the perspectival cluster at the end of a long central fascicle of polyphonic motets reinforces the monophonic motet's playful connections of regional, gender, codicological, and musical peripheries.

GENRE TROUBLE AND THE *MOTET ENTÉ*

Earlier I noted that the collection of monophonic motets in trouv. *N* functions as a musical graft onto the end of that manuscript, supplementing and distinguishing an otherwise standard collection of *chansons*. Indeed, most of these monophonic motets can be characterized as accessories to the more homogeneous core repertories of strophic *chansons* or polyphonic motets—grafted buds onto a stock, if you will. This aspect is borne out more fully and multifariously in the case of *Bone amourete m'a souspris*, one of the many additions to trouv. *M* discussed in chapter 3. As noted there, the same scribe also added two stanzas of the trouvère *chanson Se j'ai chanté sans guerredon avoir*, set to a free, heterostrophic melody in mensural notation.[67] All of the additions to trouv. *M* were written in Franconian mensural notation, and many on pre-ruled five-line staves common to polyphonic collections. The new notational lingua franca of differentiated longs and breves, oblique and *cum opposita proprietate* ligatures, and measured rests made its way into other collections of trouvère songs as well, most notably trouv. *O* and *R*, both of which contain sizeable numbers of songs with mensural note shapes, though not always consistently or logically applied.[68] Nevertheless, these mensural or quasi-mensural monophonic songs reveal a permeability of stylistic and generic categories to polyphonic rhythmic and notational practices over the course of the thirteenth and early fourteenth centuries. It is also significant that the single largest subgroup of the

---

66. *Cil brunes ne me meine mie/IN SECULUM*, fol. 268 (Gen 156).

67. These two *chanson* stanzas are linked to the monophonic motets in another, somewhat cryptic way. Faint Roman numerals appear in the left margin of both stanzas, counting the first as iiii and the second as ii. Similar roman numerals appear in the left margin for *Bone amourete m'a souspris* (vi) and *Vous me le defoidés l'amer* (viii); a different hand numbered *Hé, tres douces amourtetes* (vii) and *L'autrier lés une fontaine* (iii). The numbers are not in a discernible sequence.

68. See Haines, *Eight Centuries of Troubadours and Trouvères*, 29, for a listing of *chansonniers* with mensural melodies.

mensural additions to trouv. *M* is that of the monophonic motets, comprising nearly a third of the total additions, and representing the contribution of seven different scribes (see chapter 3). This attests to the ongoing cultivation of monophonic motets well after the collection in trouv. *N*.

Six of the nine added monophonic motets to trouv. *M* incorporate the words of identifiable refrains. For *Bone amourete m'a souspris*, the composer chose the words and the music of the preexisting refrain *Bonne amourete me tient gai*, which survive as the middle voice of a polyphonic *rondeau* by Adam de la Halle (see example 4.8 🔊 OXFORD WEB MUSIC).[69]

EXAMPLE 4.8 Adam de la Halle, *Bonne amourete me tien gai* from *W*, fol. 34

Bonne a - mou - re - te   me   tient   gai

Bonne amourete	Good love
me tient gai.	keeps me happy.
Ma compaignete	My companion,
bonne amourete	*good love,*
ma canconnete,	my little song,
vous dirai:	will say to you:
bonne amourete	*Good love*
me tient gai.	*keeps me happy.*

Bone amourete m'a souspris, like a textbook example of earlier scholars' notions of *motet enté*, splits the refrain words and melody in two (marked with the letters A and B in example 4.8), with each half framing new free lyrical and melodic material (see example 4.9 🔊 OXFORD WEB MUSIC).

---

69. This aphorism also appears as an autonomous refrain in the version of *Renart le nouvel* preserved in P-BnF fr. 1593, fol. 18v, but set to unrelated music.

EXAMPLE 4.9 *Bone amourete m'a souspris* from trouv. *M*, fol. 3ᵛ

Bone amourete m'a souspris.	*Good love* has overwhelmed me.
D'amer bele dame de pris,	To love a beautiful lady of worth,
le cors a gent et cler le vis,	with an elegant body and bright face,
et pour s'amour trai grant esmai.	and for her love I endure great dismay.
Et nepourquant je l'amerai	Nevertheless I will love her

tant con vivrai de fin cuer vrai	with a noble and true heart as long as I live,
car l'esperance ke j'ai	for the hope that I have
de chanter toujours	to sing always
me tient gai.	*keeps me happy.*

This new material decidedly points toward the high courtly rhetoric and metrical regularity of trouvère *chansons*, neatly integrating and elevating the more popular rhetoric of the refrain. The regular eight-syllable lines (set to four-bar phrases in transcription) become only slightly ruffled near the end, with one shortened penultimate phrase (mm. 25–28) followed by a final eight-syllable phrase interrupted by a midpoint rest. This rest marks a significant moment in the music: on the larger level, the pause announces the completion of the refrain; but on the lower level, the rest once again divides the refrain melody, for in mm. 30–31 the composer has tucked in the first half, but disguises the initial two notes in a ligature that appears mid-word. However, one other detail of the notation might have prompted a *reader* of this song to think of the original polyphonic refrain couplet. Despite the frequent use of *cum opposita proprietate* ligatures linking breves and semibreves, the last three-note ligature is a singular *conjunctura* comprised of a square and two *currentes* (see m. 32 and figure 4.4)—the same ligature used at the same melodic point in Adam de la Halle's polyphonic *rondeau* preserved in trouv. *W*, the "collected works" manuscript for Adam's compositions, and a source indirectly related to trouv. *M*.[70]

By writing a figure that joins two semibreves to the preceding rather than the following note, the notator went against habit, possibly to conform to the notation of the *rondeau*.[71] Coincidentally (or not?), an anonymous prologue to his dramatized *pastourelle Robin et Marion* in trouv. *W* associates Adam's name with the term *motet enté* in a passage that reads: "Nenil ains sauoit canchons faire / Partures et motes entes / De che fist il agrant plentes / Et balades ie ne sai quantes" (no one before knew how to make *chansons*, *partures*, and *motets entés*, of which he added a great amount, and *ballades*, I don't know how many). Thus the recording technology—the mensural notation—itself became a creative aspect of this composition: on one hand, the ligature and rest in measures 30–1 partially obscure the sampling and grafting of this refrain

---

70. Trouv. *M* belongs to pair of intersecting *chansonnier* groups: the related manuscripts *AMTa* and the Adam de la Halle group *APTWa*. See Karp, "The Trouvère MS Tradition," esp. 36–42.

71. The consequent reading of this *conjunctura* according to its graphic components of a breve and two semibreves implies that the scribe's three-*currentes* figure (•••) divides the breve into three equal semibreves. Given this ternary breve, a strict Franconian transcription might be in order, which would read all pairs of semibreves as unequal (semibreve minor, semibreve major). I have opted to transcribe pairs of semibreves as equal, however, as does Tischler in *The Earliest Motets*, 2:1540–41, since concerns about the simultaneous rendering of duplet and triplet semibreves do not obtain in monophony, and since changes and conflicts in late thirteenth- and early fourteenth-century theoretical sources on the rhythmic values of semibreves (duly noted by Grocheio) suggest a more flexible performance practice.

FIGURE 4.4 *Bone amourete m'a souspris* from trouv. *M*, fol. 3ᵛ (Bibliothèque nationale de France, Paris)

melody, while on the other hand the *conjunctura* in m. 32 offers a visual cue that recalls the source *rondeau*. Both notational details playfully integrate the preexisting melody in such a way that a level of musical literacy is required to fully appreciate the sampling and grafting.

This piece bears still more delightful details, for the composer also employed the melodic material of the refrain—specifically the raised leading tone—as a basis for shaping the ends of the newly composed melody, in a sense indexing the melody. The sign ♮ in measures 4, 28, and 32 establishes the F as *musica ficta*, also known in medieval treatises as *falsa musica, musica colorata, coniuncta*, and also by the Greek term *synemmenon*. All of these terms refer to notes outside the codified Guidonian diatonic gamut, but communicate subtle conceptual variations. The terms *musica ficta, musica falsa*, and *musica colorata* imply a deviation or digression from the pitch field, while *synemmenon* and *coniuncta* indicate a "hooking on" of a new tetrachord or hexachord that yields the altered pitch.[72] In his treatise *Tractatus de discantu* (ca. 1300) on composing polyphony, Anonymous 2 cites two reasons for the use of chromatic notes (*musica falsa*): "because of necessity and because of beauty in melody itself. The reason of necessity arises because we could not have a fifth, a fourth, or an octave...the reason of beauty is manifest in the *cantus coronatus*."[73] Thomas Brothers has noted that Anonymous 2 sets up *causa pulchritudinis* in opposition to *causa necessitatis*—a departure from the cause of necessity that is paralleled by his departure from the context of polyphony and shift to monophony. Monophony, of course, does not require attention to vertical intervals. The option of beautiful chromatic inflection in the *cantus coronatus* effectively sets "sophisticated polyphony alongside a sophisticated monophonic genre in order to draw attention to different styles of using musica ficta."[74] Brothers has further demonstrated that the beautiful application of *musica ficta* in monophony can be found in the redaction of trouvère melodies recorded in trouv. *O*, whose melodies show a high degree of gratuitous chromatic inflection. He likens these inflections to "digressions" in contemporaneous theories of rhetoric—"flexibility of melodic discourse" and "syntax," which were valued for their "subtlety and idiosyncrasy."[75]

The F♯ in measures 4 and 28 of *Bone amourete m'a souspris* could be explained in terms of *causa pulchritudinis*, for in both instances the chromatic note appears without clear melodic provocation (indeed, creating a melodic diminished fourth with the B♭ in m. 1) and without cadential resolution, but it creates an open phrase ending that leaves the listener in a state of suspense. Such precious melodic gestures—connecting two phrases by raising a leading tone and interrupting the resolution—occur in the polyphonic *chansons* of Guillaume de Machaut and other fourteenth-century composers, signaling a synthesis of an increasingly refined sense of melody that extended the legacy of the trouvères with the increasingly complex phraseology and harmonic environment of the polyphonic

---

72. Brothers, *Chromatic Beauty*, 1, 11, 36–37.

73. "Causa necessitatis et causa pulchritudinis cantus per se. Causa necessitatis, quia non poteramus habere diapente, diatessaron, diapason.... causa pulchritudinis, ut patet in cantilenis cornonatis." Latin and translation ibid., 1 n. 1.

74. Ibid., 5. See also 3–6.

75. Ibid., 14. See also 11–15.

motet.[76] In *Bone amourete m'a souspris* we have another type of synthesis: the subtle trans-formation of a raised penultimate leading tone in a polyphonic *rondeau* to a beautiful chromatic inflection, hooked on or grafted and left hanging at the ends of these phrases like wondrously unexpected fruit.

Bone amourete m'a souspris exemplifies a procedural interpretation of the term *motet enté*, as well as the wider conceptual interpretation, with its plethora of musical refer-ences, including a specific *rondeau*, the courtly rhetoric and metrical regularity of trou-vère *chansons*, the single-stanza dimension and the mensural notation of polyphonic motets, and *musica ficta* (or better, *coniuncta*) pointing toward a fourteenth-century melodic sensibility born from both *chansons* and motets. All these references are enclosed in a single well-crafted monophonic motet, which itself represents a late supplement or graft to an already elaborate and cosmopolitan *chansonnier*. Thus this piece, along with the other eight like it, adds yet another type of song—a rare musical hybrid—to the gen-eral collection.

As noted in chapter 3, we have evidence from Grocheio that medieval audiences knew about and comprehended musical hybrids, and that such hybrids were considered to be fundamentally something decorated or ornamented, for he describes just such a piece in his treatise, using what appears to be two Latin translations of *motet enté*. The wording of this passage is important, so I will repeat the excerpt here: "There is also another kind of *cantilena* which they call 'ornamented song' (*cantus insertus*) or 'grafted song' (*cantilenam entatam*). It begins in the manner of a *cantilena* and ends or comes to a close in their fashion."[77] In chapter 3 I identified the recomposed *A mon pooir ai servi* as Grocheio's *cantus insertus* type, in which an initial musical refrain and a concluding musico-poetic refrain frame internal free melodies that change from strophe to strophe. Though Grocheio does not specify any of the other "motet" features I have been tracing—single stanzas, free verses, and free melodies—I do think that *Bone amourete m'a souspris* conforms to another possible manifestation of such a hybrid. Grocheio seems to provide for both single-stanza and strophic options in his phrase "earum fine clauditur vel finitur"—that is, ending (*finitur*) the piece, or closing the end of each strophe (*clauditur*) with a refrain (*earum fine*). That Grocheio allowed for multiple possible manifestations of his hybrid type is further apparent in his double naming, which introduces these hybrids as the aural equivalent of shape-shifting optical illusions—now a *cantus*, now a *cantilena*—each label describing a different point of view, like the shifting regional subject-position of voice and song inscribed in *Onc voir par amours n'amai*. This conceptual duality or plurality (two fruits growing from a single tree) might in fact be the most important decorative and

---

76. I am paraphrasing Brothers, *Chromatic Beauty*, 88. See, for example, the cantus of Machaut's *Biauté qui toutes autres pere* (B4), mm. 14–15, ibid., 109. See also the conclusion of the present study for further consideration of this point.

77. "Est etiam alius modus cantilenarum, quem *cantum insertum* vel *cantilenam entatam* vocant, qui ad modum cantilenarum incipit et earum fine clauditur vel finitur." Latin and translation Page, "Johannes de Grocheio on Secular Music," 27. I have modified Page's translation of the last clause.

technological feat of the *cantilena entata* or *cantus insertus*. Though Grocheio does not spell out a "final cause" for this genre, the purpose seems embedded in its multiple names, for just as the final cause of the polyphonic motet was to adorn the festivities of refined persons, so too is *cantilena entata* or *cantus insertus*, by virtue of its cultivated hybridity and superfluidity, an ornament to the monophonic *chanson* repertory.

Until now, I have been hedging the question of whether I consider all monophonic motets to be *motets entés*. My answer is in one sense yes—in the conceptual sense, but not necessarily in the procedural sense, as in the splitting and grafting of a refrain. I believe the medieval evidence in trouv. *N* points to the fact that procedure is not what binds those pieces together most strongly. But I also believe that monophonic motets are fundamentally *enté* in concept, in that they represent something both ornamental and technological. The phenomenon of monophonic motets—these curiously dense samples of the entire field of the medieval musical imagination, is fundamentally a phenomenon encapsulating and describing a certain technologically hybrid moment. While the strophic and melodically schematic compositions of the trouvères originated and thrived in an environment of oral composition and transmission, motet compositions, in stark contrast, originated in an environment of literacy and project a delight in textual play; they make copious references to surrounding lyrical and literary genres, and plant these references in non-schematic fields. If the notion of "motet" is expanded to include monophony and refrains as well as polyphony, the monophonic motet is a signature of a post-written oral transformation and relocation.[78] Motet melodies as initially written and read within a polyphonic environment participate through performance in a wider arena of musical practice, in a way comparable to how samples operate in current popular music—received, dismantled, and transformed through oral procedures, but retaining the mark of technology, especially for those familiar enough with the repertory and the technology to fully appreciate the sample's dialogic significance. In the case of the monophonic motet, this technological mark would be twofold: its overdetermined evocation of grafted things, and its textuality—or, if you will, its "motetness," its condensed verbal and musical cross-referencing.

HEARING AND READING THE HYBRID VOICE

While the relative paucity and narrow distribution of monophonic motets suggests a limited cultivation, the *Roman de Fauvel* offers a fourteenth-century Parisian witness to their potency as emblems of refinement, hybridity, and technological transition.[79] The

---

78. This accords with the view of a complex interaction between oral and written practices proposed by Berger, *Medieval Music and the Art of Memory*.

79. Butterfield mentions a number of fourteenth-century uses of the tern *enté* in literary texts (as well as texts on literature). See "*Enté*: A Survey and Reassessment," 91–97.

Roman de Fauvel is an allegorical verse narrative of a profligate horse that the Goddess Fortuna elevates to the throne. The narrative, written in the tradition of a royal *admonitio*, refers to the troubled last decades of the reign of Philip the Fair of France (r. 1285–1314) and those of his sons Louis X (r. 1315–16) and Philip V (r. 1317–22). One manuscript, here referred to as *Fauvel*, presents a multimedia blitz of music, art, and explicitly

FIGURE 4.5 *Han, Diex! ou pourrai je trouver* from *Fauvel*, fol. 26ᵛ (Bibliothèque nationale de France, Paris)

co-authored verse in order to finesse its criticisms and anxieties, but also to explore in various ways the theme of transitions and transformations. This can be seen in the program of illuminations depicting the shifting hybrid anatomy of the horse Fauvel (see figure 4.5).

Michael Camille has noted that the depiction of Fauvel with a human head and a horse's behind corresponds to scenes of courtship, in which Fauvel hides his animal-like nature below a false courtly countenance (referencing the figure of Faus Semblant, "false seeming," of the *Roman de la rose*).[80] The reversed anatomy, with the head of the beast exposed, corresponds to scenes of Fauvel's enthronement, indicating the true nature of rulers and the terrifying reversal of God's hierarchical creation. These two anxiety-ridden depictions have many thirteenth-century antecedents in the bestial hybrids of marginalia and animal allegories, such as the enthroned trickster fox Renart in the late thirteenth-century interpolated verse narrative *Renart le nouvel*.

The numerous musical interpolations in this manuscript include older thirteenth-century genres and styles and newer fourteenth-century examples, and this musical pointing both backward and forward also contributes to the exploration of transitions. Ardis Butterfield has written on the four distinctive monophonic pieces that coincide with the midpoint shift of authorial voice from Gervais du Bus to Chaillou de Pesstain, and the announcement of Chaillou's musical and verbal *addicions*.[81] These four important pieces lie symmetrically around a central *ballade* in the forward-looking style of the *forme fixe* of the *seconde rhétorique*. Two single-stanza melodies form the outer layer, framing two semi-lyric pieces—aggregates of sung refrains and spoken verses. The formal and generic inscrutability of these four pieces amplifies the moment of authorial transition (which itself alludes to that of the *Roman de la rose*)[82] and links this polyvocality not only to the thoroughly hybrid nature of the whole musically interpolated *roman*, but also to the conceptual and pictorial hybridity of Fauvel.

The second semi-lyric composition, *Han, Diex! ou pourrai je trouver* (fol. 26ʳ), most clearly illustrates this complex dual referencing. The narrative introduces the piece as a "motet," but what follows is a series of interlocking spoken and sung verses, one vocal medium constantly disrupting the other (as excerpted below):

Par ce motet, qu'ai retenu,	By this motet, which I have retained,
que tout qu'aussi sui je tenu	I am held in all the same bonds
com cil dont ce motet acorde.	as he concerning whom this motet harmonizes.

---

80. Camille, "Hybridity, Monstrosity, and Bestiality in the *Roman de Fauvel*."

81. See Butterfield, "Refrain and Transformation of Genre."

82. See Brownlee, "Authorial Self-Representation in *Fauvel*."

Han,   Diex!   ou   pour - rai je   trou - ver   [con - seil]

Han, Diex! de tout le monde sire,	*Oh, God!* Lord of all the world,
en quel rëaume, en quel empire,	in what kingdom, in what empire,
en quelle contrée ne terre,	in what country or region,
qui est qui le me sache a dire,	who is there who can tell me,
tant lointaign païs sache eslire?	can choose a place however far away?
Ou porrai je trouver par querre	*Where can I find*, through searching,
conseil?	counsel?
De quoi trouver *conseil, confort*	Find *counsel, comfort, and relief*
n'alegement? Si me confort	for what? So help me
amour, pas cler n'i puis veoir	love, I cannot see clearly
a confort trouver; c'est moult fort!	how to find comfort; it's very hard!
mes dont vient ce grant desconfort?	But where does this great discomfort come
	from?
Il se couvendroit pourveoir	It would be right to take precautions.

Des   mauls   que   la   belle au   vis   cler

Me   fait   sen - tir   si   a - - - spre - - - ment.

Dont il vient? *Des maus que la belle*	Where it comes from? *From the woes that*
	the beauty
au vis cler, et de cors est telle,	with a bright face, and the same of body,
belle sanz per, *me fait sentir*	beautiful without peer, *makes me feel*
si *asprement* que l'estencelle	so *bitterly* that the spark
d'amour m'art tout souz la mamelle.	of love sets fire to my breast.
Qui m'en puet de mort garantir?	Who can protect me from death?

Du tout en tout a moi gre - ver se de - lite

Comment sera il que n'en muire,	How can it be that I won't die,
quant celle en qui confort deduire	if the one in whose comfort I should
me deüsse tant me despite	that in order to singe my heart
que pour moi pour faire au cuer cuire	rejoice detests me so much
(*du tout [en] tout* ce me doit nuire)	(this will surely be *utterly* harmful to me)
trop *en moi grever se delite*?	*she greatly delights in hurting me*?

Each segment of melody and poetry contributes to a free monophonic composition that has a second concordance.[83] The intermittent spoken verses provide a poetic gloss that elaborates the sentiment and incorporates the words of the preceding sung verse. In the narrative, Fauvel sings this fractured monophonic motet in an effort to woo Fortune. The two vocal mediums of speech and song perhaps represent Fauvel's braying—his inability to sustain a musical voice, which in turn registers as *faus semblant*. This implication of dubious polyvocality gains support in light of the fact that the song created by the refrains also surfaces as the motetus of the scathing four-part Latin motet *Quasi non ministerium/Trahunt in precipicia/Ve, qui gregi deficiunt/DISPLICEBAT EI* earlier in the *roman*. The miniature illustrating the monophonic motet depicts three birds surrounding Fauvel as he brays to Fortune, no doubt referring to the missing voices of the polyphonic motet and cuing the reader to turn the pages backward. Thus we have a melody from a polyphonic motet extracted and digitalized into small sound bites and each re-presented as "motets" of another type, that is, as refrains just like those in table 4.2 above. This scene in *Fauvel* visually and thematically resembles the one from *Renart le nouvel* excerpted in table 4.2, where numerous refrains appear in close succession, sung by various animals who woo and deceive one another as they process to a banquet. The monophonic motet scene-complex from *Fauvel* plays with musical, verbal, and even visual references to an earlier allegorical interpolated verse narrative.[84]

---

83. For a complete transcription see Rosenberg and Tischler, *The Monophonic Songs*, 97–100. The monophonic song appears on the guard leaf of P-BnF f. lat. 7682. The words in example 4.10 are from Rosenberg and Tischler, with the exception of the introductory lines; the musical transcriptions are my own.

84. Butterfield has also discussed the connections of this semi-lyric piece with *Renart le nouvel*; see "Refrain and Transformation of Genre," 112–20. See also Peraino, "*E pui conmencha a canter*: Refrains, Motets and Melody." The two labeled *dits entés* by Jehan de Lescurel should also be mentioned here; Butterfield discusses these pieces in light of the grafting procedure she traces; see "*Enté*: A Survey and Reassessment," 89–91.

This particular deployment of a sampled motet voice presumes quite a sophisticated reader, one who is not only literate and acquainted with a repertory of animal stories and interpolated verse narratives, but also one who can read mensural notation and recognize melodies by sight, for a hearing of the polyphonic motet would not readily leave that particular melody ringing in the ears. Rather, this musical cross-reference requires the reader to fully utilize the technology of the codex, to follow a musical hyperlink by turning the pages backward and forward. It also challenges the reader to read and hear a string of refrains polyphonically—first by closing the gaps and reconstructing the original melody, and then by recalling its original polyphonic environment.

Any fan of current popular music will tell you that there are few things more satisfying than recognizing a sample or a stylistic allusion, hearing the transhistorical integrations and dialogues, and fully appreciating the latest in sound technology. Certainly *Han, Diex! ou pourrai je trouver* in *Fauvel* offered similar potential rewards for its audience; so too did *En non Dieu c'est la rage* and other earlier examples of monophonic motets, though no doubt to a more limited degree. But that's technology for you: today's grafted fruit is tomorrow's discarded apple.

5

Machaut's Turn to Monophony

ONE QUESTION LIES at the heart of this chapter. Why did Guillaume de Machaut write so many monophonic *virelais*? Of the thirty-three *virelais*, twenty-five are monophonic, while only eight are polyphonic (seven for two voices, one for three voices); even not counting these polyphonic *virelais*, the twenty-five monophonic *virelais* constitute the second most numerous genre in his musical oeuvre, which includes forty-one polyphonic *ballades*, twenty-two polyphonic *rondeaux*, twenty-three polyphonic motets, a polyphonic setting of the Mass Ordinary, and the polyphonic instrumental *David Hocket*. Machaut also wrote fifteen monophonic *lais* (another four have alternate polyphonic realizations); three monophonic songs in *pedes-cauda* form (a *complainte*, a "*chant roial*," and a *ballade* [B37][1]) were interpolated into the narrative the *Remede de Fortune*, which is in effect a musical *summa*. These last monophonic songs, along with the *lais*, are clearly retrospective, signifying a mastery and extension of classic thirteenth-century forms much like the *chansons d'amour* of Adam de la Halle. *Virelais*, in contrast, belong to the new fashion for refrain songs as one of the three *formes fixes* of the four-teenth century.

Among the *formes fixes*, the *virelais* are distinguished by the embedding of an internal stanza between the statements of a refrain. In its fourteenth-century form, the complete internal stanza is comprised of two parts: the first is the verse, which is always in the form of a couplet, two rhyming lines each with the same syllable count and melody;

---

1. All numbers for Machaut's compositions refer to Schrade, ed., *The Works of Guillaume de Machaut*; all texts are taken from this edition unless specified.

the second is a section that has the same rhymes, syllable count, and melody of the refrain. This section was called the *vuelta* (meaning "return") in fifteenth-century Spanish *villancicos*, which use the same form of *virelais*. The term *"vuelta,"* which I use throughout this chapter, calls attention to the return of the sounds of the refrain, though not its words.

The melodic plan for the *virelai* is represented in modern times this way, with lower case letters indicating new words for each stanza: AbbaA. Unlike the *rondeau* (ABaAabAB), where the two halves of the refrain generate music for the entire form, in the *virelai* the internal couplet presents contrasting music to the refrain. And the refrains of Machaut's *virelais* are not the pithy lines of the thirteenth century that invite a choral response, or the one-line refrains of his own *ballades*; rather they are extensive four- to eight-line closed lyric statements that develop a significance of their own.[2]

Machaut knew the term *virelai* but he preferred to call his songs in *virelai* form *chanson baladée* or "danced songs," as he notes in the *Remede de Fortune* (before 1342):

LINES 3448–50
Encommenchay ce virelay   I began this *virelai*
que on claimme chançon balladée;   which is called a danced song;
ainssi doit elle estre clamée.   thus it should be proclaimed.[3]

What follows in the *Remede de Fortune* is the monophonic *virelai Dame, a vous sans retollir*, to be discussed presently. Machaut sets this song up with an extensive narrative in which the Lady (*Dame*) invites the Lover (*l'Amant*) to join a group of courtiers engaged in a festive round dance (see figure 5.1). Machaut indicates that members of the group took turns singing as they danced, without instrumental accompaniment:

LINES 3366–8
N'il n'avoient nul instrument,   There were no instruments
ne menestrelz, fors chançonnettes   or minstrels, only delightful,
deduisans, courtoyses, et nette.   bright, and courtly songs.

LINES 3437–41
Mes dansié n'ous pas longuement   But I had not danced long
quant elle me dist doucement   before she told me sweetly
qu'il couvenoit que je chantasse   that it was agreed that I should sing,

---

2. In size, these refrains equal or exceed the total number of lines of the verse, which reverses the relationship between refrain and stanza found in the *ballade* or the earlier *chanson à refrain*.

3. All texts and translations of the *Remede de Fortune* are quoted from Guillaume de Machaut, *Remede de Fortune*, ed. and trans. Wimsatt and Kibler; their base manuscript is MS C. This quotation appears on fol. 51. Machaut also calls attention to the terminological distinction in his *Prologue*: "Motès, rondiaus et virelais / qu'on claimme chansons baladées" (Motets, *rondeaux*, and *virelais*, which are called danced songs). Section V, lines 14–15. *Oeuvres de Guillaume de Machaut*, ed. Hoepffner, 1:6. Hoepffner uses source G (P-BnF fr. 22546) as the base manuscript for his edition of the *Prologue*.

FIGURE 5.1 L'Amant sings a *virelai* in the *Remede de Fortune*, P-BnF fr. 1586, fol. 51 (Bibliothèque nationale de France, Paris)

et que de chanter m'avissasse,   and that I must make ready to sing,

car venus estoie a mon tour.   for it had come to my turn.[4]

From this scene in the *Remede de Fortune*, Lawrence Earp extrapolates that "in the early 1340s, at the beginning of his occupation with the setting of lyrics to music, Machaut had reserved the genre *virelai* as the dance genre," and, further, that they were "an isolated and local phenomenon" possibly "associated with the court of Bonne of Luxembourg," for whom the *Remede de Fortune* was probably composed.[5] Wulf Arlt echoes Earp's conclusions, stressing a dichotomy between "the simple musical form of the early monophonic virelais" that serve "the old dance-song function associated with the term 'ballade'" and later "more complex musical formulations, including polyphonic settings."[6]

Yet the music of the monophonic *virelais* is far from simple, and their functionality goes beyond accompanying dance. The scene of the *virelai* in the *Remede de Fortune* must not be taken merely as a literal description of performance practice; the song also participates in the long arc of the narrative. The story unfolds from an event that is a narrative version of a common topos in troubadour and trouvère lyrics, namely the loss of speech in the presence of the beloved. Here the Lover (who is the narrator/Machaut in his youth) has composed a *lai* about his feelings for the Lady, which comes to her as an anonymous lyric. She requests that he perform the *lai*, and after the performance she asks the composer's name. Fear silences the Lover, and he runs away devastated, isolating himself from courtly society. Through an extended instruction by Hope, the Lover regains his fortitude and returns to his Lady with the intention of revealing his identity as the composer of the *lai*. Importantly, the *virelai* is the first song that the Lover sings in the company of the Lady after his return from isolation, and before his revelation as the author of the *lai*; it marks his reentry into the social world and the regaining of his identity. Thus the *virelai* represents a newly found voice. If we extrapolate from this context, then our view of monophony becomes rather more complex: its form and style function as a special type of representation of the voice. In this chapter I strive to understand that representation.

A: MACHAUT'S VOICE: THE EXCEPTIONAL VIRELAI

Machaut invites us to interpret his songs by having his characters—Hope, the Lover, and the Lady—act as audience and commentators on the content of the lyrics, especially the *lai* that precipitates the story. Scholars have noted the new concept of *fin'amors*

---

4. I have provided a translation for line 3439, which does not appear in Wimsatt and Kibler.

5. Earp, "Genre in the Fourteenth-Century French Chanson," quotes from 131 and 141 respectively; see also Earp, *Guillaume de Machaut*, 25–26. About the *virelai* in the *Remede de Fortune*, Elizabeth Leach writes, "although it is a monophonic song form and thus could theoretically be performed by one musician singing alone, it is very specifically a social dance form, as the illumination that accompanies the musical notation makes clear"; see *Guillaume de Machaut*, 159.

6. Arlt, "Machaut, Guillaume de."

TABLE 5.1

Lyric interpolations in the *Remede de Fortune*

Genre	Singer	Form	Voices	Lines
lai	Lover	12 double-versicle strophes	monophony	431–680
complainte	Lover	36 stanzas (aab)	monophony	905–1480
chant roial	Hope	5 stanzas + envoi (aab)	monophony	1985–2032
baladelle	Hope	3 stanzas (aabb)*	4 voices	2857–92
balade	Lover	3 stanzas (aabC)	2 voices	3013–36
chanson baladée	Lover	3 stanzas (AbbaA)	monophonic	3451–96
rondelet	Lover	1 stanza (ABaAabAB)	3 voices	4109–16

* Every stanza concludes with a single-line refrain.

embedded in the *lai* and brought to light by Hope, namely, the alignment of love with hope rather than desire. This breaks from the troubadours' and trouvères' construction of love by casting desire as a negative force, not generative of song, but rather generative of silence because desire is subject to the turning Wheel of Fortune. Only hope can sustain *vraie amour* as a remedy to Fortune's ups and downs, and, by extension, hope detaches love from all external experiences, including interactions with the Lady. Thus love becomes self-sustaining—"a kind of sublime solipsism."[7]

The interpolated songs in the *Remede de Fortune* explicitly espouse this "modern love" (to quote David Bowie once again), promoting *souffisance* (sufficiency) over *desire*, with one exception—the *virelai* (*chanson baladée*). The songs are distributed between the Lover and Hope, and they follow a didactic order from the most complex poetic form to the simplest; the music, however, progresses in an inverse relationship to the lyrics, from syllabic settings to melismatic settings (see table 5.1). Again, the exception here is the *virelai*, which is syllabic.[8] Furthermore, in MS *C*, every song in table 5.1 receives an illustration, and every song is represented as a written scroll—except the *virelai*. This song is represented as a spontaneous, unmediated, and *unscripted* performance (see figure 5.1). Thus this exceptional song, *Dame, a vous sans retollir*, merits a closer look.

Once asked to sing for the dance, the Lover, newly returned to society, demurs: "but I know very little about singing" ("mais petitement me sçai de chanter entremettre," lines 3444–45). The audience of the *Remede de Fortune* knows otherwise, however, for they have heard or read the *lai* and a *ballade* (*Dame, de qui toute ma joie vient*) that the Lover composed on his way to rejoin society. The *ballade* praises not love but hope as the source of desire, which the Lover ultimately finds within himself:

---

7. This observation about Machaut's new concept of love was first put forth by Kelly in *Medieval Imagination*, 130–37; quotation from Brownlee, *Poetic Identity in Guillaume de Machaut*, 6; see also 37–63.

8. Calin, "Medieval Intertextuality," esp. 7.

LINES 3021-4

Cilz douls Espoirs en vie me soustient	This sweet Hope keeps me alive
et me norrist en amoureus desir,	and nourishes me with amorous desire,
et dedens moy met tout ce qui couvient	and places within me everything that is needed
pour conforter mon cuer et resjoïr;	to comfort and bring joy to my heart;

This sentiment of *souffisance* contrasts with the more traditional configuration of love in his next lyric utterance, the *virelai*. I quote the final stanza and the framing refrain of the *virelai* below:

A

Dame, a vous sans retollir	My lady, to you without reservation
doins cuer, pensee, desire,	I give my heart, my thought, desire,
corps, et amour,	body, and love,
comme a toute la millour	as to the very best
qu'on puist choysir,	who can be seen,
ne qui vivre ne morir	or who can live or die
puist a ce jour.	in this time.

b

Dame, ou sont tuit mi retour,	My lady, my every resource,
souvent m'estuet en destour	I must often lament and mourn
plaindre et gemir,	when far from you,

b

et, present vous, descoulour,	and, near you, I grow pale,
quant vous ne savez l'ardour	since you don't know the passion
qu'ai a sousfrir	I have to suffer

a

pour vous qu'aim tant et desir,	for you whom I love and desire so much
que plus ne le puis couvrir.	that I can no longer hide it.
Et se tenrour	And if tenderness
n'en avez, en grant tristour	you do not have, in great sadness
m'estuet fenir.	I must end my days.
Nonpourquant jusqu'a mourir	Nonetheless until death
vostre demour.	I remain yours.

A

Dame, a vous sans retollir	My lady, to you without reservation
doins cuer, pensee, desire,	I give my heart, my thought, desire,
corps, et amour,	body, and love,

comme a toute la millour	as to the very best
qu'on puist choysir,	who can be seen,
ne qui vivre ne morir	or who can live or die
puist a ce jour.	in this time.[9]

In the initial position, the refrain seems pedantic, listing the physical and mental faculties engaged in courtly devotion balanced by an extended superlative that reflects the worth of his beloved. The stanza, however, harks back to the *fin'amors* of the troubadours and trouvères—a subject consumed by desire, suffering, and lamenting, dependent on the Lady for "every resource." Indeed, love and desire here threaten to expose the Lover—not through words, but through his physical appearance, his *descoulour*. Coming after this more passionate outburst, the refrain takes on a different meaning, for we know, then, the toll this complete devotion takes on the lover's heart, thought, desire, and body. The list becomes an enumeration of vulnerability, and the superlative "la millour...ne qui vivre ne morir" echoes the forlorn devotion "jusqu'a mourir" of the lover's imagined rejection.

Yet we know, too, that revealing his love (by revealing his authorship of the *lai*) is, in fact, the Lover's plan. The threat of exposure in the lyric of the *virelai* acts as a decoy, another moment of coyness and deferral. Discretion, deferral, dissimulation—these are, of course, part of the public face of *fin'amors*, played out in both the modesty and the scandalmonger topoi. This is borne out in the curious coda to the *Remede de Fortune*: after the Lover and the Lady pledge their devotion to one another, they also pledge to keep their love secret; but soon the Lover grows melancholic from the Lady's inattention in public. She explains her reasons to him:

LINES 4199–4204

Car je le fais pour le milleur	I do it for the best
et pour mieus celer vostre amour;	and in order to conceal our love better;
car qui en amour ne scet faindre,	for a lover who does not know how to feign,
il ne puet a grant joye ataindre	cannot attain great joy.

This topsy-turvy condition of love, in which words and appearances *should be* misleading, serves to drive home Machaut's point about (modern) *fin'amors*, for only through internal hope and *suffisance* can a lover withstand such outward tests of Fortune.

In contrast to the subterfuge of verbal expressions, musical expressions function as moments of distilled and truthful sentiment in a narrative full of coyness. Once the Lover has revealed his identity as the composer of the *lai*, he also reveals the meaning of the *virelai*.

---

9. Lines 3484–96. I have modified the translation.

LINES 3705–10

Et s'il vous plaist, ma dame chiere,	And if it pleases you, my dear Lady,
a regarder la dairreniere	to consider the last
chançonnette que ja chantay,	little song that I sang,
que fait en dit et en chant ay,	of which I composed both words and music,
vous pourrez de legier savoir	you can easily tell
se je ment ou se je di voir.	whether I am lying or speaking the truth.

The *virelai* figures here as a medieval polygraph, a means of detecting the underlying emotions that words alone can miss or mask. But how is this so? As I noted, the words of the *virelai* do not conform to Machaut's new concept of love; they are markedly nostalgic from the narrative's point of view, harking back to the sentiments of troubadours and trouvères. Perhaps this love rhetoric of the past lends the words credence. Perhaps, too, the music tells something more.

Several scholars have discussed the music of *Dame, a vous sans retollir* (see example 5.1 ● OXFORD WEB MUSIC), noting the clear tonal focus (F final supported by a C half-cadence in the internal couplets), melodic correspondences at the close of each section, metrical ambiguity (toggling between 6/8 and 3/4), musical enjambments of poetic lines (A section, mm. 4, 7, 8, 10; B section, m. 4), and even "implied polyphonic textures" in the registral distribution of notes (A section, mm. 9–10) and "control of sub-surface pitch structure on several levels at once." Indeed, *contra* Arlt's statement about the simplicity of the *virelais*, Daniel Leech-Wilkinson concludes that "a composer capable of manufacturing these kinds of subtleties was no beginner, nor was he simply writing down the sorts of tunes commonly used for courtly dance."[10]

A close look at the musical and poetic details of this *virelai* reveal it to be particularly expressive. Although the tonal scheme is clearly defined by the full and half-cadences, the A section begins obscurely, emphasizing G rather than F as the pitch of repose for the setting of the first three lines (mm. 1–5). This G becomes redefined as the upper neighbor to the F final through a series of eighth-note figures that wind their way through upper and lower neighbor notes, and concatenate the poetic lines (mm. 7–8), until finally settling on the F in measure 9, then followed by a long cadential confirmation (mm. 9–11). As is usual in Machaut's *virelais*, the shorter B section presents a contrasting tessitura and tonal focus, usually leaping to the fifth or octave above the refrain's final. Given its brevity, there is not much time for coyness; the complementary pitch C comes on strong as the tonal anchor in this section. This renders the A section all the

---

10. Quotations from Leech-Wilkinson, "Not Just a Pretty Tune," 30 (see also 27–31); other scholars treating this *virelai* include Earp, "Genre in the Fourteenth-Century French Chanson," 127–32; Arlt, "Aspekte der Chronologie," 263–64; and Plumley, *The Grammar of 14th-Century Melody*, 103–104.

EXAMPLE 5.1 Guillaume de Machaut, *Dame, a vous sans retollir* (V33), final stanza

more coy for its opening feint to G. Machaut has given us a melody that embodies the dilemma of discretion and expression that lies at the heart of the *Remede de Fortune*, and the moment of the Lover's *virelai*.

Ambiguities in the realm of pitch in *Dame, a vous sans retollir* are matched in rhythm. Machaut gives the performer of this *virelai* a set of articulation problems to overcome, just as the Lover had to overcome his own paralyzing silence. Melodic phrases follow longer syntactic lines rather than the shorter poetic ones artificially divided by rhyme and syllable count. This is especially true in the setting of the last stanza quoted above. In example 5.1, the beginning of a new poetic line is italicized, but the transcription follows the logic of the musical phrases. If we write out the longer syntactic lines, we see another level of play and syncopation in the alternation of internal and external rhymes, and in collisions of successive accents that fall on rhyming words and the word that follows (highlighted in bold below and in the score).

Refrain:

Dame, a vous sans retollir doins cuer, pensee, des**ir**, *corps*, et amour,

comme a toute la mil**lour** *qu'on* puist choysir, ne qui vivre ne mo**rir** *puist* a ce jour.

Rhymes:

-ir	-ir	-our,	
-our	-ir	-ir	-our.

Couplet:

Dame, ou sont tuit mi retour, souvent m'estuet en des**tour** *plaindre* et gemir,

et, present vous, descoulour, quant vous ne savez l'ar**dour** *qu'ai* a sousfrir

Rhymes:

-our	-our	-ir,
-our	-our	-ir.

In contrast to these head-on collisions of successive musical and verbal accents, the cadence of the B section (m. 16) interrupts the flow of words with a striking pause on *sousfrir*, thus leaving the singer/Lover to hang on this suffering before the clause is completed by the *vuelta*. Unlike the other stanzas, the *vuelta* in this final one is comprised of short sentences that amplify with full stops and emphatic starts the same nodes of tension written into the musical-poetic design of this song.

Vuelta:

pour vous qu'aim tant et desir, que plus ne le puis couv**rir**. *Et* se tenr**our**

n'en avez, en grant trist**our** *m'estuet* fe**nir**. *Non*pourquant jusqu'a mourir **vostre**
   demour.

In *Dame, a vous sans retollir* the rush of music through poetic lines matches the emotional urgency of the words, and the pervasive out-of-sync rhythmic articulation of words and music calls attention to a paradox inherent in Machaut's *virelais*: it is the paradox of the *chanson baladée*.

The narrator describes the performance practice of all the *chançonettes* of the convivial dance as purely vocal, without instrumental accompaniment (and without minstrels, or professional musicians). Instrumental dances survive from the fourteenth century—the earliest appear among the mensural additions to trouv. *M*—and their melodies are boisterous and immediate rather than intimate and coy, as is the *virelai* Machaut provides for a "danced song" in the *Remede de Fortune*.[11] Daniel Leech-Wilkinson argues that "hardly any [of Machaut's *virelais*] have the regular metrical structures one would expect of a dance accompaniment, or the regular mode one would expect of a popular song."[12]

---

11. See McGee, *Medieval Instrumental Dances*.

12. Leech-Wilkinson, "Not Just a Pretty Tune," 16. Eustache Deschamps, in *L'Art de dictier* (1392), defines the genre *chanson baladée* not with regard to dance, but rather by comparison to the *ballade*, which shares a

Machaut may be taking a certain "poetic license" in characterizing his own *virelai* in a particularly rustic way, adding an element of authenticity that is distinct from the rarefied clerical language of love. Yet the narrative expressly describes a woman dancing to *Dame, a vous sans retollir*, and responding with her own song, whose refrain Machaut quotes. There is a curious didacticism to the scene, as if Machaut wants to stress the origins of the *virelai* in dance, while using it in the manner of a trouvère *chanson d'amour*, where desire—not dance—is the raison d'être of the song. Here, then, we may read Machaut's term as naming a composite or hybrid genre—a *chanson* that is danced to—which is also a paradox for its mixed register of personal solo song and social, choral event. We must keep in mind that in Machaut's scene, other courtiers are singing songs for the dance, presumably *virelais*. Would their lyrics speak of love? Would their songs be equally expressive and sincere? Or does such authentic expression pertain only to Machaut's voice?

b: AUTHENTICITY AND THE *VIRELAI*: SOUTHERN TRADITIONS

Like the etymology of "*tornada*" discussed in chapter 1, the name "*virelai*" probably has something to do with turning (*virement*), from *virer* (to turn, to twist). A number of thirteenth-century refrains and other scattered references describe a dance move or a dance song with the term *vireli*, *virenli*, or *virelai*, though the latter form seems to have gained prominence only with Machaut's generation.[13] Leech-Wilkinson has looked for *virement* in the circularity of Machaut's tonal designs that allow a dual functioning of the A music to lead into the stanza as well as close the entire song; Earp believes that for Machaut, *virement* is "the sum effect of the short lines of different lengths, combined with a musical setting that features unpredictable longs and shorts that bring about misplaced word accents and headlong enjambments of lines"—in other words, a spinning around that creates dizziness and disorientation.[14] If turning is at the root of the *virelai*, then we might well ask what Machaut seems to be turning toward, or away from, in his glossing of the *virelai* as a *chanson baladée*.

A number of thirteenth-century genres share the musical and metrical form that defines the French *virelai*—Occitan *dansas*, the Spanish *cantigas* (later *villancicos*), the Italian *ballate* and sacred *laude*[15]—and this has given rise to a number of theories about the

---

three-strophe structure plus a refrain. See Earp, "Genre in the Fourteenth-Century French Chanson," 128n15.

13. See Bec, *La Lyrique française*, 1:234–40; Wilkins, "Virelai."

14. Earp, "Genre in the Fourteenth-Century French Chanson," 130–31; see also Leech-Wilkinson's comments in "Not Just a Pretty Tune," esp. 24 and 30.

15. A single thirteenth-century source of monophonic *laude* survives (Cortona, Biblioteca Comunale e dell'Accademia Etrusca 91), containing modest, largely syllabic settings notated in note shapes that defy any modal or mensural interpretation. See Barr, *The Monophonic Lauda*. The earliest source for monophonic *ballate* stems from the first half of the fourteenth century and contains highly melismatic musical settings that

form's origin. In his thorough study of the origin of the *virelai* and *villancico*, Pierre Le Gentil notes that scholars tend to split into three camps—those who argue a derivation from the eleventh- and twelfth-century Andalusian *mūwashshah* and *zajal*, those who argue a derivation from responsorial liturgical forms and paraliturgical *versus* with refrains circulating in Aquitaine ca. 1100, and those who argue an evolution from the variety of refrain-forms associated with the *carole*. The Andalusian or Hispano-Arab theory has garnered much attention because of the compelling resemblance between *mūwashshah* and *zajal* poetic forms and Spanish *cantigas*, and because it fortifies arguments that the particular ethics of *fin'amors* also originated with Arabic poetry (see the Introduction).

The metrical scheme of the *mūwashshah* and *zajal* can be loosely described as Abbba[A], with a prelude, a strophe comprised of triple monorhyme versicles or some tripartite rhyme scheme (bcbcbc), followed by a *vuelta* that recalls the rhymes of the prelude (which may or may not act like a refrain); *zajals* sometimes end with a *kharja*—a refrain-like tag in corrupt Spanish that attests to cultural cross-fertilization. In reality, the designs vary widely and can look more or less like a *virelai* (such as ABaaab[AB] or AAbcbcbcba[AA]).[16] The internal lines that precede the *vuelta* change their rhymes from strophe to strophe (AbbbaAcccaAdddaA), rendering the rhymes of the *vuelta* as equivalents to the *rims estramps* in troubadour poetry, or rhymes connected across rather than within strophes.

Some scholars see the influence of the *zajal* in the lyrics of the earliest troubadours Guilhem IX and Marcabru that use three-line rhymes followed by *rims estramps* (aaab, cccb, or aaabab, cccbcb), and especially in the lyrics of the later Spanish *cantigas*, which frequently contain triple monorhyme versicles followed by a single-line *vuelta* that recalls the rhyme of the refrain. The music of the *cantigas de Santa Maria*, compiled in the mid-thirteenth century for the court of King Alfonso X (r. 1252–84), frequently superimposes another design onto the lyrics, distributing the three versicles into a musical couplet and *vuelta* so that the song form looks like a *virelai*. The metrical and musical design of *cantiga* no. 17, *Sempre seja bèeita et loada* is as follows:[17]

---

can be compared to the *virelais* of Jehan de Lescurel more readily than to the Occitan pieces in trouv. *M*, or the *virelais* of Machaut. For a discussion of the monophonic *laude* and *ballate*, see Yudkin, *Music in Medieval Europe*, 297–301 and 523–25, respectively. These fourteenth-century *ballata*, however, use a single-line refrain and single-line couplets. Nevertheless, the term *ballata*, like *dansa* and *chanson baladée*, explicitly conveys an association with dancing. In *De vulgari eloquentia*, Dante mentions the *ballata* along with *sonitus* (sonnets) as less noble vernacular forms than the *cantiones* of the troubadours and trouvères; see *De vulgari eloquentia*, Bk. II, 3.

Despite the differences in poetic and melodic style between the monophonic *virelais* and *ballate*, polyphonists of the mid-fourteenth century—French and Italian alike—did recognize a formal similarity and found it entirely appropriate to Frenchify or Italianize the style of their compositions, as is evident in the *ballate* of Francesco Landini and the florid mimetic *virelai Par maintes foys* by Vaillant.

16. Le Gentil, *Le Virelai et le villancico*, 30–56; Harvey et al. "Zajal."

17. See Le Gentil, *Le Virelai et le villancico*, 126–29. For a transcription of *cantiga* no. 17 see also Anglés, ed., *La música de las Cantigas*, 2:25.

words:	A^{10}	A^{10}	b^{10}	b^{10}	b^{10}	a^{10}	A^{10}	A^{10}
music:	A	B	c	c	A	B	A	B

Where line lengths differ between the refrain and the versicles of the strophe, composers or scribes exercised the option to divide long note values and break or create ligatures as needed, preserving the melodic design despite the poetic one (see *cantiga* no. 36, *Muit'amar devemos en nossas voontades*).[18] Many troubadour and trouvère songs do not match rhyme scheme with melodic repetition (most obvious with the *oda continua*, and in the *cauda* portion of songs), but the "near miss" of the *cantigas* seems more suggestive, perhaps indicating that the music and the words came from different points of origin and were brought together by an observation of their shared characteristic—namely, the formal *return* of something within the strophe that signals the refrain.

Liturgical and paraliturgical repertories provide other twelfth-century models for poetic and musical designs that may have led to the French *virelai* or Occitan *dansa*. The *versus tripertitus caudatus* (aab ccb; 448 448) found in sequences and in some *sirventes*, as noted in chapter 2, also resembles the strophe of the *dansa*.[19] Margaret Switten has observed a variety of refrain forms in twelfth-century Aquitanian *versus*, ranging from single-word refrains, single-line refrains, to varied refrains and double refrains, which she believes influenced refrain practices in troubadour songs. Although Switten does not connect any of the *versus* to the later Occitan *dansa*, the *versus In hoc anni circulo* uses a "*zajal*esque" construction (aaaB cccB dddB: music, abcD), alternating Latin and Occitan strophes.[20] The Latin portion of this song enjoyed distribution well beyond the Limousin region and the medieval period; notably, a Sicilian source, dated between 1130 and 1139, contains the Latin strophes with a two-line refrain split in such a way as to provide a *vuelta* that signals a turn to the refrain (lyric, aaaB CB; music, abcD CD).[21] Thus as this song migrated, the structural importance of the refrain became reinforced; furthermore, the melodic style also shifted from lightly melismatic, in the manner of a *canso*, to rigidly syllabic. Hans Spanke lists *In hoc anni circulo* among the thirteen sacred refrain songs that bear witness to the crossover between secular and ecclesiastical dance—the latter used in lay worship and by the clergy during the festivals of Christmas, Easter, and major and local saints. On his visit to the church of Saint-Yldevert in Gournay (Normandy), sometime between 1248 and 1269, the archbishop Odo Rigaldus

---

18. Anglés, *La música de las Cantigas*, 2:44.

19. See also Le Gentil, *Le Virelai et le villancico*, 151–53.

20. P-BnF lat. 1139, fol. 48. See Switten, "*Versus* and Troubadours around 1100," 121; see also 92n2 for past studies that link Aquitanian *versus* to troubadour lyrics. See also Newcombe, "The Refrain in Troubadour Lyric Poetry."

21. For transcriptions see Treitler, "The Aquitanian Repertories of Sacred Monody," 2:10; the source is Madrid, Bibl. Nac. 289, fol. 147. See ibid., 2:10–11 for a discussion of the source, and 32–35 for critical notes on the transcription. A few Aquitanian *versus* lyrics suggest a *vuelta*, though the musical setting uses double versicles: see *In laudes innocentium* (lyrics, a^8 a^8 a^8B^4 A^8B^4; music, a^8 a^8 b^{12} b^{12}) in Spanke, "St. Martial-Studien," 12, no. 40. For other examples see Spanke, "Tanzmusik in der Kirche des Mittelalters," esp. 124–26, nos. 2, 5, 9, 12.

observed "clerics, deacons, and even priests in certain festivities...leading *caroles* through the streets and doing 'the *virelai*.'"[22]

Hispano-Arab and liturgical theories aside, Machaut's own association of the *virelai* with dance leads us directly to the French refrain songs variously called *rondets de carole* and *ballettes*, and to the Occitan *dansa* as *his* point of origin for the form. These northern and southern secular dance songs appear at roughly the same time in the middle decades of the thirteenth century (along with the *cantigas*), yet there is evidence to suggest that the *virelai-dansa* form in particular retained—or perhaps acquired—an association with Occitan in the latter half of the century and into the next.

Among the northern examples of the *rondets de carole* two formal options appear regularly—the splitting of a refrain and its interpolation within the strophe, yielding the prototype for a *rondeau* form (aAabAB); and adding a refrain to a short couplet with a transitional couplet, yielding the prototype for the *virelai* (aa ab AB). The proto-*rondeau* form was most common, as borne out in the ratio of *virelai* to *rondeau* forms (1:17) quoted in the early thirteenth-century narrative *Guillaume de Dole*, and among the monophonic refrain songs of Willammes d'Amiens (1:9) and the polyphonic refrain songs of Adam de la Halle (2:13). In Friedrich Gennrich's comprehensive collection of *rondeaux, virelais,* and *ballades* from the late twelfth to the early fourteenth centuries, the number of *rondeaux* far exceed *virelais*.[23] Looking ahead to Jehan de Lescurel, only five of his thirty-four monophonic songs, preserved uniquely in *Fauvel* (ca. 1316–17), are in *virelai* form.[24] *Fauvel* itself contains two examples of *virelai* forms among its monophonic interpolations: for *Douce et de tout noble afaire* (no. 44) the melodic form matches the rhyme scheme, providing a rare example of a musical *zajalesque* construction (ABCaaabcABC), while *Providence, la senee* (no. 26, introduced as a *ballade* in the narrative) uses a double-versicle melodic

---

22. "Clerici, vicarii, ac etiam capellani in festivitatibus quibusdam...ducendo choreas per vicos et faciendo *le vireli*." Quoted in Spanke, "Tanzmusik in der Kirche des Mittelalters," 128; and also Pfuhl, *Untersuchungen über die Rondeaux und Virelais,* 66. For a thorough study of the relationship between Latin and Romance lyric see Spanke, *Beziehungen zwischen romanischer und mittellateinischer Lyrik.* For more on liturgical dancing see Stevens, *Words and Music in the Middle Ages,* 178–86. For a study of the fraught relationship between the church and the *carole,* see Page, *The Owl and the Nightingale,* 110–33. Page identifies the Old French equivalent of *corea* as carole in *Voices and Instruments,* 80.

23. See Gennrich, *Rondeaux, Virelais und Balladen* I; the *virelai* forms are no. 13 (rhyme scheme abacbC from *Guillaume de Dole*), no. 49 (Guillaume d'Amiens); those by Adam de la Halle are no. 69, *Fines amouretes ai,* which comes closer to the *virelais* of the fourteenth century, showing a musical pattern of AbccabAB, and no. 81, *Dieus soit en cheste maison,* with the musical scheme ABccde [AB]. This last song also uses a zajalesque three-line monorhyme in the stanza.

    Gennrich argued that the *rondeau* and the *virelai* emerged from the same pool of refrain forms—a view shared by Gilbert Reaney. Willi Apel believed the *virelai* was not indigenous to northern France. See Gennrich, *Grundriss einer Formenlehre des mittelalterlichen Liedes,* 69–77; Apel, "Rondeaux, Virelais, and Ballades in French 13th-Century Song," 128–29; Reaney, "Concerning the Origins of the Rondeau, Virelai, and Ballade Forms," 161–63.

24. See Wilkins, ed., *The Works of Jehan de Lescurel.*

construction for the refrain (ABAB′cdcd abab′ABAB′).²⁵ Although the *virelai* had become formally differentiated from *ballades* and *rondeaux* by the time of these compositions, the index for the manuscript only lists "balades, rondeaux et diz entez sus refroiz de rondeaux, les quiex fist Jehannot de Lescurel" (*ballades, rondeaux*, and grafted *dits* onto the refrains of *rondeaux*, those made by Jehan de Lescurel); the word *virelai* does not appear. Nor did earlier compilers make a distinction between *virelais* and *rondeaux*; as mentioned in the previous chapters, the table of contents for trouv. *a* lists *chancons, pastoureles, motet et roondel*, and Adam de la Halle's collected works manuscript trouv. *W* similarly lists only *cançons, partures, roundiaus, motes*. Wulf Arlt states unequivocally that the *virelai* "is not conceived as a distinct genre till Machaut."²⁶

Arlt and Page both argue that the *virelai* emerged out of a "*ballade-virelai* matrix" to be found in trouv. *I*, where scribes rubricated the section of *ballete*, but not the section of *rondeaux* and motet lyrics. Various refrain designs appear among the *ballete*, including *chanson à refrain* and *chanson avec des refrains*, and songs that begin with refrains not metrically linked to the stanzas but presumably repeated after each. Very few of these lyrics (by my count only six out of 188) look like *virelais* with a substantial refrain that equals or exceeds the length of the couplet, and with a fully-formed *vuelta* that reflects the rhyme and syllable count of the refrain.²⁷ Thus it seems the *virelai* form was a less chosen option among many refrain procedures; it did not fit well with the practice of pithy refrain quotation found in the *chanson à refrain* or *chansons avec des refrains*, or dance-song practices that interleave half a refrain into the verse, as found in the *rondet de carole*. In sum, the form does not appear to be favored in—or "indigenous" to—the north.

Only about thirty Occitan songs identified as *dansas* by scholars survive, the majority of which are attributed to two mid-thirteenth-century troubadours: István Frank lists thirteen by Guiraut d'Espanha (de Tholosa) (fl. 1245–65), five by the Catalan Cerverí de Girona (fl. 1259–85), and one each by Uc de Saint Circ (fl. 1217–53) and Paulet de Marselha (fl. 1260s).²⁸ The remaining ten are anonymous, and three of these appear among the five

---

25. Fauvel sings both songs in his effort to woe Fortune; their melodies are heavily ornamented. The numbers refer to the edition by Rosenberg and Tischler, *The Monophonic Songs*. For the date of the *Fauvel* manuscript see Bent and Wathey, introduction to *Fauvel Studies*, 16.

26. Arlt, "Jehannot de Lescurel and the Function of Musical Language," 26.

27. See Atchison, *The Chansonnier of Oxford Bodleian MS Douce 308*. The six *ballete* in clear *virelai* form are nos. 12, 23, 53, 60 (although the refrain does not appear before the first strophe), 63, and 77. In his investigation of the songs in Douce 308 Christopher Page writes of a "*ballade-virelai* matrix" in which the placement of the refrain in relation to the verse could yield the prototype for either form—refrain-verse for *virelais* and verse-refrain for *ballades*. This places the *virelai* in relation to the *chanson à refrain* rather than the *rondet de carole*. More importantly for Page, sixteen of these songs foreshadow the *ars nova ballade* with their three isometric and monorhymed stanzas and the same concluding refrain. See Page, "Tradition and Innovation," 378–83.

28. Frank 2:70–71. *Amors m'art con fuco* (PC 461-20) is not listed among the *dansas* in Frank; he lists it as *canso* fragment 624:88, despite its *dansa* musical and poetic form. Although the name Guiraut d'Espanha would seem to indicate an association with Spain, troub. *C* gives his name as "de Tholosa," suggesting he was a native of or associated with Toulouse.

mensural *dansas* added to trouv. *M*. These five *dansas* are the only ones to survive with music. (As mentioned in chapter 3, the *tornada* of *Ben volgra s'esser poges*, which has been attributed to Guiraut d'Espanha by some scholars, identifies itself as a *dansa*.[29])

The term *dansa* as a generic designation first appears in two twelfth-century Occitan sources, where it is associated with performance on a fiddle (along with other genres such as *descorts*, *lais*, and *cansonz de gesta*),[30] and later in a didactic verse epistle by Guiraut Riquier (dated 1274), which lists "*coblas, sirventes, dansas*" but gives no details about poetic or musical form.[31] Two treatises, the *Doctrina de compondre dictats* (ca. 1290) and *Las Leys d'Amors* (ca. 1330), describe the *dansa* as a song with a refrain and three stanzas, plus one or more *tornadas*; both describe the option of ending the stanzas with the same rhymes and line lengths as the refrain—in other words, a *vuelta*.[32] *Las Leys d'Amors* further specifies that the length of the refrain (*repos*) should be about half the length of the stanza (*cobla*), presumably so the verse and *vuelta* are more or less balanced, and that none of the line lengths should exceed eight syllables (those that do are "irregular").

The author of *Las Leys d'Amors* also pointedly criticizes current trends in performance that wrongly make the *dansas* sound like the *redondel*: "Han mudat lo so de dansa en so de redondel am lors minimas et am lors semibreus de lors motetz" (They change the music of the *dansa* into the music of the *redondel* with the minims and semibreves of their motets). A later marginal annotation explains that *redondels* and songs called *viandelas* are made *en frances* (in French).[33] The notation and rapid melodic style that characterize the French compositions for these Occitan writers strongly suggests *ars nova*-style motets and *formes fixes*. The monophonic pieces by Jehan de Lescurel, which

---

29. The song is listed twice in PC as both attributed and anonymous; Elizabeth Aubrey adopts the attribution to Guiraut d'Espanha in *The Music of the Troubadours*, 124. The Becks note that other lyrics by Guiraut d'Espanha reference *coms d'Anjous* (PC 244-9) and *lo coms Karles* (PC 244-1) but not *reys Karles* as in *Ben volgra s'esser poges* (*Le Manuscrit du roi*, 2:170). Given that Guiraut's flourishing dates precede Charles's ascension to the throne of Sicily in 1270, it seems unlikely that Guiraut composed the *dansa*. Otto Hoby also doubts that Guiraut composed *Ben volgra s'esser poges*; see his "Die Lieder des Trobadors Guiraut d'Espanha," 120. Scholars have linked the nine *dansas* that appear anonymously in troub. *E* to the attributed *dansas* and *cansos* of Guiraut d'Espanha through shared *senhals* and metrical schemes. In Hoby's edition of the texts he does not indicate that the opening refrain repeats at the end of each stanza. One *dansa*, *Gen m'ausi* (PC 244-2), contains a *zajal*esque metric scheme: aab cccab dddab eeeab plus two *tornadas* that repeat the rhymes of the refrain.

30. See Page, *Voices and Instruments*, 22–23.

31. The epistle by Riquier is titled *Pus Dieus m'a dat saber* (no. 10 or 11 depending on the catalog) written during his stay in the courts of Castile. For text see Linskill, *Les Épîtres de Guiraut Riquier*, 187, line 817. See the *vida* of Raimond de Miraval, which mentions the composition of *dansas*; s.v. "Dansa," *LR*, 3:8.

32. See Aubrey, *The Music of the Troubadours*, 123, for a quotation of the *Doctrina* passage concerning the *dansa*; see also Chambers, *An Introduction to Old Provençal Versification*, 217–22 for a discussion of the *dansa* in *Las Leys d'Amors*; Marshall, *The Razos de trobar of Raimon Vidal*, 138 and 141–42; and Page, *Voices and Instruments*, 24 and 247n22.

33. Gatien-Arnoult, ed., *Las Leys d'Amors*, 1:342 (text). These rules are found in both the prose (340–43) and verse redactions (354–59) of the treatise; see 350–51 for the section on the *redondels* and *viandelas*. Page discusses the marginal annotations in *Voices and Instruments*, 42–46.

TABLE 5.2

Dansas and the *rondeaux* added to trouv. *M*

Scribe	Beck fol.	Current fol.	Incipit	PC number
Dansas				
1	170bis	186*	Ben volgra s'esser poges	461-51a/244-1a
3	XXI^v	78^v*	Tant es gay et avinentz	461-230
5	3^v	1^v	Donna, pos vos ay	461-92
6	3^v	1^v	Pos qu'ieu vey la fualla	461-196
7	170^terv	187^v*	Amors m'art con fuoc	461-20a
Rondeaux				B-rond number
18	6^v	4^v	Trop ai esté lonc tans mus	154
20	7^v	5^v	J'ai bele dame amée	155
21	3	1	U despit des envïeus	153
21	7^v	5^v	Se je chant et sui envoisiés	156

* denotes a position at the end of a gathering.

I will discuss in the following section, are particularly relevant. Here I want to point out that in *Las Leys d'Amors*, it is language and melodic style that most distinguish the *dansa* from the *redondel*.[34] This alignment of language and genre occurs in the mensural additions to trouv. *M* (see table 5.2). Furthermore, they lie on opposite ends of the spectrum in terms of chronology, formality, rhetoric, and musical scope. Thus, at the turn of the fourteenth century, the *rondeau* and the *dansa* seem to display distinct characters and perhaps also meanings.

We know that at least one of the *dansas*, *Ben volgra s'esser poges*, was probably composed and recorded between 1265 and 1285 because the final *tornada* makes an unusual reference to "*reys Karles*"; the other four *dansas* were probably added shortly thereafter, judging by their similar bookhand and their clustering with other early entries.[35] The fact that these later *dansas* have lost their multiple stanzas and *tornadas* suggests that they function as examples of a more purely *musical* genre, rather than songs bound by words

34. Page also cites this passage as evidence that Guilhem Molinier "denounces the influence of rhythmic style that he associates with the motet" ("Tradition and Innovation," 368). Le Gentil believes that the *dansa am refranh* or *cobla retronchada* as described in *Las Leys d'Amors* came late to the troubadour tradition, and may reflect the influence of refrain practices from the north (*Virelai et Villancico*, 57).

35. *Tant es gay et avinentz* shows some cursive characteristics with exaggerated loops. This *dansa* had to be entered before the *cobla Ben volgra quem venques* (though the *cobla* is written in a more formal bookhand) because the *cobla* was entered in the remaining portion of the right column following the last lines of the *dansa*. Thus the degree of formality of the hands does not necessarily map onto the chronology of the entry. Furthermore, the prior *dansa* is written in mensural notation whereas the *cobla* is written in undifferentiated neumes.

to a time or place or persona. All are neatly executed over a generous amount of parchment. The French *rondeaux*, on the other hand, were among the latest additions to the manuscript, written in cursive and hastily executed, crowded on hand-drawn staves or the leftover staves of other mensural additions (*U despit des envïeus* is crammed into a small area despite plenty of blank parchment, presumably to save room for another addition that was never executed).

The five *dansas* have greater musical and poetic dimensions than the *rondeaux*: the *dansa* refrains are mostly quatrains (the refrain for *Pos qu'ieu vey la fualla* is a tercet), and the verses generally consist of four lines with alternating rhymes. Thus the expanded form for these *dansas* is ABAB cdcd abab ABAB, which is similar in scale to the *virelais* of Machaut. *Ben volgra s'esser poges* has an unusual internal tercet that is not, however, "*zajal*esque" (rhyme, ABBA ccd ccd abba ABBA; melody, ABCD efg efg abcd ABCD); it is the only *dansa* of the five in trouv. *M* that has three stanzas and multiple *tornadas* as described in *Las Leys d'Amors*. The refrain is not cued after each stanza, but only after the final *tornada*. Of the four remaining *dansas* only *Donna, pos vos ay chausida* cues the refrain after the *vuelta*. Given that these *dansas* only have one stanza, we can safely assume that the performance of the refrain at the song's conclusion was simply understood.[36]

In contrast to the length of the *dansas*, three of the four *rondeaux* are comprised of only eight lines total (with two-line refrains), while *Trop ai esté lonc tans mus* has a notable three-line refrain. A comparison of *Donna, pos vos ay chausida* and *U despite des envïeus* illustrates the difference in scale and rhetoric of the *dansas* and the *rondeaux* added to trouv. *M*:

A

Donna, pos vos ay chausida,	a7′	Lady, since I have chosen you,
faz me bel semblan	b5	look kindly upon me
qu'ieu suy, a tota ma vida,	a7′	for I am, all my life,
a vostre coman.	b5	at your command.

b

A vostre coman seray	c7	I will be at your command
a totz los jors de ma via,	d7′	every day of my life,

b

e ja de vos non partray	c7	And I will never leave you
per degun'autra, que sia.	d7′	for any other, whomever it may be.

---

36. Page, *Voices and Instruments*, 247n22, suggests that the repeat of the refrain at the end may have been a "Gallicanism." *Donna, pos vos ay chausida* is followed on the same folio by another *dansa*, *Pos qu'ieu vey la fualla*, which does not cue the final refrain. Page's question echoes those of Le Gentil and others who are uncertain about the repeat of the prelude in the *zajal*.

a

Que Erex non amet Henida	a7′	Erec did not love Enide
tan, ni Ysuetz Tristan	b5	as much, nor Tristan Iseult
con yeu vos, donna grasida,	a7′	as I you, gracious lady,
qu'ieu am sens engan.	b5	whom I love without guile.[37]

A

Donna, [pos vos ay chausida
faz me bel semblan
qu'ieu suy, a tota ma vida.
a vostre coman.]

U despit des envïeus	a7	*In spite of the envious people*
serai je toudis jolis.	b7	*I shall always be merry.*
Et si vuell estre amoureus,	a7	And so I want to be loving,
u despit des envïeus,	b7	*in spite of the envious people,*
pour noble cors gracïeus,	a7	because of a noble and gracious person,
car amours m'en a espris.	b7	for love has inflamed me.
U despit [des envïeus	a7	*In spite of the envious people*
serai je toudis jolis]	b7	*I shall always be happy.*

The *dansa* lyric conveys a high literary tone, with its references to the classic couples Erec and Enide (from Chrétien de Troye's Arthurian *roman* ca. 1170), and Tristan and Iseult (a Celtic legend circulating in various forms and languages from the twelfth century on). It is not unusual to find these literary figures in troubadour lyrics; Bernart de Ventadorn mentions the legendary Tristan in a number of his lyrics (see chapter 1), and Raimbaut de Vaqueiras compares his love to Erec's for Enide at the end of *Kalenda maia*—the only *estampida* to survive with words.[38] The *rondeau U despit des envïeus*, which was certainly added in the first quarter of the fourteenth century, employs the short and direct rhetoric of thirteenth-century refrain songs; and, though not without musical ingenuity, the simple modal rhythm, short regular phrases, and lightly ornamented setting also hark back to the earliest *rondets de carole* (see example 5.2 🎵 OXFORD WEB MUSIC). Machaut would later transform the *rondeau* into a venue for imagistic and imploring language set to long melismatic lines within a dense polyphonic texture—far removed, it would seem, from *U despit des envïeus*.

---

37. For text and translation (modified) see Page, liner notes to *The Spirits of England and France 2*, Gothic Voices (Hyperion CDA66773, 1995), 12–13. In these notes (5), Page suggests a date of 1310 for the *dansas* in trouv. *M*, though he offers no reasoning in support of it.

38. The scribe of *Donna, pos vos ay chausida* actually writes "Herida," suggesting a lack of familiarity with the literary figures Erec and Enide. For a discussion of *Kalenda maia* (PC 392-9) and the reference to Erec and Enide, see Aubrey, "The Dialectic between Occitania and France," 43–44. For more references to these couples in troubadour lyrics see Chambers, *Proper Names*.

EXAMPLE 5.2 *U despit des envïeus* from trouv. M, fol. 1/B3

Donna, pos vos ai chausida (see example 5.3 ⊘ OXFORD WEB MUSIC) merits a closer look, for it foreshadows key elements of Machaut's *virelais* far more than the ornate, melismatic *virelais* of Jehan de Lescurel written in Paris ca. 1316. It resembles Machaut's *virelais* in its syllabic to lightly ornamented setting, rhythmic vigor, and economy of melody. The music for the refrain forms a double versicle with open and closed endings (common among the Spanish *cantigas* with four-line refrains), thus the complete form is comprised of parallel phrases (AA'bb'aa'AA') that correspond with the rhyme scheme. (*Tant es gay et avinetz* also uses a double versicle melodic construction for the refrain). On the smaller scale, however, the composition is rich with invention. Varied groupings of semibreves, and quick switches of mode using *puncta* and carefully placed *cum opposita*

proprietate ligatures, keep the melody dancing with low-level syncopations, while the succession of phrases of unequal lengths in the refrain and *vuelta* produce syncopations of a higher order. A shift in tessitura and tonal focus marks the verse from refrain, as in Machaut's *virelais*: the entire melody spans a C octave, with a concentration on the lower fifth of the octave in the refrain (C to G), and the upper end in the couplet (A to high C). The local melodic focal points—C in the refrain, and A in the couplet—provide contrasts to the D final used to close each major section (the refrain, the verse, and the *vuelta*).

EXAMPLE 5.3 *Donna, pos vos ay chausida* from trouv. M, fol. 1ᵛ/B3v

EXAMPLE 5.4 Guillaume de Machaut, *Dame, a qui m'ottri* (V12)

Donna, pos vos ay chausida is comparable in many respects to Machaut's *Dame, a vous sans retollir* from the *Remede de Fortune*; another of Machaut's *virelais*, *Dame, a qui m'ottri* also makes a good comparison (see Example 5.4 ⊛ OXFORD WEB MUSIC).

This *virelai* similarly uses a double versicle construction for the refrain melody, with an open cadence on A and a closed cadence on F; the verse shifts the tessitura and tonal focus dramatically from F to high C by way of a tritone leap to a signed B♮. The rhythmic flow moves from equal semibreves (mm. 1–3), to unequal minims either in "Scots snap" figures (mm. 4, 8) or swung melismatic notes (m. 13), thus shifting the modal feel. An alternation of short lines sung to longer note values (mm. 1–3, setting oxytonic rhymes), and long lines sung to shorter note values (mm. 4–7, setting paroxytonic lines), further adds to the off-kilter rhythmic environment, which, as with *Donna, pos vos ay chausida*, results in a lively tune that dances itself, though it may not be itself fit for dancing.[39]

---

39. For other discussions of this *virelai* see Leech-Wilkinson, "Not Just a Pretty Tune," 20–24; and id., "The Well-Formed Virelai," 129.

The resemblance between the Occitan *Donna, pos vos ay chausida*, or any of the *dansas* added to trouv. *M*, and select Machaut *virelais* does not prove a direct relationship, or that Machaut understood the form as particularly "southern." Yet additional circumstantial evidence offers tantalizing possible intersections and associations. As discussed in chapter 3, the content of trouv. *M* reveals its ties to Champagne and Artois, and the Occitan additions can be linked to both regions through the Mediterranean empire of Charles d'Anjou, and through Charles's own strong ties to Artois. Machaut hailed from the county of Champagne, perhaps Reims, and received his primary education at the cathedral of that city. His first post was a chaplaincy at Houdain in the diocese of Arras prior to 1330, and in 1332 he was made a canon at the cathedral of Arras.[40] Machaut could have encountered Occitan *dansas* circulating in Champagne during his youth from 1300 to 1315, or later in Arras, which is the most likely place for trouv. *M* to have been housed and utilized as a repository for new monophonic compositions. We know that Machaut quoted from the Artesian trouvères Moniot d'Arras, Perrin d'Angicourt, and Adam de la Halle, and Machaut's singular *chant roial* may be a reference to the name given to Adam's *chansons* or other "crowned" *chansons*.[41] Could it be that Machaut encountered Occitan *dansas* in Arras as well? And that his preferred term *chanson baladée* was a translation or transformation of *dansa*? The paucity of northern examples of the form and its seeming

---

40. See Earp, *Guillaume de Machaut*, 3–8, 17–18; see also Robertson, *Guillaume de Machaut and Reims*, 2–4, 35–37, and 171. Robertson suggests that Machaut may have been educated in the Collège d'Arras in Paris, perhaps starting in 1316. If we adopt Christopher Page's date of 1310 for the *dansas*, then it is not impossible that Machaut may have heard or learned about such songs there as well. Based on archival evidence and the autobiographical prologue to Machaut's *dit Jugement dou roy de Navarre*, Roger Bowers has argued that Machaut spent from 1349 until about 1358 in the service of Charles, king of Navarre, and that Machaut can be placed in Pamplona in 1349 to prepare for Charles's coronation. Although this puts Machaut squarely in the region of *dansas*, *cantigas*, and perhaps proto-*villancicos*, the accepted chronology of his compositions, which date the bulk of his *virelais* in the 1340s, points to an earlier encounter with songs in *virelai* form. See Bowers, "Guillaume de Machaut and His Canonry of Reims," 10–16.

   That southern lyrics and melodies circulated in the region of Burgundy, Champagne, Picardy-Artois, and Lorraine is evident in the northern *chansonniers* that contain troubadour sections (trouv. *U* and *M*), Occitan *lais* in trouv. *T* and *M*, as well as *contrafacta* of troubadour melodies that appear scattered in all trouvère sources (PC 70-7 = RS 1057; PC 70-43 = RS 1934, 365, 349; PC 392-9 = RS 1506; PC 404-4 = RS 388, 1459, 333). Three of these *contrafacta* appear in the Burgundian source trouv. *O*. The melody given for the Occitan song *Lo clar temps vei brunezir* (PC 404-4, attributed to Raimon Jordon elsewhere) in trouv. *M* also serves as the melody for one of the vernacular songs to the Virgin that opens the anthology—*Virgen pucele roiauz* (RS 388) attributed to Willaumes li Viniers—as well as a *jeu-parti* involving Thibaut de Champagne (RS 333) in trouv. *K*, *Mt*, *O*, and *X*. See the relevant entries in van der Werf, *The Extant Troubadour Melodies*.

41. See Machabey, *Guillaume de Machault*, 1:133–36 (on the *chant roial*), and 2:26 and 37–38 on other Adam de la Halle quotations. *Tres douce dame que j'aour* (B24) and *N'en fait n'en dit n'en pensee* (B11) quotes the refrain of Adam's *rondeau Tant con je vivrai*; the *lai Qui bien aimme a tart oublie* (L16) quotes the same proverb that begins the vernacular Marian song *Qui bien aime, a tart oublie* by Moniot d'Arras (RS 1188). On literary quotations from Perrin d'Angicourt see Boogaart, "Encompassing Past and Present," 23–31. Boogaart also discusses Machaut's quotation of trouvères Thibaut de Champagne and Gace Brulé (also from Champagne). See also the relevant entries in Earp, *Guillaume de Machaut*, and van der Werf, "Cantus coronatus." A few crowned (presumably prize-winning) *chansons* are indicated in trouv. *N*, *T*, and *X*.

independent development from the *rondeaux*—including its persistent monophony—suggests that the *virelai* retained or acquired "otherness." In the Parisian source *Mo*, the triplum and motetus of the three-part motet *Li jalous part tout sunt fustat/Tuit cil qui sunt enamourat/VERITATEM* are written in a "Gallicanized" Occitan and their melodies follow a rudimentary *virelai* pattern (abccabab).[42] Although neither lyric uses a corresponding *virelai* poetic form, both mention dancing, and the motetus lyric is, in fact, a *rondeau* set to a *virelai* scheme. Thus the motet encapsulates the web of associations that link the *virelai* musical form, southern languages or dialects, and dancing—here given a particularly northern twist in the motetus, which fits a *rondeau* poem written in a southern dialect into a *virelai* musical form.

A further web of associations merits attention. The triplum and motetus evoke the genre of the *chanson de mal mariée* with the figure of the jealous, cuckolded husband (*le jalous...portent corne*) who is to be driven away from the dance, according the commands of *la regine*. The *chanson de mal mariée* is usually written in a woman's voice, here given regal power in an inversion of the normal complaint. The music for *Mo* no. 169 has a concordance in an earlier fascicle of the same codex, *Post partum virgo mansisti/Ave, regina glorie/VERITATEM* (*Mo* no. 64), and the two motets are thematically related by the figure of the queen—in *Mo* no. 64 the Virgin Mary, "queen of glory and mirror of the angels" (*Ave, regina glorie, et angelorum speculum*), who miraculously remains inviolate after the birth of Christ.[43] This nexus of the *virelai*, *chanson de mal mariée*, and religious allegory reappears in Machaut's motet *Lasse! Comment/Se j'aim/POUR QUOY ME BAT MES MARIS* (no. 16), which features a *virelai de mal mariée* tenor. Anne Robertson has revealed the allegory of a spiritual journey embedded in the courtly love language of Machaut's first seventeen motets; in the penultimate motet, the *mal mariée* represents the Sponsa of the Song of Songs, allegorized as the feminine soul who must endure the tribulations of the world in order to achieve union with her true Lover, Christ.[44]

In both *Mo* no. 64 and Machaut's motet M16 we find a paradoxical combination of an iconic song of physical dance with a metaphysical miracle of the virgin birth or the soul's unification with Christ. We will see an association of the female voice in other *virelais* in this chapter, which lends weight to the *virelai* as a form of otherness—of voice, of language, of region, of physical desire in relation to metaphysical hope.

The *dansas* added to trouv. *M* participate in the back story of Machaut's *virelais* and the form's particular expressivity. By the time of their writing, the Occitan of their lyrics

---

42. *Mo* no. 169; Gen 467–68. The only clearly Occitan word forms in the two texts are the past participles *fustat*, *huat, frapat*, and *enamourat*. See Tischler, *The Montpellier Codex*, 2:188 (music) and 4:62–63 (text and translation). The refrain *Tuit cil sunt enamorat* (B-ref 1822) also appears in the old French interpolated *roman La Court de paradis*. Gennrich lists four motets with Occitan lyrics: Gen 319 and 537 in *W2*, Gen 467–68 in *Mo*, and Gen 674 in trouv. *T*.

43. Gen 469–70; see Tischler, *The Montpellier Codex* 2:55–56 (music) and 4:26 (text and translation). Huot discusses both *Mo* nos. 169 and 64 in *Allegorical Play*, 103–106.

44. See Robertson, *Guillaume de Machaut and Reims*, 165–68.

(and of the *descorts*), in the context of a French-dominated *chansonnier*, may have functioned to add literary weight as well as a hint of exoticism. William Paden has investigated the use of Occitan within French romance, where the opacity or "noise" of the foreign language (though Gallicanized) represents a non-native "lyric language" that could then take on wider meaning within the narrative.[45] The troubadours were already represented in the collection (their language also Gallicanized as in French romances), thus providing the literary back story to the French songs and motets in this musical *summa*. Both the added *descorts* and the *dansas* extended the repertory of the troubadours into the next generation, combining the noise of a belated lyric language with the noise of experimental and newly emerging musical compositions. While the *descorts* reinterpreted an older lyric genre, the *dansas* projected current trends: one of these trends was the changing nature and meaning of refrains.

b: AUTHENTICITY AND THE *VIRELAI*: PUBLIC VS. PRIVATE REFRAINS

As discussed in chapter 1, Bernart de Ventadorn's *En cossirer et en esmai* indicates that songs were occasionally read rather than performed, creating an intimate exchange between author and reader. Centuries later, Dante, in *De vulgari eloquentia* (ca. 1305), notes that songs may be performed without musical accompaniment, or not performed at all, and still retain their identity as "songs."[46] By the early 1330s, as Lawrence Earp argues, few poets writing in the new *formes fixes* had the technical expertise to set their lyrics to the fashionable *ars nova* style of court music, and thus emerged a distinction between "lyrics for reading and lyrics for singing."[47] Machaut's manuscripts attest to this development as well: they contain a section of nearly 200 lyrics, referred to as the *Loange des dames* (Praise of Ladies), which were never intended to be set to music, far outnumbering those that were.[48] This distinction has less to do with a change in the formal properties of the poetry than with a change in concept, namely, that a lyrical poem with a refrain and an origin in public dance songs could be a complete expression as read—without musical performance. And this casts the refrain song as a wholly private communication between poet and reader, as Bernart de Ventadorn posited for his *canso*. Similarly, in the *Voir Dit*, Machaut sends his young correspondent Toute Belle nine *virelai* lyrics, but he never responds to her repeated requests that she set the *virelais* to music.[49] By his silence, and the silence of his *virelais*, Machaut kept their impact in the realm of the private.

---

45. See Paden, "Old Occitan as a Lyric Language." As mentioned in chap. 3, the Occitan of the *dansas* and the *descorts* show some orthographic irregularities but are for the most part not Gallicanized.

46. Peraino, "Re-placing Medieval Music," 227–28.

47. Earp, "Lyrics for Reading," 110–12.

48. Earp notes that more than 80% of Machaut's *ballades* lack music (ibid., 115).

49. Noted in Earp, "Machaut's Role," 471. Machaut's *Le Livre dou voir dit* ("The Book of the True Story," henceforth *Voir Dit*) was written ca. 1363–65.

An analogous shift from public to private occurs in the nature and meaning of the refrain itself, from its cuing of a public, choral response as part of the *rondet de carole*, to its insistent expression of a private plea in the fourteenth-century *formes fixes*. The story of the differentiated *virelai* in the north parallels the shifting role of the refrain. As discussed in the previous chapter, Ardis Butterfield argues that refrains represent "the image of another's language" (quoting Bakhtin), and she sees a continuity between the fourteenth-century *forme fixe* and the practice of refrain-citation found in interpolated narratives; in other words, the voice of the public from the *rondet de carole* still haunts the repeating refrains of the *formes fixes*, giving them citational weight, so to speak, and inter-rupting the solo voice of the strophe that replaces the narrative context.[50] But at the same time that verse narratives and song genres profile refrains as the public, choral responses (especially in *Guillaume de Dole*), they also use refrains to portray individual musical expressions. Indeed, the rhetoric of refrains, however "common" or public, is often point-edly personal, such as this one from chapter 4: "In the name of God, this lovesickness is madness if I have no relief!" The shift in the expressive weight of refrains began in the thirteenth century with their citation in verse narratives. Ardis Butterfield notes this in the *Roman de la violette* (ca. 1240) in this passage:

La damoisiele de Couchi,   The lady of Couci,
cui Dex fache vrai merchi,   to whom God grant true mercy,
qui molt fu avenans et biele,   who was very attractive and pretty,
a dit ceste canchon nouviele,   uttered this new song,
car ele amoit bien par amor: for she was very much in love:
Seulete vois a mon ami;   *I go alone to my lover;*
s'ai grant paor.   *I am terrified.*
Li castelainne de Nïor,   The châtelaine of Nior,
c'on apieloit Alïenor,   who was called Alïenor,
molt estoit cointe, un poi brunete.   was very delicate, and somewhat
                                                              dark-haired.

Puis a dit cest cançonnete,   She then uttered this song,
qu'ele n'estoit mie esperdue: for she was not at all dismayed:
Aprendés a valoir, maris,   *Learn to be worthy, husband,*
ou vous m'avés perdue.   *or you have lost me.*

As Butterfield points out, the narrative gives the identity (name and region), a physical description of each woman, and then "a brief emotional reason for her refrain."[51] Thus,

---

50. Butterfield, *Poetry and Music*, 243 (quotation) and 278.

51. Ibid., 54–55.

like the *vidas* and *razos* of the troubadours, the poet connects the refrain to an individual voice and a private experience, turning a generic expression into a specific one. These refrains, then, encapsulate the imagined circumstance of the courtly trouvère *chansons*—the professions of love or fear by an individual in the throes of the experience. As mentioned in the previous chapter, later verse narratives, such as the animal fable *Renart le nouvel* and the *Roman de Fauvel*, continue this expressive use of refrains, even in ridiculous scenarios that satirize the sincerity of the courtly expressions.

Most scholars investigating the change of fashion from the trouvère strophic *chanson* to the *formes fixes* follow the trail of poetic and musical developments. Earp, for example, notes that the expansion and standardizing of thirteenth-century dance songs with four-line refrains, isometric stanzas, and octo- or decasyllabic lines allowed for "the gradual adaptation of the old dance lyrics into poetical forms suitable to carry the more elevated conceits formerly reserved for the high trouvère chansons."[52] It is instructive to compare refrains from successive generations of poets on either side of this transition to illustrate the expansion of the refrain.[53]

Adam de la Halle
>rondeau: B-ref 823 (three concordances)

>>*He, Diex! Quant verrai* Oh, God! When will I see
>>*cheli que j'aim?* the one I love?

>virelai: B-ref 747 (no concordances)

>*Fines amouretes ai* I have perfect little loves.
>*Dieus! Si ne sai* God! I do not know
>*quant les verrai.* when I will see them.

Jehan de Lescurel
>rondeau: B-ref 204 (one related refrain)

>*A vous, douce debonnaire,* To you, sweet gentle lady,
>*ai mon cuer donné,* I have given my heart,
>*ja n'en partiré.* never shall I leave you.

>virelai: B-ref 601 (no concordances)

>*Douce Amour, confortez moi,* Sweet Love, comfort me,
>*dolente et desconfortée;* sorrowful and in despair;
>*humblement je vous en proi,* humbly I ask you,
>*ou de malle eure fui née.* why was I born of such misfortune.

---

52. Earp, "Lyrics for Reading," 109.

53. See Wilkins, ed., *The Lyric Works of Adam de la Halle*, 56 (*rondeau*), and 52 (*virelai*); Wilkins, ed., *The Works of Jehan de Lescurel*, 2 (*rondeau*), and 12 (*virelai*).

Guillaume de Machaut
    rondeau (no. 12)

Ce qui soustien moy,	What sustains me,
m'onneur, et ma vie;	my honor, and my life;
aveuc Amours	with [the aid of] Love,
c'estes vous, douce dame.	it is you, sweet lady.

    virelai (no. 12)

Dame, a qui	Lady, to whom
m'ottri	I give myself
de cuer, sans penser laidure.	from the heart, without any evil thought.
Je n'ay mie desservi	I have not deserved
qu'en haï	that your heart
m'ait si	has such dislike
vos cuers, qu'a desconfiture	for me, that I am undone
soie pour l'amour de li.	by my love for it.

With Adam de la Halle, the refrains from his *virelai* and *rondeau* appear indistinguishable; both are short and exclamatory. The main difference is that many of Adam's refrains from his *rondeaux* circulated widely, while the refrains of his two proto-*virelais* are unique. Similarly, Lescurel's *rondeau* refrain, while elevated in tone from Adam's, still shares a pithy rhetoric with thirteenth-century refrains such as *Tos jors vos servirai, ne ja de vos ne partirai* (B-ref 1778; Every day I will serve you, never will I part from you). His *virelai* refrain, however, presents a more emotionally expressive register.[54] Despite the clichéd sentiment, an individual voice takes shape in the expanded sentence—here, notably, the voice is a woman's, as indicated by the feminine endings of *donente* and *desconfortée*, and *née*. With Machaut's refrains, all resemblance to the thirteenth-century exclamations and aphorisms are gone. As refrains begin both the *virelai* and the *rondeau* forms, they set the tone of the lyric. There is a formal constraint on the *rondeau* refrain, however: *rondeau* refrains must be divisible into two related syntactic halves; therefore, they are never more than a single sentence, and rarely exceed four lines of verse.[55] The *virelai* refrains, however, can encompass more sentences, and hence more sentiments, creating a complex psychology at the outset. *Dame, a qui m'ottri*, for example, offers conflicting statements: it begins with pure devotion, without evil thoughts, but ends with an admonishment in a comparison of the lover's and beloved's respective hearts—one offering love, the other hatred (see the discussion of example 5.4 above).

---

54. Arlt, "Jehannot de Lescurel," notes the wide range of register and formal patterns in Lescurel's lyrics, "from the light tone of dance-songs to the high register of the *grand chant*" (26). Such distinctions in refrain registers are corroborated by the additions to trouv. *M*, as noted above.

55. Only Machaut's *rondeau* no. 5, *Quant j'ay l'espart*, contains a refrain of six poetic lines, but only one sentence.

The monophonic songs in *Fauvel*, including those by Jehan de Lescurel, had absorbed the musical trends of the polyphonic *ars nova* motet, specifically ornate or melismatic settings and the new range of note values and rhythmic relationships. Earp sees this new style of music as the definitive break from the dance, and I would add from any hint of a public voice in the role of the refrain.[56] Arlt describes a new element of "extreme individualization" in the songs of Lescurel; beneath an ornamental surface Lescurel produced varied text-settings in which poetic "tone" is matched by the underlying pace of the syllables—breves and semibreves for a lighter tone, and longs and breves for a serious tone. He goes on to argue that "without the ornamental notes," the serious songs reveal an underlying "*grand chant* idiom" with opening melodic descents through the octave.[57] Only three songs of the thirty-two in the collection, however, use the semibreve as the underlying syllabic unit: these are the *rondeaux Douce dame, je vous pris* and *Guilleurs me font mout souvent*, and the *virelai Gracïeusette*. The degree of ornamentation and the melismatic extensions may also serve to "individualize" songs. Although I do not see a rigorous correlation between poetic form or tone and melodic style, it may be significant that the *Douce Amour, confortez moi*, the *virelai de femme* quoted above, is one of the least decorated melodies (though still more than most Machaut *virelais*), with short melismas ending each line in the "*grand chants* idiom" (see example 5.5 ◐ ᴏxꜰᴏʀᴅ ᴡᴇʙ ᴍᴜsɪᴄ). As *Donna, pos vos ay chausida* and *Dame, a qui m'ottri* discussed above, this *virelai* also sets the refrain to a double-versicle melodic construction with open and closed cadences, and the verse begins with a leap to the upper range of the central F octave. The rhythm hints at a lilting first-mode background, but freely breaks this pattern (mm. 3, 13, and 26) for a subtle syncopation against the expected flow.

Another striking feature of this song is the constant outlining of the tritone F–B♮ in the A section; the distinctive Lydian tetrachord provides a restless and plaintive musical setting of the sorrowful words. This is not a *mal mariée* lyric, but rather one that echoes the troubadours' and trouvères' classic rhetoric of suffering (unto madness and death!) from unrequited love.

Though Arlt insists that at this time the *virelai* was not differentiated from the *ballade*, we can perhaps see certain tendencies taking shape: a serious courtly poetic tone set out with a substantial refrain, a modestly decorated but well-contoured melody, a cycling of musical couplets with open and closed cadences. Given that the *Fauvel* manuscript is the unique source for Lescurel's compositions, they represent for the most part a Parisian style of song; it is a style strongly marked by the *ars nova* of musical composition, which provided the means for a clearer individuation of songs with the semibreves and minims that the author of *Las Leys d'Amors* deemed unsuitable for the *dansa*. If Lescurel's songs call attention to their own individuality and novelty within a long

---

56. See Earp, "Lyrics for Reading," 104 and 113–14.

57. Arlt, "Jehannot de Lescurel," 26–29; see also id., "Aspekte der Chronologie," 209–27.

EXAMPLE 5.5 Jehan de Lescurel, *Douce Amour, confortez moi*

tradition of the *chanson*, then *Douce Amour, confortez moi* is set apart from the rest by sounding "old school"—not the fancy Parisian style of the day, but an updated troubadour style (and form) in which the refrain establishes and dominates the subjective poetic and musical voice.

a: MACHAUT'S DISCORDANT *VIRELAIS*

Thus far I have argued that by the time of Machaut's compositions, the *virelai* form had particular associations that made it exceptional among the *formes fixes*: as a less-favored form in the north, and with strong ties to the Occitan *dansa*, the *virelai* had an air of temporal and geographical "otherness" such that its form alone provided a distinctive poetic and musical vehicle for self-expression; furthermore, the form allowed for a particularly developed and personalized refrain, one that could convey a complex psychology or a new take on traditional love themes. The *virelai*, then, may have represented a more direct and "authentic" voice among the emerging *formes fixes*—less affected and diluted by the rhythmic and polyphonic contrivances of the day. This accords with Machaut's choice of the *virelai Dame, a vous sans retollir* to reveal his true emotions in the *Remede de Fortune*.

Sounding "old school" or "old world" can be innovative in context, and Machaut's conservation of monophony for his *virelais* is certainly a novelty among his *formes fixes* in the context of the "collected works" anthologies put together under his supervision. Earp argues that Machaut's polyphonic *formes fixes* represent some of the earliest efforts to set the new forms of lyric to the new style of music, but that with the *virelai* "it appears that Machaut was quite self-consciously preserving the genre for the dance," and further that "Machaut's oddly emphatic assertion of his label *chanson baladée* may indicate that he was fighting to preserve something lost."[58] Although the suitability of the *virelais* for dancing has been questioned (as noted above), their self-consciousness seems indisputable. But rather than fighting for a "lost" tradition, Machaut's *virelais* seem to fight for a new musical approach to that self-consciousness. Like the melodic individuality of Jehan de Lescurel's songs, no two *virelais* by Machaut are alike in their combination of rhyme, metrical, and musical patterns.

The context of the *Remede de Fortune* shows Machaut to be composing polyphonic *ballades* and *rondeaux*, yet twenty monophonic *virelais* (plus three without music) appear in the earliest layer of MS *C*, which collects literary and musical compositions before 1349 (see table 5.3). Other musical settings of the 1340s include sixteen polyphonic *ballades* and eight monophonic *lais*. Four more monophonic *virelais* and one polyphonic *virelai* appear in the second layer of the manuscript dated 1350–56, along with the addition of two monophonic *lais*, eight *ballades*, nine *rondeaux*, and nineteen motets (all polyphonic).[59]

The *compilatio* of the manuscripts that transmit Machaut's "collected works" has been much studied by musicologists, art historians, and literature scholars.[60] Although a mixture of trends is found in thirteenth-century narrative and lyric compilations (see chapter 3), the ordering of genres and even specific pieces, as well as the program of illustrations, conveys a new level of self-consciousness about the twin roles of poet and lyric protagonist, and about the creation of coherent "books" that reflect the author's particular subjectivity and identity, expressed on all levels of composition.

---

58. Earp, "Lyrics for Reading," 115; see also 113–14.

59. The chronology of Machaut's compositions has been meticulously worked out by a number of scholars from literary, art historical, and musicological angles. For a thorough summary of the scholarship see Earp, *Guillaume de Machaut*, 273–77. For some reason, and though it does not contain the *Judgement dou roy de Navarre*, in the seventeenth century MS *C* was mistakenly catalogued as "les chansons de Thibault, comte de Champagne, roy de Navarre"—a curious coincidence for the present study (see ibid., 78). See also Günther, "Chronologie und Stil der Kompositionen Guillaume de Machauts."

60. The key studies include Williams, "An Author's Role in Fourteenth-Century Book Production"; Avril, "Les Manuscrits enluminés de Guillaume de Machaut"; Günther, "Contribution de la musicologie à la biographie et à la chronologie de Guillaume de Machaut"; Huot, *From Song to Book*, esp. chaps. 8 and 9 on Machaut; see also Earp, "Machaut's Role" and Leach, *Guillaume de Machaut*, 82–131.

TABLE 5.3

Machaut's monophonic *virelais*

Schrade no.	Incipit	Date	Style	Musical design Refrain/Couplet	Poetic design Refrain/Couplet
1	He! Dame de vaillance	1340s	syllabic	ABCDE/FG FG	a6′a6′a6′b6/|:c8d6′:|
2	Loyaute weil tous jours	1340s	syllabic	ABC/DE DE	a9a5b6′/|:a8b5′:|
3	Ay mi! dame de valour*	1340s	syllabic	ABAB′/CD CD′	|:a7 b5:|/|:c6 a8:|
4	Douce dame jolie	1340s	syllabic	ABA′C/DE DE′	a6′a6′a6′b7/|:a6′a6′b6:|
5	Comment qu'à moy	1340s	syllabic	ABCD/EF EF	a6′b6a6′b6/|:a6′b6:|
6	Se ma dame	1340s	syllabic	ABCD/EFG EFG′	a7a7b5′b8′/|:c8c3a7:|
7	Puis que ma dolour*	1340s	syllabic	ABAB′/CDE CDE′	|:a7′a7′a7′b5:|/|:b7b7a5′:|
8	Dou mal qui m'a	1340s	syllabic	ABCD/EF EF′	a7a6a5b5′/|:a7a6′:|
9	Dame, je weil endurer	1340s	syllabic	ABCD/EF EF	a7a7b5′b2′/|:c8a7:|
10	De bonté, da valour*	1340s	syllabic	ABCAB′/DEF DEF	a6a6b5′a6b8′/|:b5′b5′a3:|
11	He! dame de valour	1340s	syllabic	ABCDE/FG FG	a6a7a7a6b7/|:c8a7:|
12	Dame, a qui m'ottri*	1340s	syllabic	ABCABC′/DEF DEF′	|:a3a2b7′a7:|/|:c7c2a7:|
13	Quant je sui mis†	1340s	syllabic	abcdAB	a7b5′a7b5′ B9A5
14	J'aim sans penser†	1340s	syllabic	abcdefABCABC′	a6′b6a6′b6a6′/|:A3′A3′B5:|
15	Se mesdisans	1340s	syllabic	ABCDEF/GHI GHI′	a7a7b5′b7′b7′a5/|:c7c7b5′:|

Schrade no.	Incipit	Date	Style	Musical design Refrain/Couplet	Poetic design Refrain/Couplet
16	C'est force, faire	1350–56	neumatic	ABC/DEF DEF'	a7b4b7a4b7a4/|:b7b4c7:|
17	Dame, vostre doulz*	1340s	melismatic	ABAC/DEF DEF'	|:a7'a3'b7:|/|:b7b3a7':|
18	Helas! et comment*	1340s	neumatic	ABCABC'/DEF DEF'	|:a7'a3'b7:|/|:c7c3b7:|
19	Dieus, Biauté, Douceur*	1340s	syllabic	ABCDABCD'/EFG EFG'	|:a7'a7'a7'b5':|/|:b7'b7'c5':|
20	Se d'amer me repentoie*	1340s	neumatic	ABCABC'/DE DE	|:a7'a3'b7:|/|:b7a7':|
21	Je vivroie liement	1340s	neumatic	ABCD/EF EG	a7b5'a7a7b2'/|:c7b5:|
22	Foy porter	1350–56	melismatic	ABCDEFGH/IJIJ'	a3a4b4b3b4a4b7a4/|:b7b7a4:|
25	Tuit mi penser	1350–56	neumatic	ABCDE/FGHI FGHI	a4a4a4b6'/|:a7a4a4b6':|
27	Liement me deport*	1350–56	melismatic	ABCDABCD'/EFG EFG'	|:a6a6a6b6':|/|:b6'b6'a6:|

* Denotes double versicle refrain design.
† Chanson à refrain with oda continua form.

The *Remede de Fortune* contains its own miniature lyric anthology in which the musical interpolations are systematically organized in a decreasing order of poetic complexity and prestige, with the major genres as follows: *lai, ballade, virelai, rondeau*. In the earliest music section of MS *C*, Machaut reversed this plan, ordering the genres from the least to the most complex: *virelais, ballades,* and *lais* only (the second music section inserts somewhat haphazardly new *ballades, virelais, lais,* and *rondeaux* before the motet collection). Eventually, for later anthologies, he reordered the genres according the scheme of the *Remede*, with a list that was somewhat altered and expanded: *lais*, motets, the Mass, the *David Hocket, ballades, rondeaux, virelais.*[61] Thus Machaut reassessed the *virelai* in particular, deeming it weightier than the *rondeau* in the *Remede de Fortune*, and then less so after 1350, when he began to compose many more *rondeaux*.

It seems clear, and as Earp has suggested, that musical rather than poetic considerations played a role in "demoting" the *virelai*, for, as discussed above, the poetic form in fact offered greater breadth of emotional expression.[62] Furthermore, in his study of Machaut's "poetic elements of rhythm," Robert L. Gieber notes that "[t]he virelai is by far the most interesting poetic form as far as metric variety is concerned. With the exception of *virelais* 5 and 30, which are hexasyllabic throughout, all others are heterometric with verse lines ranging in length from two to nine syllables." Gieber goes on to conclude that

> since the structure of the *chanson baladée*, as Machaut called the virelai, is much freer than that of the ballade or rondeau, it is probably in this genre that Machaut shows the most rhythmic ingenuity; the varying combinations of rhymes show a definite search for variety, yet the poet always ends up with remarkable symmetry in a sort of compromise between fantasy and order.[63]

Fantasy and *disorder* may be a more appropriate description for the effect of the peculiar *De bonté, de valour* (V10). The *virelai* is remarkably full of contrasts and conflicts—of musical and poetic rhythms, of melodic contours, of lyric subject and object. We can add to this the odd combination of the consistently high-minded lyrics set to a playfully erratic melody. This *virelai* features an asymmetrical refrain of five lines, all of varying lengths, as shown below with the poetic scheme and corresponding melodic phrases:[64]

De bonté, de valour,	a6	A	With goodness, with merit,
de biauté, de douçour	a6	B	with beauty, with sweetness
ma dame est parée;	b5′	C	my lady is adorned;

---

61. See Earp, "Machaut's Role," 466–70. The final order of genres reflects that of Machaut MS *A* from the 1370s; see Hoppin, *Medieval Music*, 400 for a complete list of contents for that manuscript.

62. Earp, "Machaut's Role," 470–71.

63. Gieber, "Poetic Elements of Rhythm," 8–9.

64. Text and translation (modified) from Hoppin, *Anthology of Medieval Music*, 146–47.

| de maniere, d'atour, | a6 | A | with manners, with character, |
| de sens, de grace est couronnée. | b8′ | B-extended | with wisdom, with grace she is crowned. |

Yet Machaut chose to use a double-versicle melodic construction, resulting in a curious collision between poetic and melodic design (see example 5.6  OXFORD WEB MUSIC). Here are the "musical sentences":

De bonté, de valour	a6	A
de biauté, de douçour ma dame est parée;	b11′	B
de maniere, d'atour,	a6	A
de sens, de grace est couronnée.	b8′	B-extended

EXAMPLE 5.6   Guillaume de Machaut, *De bonte, de valour* (V10)

To accommodate the two conflicting designs, Machaut follows the sense of the words, "correcting" the poetic enjambments with musical settings of meaning rather than form. Musical phrases concatenate poetic lines with pitch rather than rhythm; the signed F♯ at the end of the second line leads the ear directly to its brief resolution and subsequent cadential extension for the third line. From measure 3 on, the refrain melody features a snaking ascent of oscillating semitones, E–F, F–F♯, F♯–G, and A–B♭ in the first ending. Thus the third or "C" melodic phrase functions as the first ending, while an extended "B" phrase turns into the second ending. With this new disposition of words the listener expects melodic symmetry but is caught short by the literally shortened second ending: the verbal effect of acceleration requires melodic compression.

The couplet of the verse is similarly heterometric, though symmetrical:

b
Dame desirée,	b5′	Desired lady,
richement aournée	b6′	richly adorned
de colour,	a3	with color,

b
bien endoctrinée,	b5′	well instructed,
de tous a droit loée	b6′	by all rightly praised
par savour,	a3	for taste,

Yet Machaut again creates long musical phrases by setting the -ée verbal rhymes in decidedly non-rhyming rhythmic patterns (see mm. 10 and 12). Furthermore, the articulation of the first rhyme in measure 10 is undermined by the melodic leaps of a fifth, and the final short note that launches us into the next musical phrase. Thus the three heterometric segments converge into two homometric lines, which flow seamlessly into the *vuelta* to form one long sentence:

Dame desirée, richement aournée de colour,		a14	
bien endoctrinée, de tous a droit loée par savour,		a14	
jeunette, sans folour,	a6		youthful, without folly,
simplette, sans baudour,	a6		simple, without boldness,
de bonne heure née,	b5′		born in a happy hour,
parfaite en tout honnour,	a6		perfect in all honor,
nulle n'est a vous comparée.	b8′		none can be compared to you.

De bonté, de valour...

The tone of the poem changes abruptly in the last stanza, from the long list of the beloved's attributes to the "sweet suffering" topos of the trouvères, as the *vuelta* illustrates:

Si vueil je la dolour	So I wish the pain
et l'amoureuse ardour	and the amorous ardor
qu'en moy est entrée,	that has entered within me
endurer nuit et jour,	to endure night and day,
ne ja n'en serez miens amée.	nor will you ever be loved less for that.

This *vuelta* casts the words of the refrain that follow in a different light; placing the lover's masochistic ardor beside the beloved's virtuous adornments highlights the division between subject and object—the sentimental voice of the poet and abstract silence of the lady. We again see a tension between narrative and cyclic forces that yields new interpretations of the refrain, as with *Dame, a vous sans retollir*. The meaning of the refrain changes over the course of the three stanzas. This is a fundamental expressive feature of the *virelai*.

I want to follow another disorderly detail of Machaut's expressive musical vocabulary that appears frequently in the *virelais*: it is the dramatic and sometimes awkward melodic leap between phrases. This is a favorite device separating the refrain and verse; for example, in *De bonté, de valour* the major sixth leap from the final G of the refrain to the high E of the couplet startles the listener and foreshadows the contrasting musical properties of its relative tonal stasis and angularity as compared to the semitone motion of the refrain. Below is a list of such leaps (always ascending) greater than a third:

V1	fifth (G–D)
V2	octave (F–F)
V3	fifth (G–D)
V4	major sixth (G–E)
V5	major sixth (G–E)
V6	major sixth (F–D)
V7	major sixth (G–E)
V10	major sixth (G–E)
V12	tritone (F–B♮)
V15	octave (F–F)
V16	major ninth (D–E)
V18	major ninth (G–A)
V20	octave (G–G)
V22	octave (F–F)
V25	fourth (C–F')
V33	octave (F–F)

Thus over half of the monophonic *virelais* contain a dramatic leap between the refrain and verse, which is, to be sure, an expedient way to get to the upper range of the scale. Octaves and fifths provide the smoothest of such transitions, without disrupting the centrality of the final that closes the refrain, but Machaut prefers the major sixth, and a couple of other more disorienting intervals—major ninth and tritone—also stand out.

Aymi! dame de valour (V3) opens with a remarkable gesture that imbues the major sixth leap with particular significance as a sonic emblem of courtly suffering (see example 5.7 ⊘ OXFORD WEB MUSIC). Machaut sets the exclamation "*Aymi!*" over a prolonged D that bends upward to E via a plicated breve, before plunging down a sixth to G. The gesture is elaborated in measure 6, where the high E changes from an ornamental note to the goal-note of the short melisma. We can hear it as an overshooting of the fifth, from emotions or exuberance. And although this song contains the relatively smooth leap of a fifth between

EXAMPLE 5.7 Guillaume de Machaut, *Aymi! dame de valour* (V3)

the refrain and verse, an internal leap of a minor seventh (G–F) occurs within the verse melody (mm. 13–14).

The words to this *virelai* provide a study in enjambment for lines between and within sections; the first strophe sets the pattern:

A

Aymi! dame de valour,	Alas, lady of merit,
que j'aim et desir,	whom I love and desire,
de vous me vient la dolour	from you comes pain
qui me fait languir.	that makes me languish.

b

Tres douce creature,	Very sweet person,
comment puet vo fine douçour	how can your pure sweetness

b

estre vers moy si dure,	be so harsh toward me
quant mon cuer, mon corps et m'amour	when my heart, my body, and my love

a

vous ay donné sans retour	I have given you without return
et sans repentir?	and without regret?
Or me tenez en langour	Now you hold me in languor
dont je criem morir.	from which I fear to die.

A

Aymi! Dame de valour...

As an early *virelai* in the series (and perhaps chronologically), *Aymi! dame de valour* establishes several details characteristic for the collection, including the poetic circularity of enjambments and the musical emblem of the major sixth.

Another closely related gesture within the collection of *virelais* is the neighbor-note decorations. These appear in other song-types as well, where oscillating figures extend harmonies with surface motion, and lock or weave lines together; in a monophonic context they can call to mind the easy finger work of instrumentalists. Such continuity is especially clear in *He! dame de vaillance* (V1), whose refrain goes for ten measures with few poetic and no melodic breaks, and in *Loyaute weil tous jours* (V2), which highlights and heightens the neighbor-note motif with a play of semitone relationships (C♯–D, B–C).

Along with metrical variety in the *virelais*, Machaut presents different registers and ideologies of love. The rhetoric of *Aymi! dame de valour* contrasts with that of *De bonté, de valour*, for example; the former is more blame than praise, with sharper, more direct emotional statements, while the latter is all praise in a loftier courtly tone.

A confrontation of two registers of love appears in *Liement me deport* (V27, composed between 1350 and 1356). Though presumably written well after the *Remede de Fortune*, *Liement me deport* encapsulates, over several stanzas, that narrative's ideology of love as *souffisance* secured in Hope, in contrast to the old trouvère ideology of love as rooted in fickle Fortune and desire. The lyric presents a vivid account of Desire's effect: the refrain opens with the theme of a wounding sting and death, to which the first stanza adds burning and despairing ardor; the second stanza provides an account of Desire's piercing bite, and then moves to the remedy of Hope. After this, the restatement of the refrain acts as a reminder of the pitfalls without Hope.

A

Liement me deport	Cheerfully I comport myself
par samblant, mai je port,	in appearance, but I bear,
sans joie et sans deport,	without joy or pleasure,
une si grief pointure	a sting so grievous
que je sui au droit port	that I am at the very gates
de mort, sans nul deport,	of death, without any relief,
se d'Amours n'ay tel port	if from Love I do not have such assistance
qu'il me preigne en sa cure.	that he takes me into his care.

b-1

Car quant de vo figure	For when the sweet image
la douce pourtraiture	of your face
dedens mon cuer recort,	I remember in my heart,

b-1

espris sui d'une arsure,	I am enflamed with a burning,
ardant, crueuse, et sure,	ardent, cruel, and bitter,
pleinne de desconfort;	full of despair;

a-1

car Desirs son effort	for Desire directs his force
fait de moy grever fort,	to tormenting me harshly,
mais j'ay cuer assez fort	but my heart is strong enough
contre sa blesseure.	against the wound.
Si ne me desconfort,	So I do not despair,
car d'espoir me confort	for I console myself with hope
qui me donne confort	which gives me comfort
en vostre douceur pure.	in your pure sweetness.

A

Liement me deport...

b-II

Si qu'einsi m'asseure	So that I am thus protected
Espoir, qui en moy dure,	by Hope, who endures in me,
vers Desirs, qui a tort,	against Desire, who is wrong,

b-II

quant sans nulle mesure	when beyond all measure
quiert ma desconfiture,	he seeks my defeat,
qu'a moy toudis s'amort;	for to me he is always deadly;

a-II

n'en riens ne s'en remort.	nor does he show any remorse for it.
Il ne tent qu'a ma mort;	He only seeks my death;
il me point, il me mort,	he pierces me, he bites me,
trop me nuit sa morsure.	and his bite harms me so.
Il m'aroit tantost mort	He would soon have killed me
par son mervilleus sort	by his wondrous spell
se n'estoit le ressort	if there was not the support
d'esperence seure.	of certain hope.

A

| Liement me deport... | |

The third stanza mentions neither Hope, nor wounds, nor bites, but rather trots out the standard topoi of endurance, loyalty, and service; the *vuelta* confirms the full conversion of the subject to the chaste love of the later *Remede de Fortune*, as the lover equates the ripening of his joy with the lulling of desire by Pity:

b-III

Mais pour peinne qu'endure,	But for all the pain I endure,
tant soit a porter dure,	however hard it maybe to bear
n'orrez vilain rapport	you will not hear a base report

b-III

que je pense laidure,	that I think insult,
barat ne mespresure	deceit, or misdeed
vers vostre gentil port:	toward your noble conduct:

a-III

a Amours m'en raport.	I rely on Love.
Et se Pitez endort	But if Pity lulls
mon desir, qui ne dort,	my desire, which never sleeps,
joie ert pour moy meure.	joy will ripen for me.

Dieu pri qu'il vous enort,	I pray God that he advises you,
si qu'en soiez d'acort,	so that you will be in accord,
Belle, qu'a vous m'acort	Beauty, that I give myself to you
sur toute creature.	above all creatures.

A

Liement me deport...

Closing with the refrain after this third stanza sends the audience once again to the realm of stinging wounds and unhappiness—and it ends there! Thus the final refrain caps the song with a return to an experience of love that is in the distant psychological past; in other words, the refrain becomes itself a belated love song.

The music of *Liement me deport*, however, is *au courant* with a refined, melismatic melody. For the lengthy refrain, Machaut set an asymmetrical couplet to an asymmetrical pair of melodic phrases in which the second ending extends the line-end melisma for an extra measure (see example 5.8 🅐 OXFORD WEB MUSIC).

Although the poetry is nearly isometric (a6a6 a6b6 ʹ), modest melismas appear unpredictably throughout the refrain music—in the middle of line 1 (m. 2), at the beginning of line 3 (mm. 6–7), at the beginning and end of line 4 (m. 10)—thus creating musical phrases of differing lengths (4, 2, 3, and 4 or 5 measures respectively). The verse follows suit with its own set of unbalanced internal phrases (2, 2, and 5 measures), for nearly isometric lines (b6 ʹb6 ʹa6). Machaut does not use an expressive leap to separate the refrain and verse; rather, he places two such ascending leaps in more surprising positions: there is a major ninth (G to A) between the first and second phrases (m. 4), and a major sixth (G to E) between the third and fourth phrases (mm. 9–10). Furthermore, the ascending leap of a fourth (D–G in m. 6) divides the second and third phrases. Thus every phrase of the refrain begins high and tumbles downward, sometimes precipitously, as with the downward leap of a fifth (D–G) in measure 9. The verse begins with a melodic ascent, but soon echoes several of the dramatic melodic gestures in the refrain, including ascending leaps between phrases (the fourth D–G in m. 19; and the major sixth G–E in mm. 21–22), and ending a phrase with a plunging fifth (D–G in m. 21).

Two more details merit attention. The short melismas in measures 2 and 5–6, each marked off by a minim rest, create a momentary conflict between sound and sense. The rests disconnect the melismatic notes from the previous phrase, creating an anacrusis to the next; yet the previous syllable (-ment, -port) is retained. Thus the music pushes forward while the words pull backward. (This can be compared to the effect produced by the monosyllabic trailing rhymes in the Occitan *descorts* discussed in chapter 2, where the isolated and belated rhyme conflicted with the forward-looking syntax.) With *Liement me deport*, it is the musical syntax that charges ahead of the words. We can see confusion on the part of the scribes about this curious gesture. The first melisma in measure 2 is a five-note decoration and prolongation of B♭; in MS *C*, the scribe created a parallel

EXAMPLE 5.8 Guillaume de Machaut, *Liement me deport* (V27)

five-note melisma over the word *port*, writing *sans*, which begins line 3, on the high F minim (see m. 7). The intentional layout of the song makes the parallelism of the melismas clear, for the scribe coordinated the change of poetic line with a change in staff line. Yet in the later manuscripts *Vg* and *A*, the parallel is disturbed, and the word *sans* has been entered in the middle of the five-note figure. This placement is also clear and seemingly intentional, especially since it is verified in two sources. Perhaps this was not scribal interference but Machaut's own revision of a detail. The musical effect is subtle yet important: the "premature" entrance of a word mid-melisma produces just enough unpredictability in the relationship of notes and words that our ear hears the conflict of sound and sense more acutely.

The lyrical and musical contents of *Liement me deport* take on greater meaning when considered in the context of the surrounding *virelais* in the compilations. *Liement me deport* appears in the second part of MS *C*, containing compositions from 1350–56, and thought to be "disordered" by comparison to the first part of MS *C*, and the other "collected works" manuscripts close in time to Machaut (MSS *A* and *Vg*). The second part of MS *C* may have a trace of a plan, however, for it begins with six *lais* (extending the genre collection of the previous gathering) followed by two large monophonic *virelais*, *Foy porter* (V22) and *Tuit mi penser* (V25). This ordering of *lais* followed by *virelais* prefigures the organization of the later anthologies. Clusters of *ballades* and *rondeaux* then follow, and the whole section of *forme fixe chansons* ends with two monophonic *virelais* and a *rondeau—Liement me deport, Mor sui, se je ne vous voy* (V26), which was given a tenor in the other sources, and *Rose, lis, printemps, verdure* (R10), entered late and missing its triplum.[65] The linking of the last two *virelais* stands even in the later collections of MSS *Vg* and *A*, where the order of this pair is switched so as to end with a piece of monophony just before the grouping of the later five polyphonic *virelais*. Given the images of wounds and death in the refrain of *Liement me deport*, the proximity of *Mors sui, se je ne vous voy* (I die, if I do not see you) and *Liement me deport* in the manuscripts makes thematic sense. Other thematic connections can be found: the second stanza of *Mors sui, se je ne vous voy* begins with Pity and Good Faith asleep, allowing Desire to *estanche sa soy* (quench his thirst), continuing the motif of Desire as a consuming mouth that drinks and eats its victims. There is no hope, or Hope, in the lyric at all. Musically the two *virelais* share the final G, and melodic prolongations of B♭. *Mor sui, se je ne vous voy* also contains melodic features that recall the first three *virelais* in the first section of MS *C*: the opening short melisma of the otherwise predominantly syllabic cantus begins with a stepwise melodic descent from E to D, which echoes the first two notes of *He! dame de vaillance* (no. 1), followed by a chromatic C♯–D–C♯ neighbor-note decoration, which reverses the D–C♯–D of *Loyaute weil tous jours* (no. 2). Furthermore, in the later polyphonic version of *Mor sui, se je ne vous voy*, the initial harmonic interval is the major sixth E–G, which quickly resolves to the fifth D–G—a vertical rendition of the opening melodic gesture of *Aymi! dame de valour* (V3).[66] Hence, *Mor sui, se je ne vous voy*, the only *virelai* in MS *C* to

---

65. Space for the triplum was provided at the bottom of fol. 205v, which contains *Mor sui, se je ne vous voy*. See also Earp, "Scribal Practice," 138–42. For a comparison of the contents of the manuscripts see Chichmaref, introduction to *Guillaume de Machaut*, 1:lxxx–c (MS *C* is here MS *E*).

66. For a comparison of the monophonic and polyphonic versions of this *virelai* see Fuller, "Machaut and the Definition of Musical Space." Fuller makes an elegant analogy to art: "A parallel in the visual sphere, much

be "updated" later with a tenor, and perhaps the first polyphonic *virelai* Machaut undertook, presents a thematic and sonic back story to *Liement me deport*, and this may be the reason for the addition of a tenor and the switch in order of these two *virelais. Mor sui, se je ne vous voy* recalls in music and words the early *virelais* and their anguished desire, yet also signals with polyphony something new—the "enlightenment" to be heard in the monophonic voice in *Liement me deport*.

Two monophonic *virelais*, *Se mesdisans en acort* (V15) and *Se d'amer me repentoie* (V20), adopt a female voice; they appear as a trick of ventriloquism, giving voice to the "Dame" addressed in so many of the *virelais*. What these ladies say and sing contrasts with the love declarations of the male voices around them. In *Se mesdisans en acort* the lady complains about slanderers and plans her recourse of dignity and even revenge. As William Mahrt notes, Machaut seems to distinguish the voice of the lady from her detractors with an "inharmonious juxtaposition" of the hard and soft hexachords; the first phrase of the refrain ("If slanderers in agreement") begins in the hard hexachord with a meandering stepwise descent from E to G that pauses on B, while the second phrase ("are tormenting me wrongly") begins with a jarring leap upward from F to B♭. The resulting melodic clash of B♮ and B♭ and the abrupt shift in tonal focus from G to F seem an ironic musical response to the word *acort*.[67] The rest of song, both refrain and verse, continues as an F-centered melody, cyclically interrupted by that one phrase of slanderous melodic discord. In *Se d'amer me repentoie*, the lady considers the good qualities of her male suitor and pledges to love him in return. The poem is remarkably matter-of-fact in tone, without emotional exclamations of suffering, longing, or even superlatives of joy. She coolly rationalizes her love based on her lover's service, fidelity, and discretion. In the *vuelta* of the last stanza she concludes:

Pour quoy dont ne l'ameroie?	Why then should I not love him?
Trop aroie	My heart would be
le cuer divers et failli.	far too cruel and erring
s'il m'aimme et je ne l'amoie.	if he loved me and I did not love him
et creoie,	and believe in him,
quant il l'a bien desservi.	when he has so well deserved it.

The music further distinguishes the lady's voice from the other *virelais*, for the setting is not syllabic: groups of two to four notes separate and extend syllables, and run musical phrases together. This constant, light ornamentation renders the melody restless and tonally evasive. As with *De bonté, de valour*, the two versicles of the refrain melody are not

---

closer to the present, would be the images on Monet's series of haystacks or the Rouen cathedral facade. Two canvases in a series will share the same subject and artistic presence but be recognized as different realizations, each of which enhances the special vision of the other" (8).

67. Mahrt, "Male and Female Voice," 226–27.

equal; the second ending comes up a measure shorter than the first. Machaut emphasizes his asymmetry with an "across-the-bar" syncopation, creating a hemiola that brings the refrain music to a sudden decisive close on the elusive final.[68]

We may hear in these songs Machaut's attempt to convey gender difference through the juxtaposition of hexachords or an ornamented melody. Yet the verbal and musical vocabulary is, of course, his own. And it is an odd melodic language overall. As Daniel Leech-Wilkinson notes, "while a few, like *Douce dame jolie*, are certainly simple and tuneful, easy to sing and dance, there are also some very strange and difficult pieces among Machaut's virelais."[69] I have highlighted the ways in which the monophonic *virelais* feature musical emblems of conflict and discord that recall in spirit, if not more directly, the Occitan *descorts* discussed in chapter 2. Awkward melodic leaps, unbalanced phrases and asymmetrical double versicles, disorienting chromatic notes, and even the banality of the neighbor-note decorations and the frequent "mode 2" low-level rhythms create a collection of songs that as a whole seems designed to challenge as much as entertain. In the monophonic *virelais*, Machaut developed an expressive musical vocabulary to convey the lyric subject's internal battle between Desire and Hope, or between old love and new, or to convey a difference between male and female voices.

A final example makes a more explicit connection between *virelais* and *descorts*—the polyphonic *virelai En mon cuer a un descort* (V24). This composition first appears in MS *Vg* (dated 1360–70), embedded between two monophonic *virelais* along with the three-part *virelai Tres bonne et belle* (V23), which precedes it. (Both *virelais* were formatted for three parts, although *En mon cuer a un descort* is not preserved as a three-part piece in any subsequent source.) For *En mon cuer a un descort*, as well as other two-part *virelais* (V28 and V29), Machaut returned to the metrical scheme of *Dame, a vous sans retollir* from the *Remede de Fortune*.[70] The refrain contains the typical wordplay between *descort* and *acort* familiar in both Occitan and French *descorts* of the previous century:

En mon cuer a un descort	In my heart I have a discord
qui si fort le point et mort	that so strongly pricks and bites it
que, sans mentir,	that, in truth,
s'amours par son doulz plaisir	if love by its sweet pleasure
n'i met accort	does not make an accord there
aveuc ma dame, pour mort	with my lady,
me doy tenir.	I must consider myself dead.

---

68. About this *virelai* Yolanda Plumley observes that "[t]he run-on nature of the musical phrases prevents any clear articulation of the basic melodic frames outlining pentachord and tetrachord, and the identity of the final is only established at the *clos* cadence." See Plumley, *The Grammar of 14th-Century Melody*, 98–99. The serpentine descent through a central octave, the run-on musical phrases, and the tonal indecision of *Se d'amer me repentoie* resemble another *virelai*, *He! dame de valour* (V11).

69. Leech-Wilkinson, "The Well-Formed Virelai," 125.

70. Noted by Hoppin, *Medieval Music*, 430.

As with the pairing of *Mor sui, se je ne vous voy* and *Liement me deport*, this *virelai* links with its neighbor *Tres bonne et belle* in text as well as texture. The third stanza of *Tres bonne et belle* provides the image of Desire's *pointure*, yet the overall sentiment of *Tres bonne et belle* is one of cheerful acquiescence; indeed, in the first verse the lady actually rewards the lover with a smiling gaze. Thus *Tres bonne et belle* presents love as *acort* to the next song's *descort*.

Given the musical implications of *descort*, Gilbert Reaney looked for signs of text-painting in the counterpoint and concluded "unfortunately there is nothing which one could consider very discordant."[71] The lack of harmonic discord is due to the slow-moving tenor and the simple, relatively unsyncopated rhythms of the cantus; there are no startling chromatic alterations, and most dissonances are fleeting. Machaut perhaps intended the calm-surface demeanor of simple melody and counterpoint to play against the legacy of complicated poetry and discordant music associated with the word *descort*. But one contrapuntal peculiarity stands out: the piece begins oddly, with the tenor launching its first pitch A before the cantus, which then enters on the E *below* the tenor note, to form an initial harmonic fourth, as the cantus emerges from the depths, so to speak. This can be heard as an emblem of *descort*, encoded in the ambiguous and somewhat inharmonious relationship of the voice parts and the outset. The same voice-crossing counterpoint returns in the refrain, thus rounding the song with that subtle polyphonic discord.

The genealogy of Machaut's *virelais*, then, may include both the Occitan *dansa* and the Occitan and French *descort*. The other important monophonic repertory in Machaut's oeuvre, the *lai*, lends further credence to this familial relationship, for the *lai* has formal and perhaps conceptual ties to the *descort*, especially in the fourteenth century. Musicologists speculate that Machaut's *lais*, with their twelve strophes of quadruple versicles—seemingly monumental proportions compared to his other secular songs— would last up to twenty-five minutes in performance.[72] Their extensive length and challenge to the performer relates them to the *descorts* added to trouv. *M* discussed in chapter 2. In Machaut's anthologies (though, again, not in the *Remede de Fortune*) he consistently placed the *lais* in the position of greatest prestige, counterbalanced by the *virelais*. In MS *C* this means the *lais* came last, but in all other major manuscripts it means that the *virelais* came last. It is the *virelais* that get the "final word"—or rather, the final song. Linked by texture and *compilatio*, the monophonic *lais* and *virelais* work together to present Machaut's voice in musically dialogic ways.

A: MACHAUT'S VOICE

In order to understand Machaut's monophonic voice fully, we must take a detour with the *lais*. Manuscript evidence suggests that in the thirteenth century *lais* and *descorts* were

71. Reaney, "Guillaume de Machaut," 42.

72. See Fallows, "Guillaume de Machaut and the *Lai*," 477; and Reaney, "The *Lais* of Guillaume de Machaut," 31.

generally understood as separate genres, though they share a heterostophic poetic form and the tendency toward parallel-versicle melodic constructions. Both genres often name themselves within their texts, and the *descorts* are integrated into the general collection of authors, whereas *lais* are frequently set apart and given individual rubrics in the *chanson-niers* (as in trouv. *M, N,* and *T*). Musical style also distinguishes the two genres; *lai* melodies tend toward syllabic and recitational style whereas *descort* melodies tend toward a more decorated and contoured style. The trouvère Willaumes li Viniers, however, reveals the potential for generic confusion in his playful song *Se chans ne descors ne lais* (This song is neither *descort* nor *lai*).

As the mensural additions to trouv. *M* attest, melodic distinctions between *lai* and *descort*, and even *chanson*, became fuzzier by the late thirteenth century. In chapters 2 and 3, we saw composers experimenting with various forms of heterostrophic melodic construction—through-composed, sequential, or serial *pedes-cauda*—no matter the genre of the lyric. *Fauvel* contains four vernacular *lais* (so called in the table of contents); all are written in the *ars nova* decorated melodic style.[73] One, however, names itself as a *descort*— *En ce dous temps d'esté* (no. 64). This song is a fascinating melting-pot of genres: it begins with the narrative language of a *pastourelle* or a *dit*, setting the stage in the first strophe for the scene in which the White Princess asks her ladies to compose a *descort* on her proposed topic. The remaining eleven strophes become a *jeu-parti* on the question whether it is sensible or foolish to commit one's heart to love. Unlike the *lais*, this song displays a self-consciousness about the conditions of its own making, and the differentiation of the many voices contained within it, as these lines from the first strophe indicate:

Je, qui sui leur mestresse, avant le commençai	I, who am their mistress, began the composition
et en le faisant non de descort li donnay,	and in doing so I gave it the name descort,
quar selon la matere ce non si li est vrai.	for, given the subject, that name was appropriate.[74]

This song may be the last example of a self-named *descort*. Though it has been appointed to the genre of the *lai*, it is far grander in scale and concept than the other *Fauvel lais*, with its twelve strophes (Machaut's standard) and Alexandrine versification (twelve-syllable lines). One of Machaut's unnotated *lais*, *On parle de richesses et de grant signorie*, may have been directly influenced by this *Fauvel descort* for it begins with three strophes of double versicles with Alexandrine lines (unique among Machaut's *lais*) and features an

---

73. *Talant que j'ai d'obeïr* (no. 21) is exceptional in that it is slightly more conservative and monotonous in its rhythmic language. The Latin *lais* are much more conservative, perhaps archaic, in their style. See Rosenberg and Tischler, *The Monophonic Songs.*

74. Text and translation from Rosenberg and Tischler, *The Monophonic Songs,* 138.

exchange between male and female subjects on the topic of love. The male voice speaks of love in didactic ways, as its "codifier," while the female voice speaks of love in typical lyric fashion, as its subject, or "participant."[75]

On parle de richesses appears as the penultimate *lai* in the series of fifteen in MS *C*. In line with the thirteenth-century *compilatio* that placed the *lais* at the ends of anthologies with separate rubrication, MS *C* begins each *lai* with an illustration. No other musical genre receives such treatment, and in the other Machaut manuscripts, where the *lais* appear first among the notated lyrics, they do not receive such illustrations. Examining these illustrations along with the poetic content, Sylvia Huot argues that the series of fifteen *lais* in MS *C*, which mix notated and unnotated *lais*, present a "unified poetic construct"—a program that, as it unfolds, identifies the male lyric "I" "as writer, poet, and codifier of love, more so than as lover."[76] The series fall into subsections: in the first six *lais* the lyric "I" is male, and the activity of composing is prominent either within the lyric (L1, L4, L5, L6) or in the illustration (L1, L3). The next three alternate between male and female lyric subjects, and "return to a pure articulation of love, here presented from both sides."[77] The early layer of the collection ended here, with this display of Machaut's manipulation of the lyric persona. Yet the next part of the collection continues the alternation of differently gendered subject-positions, creating dialogic pairs of songs. With the final three *lais*, however, the female voice dominates. The following is an outline of the *lais* as they appear in MS *C*, grouped according to Huot's observations (nos. 1, 2, 5, and 9 are in Franconian notation):

Group 1: male voice
1. (blank staves) **Loyaute, que point ne delay**
2. **J'aim la flour de valour**
3. Pour ce qu'on puist
4. (unnotated) Aus amans pour exemplaire
5. **Nuls ne doit avoir**
6. Par trois raisons

Group 2: alternating male and female voices
7. Amours doucement – male
8. Amis t'amour (Le lay des dames) – female
9. **Un mortel lay weil commencier** (Le lay mortel) – male
   [ballade] – ends first collection
10. Qui bien aimme a tart oublie (Le lay de plour) – female

---

75. Huot, *From Song to Book*, 269–70. Gilbert Reaney observed: "it seems likely that the *Fauvel lais* had some influence on [Machaut], since there are undoubted traces of *Fauvel* motet influence in Machaut's motets." See Reaney, "The *Lais* of Guillaume de Machaut," 23.

76. Huot, *From Song to Book*, 271.

77. Ibid., 265.

11. Ne say comment commencier (Le lay de l'ymage) – male
12. (unnotated) Se quanque Diex en monde a fait – female

Group 3: predominantly female voices
13. (unnotated) Maintes foys oy recorder – female
14. (unnotated) On parle de richesses et de grant signorie – male and female
15. (unnotated) Amours se plus demandoie – female

From this Huot concludes that "the use of the female voice in the last three lays stresses the withdrawal of the poet as lover from the picture, giving way instead to lover and poet as distinct voices."[78] The adoption of a female subject-position increases the artifice of the lyric voice, severing it decisively from Machaut's autobiographical "I." Troubadours and trouvères sometimes wrote songs with a female subject-position (the *chanson de mal mariée*, *chanson de femme* and *aube*); recall, too, the *virelai de femme* by Jehan de Lescurel and the two by Machaut discussed above (as well as his *virelai de mal mariée* tenor for motet M16). These are brief forays into the voice on the *other* side of love. With the *lais*, Machaut made a project of demonstrating and particularizing his poetic voice through a systematic manipulation of gendered subject-positions.

There is another level of artifice and voice to these *lais* provided by the notation. Four of the ten *lais* in MS *C* transmitted with music are written in Franconian notation, with longs, breves, and semibreves (see bold titles above; *Loyaute, que point ne delay* is notated elsewhere in Franconian notation). Many scholars have observed that this archaic notation simply complements the archaic genre of the *lai*,[79] but it seems to me that for Machaut the turn back to earlier notation has a more nuanced meaning: it provides yet another encoding of self-consciousness in and about writing and reading. Machaut does not simply use this voice of the *ars antiqua* to convey dignity or loftiness, for he does not use it for all the *lais*. Rather, it is the contrast of the old with the new that is important here. The first set of six *lais*, which emphasizes the poet as writer and creator, offers all formats of the written *lai*, in old and new notation, and entirely without notation. In the next set of four *lais*, which offers heterosexual pairings, only the despairing *lay mortel* is written in what can easily be understood as expressively slow note values.

78. Ibid., 271. Sarah Kay argues that Machaut pursued the issue of gender and sexual difference in *Jugement dou roy de Navarre* (ca. 1349), which he used to complicate and critique the concepts of universals. In that narrative "Guillaume" is put on trial for slandering women (presumably in an earlier *dit*), and he receives the punishment to compose a *lai*, a *virelai*, and a *ballade*. In some manuscripts (notably MSS *A* and *Vg*) *Qui bien aimme a tart oublie* follows the *dit* presumably as an illustration of Machaut's atonement, though the *virelai* and the *ballade* are unaccounted for. The sequence of predominantly female-voiced *lais* that follow the *ballade* were presumably written after this *dit*, and suggest, if not atonement for misogyny, then at least an extended fascination with writing lyrics from a female subject position. See Kay, *The Place of Thought*, 93–122, and also Newes, "'Qui bien aimme a tart oublie.'"

79. Reaney, "The *Lais* of Guillaume de Machaut," 25. Two of the ten *lais* listed above, *Pour ce qu'on puist* (L3) and *Amours doucement* (L6) begin with longs and breves but also include semibreves and minims as well. On the use of older notational styles for the *chant roial*, the *complainte*, and the *lai* in the *Remede de Fortune*, see Leach, *Guillaume de Machaut*, 153–54.

Machaut's choice to turn back to past musical vocabularies distinguishes the present from the past as well as showing off his musical versatility; he commands both the *ars nova* and the *ars antiqua*, and thus, in a way, transcends the boundary between present and past. As we saw in chapter 3, details of *compilatio* over time recorded changing conceptions of the lyric voice (in trouv. *T*) and modes of self-expression (in trouv. *M*). Machaut's collected works manuscripts contain within them a *chansonnier* of notated songs that transmits its own metanarrative of the lyric voice, which links to the actual narratives in the manuscript, especially the *Remede de Fortune*. The explorations of voice in the *lais* in MS *C* reflect back on the *virelais*. In light of the *lais'* ever-changing self-conscious stances, the *virelais* appear pure in their lyricism. Although the ideology of love changes over the course of the *virelai* collection, the lyric persona firmly remains a lover, with no pretense to poet or even composer. Indeed, the *virelais* lack such self-referentiality; they rarely refer to their own making, or the activity of composing. Only one *virelai*, *Dame, voustre doulz viaire* (V17), borrows language from the trouvère *envoi* in its final *vuelta*, ending the strophe with the line, "C'est tout. Mon chant vous envoy." The form of the *virelai* itself prevents such literary self-referencing, for the refrain takes the place of both the *exordium* and *envoi* of the trouvère songs, where contemplation of the making of song traditionally takes place. Given the pure lyricism of the *virelais*—by comparison to the *lais* with their links to an Occitan past—it makes sense, then, that Machaut used the *virelai* in the *Remede de Fortune* to express the true feelings of the lover *qua* lover.

Though syllabic, the *virelais* are consistently written in the lower and newer rhythmic values of semibreve and minim. Thus with the *virelais* Machaut dresses the old lyric persona in newer formal and notational garb, while with the *lais* he dresses the newer poetic persona in older formal and notational garb. It is a grafting of stalk and bud—selves and songs—that joins generations of poets and composers, as well as scribes and notators.

Men and women, too, are joined together. Huot writes: "the alternation of male and female voices in the progression of the lays imitates the format of the carol" and this "captures with extraordinary sensitivity the creative tension between song and book. Machaut explores the dynamics by which singing is replaced by writing as the lyric activity: the carol is projected into the book, the trouvère becomes the author."[80] The depiction of the *carole* in the *Remede de Fortune* (see figure 5.1 above), however, is directly associated with the performance of the *virelai*. And there we see the singer Machaut hand in hand with women in the dance. His voice in the *virelai*(s) enables the *carole* and the round-dance of male and female voices in the *lais*.

In Machaut MS *C*, the *lais* end the collection of notated lyrics with a woman's voice. Later manuscripts switch the order of *virelais* and *lais*, so the *virelais* come last, and they also scramble the *carole* of men and women after the first seven *lais*. But in MS *A* (from the 1370s), perhaps the last anthology to have been supervised by the composer, the lyric

---

80. Huot, *From Song to Book*, 272 and 273, respectively.

collection ends with two polyphonic *virelais* in the female voice—*Moult sui de bonne heure née* (V31) and *De tout sui si confortée* (V32).[81] This is also the earliest manuscript to contain *Le Livre dou voir dit*, Machaut's monumental exploration of love, voice, and poetic identity in conjunction with age and gender. The *Voir Dit* has garnered much scholarly attention for its "literary self-consciousness," undoing the conventions and motifs of past love literature in a seemingly postmodernist weave of genres (lyric, narrative, epistle), intertextual allusions and self-references, and, above all, a blurring of truth and fiction.[82] The narrative events tell of a young woman's pursuit of a distant, aged poet, which turns the conditions of love and song found in the troubadour and trouvère lyric on its head. Indeed, the narrative takes as its starting point the *tornadas* and *envois*, but in reverse: the lady first sends a song to Machaut, who is the unseen "far away love"; she calls him into his identity as a lover-poet. Machaut interrogates and burlesques that combinatory identity, however, by structuring his narrative around a central conflict between the old figure of the aristocratic trouvère-lover, who experiences love as an embodied condition and who sings because he must—because love demands it—and the new figure of the cleric-poet, who displaces and sublimates the experience of love into writing, and who composes and loves by request after he appears to be past his prime for both.[83]

Throughout the story Machaut deploys lyric topoi (springtime settings, praise and blame, slanderers, Ovidian lovesickness and cures, the desired embrace) as both "real" scenarios and literary conventions. And in every scenario, Machaut fails as a lover (Toute Belle initiates the embrace) but he succeeds as a poet nevertheless. William Calin notes: "realism is a manifestation of antiromance. The author exposes traditional courtly artifice, indulges in a parody of *fin'amors*. The courtly and the noncourtly, the romantic and the down-to-earth, are juxtaposed, one convention played off against another for literary purposes, to create a mood of laughter and sophisticated, ironic detachment."[84]

As many scholars have noted, the primary story in the *Voir Dit* is the story of its own making, "the writing and construction of the book itself."[85] But Machaut does not write the book alone, for Toute Belle composes letters and lyrics in nearly equal measure. Indeed, their relationship at times appears to be one of teacher and apprentice, or two equal participants in a scholastic dialogue or *jeu-parti,* rather than the traditional roles of lover and

---

81. Machaut MS *A* is also the first manuscript to contain the *Prologue*; see Earp, "Machaut's Role," 480 and 488.

82. For the text, translation, and informative introduction see Guillaume de Machaut, *Le Livre dou Voir Dit*, ed. Leech-Wilkinson. For an extensive summary and discussion the *Voir Dit* see Brownlee, *Poetic Identity in Guillaume de Machaut*, 94–156.

83. Brownlee notes that the "courtly diction (as well as the constructs and topics of the grand chant courtois qua literary tradition) predominates" in Part 1, while in Part 2, the clerkly diction (as well as typically clerkly attitudes, stances, and bookishness) predominates; see *Poetic Identity in Guillaume de Machaut*, 95. On the matter of Machaut being too old for love, see Calin, *A Poet at the Fountain*, 180.

84. Calin, *A Poet at the Fountain*, 178–79.

85. Brownlee, *Poetic Identity in Guillaume de Machaut*, 94.

beloved. This "pluralization of the voice" also places the *Voir Dit* in line with the most famous double-authored narrative, the *Roman de la rose*, which contrasts the romantic language of Guillaume de Lorris with the clerkly, caustic, and didactic continuation by Jean de Meun.[86] The double-authored nature of Machaut's *Voir Dit* is made explicit in the narrative when Toute Belle refers to *nostre livre*.[87] Scholars have debated the existence of Toute Belle, whether her distinct voice is part of the "true story" or an alter ego formed for the elaborate and ingenious literary fiction.[88] Fiction or no, the *Voir Dit* continues in an extended and thorough way Machaut's exploration of gender and lyric voice, which he began with the *lais*, and perhaps completed with the final polyphonic *virelais*.

Early in the story, before they meet, Machaut sends Toute Belle the words to three *chansons baladées* "that have never been sung" (lines 942–43). In three letters (nos. 5, 28, and 32) Toute Belle requests that he set to music "des virelais que vous feistes avant que vous meussez veue" (the virelais you composed before laying eyes upon me), especially one, *L'ueil, qui est le droit archier* (the eye, which is the true archer).[89] Machaut ignores her request, responding in letter 33 only to say that he has been busy working on *vostre livre*. This tacit power struggle is laced with irony in the play of the *virelai*'s title, which specifies sight as the instigator of love, and the identity of the *virelais* as those composed before his eyes had seen her (thus calling into question their expressive truth-value). Yet his refusal seems significant from a musical standpoint. Machaut set few new *virelais* to music between 1360 and 1370—only seven total, with six in two-part polyphony, and one in three-part polyphony (none as monophonic songs). Five more unnotated *virelais* are incorporated into the *Voir Dit* (another four are attributed to Toute Belle). Machaut either lost interest in the *virelai* as a lyric genre "for singing," caught up instead in the growing vogue for polyphonic *rondeaux*, or the genre itself came to signify a compositional problem—how to reconcile the expressive musical language of the *virelai*, established in monophony, within a polyphonic texture. The *Voir Dit* includes one piece of monophony; it is the central *lay d'Esperence*, referencing the ideology and preeminent lyric genre of the *Remede de Fortune*. Thus the association between monophony and genre still held to some degree, with its attendant symbolic significance of prestige and purity. We do not know whether the *virelais* of the *Voir Dit* would have been monophonic or polyphonic, though we do know that the genre posed this choice of

---

86. See ibid., 98, on the apprentice–teacher relationship. For "pluralization of the voice" see Cerquiglini, *"Un Engin si soutil": Guillaume de Machaut et l'écriture*, esp. 91–103. She compares the exchange to dialogues, *jeux-partis*, and the letters of Abelard and Heloïse. See also Huot, "Reliving the *Roman de la rose*"; and Devaux, "Le *Voir Dit* de Guillaume de Machaut.

87. For the Lady's claim of *nostre livre* see letter 26, *Voir Dit*, 326. The base text comes from MS *A*; the later and less reliable Machaut MS *E* reads *vostre livre*.

88. Calin, *Poet at the Fountain*, 169–71 argues for Toute Belle as a literary fiction; see Leech-Wilkinson, introduction to *Voir Dit*, xxxviii–l.

89. For the relevant passages see letter 5 (p. 87), letter 28 (p. 347), letter 32 (p. 417) in *Voir Dit*. The quotation is from letter 32, although letter 28 uses similar language.

texture—the single voice, bearing the weight of past troubadour and trouvère songs and Machaut's own earlier reworking of those traditions, or a plurality of voices, associated with artful manipulations of newly standardized forms. The dialectic of monophony and polyphony speaks to one central theme of the *Voir Dit*: it is the unification of the pluralized voice through love lyrics and their *compilatio*.

The *virelais* of the *Voir Dit* never received a musical setting, though the lyrics do appear in the music section of the manuscripts, as if a testimony to Toute Belle's unfulfilled request.[90] However, Machaut included the two presumably new polyphonic *virelais* at the end of the musical anthology in MS *A*. As their first lines announce, *Moult sui de bonne heure née* (I was born of a happy hour) and *De tout sui si confortée* (I am so comforted in all things) form a pair of cheerful and celebratory love lyrics, where the female subjects extol the male lovers for their honor and for loving them well. In *De tout sui si confortée*, the lady awaits the return of her male lover from a foreign land (*d'estrange contree*), and in the meantime she concentrates on pleasant thoughts and pledges her loyalty. *Moult sui de bonne heure née* explicitly articulates the *Remede de Fortune*'s ideology of love, especially in the first stanza:

b-1

Nos cuers en joye norry	Our hearts by joy
sont, si que soussi,	are nourished, so that care,
ne riens qui nous disagree,	or anything that displeases us,

b-1

n'avons, pour ce que assevi	we do not have, because we are sated
sommes de mercy,	by total mercy,
qu'est souffisance appellee;	which is called sufficiency;

a-1

un desir, une pensee,	one desire, one thought,
un cuer, une ame est entee	one heart, one soul is grafted
en nous, et aussi	in us, and also
de voloir sommes uni.	we are one in our wishes.
Onques plus douce assamblee,	Never was a happier couple
par ma foy, ne vy.	seen, in truth.

Machaut puts a post-*Voir Dit* spin on the *Remede de Fortune*'s ideology of sufficiency, for sufficiency here is achieved not in Hope, but in the unity between lover and beloved,

---

90. Eight of the sixty-three lyric poems in the *Voir Dit* have been set to music (nine if counting the double ballade as two lyrics). These include three three-part *ballades* (B32, B33, B36), one four-part double *ballade* (B34), two three-part *rondeaux* (R13, R17), one two-part *rondeau* (R4), and one monophonic *lai* (L13). These eight pieces are included in the music anthologies of MSS *Vg* (ca. 1360–70, but which does not include the *Voir Dit*), *A*, *B* (ca. 1370–72), and *G* (ca. 1390). See also Ragnard, "Le *Voir Dit*."

poetically depicted in the syntactic enjambments that unite one line to the next and the verse to the *vuelta*. Indeed, these lovers are so in agreement, so without discord, so grafted together that the lyric reads as a new type of anti-*canso*, a *descort* on the scale of the whole *canso* tradition. The sentiment of sufficiency and contentment, ruffled only by the grief of distance, jettisons the foundational paradox of the love songs of the twelfth and thirteenth centuries—subjecthood born of subjugation, the voice that emerges from the impossibility of achieving the fulfillment of desire. This literary merging of self and other in the *Voir Dit*, and its lyric counterparts in these two female-voiced polyphonic *virelais*, signals the decisive end of the troubadour and trouvère love song and its monophonic subject. With Machaut's late *virelais*, monophony, once a sonic emblem of *fin'amors* and self-expression, finally yields to the polyphony of its manifold subjects—lover, beloved, composer, scribe, performer, and audience—united in the enterprise of giving voice to love.

Conclusion

MEDIEVAL EXPRESSIONISM

I WILL CONCLUDE this study with several returns, beginning with the frontispiece and the first song considered in the introduction. With the image of his beloved inscribed on his chest, the troubadour Folquet de Marselha gestures toward the song *En chantan m'aven a membrar.* Medieval readers would understand this marginal illustration in troub. *N* to depict the activities of the heart—to remember the beloved, to contemplate love, and to lead the troubadour to self-expression, just as his hand leads the readers' eyes to the lyric. If we follow the line from his fingertips to the song, we are directed to two particular lines:

mas per so chant qu'oblides la dolor	but I sing in order to forget
e·l mal d'amor.	the pains of love.

These lines are a contradiction, for the troubadour's voice is animated by his desire for the beloved, by the *mal d'amor.* Should he forget this pain, should the beloved's face be erased from his heart, he would cease to sing. We might also view this visual graft of lover and beloved with an eye toward the multiplicity of "selves" and voices that generate the love song—the troubadour, the performers, the compilers, and the scribes. Indeed, the mono-phonic love song is a contradiction: it is the representation of a single voice that points to the polyphony of voices in its making. And it does so in musical ways.

The lyrics of love songs from the troubadours to Guillaume de Machaut are characteristically self-conscious, reflecting on the materials and event of their making, frequently in paradoxical formulations—in the songs of nature that the troubadour transforms into artifice, in agency (singing) born of subjugation (desiring), in the historical and irreducibly social condition of the subjective voice and lyric "I," and in the love song as an end in itself in which the beloved becomes a literary device (and literary devices are beloved). Through these paradoxes, the self emerges as the subject, and song as the predicate; in other words, the song is expressive in the abstract as an emblem or event of self-expression. This study was prompted by the question: can we find such self-conscious self-expression in the details of music? I have argued that we can, especially in moments and examples where the specifically musical properties of the song—voice, melody, rhythm, form, and genre—come dramatically to the fore and seem to comment or reflect on music itself.

Why set love poetry to music? Music muddies the articulation of words; it competes with the poem's artful design of rhymes and rhythm of the syllables and accents. Poetry already sets up a conflict between sound and sense with inventive word choices, syntax, and enjambments that delight the ear with a syncopation formed from the flow of words clashing with breaks between lines and stanzas. It may not be surprising, then, that the monophonic settings of love songs should extend this verbal music with its own insistent organization of sound. Music superimposes onto words yet another artful design of formal repetition and phrases parsed by pitch content and melodic contour. What becomes evident in performance is not necessarily the harmony of words and music, but rather their frequent discord, which the bare monophonic settings highlight. Our tools for measuring musical expression are largely based on Renaissance and Romantic models; we look for the coincidence of significant verbal and musical events, mimetic gestures of word painting, affective association of harmonies, and an organic form that can show changing psychological states. Words and music in the Middle Ages—by these standards, and possibly by the standards of medieval composers—comprise parallel, if not outright conflicting, systems of expression that may cooperate at some times, and not at all at other times.

I noted in chapter 3 how consistently in the first stanza of Robert de Castel's *chanson Se j'ai chanté sans guerredon avoir* (example 3.3) poetic enjambments that connect lines of verse run roughshod over rhyme sound and musical cadence, and how mid-line syntactic pauses do not correspond to the melodic logic of the phrase. This non-mensural melody amplifies the tension between sound and sense already present in the sonic, musical properties of the lyrical words. Yet the pitches take the ear further afield from apparent meaning, for what does it mean to hear a closed melodic cadence on a word that does not signal closure but necessarily points forward? Or to hear modal rhythm tear through the end of a verbal statement before the listener can fully comprehend it? Such conflicts occur time and again in the examples featured in this book—in the trailing rhymes of the Occitan *descorts*, and the traffic jams of accents or the run-ons between verse and *vuelta* in the *virelais* of Machaut. In all these cases, the music is expressive, or gives the impression of being expressive, but it seems not to be expressing anything but itself. The challenge to performers in such situations of conflict is to render a temporal paradox—to cadence without ending, or to pause while moving forward; the performer must reach a compromise between the push and pull of these parallel systems, between musical and verbal expression. Setting words to music thus challenges their expression with another voice, as it were. This may be one answer to the "why" of the music of these love songs: music inscribes the Other, the beloved, onto the heart of the words.

The *tornadas*, *descorts*, recomposed *chansons*, monophonic motets, and *virelais* considered in this study are all expressive of this temporal paradox and musical self-consciousness, on formal and historical levels. I use the word "expressive" as art and literary historians do, to refer to compositions that display a "personalized" or subjective musical language that breaks with convention and calls attention to the unique features of the medium. In *Expressionism in Twentieth-Century Music* the authors John C. Crawford and Dorothy L. Crawford pursue the question of musical self-expression in the works of early twentieth-century composers—Schoenberg, Webern, Berg, Stravinsky, Bartók, and Ives—roughly contemporaneous with the era of expressionist painters and writers. The subjective, direct expression of emotions that characterized artworks in this era necessarily broke with conventions of representation and form.[1] The Crawfords describe a number of musical analogs for "expressionism," including chromaticism, improvisatory and non-repeating forms, aphoristic forms, melodies with wide intervals, extreme ranges, and abrupt shifts in direction, the distortion of well-known songs, and highly syncopated or obsessively repeating rhythms.[2] Many of the songs I examine here display similar expressive strategies. In its most conventional and abundant form, the medieval love song is a strophic, *pedes-cauda* melody, recorded in non-mensural notation, setting words that convey a first-person subject—perhaps even an identifiable author—who nonetheless gives voice to love in rhetorical clichés. Against this background of conventions we can hear medieval expressionism in the disruptive voice and partial formal returns of the *tornadas* (a conventional feature that breaks convention); in the seemingly spontaneous free melodies, obsessive modal rhythms, and interrupted lines of the *descorts*; in the distortion of well-known songs in the recomposed *chansons*; in the grafted voices and genres of the aphoristic monophonic motets; and in the wide intervals, chromatic surprises, and fusion of old and new melodic and amorous sensibilities in Machaut's monophonic *virelais*.

Though some important conceptual aspects of early twentieth-century expressionism—the interest in the exploration of the psyche or the unconscious, rebellion against bourgeois culture, and anxiety about industrialization—have no correspondence in the

---

1. The idea of "expressionistic" composition has been attached to repertories throughout the centuries; the Crawfords list the madrigals of Don Carlo Gesualdo (ca. 1560–1613), the fantasies of Carl Philipp Emanuel Bach (1717–88), and the late works of Beethoven (1714–1827). See *Expressionism in Twentieth-Century Music*, 2.

2. Ibid., 17–18. Aphorism was also a strategy of German expressionist literature; see Sokel, "The Prose of German Expressionism," esp. 83–85.

medieval world, both eras were marked by a sense of belatedness and a worry over spiritual decay. The correlation of modern and medieval musical expressionism lies in this shared sense of an end-game to the old forms, their loss of meaning, effectiveness, and expression. The subjective distortion of forms, techniques, and materials admits that, as Wassily Kandinsky wrote, "form is the outer expression of the inner content."[3] From this stance emerges expressionism's seemingly paradoxical tendency toward formalism and abstraction, which we can observe in both modern and medieval expressive turns.[4]

The theme of turning and returning has pervaded this inquiry into musical self-expression, on formal, cultural, and theoretical levels. The *tornadas, descorts,* recomposed *chansons,* monophonic motets, and *virelais* considered here all combine a turning backward with a looking forward—or rather, a turning backward as a means of looking forward. In chapters 2 and 3 we saw that many of the late mensural additions to trouv. *M* that eschewed or parodied the strophic repetition of the classic *chanson d'amour* were nevertheless yoked to another form of return—that of recycling an older lyric. What, then, is the role of belatedness and nostalgia in "innovation"? Sarah Kay observes in troubadour songs that "the claim to novelty is in itself a conventional *topos;* as such it carries with it its own irony, and is often used to signal not innovation but return," and she remarks that "the new cannot escape the old, it is only intelligible in function of the old, and becomes old as soon as it is pronounced."[5] As the late troubadour Guilhem de Montanhagol (ca. 1233–57) insists:

Non an tan dig li primier trobador	The early troubadours have not said
ni fag d'amor,	or composed so much about love,
lai el temps, qu'era guays,	in times past, which were gay,
qu'enquera nos no fassam, apres lor,	that we cannot yet, after them, compose
chans de valor,	songs of worth,
nous, plazens e verais;	that are new, pleasing, and true;
quar dir pot hom so qu'estat dig	for one can say what may not have
no sïa,	been said,
qu'estiers non es trobaires bos	and in no other way is a troubadour good
no fis	or fine
Tro fai sos chans guays, nous	but in making his song gay, new, and nobly
e gent assis,	fashioned,
ab nöels digz de nova mäestrïa.[6]	with new words and new mastery.

---

3. Qsuoted in Crawford and Crawford, *Expressionism in Twentieth-Century Music,* 16. Kandinsky turned to music as a conceptual model for his paintings. For a discussion of expressionism in art and its relationship to literature and other modernist see also Donahue, introduction to *A Companion to the Literature of German Expressionism,* 11–15.

4. See the discussion in Crawford and Crawford, *Expressionism in Twentieth-Century Music,* 12–13.

5. *Subjectivity in Troubadour Poetry,* 167 and 169, respectively.

6. PC 225-7, stanza I; text and translation (modified) from *Anthology,* 264–67.

Guilhem proclaims that novelty resides in new mastery of an old art form; as Kay para-phrases, "to innovate, you have to be learned at it."[7] And in the second stanza, which continues in an extended riff on novelty, Guilhem inserts his own particular voice: "E nou, qu'ieu dic razo qu'om mais no dis" (And new it is, when I say things which no one has said before, [line 18]). Yet beyond the first two stanzas the song becomes quite con-ventional. Novelty is thus haunted by belatedness, and the troubadour's voice is never entirely his own: it is a graft onto the stalk of convention and tradition.

My concern in this study has been with monophony. On the surface, monophony rep-resents an autonomous "self," which is nevertheless rendered complex and unstable by artfully self-conscious words and melodies. Can we see anything of this monophonic self-expression in polyphonic motets and later *chansons*? What, indeed, does it mean to express the self in multiple voices, or parts composed for voice and instruments? Present-day listeners are in the habit of reconciling many voices singing in harmony or polyphony as representing a coherent, unified "self" as long as the voices sing the same words. And we assume medieval listeners did so as well, as evident in the polyphonic *versus* and *con-ductus*. They would also have encountered the aural and conceptual density of selves in sacred chant—multiple voices joined in monophony (most likely a ragged unison, or blending more perfectly aided by fifths) representing the ideal of a collective becoming one sounding body. In the mid-thirteenth century, alongside the collecting and continued composition of monophonic love songs, anonymous medieval composers pursued the idea of representing multiple selves, or points of view, with multiple, clearly heteroge-neous lyric voices unified into a musical whole in the polyphonic motet. Sylvia Huot's study of these motets concentrated on a dialogue between sacred and profane registers (the former encoded in the chant tenors) that unifies these heterogeneous voices via reli-gious allegory. But if the all parts are secular songs, then we have a different topic of

---

7. *Subjectivity in Troubadour Poetry*, 170. Kay also proposes that "the 'newness' of song marks the importance of performance as process and interaction between the singer and his audience, and between the poet and his literary inheritance." It is a truism that performances present songs "anew," as in "immediate," even if they are adhering strictly to received tradition, but it is not to be assumed that the audience understands a given performance as something new, as in "novel." The idea that performers embody the troubadours' topos of nov-elty is somewhat problematic given the *tornadas* and stanzas that decry jongleurs for their bad performances or changes. Peire d'Alvernha begins one lyric with this stanza (PC 323-2; text and translation (modified) from *Anthology*, 88–89; see also the *tornada* to Jaufre Rudel's *No sap chantar quiso non di*):

Ab fina joia comenssa	With noble joy begins
lo vers, qui bels motz assona,	the song, which rhymes fair words,
e de re no·i a faillenssa;	and there's no fault in anything therein;
mas no m'es bon qe l'apreigna	but it pleases me not that it should be learned
tals cui mos chans non coveigna,	by such a one whom the song does not befit,
q'ieu non vuoill avols chantaire,	for I've no wish that some wretched singer,
cel qui tot chan desfaissona,	the sort who ruins any song,
mon doutz sonet torn'en bram.	should turn my sweet melody into braying.

conversation, one that may extend the topics of song and self-expression posed by the secular *chanson* tradition.

My second return is to the polyphonic motet *S'on me regarde/Prennés i garde/HÉ, MI ENFANT*, briefly considered in chapter 4 (see example 4.3). This motet was recorded in *Mo* ca. 1300, alongside more "progressive" motets with rhythmically stratified voices and syllabic semibreves, as well as Anglo-Norman compositions with their "progressive" tertiary harmonies. Although stylistically conservative (or downright *antiqua*) by comparison, this motet contains its own forward-looking elements in a tightly wrought musical contemplation of the voice in monophony and polyphony. As noted in chapter 4, the triplum and motetus convey women's subject-positions, or perhaps more accurately, one woman's subject-position split in two, for the lyrics are slightly different combinations of the same set of aphoristic verbal phrases with only three unique phrases at the end of the motetus (see chapter 4, table 4.3, for the text and translation). The tenor ("Hey, my child") has no known concordance, and in this context conveys a paternalistic voice—perhaps that of the lover, or the jealous rival, or the audience who overhears the woman's words to another. With its drone-like melody, the tenor provides a harmonic underpinning for the top voices as they distort a well-known *rondeau*.

With the first four measures, the words are coordinated with the musical phrases of the *rondeau*, and they participate in a brief voice exchange (a venerable polyphonic technique by this time) that here presents one song—the *rondeau* refrain—in two dimensions, as telescoped vertical layers and as a fleeting horizontal stream.[8] After these first four phrases, however, the top voices become differentiated; though they sing the same words, the lines are cleverly scrambled to avoid the close echo of whole phrases. Yet the music continues to pull the wandering voice(s) back into the fold of a single song. Importantly, the old technique of voice exchange transforms into something new: the recombinations of the *rondeau* phrases become recurring musical motifs that the ear tracks through their changing contrapuntal contexts and in their transposed and staggered entrances. We can think about *S'on me regarde/Prennés i garde/HÉ, MI ENFANT* in the context of Guilhem de Montanhagol's contemplation of novelty. The words are not new, they are not even unique to the different voices, yet their musical presentation is (always) new. Using preexisting words and tune, and a *nova mäestrïa* rendered through the abstract musical returns, the composer of this motet created a thoroughly "modern" piece of imitative polyphony that seems to look ahead to expressive musical techniques in generations beyond Machaut.

As a late thirteenth-century composition, this motet clearly speaks to the musical and conceptual dynamic between monophony and polyphony: it is a monophonic song refracted through a prism of polyphony, which serves to orchestrate the plurality of voices

---

8. See also *Trois serors sor rive mer...La jonete/Trois serors sor rive mer...La moiene/Trois serors sor rive mer... L'aisnee*/PERLUSTRAVIT (Gen 343) and Huot, *Allegorical Play*, 53–55.

inherent in the *rondeau* form.[9] Yet the motet also pulls the many voices, through musical repetition and imitation, and a preponderance of perfect sonorities, back into the orbit of a single organizing song, as if to propose that polyphony might also be considered a type of enhanced monophony.

What if we approach the polyphonic *chansons* of Machaut as enhanced monophony? What is Machaut's *nova mäestrïa* of the *art de trobar*, of the expressive complexities of melody and "song" in the context of polyphony? This is not to deny Machaut's attention to vertical sonorities and the principles of discant, or to designate his polyphonic *chansons* as accompanied songs for the purposes of performance practice (although such a determination certainly may follow). Rather it is to think about the musical legacy of the troubadours and trouvères that may still be in play in the cantus lines embedded within or floating above other composed parts, whether vocal or instrumental. Scholarly approaches to fourteenth-century polyphonic *chansons*, and Machaut's in particular, have swung between an emphasis on linear thinking, where vertical sonorities are deemed accidental, to an emphasis on harmonic thinking, where melodic lines are deemed surface decorations of a deep discant structure.[10] My proposal to think "monophonically" may seem an attempt to turn the clock back to a linear bias, but this would be only partially true. It is a partial return that Machaut himself invites with his demonstrable interests in exploring the expressive possibilities of monophony, even in its twilight.

Within a polyphonic context, singers sing but one part though they hear and interact with others; they experience their line as determined to some extent by counterpoint and sonority, and yet they must attend to its own linear logic. From this vantage point, the cantus of *Rose, lis, printemps, verdure*, for example, presents an expressively tentative lyric voice, remarkably delicate, halting, and highly refined as a melody. Machaut's "advanced" melodic sensibility was no doubt encouraged by polyphony. In such a context, performers and listeners alike hold in balance an experience of the self or the subject as not altogether autonomous, just as the troubadour's voice depended on that of the jongleur, or the pen of a scribe. In her analysis of Machaut's early two-part *ballade J'aim miex* (B7), Sarah Fuller calls attention to the perspectives of performer and listener—the former attuned to line, and the latter to *contrapunctus*—and Machaut's attention to both.[11] She concludes

---

9. The motet makes use of a *rondeau* in ingenious ways that are distinct from the *rondeau* motets or early polyphonic *rondeau* examined by Everist (he does not consider this motet in either study listed below). In the *rondeau* motets (all with chant tenors), the musical shape of the *rondeau* is displayed in one or more voices (Everist distinguishes between eight two-part motets appearing only in trouv. *M* and *T* in which both tenor and motetus reflect the *rondeau* form, and five other two- and three-part motets that use the form in one voice). Polyphonic *rondeaux* contain one lyric sung by all voices. See Everist, "The Rondeau Motet," "The Polyphonic Rondeau," and *French Motets*, 90–108, esp. 101, where he notes that *Prendés i garde* does not quite fit the thematics typical of *rondeaux*.

10. For an early argument for vocalization of all parts (and a harmonic orientation), see Page, "Machaut's 'Pupil' Deschamps on the Performance of Music." The issues of performance practice and musical analysis are carefully considered and historicized in Leech-Wilkinson, *The Modern Invention of Medieval Music*.

11. "Line, 'Contrapunctus,' and Structure in a Machaut Song," 39.

her study by describing the composition as a "multi-faceted structure, a sort of cubist construct with intersecting planes of reference, association, process."[12] Fuller's "cubist" polyphony—where different perspectives (linear and harmonic) are present simultaneously—fits well with my pursuit of "expressionist" monophony, for the abstraction of the former has roots in the subjectivism of the latter. Polyphony seems a logical extension of the monophonic love song and its belated contributors, which include Machaut. In the illustration of the *virelai* in the *Remede de Fortune* (figure 5.1), Machaut sings alone, yet clasps the hands of his audience, who will sing in turn. It is a scene of monophony with polyphonic implications—the social condition of song and self-expression.

---

12. Ibid., 54. This description also fits *S'on me regarde/Prennés i garde/Hé, MI ENFANT*: the top voices present their own slightly different angles of perspective on the same words and melodic material.

BIBLIOGRAPHY

FACSIMILE EDITIONS

Trouv. A

Jeanroy, Alfred. *Le Chansonnier d'Arras: Reproduction en phototypie.* Paris: Société des Anciens Textes Français, 1925.

Trouv. K

Jeanroy, Alfred. *Le Chansonnier de l'Arsenal: Trouvères du XIIᵉ–XIIIᵉ siècle. Reproduction phototypique du manuscrit 5198 de la Bibliothèque de l'Arsenal.* Paris: Geuthner, 1909.

Trouv. M; *troub.* W

Beck, Jean, and Louise Beck. *Les Chansonniers des troubadours et des trouvères: Le manuscrit du roi, fonds français no. 844 de la Bibliothèque nationale.* Corpus cantilenarum medii aevi, ser. 1, no. 2. 2 vols. 1938. Reprint, New York: Broude Brothers, 1970.

Trouv. O

Beck, Jean. *Les Chansonniers des troubadours et des trouvères: Chansonnier Cangé, Paris, Bibliothèque nationale, ms. français no. 846.* Corpus cantilenarum medii aevi, ser.1, no 1. 2 vols. 1927. Reprint, New York: Broude Brothers, 1964.

Trouv. U; *troub.* X

Meyer P., and G. Raynaud. *Le Chansonnier français de Saint-Germain-des-Prés (Bibl. Nat. Fr. 20050). Reproduction phototypique avec transcription.* Société des Anciens Textes Français 1. Paris: Didot et Cⁱᵉ, 1892.

Fauvel

Roesner, Edward, François Avril, and Nancy Freeman Regalado. *Le Roman de Fauvel in the Edition of Mesire Chaillou de Pesstain: A Reproduction in Facsimile of the Complete Manuscript, Paris, Bibliothèque Nationale, Fonds Français 146.* New York: Broude Brothers, 1990.

Mo

Rokseth, Yvonne. *Polyphonies du XIIIᵉ siècle: Le manuscrit H 196 de la Faculté de Médecine de Montpellier.* 4 vols. Paris: Éditions de L'Oiseau Lyre, 1935–9.

P-BnF f. lat. 3719

Gillingham, Bryan. *Paris, Bibliothèque Nationale, Fonds Latin 3719.* Ottawa, Ont.: The Institute of Mediaeval Music, 1987.

W2

Dittmer, Luther. *Faksimile-Ausgabe der Handschrift Wolfenbüttel 1099 (1206).* Brooklyn: Institute of Mediaeval Music, 1960.

Works Cited

Text editions are listed under the first name of the medieval authors, indicated by small capitals. For frequently cited editions, bibliographies, dictionaries, and anthologies see the Abbreviations.

ADAM DE LA HALLE. *The Lyric Works of Adam de la Hale.* See Wilkins, Nigel.

Adorno, Theodor W. "Alienated Masterpiece: The *Missa Solemnis.*" In *Essays on Music,* edited by Richard Leppert and translated by Susan H. Gillespie, 569–83. Berkeley: University of California Press, 2002.

———. *Beethoven: The Philosophy of Music.* Edited by Rolf Tiedmann. Translated by Edmund Jephcott. Stanford: Stanford University Press, 1998.

———. "Late Style in Beethoven." In *Essays on Music,* edited by Richard Leppert and translated by Susan H. Gillespie, 564–68. Berkeley: University of California Press, 2002.

AIMERIC DE BELENOI. *Poésies du troubadour Aimeric de Belenoi.* Edited by Maria Dumitrescu. Paris: Société des Anciens Textes Français, 1935.

Ainsworth, Peter. "Legendary History: *Historia* and *Fabula.*" In *Historiography of the Middle Ages,* edited by Deborah Mauskopf Deliyannis, 387–416. Leiden: Brill, 2003.

Alfonsi, Sandra Resnick. *Masculine Submission in Troubadour Lyric.* New York: Peter Lang, 1986.

Allen, Michael I. "Universal History 300–1000: Origins and Western Developments." In *Historiography in the Middle Ages,* edited by Deborah Mauskopf Deliyannis, 17–42. Leiden: Brill, 2003.

Almén, Byron. *A Theory of Musical Narrative*. Bloomington: Indiana University Press, 2008.

Althusser, Louis. "Ideology and Ideological State Apparatuses (Notes towards an Investigation)." In *Essays on Ideology*, translated by Ben Brewster and Grahame Lock, 1–59. London: Verso, 1984.

Altieri, Charles. *Subjective Agency: A Theory of First-Person Expressivity and its Social Implications*. Oxford: Blackwell, 1994.

Anderson, Gordon A., ed. *The Las Huelgas Manuscript: Burgos, Monasterio de Las Huelgas*. 2 vols. Corpus Mensurabilis Musicae 79. Neuhausen-Stuttgart: Hänssler-Verlag; American Institute of Musicology, 1982.

Anglade, Joseph, ed. *Las Leys d'Amors: Manuscrit de l'Académie des Jeux Floraux*. 4 vols. Toulouse: Privat, 1919–20.

Anglés, Higinio, ed. *La música de las Cantigas de Santa María del Rey Alfonso El Sabio: Facsímil, Transcripción y Estudio Crítico*. 3 vols. Barcelona: Diputación Provincial de Barcelona, 1943.

Anthology of the Provençal Troubadours. 2 vols. Edited by R. T. Hill and T. G. Bergin. New Haven: Yale University Press, 1973.

Apel, Willi. "Rondeaux, Virelais, and Ballades in French 13th-Century Song." *Journal of the American Musicological Society* 7 (1954): 121–30.

Appel, Carl. *Provenzalische Chrestomathie mit Abriss der Formenlehre und Glossar*. Leipzig: O. R. Reisland, 1920.

———. "Vom Descort." *Zeitschrift für Romanische Philologie* 11 (1887): 212–30.

Arbois de Jubainville, M. H. d' *Histoire des ducs et des comtes de Champagne, Tome IV (1181–1285) première partie*. Paris: Aug. Durand, 1865.

Arlt, Wulf. "Aspekte der Chronologie und des Stilwandels im französischen Lied des 14. Jahrhunderts." In *Aktuelle Fragen der musikbezogenen Mittelalterforschung: Texte zu einem Basler Kolloquium des Jahres 1975*, 193–280. Winterthur: Amadeus, 1982.

———. "Jehannot de Lescurel and the Function of Musical Language in the *Roman de Fauvel* as Presented in BN fr. 146." In *FS*, 25–52.

———. "Machaut, Guillaume de." In *Grove Music Online. Oxford Music Online*, http://www.oxfordmusiconline.com/subscriber/article/grove/music/51865.

ARNAUT DANIEL. *The Poetry of Arnaut Daniel*. Edited by James J. Wilhelm. New York: Garland, 1981.

Atchison, Mary. "*Bien me sui aperceuz:* Monophonic Chanson and Motetus." *Plainsong and Medieval Music* 4, no. 1 (1995): 1–12.

———. *The Chansonnier of Oxford Bodleian MS Douce 308: Essays and Complete Edition of Texts*. Burlington, VT: Ashgate, 2005.

Aubrey, Elizabeth. "The Dialectic between Occitania and France in the Thirteenth Century." *Early Music History* 16 (1997): 1–53.

———. "Genre as a Determinant of Melody, in the Songs of the Troubadours and the Trouvères." In *ML*, 273–96.

———. "Issues in the Musical Analysis of Troubadour *Descorts* and *Lays*." In *The Cultural Milieu of the Troubadours and Trouvères*, edited by Nancy van Deusen, 67–98. Ottawa, Ont.: The Institute of Mediaeval Music, 1994.

———. *The Music of the Troubadours*. Bloomington: Indiana University Press, 1996.

———. "References to Music in Old Occitan Literature." *Acta Musicologica* 61, no. 2 (1989): 110–49.

———. "Sources, MS, §III: Secular monophony, 4: French." In *Grove Music Online. Oxford Music Online*, http://www.oxfordmusiconline.com/subscriber/article/grove/music/50158pg3.

Augustine. *The City of God*. Translated by Marcus Dods. New York: The Modern Library, 1993.

Avril, François. "Les Manuscrits enluminés de Guillaume de Machaut: Essai de chronologie." In *Guillaume de Machaut: Poète et compositeur*. Actes et colloques, no. 23, 117–33. Paris: Éditions Klincksieck, 1982.

Bakhtin, Mikhail. *Problems of Dostoevsky's Poetics*. Translated by Caryl Emerson. Minneapolis: University of Minnesota Press, 1985.

Baldwin, John W. *The Government of Philip Augustus: Foundations of French Royal Power in the Middle Ages*. Berkeley: University of California Press, 1986.

Baltzer, Rebecca A. "Lambertus, Magister." In *Grove Music Online. Oxford Music Online*, http://www.oxfordmusiconline.com/subscriber/article/grove/music/15893.

Baron, Hans. "Towards a More Positive Evaluation of the Fifteenth-Century Renaissance." *Journal of the History of Ideas* 4, no. 1 (1943): 21–49.

Barone, Anthony. "Richard Wagner's 'Parsifal' and the Theory of Late Style." *Cambridge Opera Journal* 7, no. 1 (1995): 37–54.

Barr, Cyrilla. *The Monophonic Lauda and the Lay Religious Confraternities of Tuscany and Umbria in the Late Middle Ages*. Kalamazoo: Medieval Institute Publications, 1988.

Barth-Wehrenalp, Renate. *Studien zu Adan de le Hale*. Tutzing: Schneider, 1982.

Baum, Richard. "Le Descort ou l'anti-chanson." In *Mélanges de philologie romane dédiés à la mémoire de Jean Boutiere*, edited by Irénée Cluzel and François Pirot, 1:75–98. 2 vols. Liège: Éditions Soledi, 1971.

———. "Les Troubadours et les lais." *Zeitschrift für romanische Philologie* 85 (1969): 1–44.

Baumgartner, Emmanuèle. "Présentation des chansons de Thibaut de Champagne dans les manuscrits de Paris." In *Thibaut de Champagne: Prince et poète au XIIIᵉ siècle*, edited by Yvonne Bellenger and Danielle Quéruel, 35–44. Lyon: La Manufacture, 1987.

Baxandall, Michael. *Giotto and the Orators: Humanist Observers of Painting in Italy and the Discovery of the Pictorial Composition, 1350–1450*. Oxford: Clarendon Press, 1971.

Bec, Pierre. *La Joute poétique: De la tenson médiévale aux débats chantés traditionnels*. Paris: Société d'Édition Les Belles Lettres, 2000.

———. *La Lyrique française au moyen âge (XIIᵉ-XIIIᵉ siècle): Contribution à une typologie des genres poétiques médiévaux*. 2 vols. Paris: A. and J. Picard, 1977.

Beck, Jean, and Louise Beck. *Le manuscrit du roi*. See the entry for trouv. *M* in facsimile list.

Behr, Shulamith. *Expressionism*. London: Tate Gallery Publishing, 1999.

Beiche, Michael. "Motet/motetus/mottetto/Motette." In *Handwörterbuch der musikalischen Terminologie*, edited by Hans Heinrich Eggebrecht. Mainz: F. Steiner, 2004.

Bent, Margaret, and Andrew Wathey. Introduction to *FS*, 1–24.

Benton, John F. "The Court of Champagne as a Literary Center." *Speculum* 36, no. 4 (1961): 551–91.

Berger, Anna Maria Busse. *Medieval Music and the Art of Memory*. Berkeley: University of California Press, 2005.

Berger, Karol. "*Diegesis* and *Mimesis*: The Poetic Modes and the Matter of Artistic Presentation." *Journal of Musicology* 12, no. 4 (1994): 407–33.

Berger, Roger. *Littérature et société arrageoises au XIIIᵉ siècle: Les chansons et dits artésiens.* Mémoires de la Commission Départementale des Monuments Historiques du Pas-de-Calais [CdMhPC], no. 21. Arras: Commission départementale des monuments historiques du Pas-de-Calais, 1981.

Berman, Art. *From the New Criticism to Deconstruction: The Reception of Structuralism and Post-Structuralism.* Urbana and Chicago: University of Illinois Press, 1988.

BERNART DE VENTADORN. *Bernart von Ventadorn: Seine Lieder.* Edited by Carl Appel. Halle: Max Niemeyer, 1915.

———. *Bernard de Ventadour, troubadour du XIIᵉ siècle: Chansons d'amour.* Edited by Moshé Lazar. Paris: Klincksieck, 1966.

BERTRAN DE BORN. *The Poems of the Troubadour Bertran de Born.* Edited by William D. Paden, Tilde Sankovitch, and Patricia H. Stäblein. Berkeley: University of California Press, 1986.

Billy, Dominique. "Le Descort occitan: Réexamen critique du corpus." *Revue des langues romanes* 87 (1983): 1–28.

———. "*Lai* et *descort*: La théorie des genres comme volonté et comme représentation." *Actes du premier congrès international de l'Association Internationale d'Études Occitanes,* edited by P. T. Ricketts, 95–117. London: The Association, 1987.

Bischoff, Bernhard. *Latin Paleography: Antiquity and the Middle Ages.* Translated by Dáibhí Ó Cróinín and David Ganz. Cambridge: Cambridge University Press, 1993.

Black, Nancy. "The Politics of Romance in Jean Maillart's *Roman du comte d'Anjou.*" *French Studies* 51, no. 2 (1997): 130–37.

Black, Robert. "Ancients and Moderns in the Renaissance: Rhetoric and History in Accolti's Dialogue on the Preeminence of Men of his own Time." *Journal of the History of Ideas* 43, no. 1 (1982): 3–32.

Bloch, R. Howard. *Etymologies and Genealogies: A Literary Anthropology of the French Middle Ages.* Chicago: University of Chicago Press, 1983.

———. *Medieval Misogyny and the Invention of Western Romantic Love* (Chicago: University of Chicago Press, 1991).

———. "Miex vaut jamais que tard: Romance, Philology, and Old French Letters." *Representations* 36 (1991): 64–86.

Bloom, Harold. *Anxiety of Influence: A Theory of Poetry.* 2nd ed. New York: Oxford University Press, 1997.

Boase, Roger. *The Origin and Meaning of Courtly Love: A Critical Study of European Scholarship.* Manchester: Manchester University Press, 1977.

Bond, Gerald A. *The Loving Subject: Desire, Eloquence, and Power in Romanesque France.* Philadelphia: University of Pennsylvania Press, 1995.

———. "Origins." In *HT,* 237–54.

Boogaart, Jacques. "Encompassing Past and Present: Quotations and their Function in Machaut's Motets." *Early Music History* 20 (2001): 1–86.

Boswell, John. *Christianity, Social Tolerance, and Homosexuality: Gay People in Western Europe from the Beginning of the Christian Era to the Fourteenth Century.* Chicago: University of Chicago Press, 1980.

Bouwsma, William J. *The Waning of the Renaissance, 1550–1640.* New Haven: Yale University Press, 2000.

Bowden, Darsie. "The Rise of a Metaphor: 'Voice' in Composition Pedagogy." *Rhetoric Review* 14, no. 1 (1995): 173–88.

Bowers, Roger. "Guillaume de Machaut and His Canonry of Reims, 1338–1377." *Early Music History* 23 (2004): 1–48.

Breisach, Ernst. *Historiography: Ancient, Medieval, and Modern.* Chicago: University of Chicago Press, 1983.

Brothers, Thomas. *Chromatic Beauty in the Late Medieval Chanson: An Interpretation of Manuscript Accidentals.* Cambridge: Cambridge University Press, 1997.

Brownlee, Kevin. "Authorial Self-Representation in *Fauvel.*" In *FS*, 73–103.

———. *Poetic Identity in Guillaume de Machaut.* Madison: University of Wisconsin Press, 1984.

———. "The Poetic Oeuvre of Guillaume de Machaut: The Identity of Discourse and the Discourse of Identity." In *Machaut's World: Science and Art in the Fourteenth Century*, edited by Madeleine Pelner Cosman and Bruce Chandler, 219–33. New York: New York Academy of Sciences, 1978.

Burgwinkle, William. "The *Chansonniers* as Books." In *TI*, 246–62.

———. *Razos and Troubadour Songs.* New York: Garland, 1990.

Butler, Judith. *The Psychic Life of Power: Theories in Subjection.* Stanford: Stanford University Press, 1997.

Butterfield, Ardis. "*Enté*: A Survey and Reassessment of the Term in Thirteenth- and Fourteenth-Century Music and Poetry." *Early Music History* 22 (2003): 67–101.

———. *Poetry and Music in Medieval France from Jean Renart to Guillaume de Machaut.* Cambridge: Cambridge University Press, 2002.

———. "Refrain and Transformation of Genre." In *FS*, 105–59.

Bynum, Caroline Walker. *Jesus as Mother: Studies in the Spirituality of the High Middle Ages.* Berkeley: University of California Press, 1982.

Cabré, Miriam. "Italian and Catalan Troubadours." In *TI*, 127–40.

Cadier, Léon. *Essai sur l'administration du royaume de Sicile sous Charles Ier et Charles II d'Anjou.* Paris: Ernest Thorin, 1891.

Cahoon, Leslie. "The Anxieties of Influence: Ovid's Reception by the Early Troubadours." *Medievalia* 13 (1987/1989): 119–55.

Calin, William. "Medieval Intertextuality: Lyrical Inserts and Narrative in Guillaume de Machaut." *French Review* 62, no. 1 (1988): 1–10.

———. *A Poet at the Fountain: Essays on the Narrative Verse of Guillaume de Machaut.* Lexington: University Press of Kentucky, 1974.

Camille, Michael. "Hybridity, Monstrosity, and Bestiality in the *Roman de Fauvel.*" In *FS*, 161–74.

———. *The Medieval Art of Love: Objects and Subjects of Desire.* New York: Harry N. Abrams, 1998.

Cappelli, Adriano. *Dizionario di abbreviature latine ed italiane.* Milan: Ulrico Hoepli Editore, 1987.

Carruthers, Mary. *The Book of Memory: A Study of Memory in Medieval Culture.* Cambridge: Cambridge University Press, 1990.

Cerquiglini, Jacqueline. *"Un Engin si soutil": Guillaume de Machaut et l'écriture au XIVe siècle.* Paris: Librairie Honoré Champion, 1985.

Cézanne and Beyond. Organized by Joseph J. Rishel and Katherine Sachs. Philadelphia: Philadelphia Museum of Art, 2009.

Chambers, Frank. "Imitation of Form in Provençal Lyric." *Romance Philology* 6, nos. 2 and 3 (1952/3): 104–20.

————. *An Introduction to Old Provençal Versification*. Philadelphia: American Philosophical Society, 1985.

————. *Proper Names in the Lyrics of the Troubadours*. Chapel Hill: University of North Carolina Press, 1971.

Chichmaref, Vladimir F. Introduction to *Guillaume de Machaut: Poésies lyriques. Édition complète en deux parties*. 2 vols. 1: vii–cxvi. Paris: Champion, 1909.

Cholakian, Rouben C. *The Troubadour Lyric: A Psychocritical Reading*. Manchester: Manchester University Press, 1990.

Clark, Suzannah. "'S'en dirai chançonete': Hearing Text and Music in a Medieval Motet." *Plainsong and Medieval Music* 16, no. 1 (2007): 31–59.

Cnyrim, Eugen. *Sprichwörter, sprichwörtliche Redensarten und Sentenzen bei den provenzalischen Lyrikern. Ausgaben und Abhandlungen aus dem Gebiete der romanischen Philologie* 71. Marburg: N. G. Elwert, 1888.

Cone, Edward T. *The Composer's Voice*. Berkeley: University of California Press, 1974.

Coolidge, Sharon Ann. "The Grafted Tree in Literature: A Study in Medieval Iconography and Theology." Ph.D. diss., Duke University, 1977.

————. "The Grafted Tree in Sir Orfeo: A Study in the Iconography of Redemption." *Ball State University Forum* 23 (1982): 62–68.

Cotter, Holland. "My Hero, the Outlaw of Amherst." *New York Times*: Arts and Leisure, (Sunday, May 16, 2010): 1, 28.

Courtenay, William J. "*Antiqui* and *Moderni* in Late Medieval Thought." *Journal of the History of Ideas* 84, no. 1 (1987): 3–10.

Crawford, John C., and Dorothy L. Crawford. *Expressionism in Twentieth-Century Music*. Bloomington: Indiana University Press, 1993.

Crocker, Richard L. *An Introduction to Gregorian Chant*. New Haven: Yale University Press, 2000.

Cropp, Glynnis M. *Le Vocabulaire courtois des troubadours de l'époque classique*. Geneva: Droz, 1975.

Culler, Jonathan. *Structuralist Poetics: Structuralism, Linguistics, and the Study of Literature*. New York: Routledge, 1975; reprint, 2002.

Cumming, Julie E. "Concord out of Discord: Occasional Motets of the Early Quattrocento." Ph.D. diss., University of California, Berkeley, 1987.

Curtius, Ernst Robert. *European Literature and the Latin Middle Ages*. Translated by Willard R. Trask. Princeton: Princeton University Press, 1953.

Cyrus, Cynthia J. "Musical Distinctions between Descorts and Lais: Non-Strophic Genres in the Troubadour and Trouvère Repertory." *Ars Musica Denver* 4 (Fall 1991): 3–19.

Dagenais, John. "Genre and Demonstrative Rhetoric: Praise and Blame in the *Razos de trobar* and the *Doctrina de compondre dictats*." In *ML*, 242–54.

Dalglish, William E. "The Hocket in Medieval Polyphony." *Musical Quarterly* 55, no. 3 (1969): 344–63.

————. "The Origin of the Hocket." *Journal of the American Musicological Society* 31, no. 1 (1978): 3–20.

Dane, Joseph A. "Parody and Satire in the Literature of Thirteenth-Century Arras, Part I." *Studies in Philology* 81, no. 1 (1984): 1–27.

———. "Parody and Satire in the Literature of Thirteenth-Century Arras, Part II." *Studies in Philology* 81, no. 2 (1984): 119–44.

DANTE. *De vulgari eloquentia*. Edited and translated by Steven Botterill. Cambridge: Cambridge University Press, 1996.

Davidson, Donald. *Subjective, Intersubjective, Objective*. Oxford: Clarendon Press, 2001.

Davis, J. Cary. "Acordar(se): One Verb, or Two?" *Hispania* 54, no. 1 (1971): 120–24.

Deliyannis, Deborah Mauskopf. Introduction to *Historiography in the Middle Ages*, edited by Deborah Mauskopf Deliyannis, 1–13. Leiden: Brill, 2003.

Dembowski, Peter F. "Vocabulary of Old French Courtly Lyrics: Difficulties and Hidden Difficulties." *Critical Inquiry* 2, no. 4 (1976): 766–71.

Denomy, A. J. "Courtly Love and Courtliness." *Speculum* 28, no. 1 (1953): 44–63.

———. "*Fin'amors*: The Pure Love of the Troubadours: Its Amorality and Possible Source." *Medieval Studies* 7 (1945): 139–207.

Derrida, Jacques. *Of Grammatology*. Translated by Gayatri Chakravorty Spivak. Baltimore: Johns Hopkins Press, 1997.

Devaux, Jean. "Le *Voir Dit* de Guillaume de Machaut dans la tradition du *Roman de la Rose*." In *Guillaume de Machaut*, Le Livre du Voir Dit, edited by Danielle Quéruel, 22–34. Paris: Ellipses, 2001.

Dictionnaire de l'ancienne langue française et tous ses dialectes du IXe au XVe Siècle. Edited by Frédéric Godefroy. Paris: F. Vieweg, 1881–1902.

Dictionnaire de l'occitan médiéval. Tübingen: Max Niemeyer, 1996.

Diez, Friedrich. *Leben und Werke der Troubadours*. Leipzig: J. A. Barths, 1882.

Dillon, Emma. *Medieval Music-Making and the "Roman de Fauvel"*. Cambridge: Cambridge University Press, 2002.

Dinguirard, J. -C. "*So ditz la gens anciana*." *Via Domitia* 28, no. 1 (1982): 109–20.

Dinshaw, Carolyn. *Getting Medieval: Sexualities and Communities, Pre- and Postmodern*. Durham, NC: Duke University Press, 1999.

Donahue, Neil H. Introduction to *A Companion to the Literature of German Expressionism*, edited by Neil H. Donahue, 1–35. Rochester: Camden House, 2005.

Dosse, François. *The History of Structuralism*, 1: *The Rising Sign*, 1945–1966. Translated by Deborah Glassman. Minneapolis: University of Minnesota Press, 1997.

Doss-Quinby, Eglal. *Les Refrains chez les trouvères du XIIe siècle au début du XIVe*. New York: Peter Lang, 1984.

Dragonetti, Roger. *La Technique poétique des trouvères dans la chanson courtoise*. Bruges: De Tempel, 1960.

Dronke, Peter. *Medieval Latin and the Rise of European Love-Lyric*. 2 vols. Oxford: Clarendon Press, 1964.

Du Cange, Charles du Fresne, sieur. *Glossarium Mediae et Infimae Latinitatis*. Edited by G. A. L. Henschel. Niort: L. Favre, 1883.

Dunbabin, Jean. *Charles I of Anjou: Power, Kingship and State-Making in Thirteenth-Century Europe*. London: Longman, 1998.

Durand, Dana B. "Tradition and Innovation in Fifteenth Century Italy: '*Il Primato dell'Italia*' in the Field of Science." *Journal of the History of Ideas* 4, no. 1 (1943): 1–20.

Duys, Kathryn A. "Minstrel's Mantel and Monk's Hood: The Authorial Persona of Gautier de Coinci in his Poetry and Illuminations." In *Gautier de Coinci: Miracles, Music, and Manuscripts*, edited by Kathy M. Krause and Alison Stones, 37–63. Turnhout : Brepols, 2006.

Dyggve, Holger Petersen. *Onomastique des trouvères*. 1934. Reprint, New York: Burt Franklin, 1973.

———. "Personages historiques figurant dans la poésie lyrique française des XIIᵉ et XIIIᵉ siècles: Charles, comte d'Anjou." *Neuphilologische Mitteilungen* 50 (1949): 144–74.

Earp, Lawrence. "Genre in the Fourteenth-Century French Chanson: The Virelai and the Dance Song." *Musica Disciplina* 45 (1991): 123–41.

———. *Guillaume de Machaut: A Guide to Research*. New York: Garland, 1995.

———. "Lyrics for Reading and Lyrics for Singing in Late Medieval France: The Development of the Dance Lyric from Adam de la Halle to Guillaume de Machaut." In *The Union of Words and Music in Medieval Poetry*, edited by Rebecca A. Baltzer, Thomas Cable, and James I. Wimsatt, 101–31. Austin: University of Texas Press, 1991.

———. "Machaut's Role in the Production of Manuscripts of his Works." *Journal of the American Musicological Society* 42, no. 3 (1989): 471.

———. "Scribal Practice, Manuscript Production and the Transmission of Music in Late Medieval France: The Manuscripts of Guillaume de Machaut." Ph.D. diss., Princeton, 1983.

Edwards, Robert R. *Ratio and Invention: A Study of Medieval Lyric and Narrative*. Nashville, TN: Vanderbilt University Press, 1989.

Egan, Margarita, trans. *The Vidas of the Troubadours*. New York: Garland, 1984.

Eliot, T. S. *The Three Voices of Poetry*. London: Cambridge University Press, 1953.

Espiner-Scott, Janet. *Documents concernant la vie et les oeuvres de Claude Fauchet*. Paris: Librairie E. Droz, 1938.

Evans, Beverly J. "Women *Trouvères*: Just the Same Old Refrains?" *Neophilologus* 90 (2006): 1–11.

Everist, Mark. *French Motets in the Thirteenth Century: Music, Poetry and Genre*. Cambridge: Cambridge University Press, 1994.

———. *Polyphonic Music in Thirteenth-Century France*. New York: Garland, 1989.

———. "The Refrain Cento: Myth or Motet?" *Journal of the Royal Musical Association* 114 (1989): 164–88.

———. "The Rondeau Motet: Paris and Artois in the Thirteenth Century." *Music & Letters* 69 (1988): 1–22.

———. "'Souspirant en terre estrainge': The Polyphonoic Rondeau from Adam de la Halle to Guillaume de Machaut." *Early Music History* 26 (2007): 1–26.

Falck, Robert. "Gautier de Coincy." In *Grove Music Online. Oxford Music Online*, http://www.oxfordmusiconline.com/subscriber/article/grove/music/10762.

Fallows, David. "Guillaume de Machaut and the *Lai*: A New Source." *Early Music* 5, no. 4 (1977): 477–83.

———, et al. "Sources, MS, §III: Secular Monophony." In *Grove Music Online. Oxford Music Online*, http://www.oxfordmusiconline.com/subscriber/article/grove/music/50158pg3.

Fast, Susan. "Bakhtin and the Discourse of Late Medieval Music Theory." *Plainsong and Medieval Music* 5, no. 2 (1996): 175–91.

Fernández de la Cuesta, Ismael, and Robert Lafont. *Las cançons dels trobadors*. Toulouse: Institut d'estudis occitans, 1979.

Ferrante, Joan M. "*Farai un vers de dreyt nien*: The Craft of the Early Troubadours." In *Vernacular Poetics in the Middle Ages*, edited by Lois Ebin, 93–128. Kalamazoo, MI: Medieval Institute Publications, 1984.

Fleischman, Suzanne. "The Non-lyric Texts." In *HT*, 167–84.

FOLQUET DE MARSELHA. *Le Troubadour Folquet de Marseille, édition critique*. Edited by Stanisław Stroński. Cracow: Académie des Sciences, 1910.

Foucault, Michel. *The Order of Things: An Archaeology of the Human Sciences*. Translated by Alan Sheridan. New York: Vintage Press, 1973.

———. "Sexuality and Solitude." In *Ethics: Subjectivity and Truth*. Edited by Paul Rabinow, 175–8. New York: The New Press, 1997.

Frappier, Jean. *Amour courtois et Table Ronde* (Geneva: Droz, 1973).

Fredriksen, Paula. "Apocalypse and Redemption in Early Christianity: From John of Patmos to Augustine of Hippo." *Vigiliae Christianae* 45, no. 2 (1991): 151–83.

Freeman, Michelle A. *The Poetics of* Translatio Studii *and* Conjointure: *Chrétien de Troyes's Cligés*. Lexington, KY: French Forum Publishers, 1979.

Fuller, Sarah. "Line, 'Contrapunctus,' and Structure in a Machaut Song." *Music Analysis* 6, no. 1 (1987): 37–58.

———. "Machaut and the Definition of Musical Space." *Sonus* 12 (1991): 1–15.

Galassi, Susan Grace. *Picasso's Variations of the Masters*. New York: Harry N. Abrams, 1996.

Gallo, F. Alberto. *Music in the Castle: Troubadours, Books, and Orators in Italian Courts of the Thirteenth, Fourteenth, and Fifteenth Centuries*. Translated by Anna Herklotz. Chicago: University of Chicago Press, 1995.

Gatien-Arnoult, A. F, ed. *Monumens de la littérature romane: Las Flors del Gay Saber estier dichas Las Leys d'Amors*. 3 vols. Toulouse: J.-B. Paya, 1841–43.

Gaunt, Simon. "Discourse Desired: Desire, Subjectivity, and *Mouvance* in *Can vei la lauzeta mover*." In *Desiring Discourse: The Literature of Love, Ovid through Chaucer*. Edited by Cynthia Gravlee and James J. Paxson, 89–110. London: Associated University Press, 1998.

———. *Love and Death in Medieval French and Occitan Courtly Literature: Martyrs to Love*. Oxford: Oxford University Press, 2006.

———. "Orality and Writing: The Text of the Troubadour Poem." In *TI*, 228–45.

———. "Sexual Difference and the Metaphor of Language in a Troubadour Poem." *Modern Language Review* 83, no. 2 (1988): 297–313.

———. *Troubadours and Irony*. Cambridge: Cambridge University Press, 1989.

Gaunt, Simon, and Sarah Kay. *The Cambridge Companion to Medieval French Literature*. Cambridge: Cambridge University Press, 2008.

———. Introduction to *TI*, 1–7.

GAUTIER DE DARGIES. *Chansons et Descorts de Gautier de Dargies*. Edited by Gédéon Huet. Paris: Librairie de Firmin-Didot, 1912.

Gehl, Paul F. "*Competens silentium*: Varieties of Monastic Silence in the Medieval West." *Viator* 18 (1987): 125–60.

Gellrich, Jesse M. *The Idea of the Book in the Middle Ages: Language Theory, Mythology, and Fiction*. Ithaca and London: Cornell University Press, 1985.

Gennrich, Friedrich. *Grundriss einer Formenlehre des mittelalterlichen Liedes als Grundlage einer musikalischen Formenlehre des Liedes*. Halle: Max Niemeyer, 1932.

———. *Die Kontrafaktur im Liedschaffen des Mittelalters*. Langen bei Frankfurt: Summa Musicae Medii Aevi, 1965.

———. *Rondeaux, Virelais und Balladen aus dem Ende des XII., dem XIII. und dem ersten Drittel des XIV. Jahrhunderts mit den überlieferten Melodien, Bande I: Texte*. Gesellschaft für Romanische Literatur 43. Dresden: Gesellschaft für Romanische Literatur, 1921.

———. *Rondeaux, Virelais und Balladen aus dem Ende des XII., dem XIII. und dem ersten Drittel des XIV. Jahrhunderts mit den überlieferten Melodien, Bande II: Materialien, Literaturnachweise, Refrainverzeichnis*. Gesellschaft für Romanische Literatur 47. Göttingen: Gesellschaft für Romanische Literatur, 1927.

———. "Trouvèrelieder und Motettenrepertoire." *Zeitschrift für Musikwissenschaft* 9 (1926–27): 8–39, 65–83.

Gieber, Robert L. "Poetic Elements of Rhythm in the Ballades, Rondeaux and Virelais of Guillaume de Machaut." *Romantic Review* 73, no. 1 (1982): 1–12.

Giraut de Bornelh. *The Cansos and Sirventes of the Troubadour Giraut de Borneil: A Critical Edition*. Edited by Ruth Verity Sharman. Cambridge: Cambridge University Press, 1989.

Goddard, R. N. B. "Marcabru, '*li proverbe au vilain*' and the Tradition of Rustic Proverbs." *Neuphilologische Mitteilungen* 88 (1987): 55–70.

Goetz, Hans-Werner. "The Concept of Time in the Historiography of the Eleventh and Twelfth Centuries." In *Medieval Concepts of the Past: Ritual, Memory, Historiography*, edited by Gerd Althoff, Johannes Fried, and Patrick J. Geary, 139–65. Cambridge: Cambridge University Press, 2002.

Goldin, Frederick. Review of *Die Dialektik des Trobar: Untersuchungen zur Struktur und Entwicklung des occitanischen und französischen Minnesangs des 12. Jahrhunderts* by Jörn Gruber. *Speculum* 16, no. 2 (1986): 422–24.

Gordon, Donald E. *Expressionism: Art and Idea*. New Haven: Yale University Press, 1987.

Gordon, George. "*Medium Aevum* and the Middle Age." *Society for Pure English*, Tract 19 (1925): 3–26.

Gössmann, Elisabeth. *Antiqui und Moderni im Mittelalter: Eine geschichtliche Standortbestimmung*. Munich: Verlag Ferdinand Schöning, 1974.

Grande Quejigio, Francisco Javier, and Bernardo Santano Moreno. "The Love Debate Tradition in the Reception of Gower's *Confessio Amantis* in the Iberian Peninsula." In *Medieval Forms of Argument: Disputation and Debate*, edited by Georgiana Donavin, Richard J. Utz, and Carol Poster, 103–26. Eugene, OR: WIPF and Stock, 2002.

Gross, Charlotte. "The Cosmology of Rhetoric in the Early Troubadour Lyric." *Rhetorica* 9, no. 1 (1991): 39–53.

Gruber, Jörn. *Die Dialektik des Trobar: Untersuchungen zur Struktur und Entwicklung des occitanischen und französischen Minnesangs des 12. Jahrhunderts*. Tübingen: Max Niemeyer, 1983.

Gruy, Henry. *Histoire d'Arras*. Arras: Dessant, 1967.

GUILHEM IX. *Guglielmo IX d'Aquitania: Poesie*. Edited by Nicolò Pasero. Modena: STEM Mucchi, 1973.

GUILLAUME DE LORRIS AND JEAN DE MEUN. *Le Roman de la rose*. Paris: Librairie générale française, 1992.

GUILLAUME DE MACHAUT. *Le Jugement du roy de Behaigne and Remede de Fortune*. Edited by J. I. Wimsatt and W. W. Kibler. Music edited by R. A. Baltzer. Athens, GA: University of Georgia Press, 1988.

————— .*Le Livre dou Voir Dit (The Book of the True Poem)*. Edited by Daniel Leech-Wilkinson. Translated by R. Barton Palmer. New York: Garland, 1998.

————— . *Oeuvres de Guillaume de Machaut*. 3 vols. Edited by Ernest Hoepffner. Paris: Librairie de Firmin-Didot et Cᵢᵉ, 1908–21.

————— . *The Works of Guillaume de Machaut*. See Schrade, Leo.

Günther, Ursula. "Chronologie und Stil der Kompositionen Guillaume de Machauts." *Acta Musicologica* 35, nos. 2–3 (1963): 96–114.

————— . "Contribution de la musicologie à la biographie et à la chronologie de Guillaume de Machaut." In *Guillaume de Machaut: Poète et compositeur*. Actes et colloques, no. 23, 95–115. Paris: Éditions Klincksieck, 1982.

Haahr, Joan G. "Justifying Love: The Classical *Recusatio* in Medieval Love Literature." In *Desiring Discourse: The Literature of Love, Ovid through Chaucer*, edited by James J. Paxson and Cynthia A. Gravlee, 39–61. London: Associated University Press, 1998.

Haidu, Peter. *The Subject, Medieval/Modern: Text and Governance in the Middle Ages*. Stanford: Stanford University Press, 2004.

Haines, John. *Eight Centuries of Troubadours and Trouvères: The Changing Identity of Medieval Music*. Cambridge: Cambridge University Press, 2004.

————— . *Medieval Song in Romance Languages*. Cambridge: Cambridge University Press, 2010.

————— . "The Musicography of the '*Manuscrit du roi*' (Thirteenth-Century)." Ph.D. diss., University of Toronto, 1998.

————— . *Satire in the Songs of* Renart le nouvel. Geneva: Droz, 2010.

————— . "The Transformation of the *Manuscrit du roi*." *Musica Disciplina* 52 (1998–2002): 5–43.

————— . "Vers une distinction *leu/clus* dans l'art muscio-poétique des troubadours." *Neophilologus* 81 (1997): 341–47.

Hanning, R. W. "'Ut enim Faber…sic Creator': Divine Creation as Context for Human Creativity in the Twelfth Century." In *Words, Picture, and Spectacle*, edited by Clifford Davidson, 95–149. Kalamazoo, MI: Medieval Institute Publications, 1984.

Harvey, John. *Medieval Gardens*. London: T. T. Batsford Ltd., 1981.

Harvey, L. P., et al. "Zajal." In *Grove Music Online. Oxford Music Online*, http://www.oxfordmusiconline.com/subscriber/article/grove/music/30794.

Harvey, Ruth. "Courtly Culture in Medieval Occitania." In *TI*, 8–27.

————— . "Rhymes and 'Rusty words' in Marcabru's Songs." *French Studies* 56, no. 1 (2002): 1–14.

————— . *The Troubadour Marcabru and Love*. London: Westfield College Publications, 1989.

Hayburn, Robert F. *Papal Legislation on Sacred Music: 95 A.D. to 1977 A.D*. Collegeville, MN: The Liturgical Press, 1979.

Hegel, G. W. F. *Elements of the Philosophy of Right*. Edited by Allen W. Wood and translated by H. B. Nisbet. Cambridge: Cambridge University Press, 1991.

Hexter, Ralph. *Ovid and Medieval Schooling: Studies on Medieval School Commentaries on Ovid's* Ars Amatoria, Epistolae ex Ponto, *and* Epistulae Heroidum. Munich: Arbeo-Gesellschaft, 1986.

Hoby, Otto. "Die Lieder des Trobadors Guiraut d'Espanha." Diss., Freiburg, 1915.

Hofmann, Klaus. "Zur Enstehungs- und Frühgeschichte des Terminus Motette." *Acta Musicologica* 42 (1970): 138–50.

Holmes, Olivia. *Assembling the Lyric Self: Authorship from Troubadour Song to Italian Poetry Book.* Minneapolis: University of Minnesota Press, 2000.

Hoppin, Richard. *Anthology of Medieval Music.* New York: Norton, 1978.

———. *Medieval Music.* New York: Norton, 1978.

Hughes, Andrew. "Franco of Cologne." In *Grove Music Online. Oxford Music Online,* http://www.oxfordmusiconline.com/subscriber/article/grove/music/10138.

Huizinga, Johan. *Autumn of the Middle Ages.* Translated by Rodney J. Payton and Ulrich Mammitzsch. Chicago: University of Chicago Press, 1996.

Hult, David F. "Gaston Paris and the Invention of Courtly Love." In *Medievalism and the Modernist Temper,* edited by R. Howard Bloch and Stephen G. Nichols, 192–224. Baltimore: Johns Hopkins Press, 1996.

Hunt, Tony. *Miraculous Rhymes: The Writing of Gautier de Coinci.* Rochester, NY: D. S. Brewer, 2007.

Huot, Sylvia. *From Song to Book: The Poetics of Writing in Old French Lyric and Lyrical Narrative Poetry.* Ithaca: Cornell University Press, 1987.

———. "Reliving the *Roman de la rose*: Allegory and Irony in Machaut's *Voir Dit.*" In *Chaucer's French Contemporaries: The Poetry/Poetics of Self and Tradition,* edited by R. Barton Palmer, 47–69. New York: AMS Press, 1999.

———. "Transformations of Lyric Voice in the Songs, Motets, and Plays of Adam de la Halle." *Romance Review* 78, no. 2 (1987): 148–64.

———. "Visualization and Memory: The Illustration of Troubadour Lyric in a Thirteenth-Century Manuscript," *Gesta* 31, no. 1 (1992): 3–14.

Hutcheon, Linda. *A Theory of Parody: The Teachings of Twentieth-Century Art Forms.* New York and London: Methuen, Inc., 1985.

Jacobus Leodiensis [Jacques de Liège]. *Speculum Musicae, Liber Septimus (VII).* Edited by Roger Bragard. N.p.: American Institute of Musicology, 1973.

Jacquemart Gielée, *Renart le nouvel par Jacquemart Gielee, publié d'aprè le manuscript La Vallière (B.N. fr. 25566).* Edited by Henri Roussel. Paris: A. & J. Picard, 1961.

Jaeger, C. Stephen. *Ennobling Love: In Search of a Lost Sensibility.* Philadelphia: University of Pennsylvania Press, 1999.

———. *The Origins of Courtliness: Civilizing Trends and the Formation of Courtly Ideals, 939–1210.* Philadelphia: University of Pennsylvania Press, 1985.

Jager, Eric. *The Book of the Heart.* Chicago: University of Chicago Press, 2000.

———. "The Book of the Heart: Reading and Writing the Mediaeval Subject." *Speculum* 71, no. 1 (1996): 1–26.

Jameson, Fredric. "On the Sexual Production of Western Subjectivity; or, Saint Augustine as a Social Democrat." In *Gaze and Voice as Love Objects,* edited by Renata Salecl and Slavoj Žižek, 154–57. Durham, NC: Duke University Press, 1996.

———. *Postmodernism or, The Cultural Logic of Late Capitalism.* Durham, NC: Duke University Press, 1991.

Jaouën, Françoise, and Benjamin Semple. "The Body into Text." In *Corps Mystique, Corps Sacré: Textual Transfigurations of the Body from the Middle Ages to the Seventeenth Century,* edited by Françoise Jaouën and Benjamin Semple, *Yale French Studies* 86 (1994): 1–4.

Jeanroy, Alfred, Louis Brandin, and Pierre Aubry. *Lais et descorts français du XIIIᵉ siècle: Texte et musique.* 1901. Reprint, Geneva: Slatkine Reprints, 1975.

JEHAN DE LESCUREL. *The Works of Jehan de Lescurel*. See Wilkins, Nigel.

JOHANNES DE GROCHEIO. *Concerning Music (De Musica)*. Translated by Albert Seay. Colorado Springs: Colorado College Music Press, 1967.

Jussen, Bernhard. *Spiritual Kinship as Social Practice: Godparenthood and Adoption in the Early Middle Ages*. Translated Pamela E. Selwyn. Cranbury, NJ: Associated University Presses, 2000.

Kaehne, Michael. *Studien zur Dichtung Bernarts von Ventadorn*. 2 vols. Munich: Wilhelm Fink Verlag, 1983.

Karp, Theodore. "Borrowed Material in Trouvère Music." *Acta Musicologica* 34, no. 3 (1962): 87–101.

———. "Guiot de Dijon." In *Grove Music Online. Oxford Music Online*, http://www.oxfordmusiconline.com/subscriber/article/grove/music/12002.

———. "A Lost Medieval Chansonnier." *Musical Quarterly* 48 (January 1962): 50–67.

———. "Three Trouvère Chanons in Mensural Notation." In *Gordon Athol Anderson, 1929–1981: In memorium von seinen Studenten, Freunden und Kollegen, Teil II*, 474–94. Henryville, PA: Institute of Mediaeval Music, 1984.

———. "Troubadours, trouvères, §III, 1: Music: Manuscript sources." In *Grove Music Online. Oxford Music Online*. http://www.oxfordmusiconline.com/subscriber/article/grove/music/28468.

———. "The Trouvère MS Tradition." In *The Department of Music Queens College of the City University of New York Twenty-Fifth Anniversary Festschrift (1937–1962)*, edited by Albert Mell, 25–52. Queens College Press, 1964.

Kay, Sarah. "Grafting the Knowledge Community: The Purposes of Verse in the *Breviari d'amor* of Matfre Ermengaud." *Neophilologus* 91 (2007): 361–73.

———. *The Place of Thought: The Complexity of One in Late Medieval French Didactic Poetry*. Philadelphia: University of Pennsylvania Press, 2007.

———. *Subjectivity in Troubadour Poetry*. Cambridge: Cambridge University Press, 1990.

Keller, Hans-Erich. "Italian Troubadours." In *HT*, 295–304.

Kelly, Douglas. *Medieval Imagination: Rhetoric and the Poetry of Courtly Love*. Madison: University of Wisconsin Press, 1978.

Kendrick, Laura. "The *Consistori Del Gay Saber* of Toulouse (1323–circa 1484)." In *The Reach of the Republic of Letters: Literary and Learned Societies in the Late Medieval and Early Modern Europe*, 2 vols., edited by Arjan van Dixhoorn and Susie Speakman Sutch, 1:17–32. Leiden: Brill, 2008.

———. *The Game of Love: Troubadour Wordplay*. Berkeley: University of California Press, 1988.

Kilgour, Raymond Lincoln. *The Decline of Chivalry as Shown in the French Literature of the Late Middle Ages*. 1937. Reprint, Gloucester, MA: Peter Smith, 1966.

Köhler, Erich. "Deliberations on a Theory of the Genre of the Old Provençal Descort." In *Italian Literature, Roots and Branches: Essays in Honor of Thomas Goddard Bergin*, edited by Giose Rimanelli and Kenneth John Atchity, 1–13. New Haven and London: Yale University Press, 1976.

———. "Observations historiques et sociologiques sur la poésie des troubadours." *Cahiers de civilisation médiévale* 7 (1964): 27–51.

———. *Trobadorlyrik und höfischer Roman*. Berlin: Rütten and Loening, 1962.

Kossmann, E. H. Postscript to *Johan Huizinga (1872–1972): Papers Delivered to the Johan Huizinga Conference, Groningen 11–15 December 1972*, edited by W. R. H. Koops, E. H. Kossmann, and Gees van der Plaat, 223–34.The Hague: Marinus Nijhoff, 1973.

Långfors, Arthur. "Mélange de poésie lyrique français VII." *Romania* 63 (1937): 474–93.

———. *Recueil général des jeux-partis français*. 2 vols. Paris: Librairie Ancienne Édouard Champion, 1926.

Latella, Fortunata. *I Sirventesi di Garin d'Apchier e di Torcafol*. Modena: Mucchi Editore, 1994.

Lazar, Moshe. *Amour courtois et fin'amors dans la littérature du XIIe siècle*. Paris: Klincksieck, 1964.

———. *"Fin'amor."* In *HT*, 61–100.

Leach, Elizabeth Eva. *Guillaume de Machaut: Secretary, Poet, Musician*. Ithaca: Cornell University Press, 2011.

Lecesne, Edmond. *Histoire d'Arras depuis les temps les plus reculés jusqu'en 1789*. 2 vols. Arras, 1880; Reprint, Marseille: Laffitte, 1976.

Leclercq, Jean. *Monks and Love in Twelfth-Century France: Psycho-Historical Essays*. Oxford: Clarendon Press, 1979.

Leech-Wilkinson, Daniel. Introduction to *Le Livre dou Voir Dit (The Book of the True Poem)*, translated by R. Barton Palmer, xi–cxi. New York: Garland, 1998.

———. *The Modern Invention of Medieval Music: Scholarship, Ideology, Performance*. Cambridge: Cambridge University Press, 2002.

———. "Not Just a Pretty Tune: Structuring Devices in Four Machaut Virelais." *Sonus* 12, no. 1 (1991): 16–31.

———. "The Well-Formed Virelai." In *Trent'anni di ricerca musicologica: Studi in onore di F. Alberto Gallo*, edited by Patrizia Dalla Vecchia and Donatella Restani, 125–40. Rome: Edizioni Torre D'Orfeo, 1996.

Le Gentil, Pierre. *Le Virelai et le villancico: Le problème des origines arabes*. Paris: Société d'Éditions, 1954.

Léglu, Catherine. *Between Sequence and Sirventes: Aspects of Parody in the Troubadour Lyric*. Oxford: European Humanities Research Centre, 2000.

Le Goff, Jacques. *Intellectuals in the Middle Ages*. Translated by Teresa Lavender Fagan. Cambridge, MA: Blackwell, 1993.

———. "Le Roi dans l'Occident médiéval." In *Kings and Kingship in Medieval Europe*, edited by Anne J. Duggan, 1–40. London: Centre for Late Antique and Medieval Studies, 1993.

———. *Time, Work, and Culture in the Middle Ages*. Translated by Arthur Goldhammer. Chicago: University of Chicago Press, 1980.

Lejeune, Rita. "La Chanson de 'l'amour de loin' de Jaufré Rudel." In *Studi in onore di Angelo Monteverdi*, 2 vols., 1:403–42. Modena: Società Tipografica Editrice Modenese, 1959.

Leppert, Richard. Introduction, Commentary, and Notes to *Essays on Music*, by Theodor W. Adorno. Edited by Richard Leppert and translated by Susan H. Gillespie. Berkeley: University of California Press, 2002.

Lerer, Seth. "Artifice and Artistry in *Sir Orfeo*." *Speculum* 60, no. 1 (1985): 92–109.

Lewent, Kurt. "Old Provençal *Desmentir sos pairis*." *Modern Language Notes* 72, no. 3 (1957): 189–93.

Ley, Graham. *The Theatricality of Greek Tragedy: Playing Space and Chorus*. Chicago: The University of Chicago Press, 2007.

Liddell, Henry George, and Robert Scott. *A Greek-English Lexicon*, revised and expanded by Sir Henry Stuart Jones, with the assistance of Roderick McKenzie. Oxford: Clarendon Press, 1940. http://www.perseus.tufts.edu/hopper/.

Linker, Robert White. *A Bibliography of Old French Lyrics*. University, MI: Romance Monographs, 1979.

Linskill, Joseph. *Les Épîtres de Guiraut Riquier, troubadour du XIIIᵉ siècle*. N.p.: Association Internationale d'Études Occitanes, 1985.

Longnon, Jean. *L'Empire latin de Constantinople et la principauté de Morée*. Paris: Payot, 1949.

――― . "Le Prince de Morée chansonnier." *Romania* 65 (1939): 95–100.

Ludwig, Friedrich. *Repertorium organorum recentioris et motetorum vetustissimi stili*. Band I: *Catalogue raisonné der Quellen*. Abteilung I: *Handschriften in Quadrat-Notation*. Revised by Luther Dittmer. New York: Institute of Mediaeval Music, 1964.

――― . *Repertorium organorum recentioris et motetorum vetustissimi stili*. Band I: *Catalogue raisonné der Quellen*. Abteilung II: *Handschriften in Mensural-Notation*. Reprint, New York: Institute of Mediaeval Music, 1978.

Lug, Robert. "Katharer und Waldenser in Metz: Zur Herkunft der ältesten Sammlung von Trobador-Liedern (1231)." In *Okzitanistik, Altokzitanistik und Provenzalistik: Geschichte und Auftrag einer europäischen Philologie*, edited by Angelica Rieger, 249–74. Frankfurt am Main: Peter Lang, 2000.

Lynch, Joseph H. *Godparents and Kinship in Early Medieval Europe*. Princeton: Princeton University Press, 1986.

McCash, June Hall Martin. "Marie de Champagne and Eleanor of Aquitaine: A Relationship Reexamined." *Speculum* 54, no. 4 (1979): 698–711.

McClary, Susan. *Modal Subjectivities: Self-Fashioning in the Italian Madrigal*. Berkeley: University of California Press, 2004.

McGee, Timothy. *Medieval Instrumental Dances*. Bloomington: Indiana University Press, 1989.

McGinn, Bernard. "The End of the World and the Beginning of Christendom." In *Apocalypse Theory and the Ends of the World*, edited by Malcolm Bull, 58–89. Cambridge, MA: Blackwell Publishers, 1995.

Machabey, Armand. *Guillaume de Machault, 130?–1377: La vie et l'oeuvre musical*. 2 vols. Paris: Richard Masse, 1955.

McKitterick, Rosamond. *Perceptions of the Past in the Early Middle Ages*. Notre Dame, IN: University of Notre Dame Press, 2006.

Mahrt, William Peter. "Male and Female Voice in Two Virelais of Guillaume de Machaut." In *Machaut's Music: New Interpretations*, edited by Elizabeth Eva Leach, 221–30. Woodbridge: Boydell Press, 2003.

Maillard, Jean. *Adam de La Halle: Perspective musicale*. Paris: Editions Honoré Champion, 1982.

――― . *Évolution et esthétique du lai lyrique des origines à la fin du XIVᵉᵐᵉ siècle*. Paris: Publications de l'Institut de Musicologie, 1963.

――― . *Roi-trouvère du XIIIᵉᵐᵉ siècle: Charles d'Anjou*. N.p.: American Institute of Musicology, 1967.

Marshall, J. H. "The Descort of Albertet and its Old French Imitation." *Zeitschrift für romanische Philologie* 95 (1979): 290–306.

――― , ed. *The Donatz Proensals of Uc Faidit*. London: Oxford University Press, 1969.

———. "The Isostrophic *Descort* in the Poetry of the Troubadours." *Romance Philology* 35, no. 1 (1981): 130–57.

———, ed. *The Razos de trobar of Raimon Vidal and Associated Texts*. London: Oxford University Press, 1972.

Martinez, Ronald. "Italy." In *HT*, 279–94.

Maus, Fred Everett. "Classical Instrumental Music and Narrative." In *A Companion to Narrative Theory*, edited by James Phelan and Peter J. Rabinowitz, 466–83. Oxford: Blackwell Publishing, 2005.

Mazzotta, Giuseppe. "Antiquity and the New Arts in Petrarch." In *The New Medievalism*, edited by Marina S. Brownlee, Kevin Brownlee, and Stephen G. Nichols, 46–69. Baltimore: Johns Hopkins University Press, 1991.

Medieval English Romances. 2 vols. Edited by Diane Speed. Sydney: University of Sydney Department of English, 1989.

Melander, Johan. "Les Poésies de Robert de Castel, trouvère artésien du XIIIe siècle." *Studia Neophilologica* 3 (1930): 17–43.

Ménard, Philippe. "Le Dieu d'amour, figure poétique du trouble et du désir dans les poésies de Thibaut de Champagne." In *Thibaut de Champagne: Prince et poète au XIIIe siècle*, edited by Yvonne Bellenger and Danielle Quéruel, 65–75. Lyon: La Manufacture, 1987.

Menocal, Maria Rosa. *The Arabic Role in Medieval Literary History: A Forgotten Heritage*. Philadelphia: University of Pennsylvania Press, 1987.

Meyer, Leonard B. *Emotion and Meaning in Music*. Chicago: University of Chicago Press, 1956.

Moi, Toril. *Sexual, Textual Politics: Feminist Literary Theory*. 2nd ed. New York: Routledge: 2002.

Mölk, Ulrich. "Deux remarques sur la tornada." *Metrica* 3 (1982): 3–14.

Momigliano, Arnold. *The Classical Foundations of Modern Historiography*. Berkeley: University of California Press, 1990.

Mommsen, Theodore E. "Petrarch's Conception of the 'Dark Ages.'" *Speculum* 17, no. 2 (1942): 226–42.

Moore, John C. *Love in Twelfth-Century France*. Philadelphia: University of Pennsylvania Press, 1972.

Mouzat, J. "De Ventadorn à Barjols: Les troubadours limousins en Provence entre 1150 et 1250." In *Mélanges de philologie romane dédiés à la mémorie de Jean Boutiere*, edited by Irénée Cluzel and François Pirot, 423–34. Liège: Editions Soledi, 1971.

Moreno, Bernardo Santano. "The Love Debate Tradition in the Reception of Gower's *Confessio Amantis* in the Iberian Peninsula." In *Medieval Forms of Argument: Disputation and Debate*. *Disputatio* 5 (2002): 103–26.

Morison, Stanley. *Politics and Script: Aspects of Authority and Freedom in the Development of Graeco-Latin Script from the Sixth Century B.C. to the Twentieth Century A.D.* Oxford: Clarendon Press, 1972.

Morson, Gary Saul, and Caryl Emerson. *Mikhail Bakhtin: Creation of a Prosaics*. Stanford: Stanford University Press, 1990.

Mouzat, J. "De Ventadorn à Barjols: Les troubadours limousins en Provence entre 1150 et 1250." In *Mélanges de philologie romane dédiés à la mémoire de Jean Boutiere*, edited by Irénée Cluzel and François Pirot, 423–34. Liège: Editions Soledi, 1971.

Murphy, James J. *Rhetoric in the Middle Ages: A History of the Rhetorical Theory from Saint Augustine to the Renaissance*. Berkeley: University of California Press, 2001.

Myerowitz, Molly. *Ovid's Game of Love*. Detroit: Wayne State University Press, 1985.

Nattiez, Jean-Jacques. "Can One Speak of Narrativity in Music?" *Journal of the Royal Musical Association*, 115, no. 2 (1990): 240–57.

Nelson, Deborah H. "Northern France." In *HT*, 255–61.

Nesbitt, Alexander. *The History and Technique of Lettering*. New York: Dover, 1957.

Neumeister, Sebastian. *Das Spiel mit der höfischen Liebe: Das Altprovenzalische Partimen*. Munich: Wilhelm Fink Verlag, 1969.

Newcombe, Terence. "The Refrain in Troubadour Lyric Poetry." *Nottingham Mediaeval Studies* 19 (1975): 3–15.

Newes, Virginia. "'Qui Bien aimme a tart oublie': Guillaume de Machaut's *Lay de plour* in Context." In *Citation and Authority in Medieval and Renaissance Music Culture: Learning from the Learned*, edited by Suzannah Clark and Elizabeth Eva Leach, 123–38. Woodbridge: Boydell and Brewer, 2005.

Nichols, Stephen G. "The Early Troubadours: Guilhem IX to Bernart de Ventadorn." In *TI*, 66–82.

——— . "Introduction: Philology in a Manuscript Culture." *Speculum* 65, no. 1 (1990): 1–10.

——— . "Voice and Writing in Augustine and the Troubadour Lyric." In *Vox Intexta: Orality and Textuality in the Middle Ages*. Edited by A. N. Doane and Carol Braun Pasternack, 137–61. Madison: University of Wisconsin Press, 1991.

Nicholson, Francesca M. "Branches of Knowledge: The Purposes of Citation in the Breviari d'amor of Matfre Ermengaud." *Neophilologus* 91 (2007): 375–85.

Nietzsche, Friedrich. *On the Genealogy of Morals*. Translated by Walter Kaufmann and R. J. Hollingdale. New York: Vintage, 1969.

Noulet, J. B., and Camille Chabaneau. *Deux manuscrits provençaux du XIVᵉ siècle, contenant des poésies de Raimon de Cornet, de Peire de Ladils, et d'autres poètes de l'école Toulousaine*. Montpellier: Bureau des publications de la Société pour l'étude des langues romanes. Paris: Maisonneuve et Charles Leclerc, 1888.

Old French–English Dictionary. Edited by Alan Hindley et al. Cambridge: Cambridge University Press, 2000.

O'Neill, Mary. *Courtly Love Songs of Medieval France: Transmission and Style in the Trouvère Repertoire*. Oxford: Oxford University Press, 2006.

Owst, G. R. *Literature and the Pulpit: A Neglected Chapter in the History of English Letters and the English People*, 2nd rev. edn. Oxford: Blackwell, 1961.

Paden, William D. *An Introduction to Old Occitan*. New York: Modern Language Association, 1998.

——— . "Old Occitan as a Lyric Language: The Insertions from Occitan in Three Thirteenth-Century French Romances." *Speculum* 66 (1993): 36–53.

——— . "The System of Genres in Troubadour Lyric." In *ML*, 21–67.

Page, Christopher. *Discarding Images: Reflections on Music and Culture in Medieval France*. Oxford: Clarendon Press, 1993.

——— . "Grocheio, Johannes de." In *Grove Music Online. Oxford Music Online*, http://www.oxfordmusiconline.com/subscriber/article/grove/music/14359.

——— . "Johannes de Grocheio on Secular Music: A Corrected Text and a New Translation." *Plainsong and Medieval Music* 2 (1993): 15–41.

———. Liner notes to *The Mirror of Narcissus*. Gothic Voices. Hyperion CDA66087, 1987.

———. Liner notes to *The Spirits of England and France*. Gothic Voices. Hyperion CDA66773, 1995.

———. "Machaut's 'Pupil' Deschamps on the Performance of Music." *Early Music* 5, no. 4 (1977): 484–91.

———. *The Owl and the Nightingale: Musical Life and Ideas in France, 1100–1300*. Berkeley: University of California Press, 1989.

———. "Tradition and Innovation in BN Fr. 146: The Background to the Ballades." In *FS*, 353–94.

———. *Voices and Instruments of the Middle Ages: Instrumental Practice and Songs in France, 1100–1300*. Berkeley: University of California Press, 1986.

Pagnin, Beniamino. "La 'littera bononiensis': Studio paleografico." *Ricerche medievali* 10–12 (1975–77): 93–168.

Painter, Karen. "On Creativity and Lateness." In *Late Thoughts: Reflections on Artists and Composers at Work*, edited by Karen Painter and Thomas Crow, 1–11. Los Angeles: Getty Research Institute, 2006.

Painter, Sidney. "The Historical Setting of Robert veez de Perron." *Modern Language Notes* 52, no. 2 (1937): 83–87.

Panofsky, Erwin. *Renaissance and Renascences in Western Art*. Stockholm: Almqvist and Wiksell, 1960.

Paris, Gaston. "Études sur les romans de la Table Ronde: Lancelot." *Romania* 12 (1883): 459–534.

Parker, Ian. "Troubadour and Trouvère Songs: Problems in Modal Analysis." *Revue belge de musicologie* 13 (1977): 20–37.

Parkes, Malcolm. "The Influence of the Concepts of *Ordinatio* and *Compilatio* on the Development of the Book." In *Medieval Learning and Literature: Essays Presented to Richard William Hunt*, edited by Jonathan Alexander and Margaret Gibson, 115–41. Oxford: Clarendon Press, 1976.

Paterson, Linda M. "*Fin'amor* and the Development of the Courtly Canso." In *TI*, 28–46.

———. *Troubadours and Eloquence*. Oxford: Clarendon Press, 1975.

———. *The World of the Troubadours: Medieval Occitan Society, c. 1100–1300*. Cambridge: Cambridge University Press, 1993.

Pattison, W. T. *The Life and Works of the Troubadour Raimbaut d'Orange*. Minneapolis: University of Minnesota Press, 1952.

PEIRE D'ALVERNHA. *Peire d'Alvernha: Liriche*. Edited by Alberto Del Monte. Turin: Loescher-Chantore, 1955.

PEIRE CARDENAL. *Poésies complètes du troubadour Peire Cardenal (1180–1278)*. Edited by René Lavaud. Toulouse: Édouard Privat, 1957.

PEIROL. *Peirol, Troubadour of Auvergne*. Edited by S. E. Aston. Cambridge: Cambridge University Press, 1953.

Peraino, Judith A. "*E pui conmencha a canter*: Refrains, Motets and Melody in the Thirteenth-Century Narrative Renart le nouvel." *Plainsong and Medieval Music* 6, no. 1 (1997): 1–16.

———. *Listening to the Sirens: Musical Technologies of Queer Identity from Homer to Hedwig*. Berkeley: University of California Press, 2006.

———. "Monophonic Motets: Sampling and Grafting in the Middle Ages." *Musical Quarterly* 84, no. 4 (2001): 644–80.

———. "New Music, Notions of Genre, and the 'Manuscrit du roi,' circa 1300." Ph.D. diss., University of California at Berkeley, 1995.

———. "Re-Placing Medieval Music." *Journal of the American Musicological Society* 54, no. 2 (2001): 209–64.

Pfeffer, Wendy. *Proverbs in Medieval Occitan Literature.* Gainesville, FL: University Press of Florida, 1997.

Pfuhl, Heinrich. *Untersuchungen über die Rondeaux und Virelais, Speciell des XIV. und XV. Jahrhunderts.* Königsberg: Ex officina Hartungiana, 1887.

Phan, Chantal. "La tornada et l'envoi: Fonctions structurelles et poïétiques." *Cahiers de civilisation médiévale (X^e–XIIe siècles)* 34, no. 1 (1991): 57–61.

Pickens, Rupert. "Jaufré Rudel et la poétique de la mouvance." *Cahiers de civilisation médiévale* 20 (1977): 323–37.

———. *The Songs of Jaufré Rudel.* Toronto: Pontifical Institute of Mediaeval Studies, 1978.

Picone, Michelangelo. "Traditional Genres and Poetic Innovation in Thirteenth-Century Italian Lyric Poetry." In *ML*, 146–57.

Piponnier, Françoise. "The World of Women." In *A History of Women in the West*, 2: *Silences of the Middle Ages*, edited by Christiane Klapisch-Zuber, 323–35. Cambridge, MA: Harvard University Press, 1992.

Plumley, Yolanda. *The Grammar of 14th-Century Melody: Tonal Organization and Compositional Process in the Chansons of Guillaume de Machaut and the* Ars Subtilior. New York: Garland, 1996.

Poe, Elizabeth W. *Compilatio: Lyric Texts and Prose Commentaries in Troubadour Manuscript H (Vat. Lat. 3207).* Lexington, KY: French Forum Publishers, 2000.

———. *From Poetry to Prose in Old Provençal: The Emergence of the* Vidas, *the* Razos, *and the* Razos de trobar. Birmingham, AL: Summa Publications, 1984.

———. "*Segon lo vers del novel chan:* The New Song of the Troubadours." Presentation given at the symposium "Etymologies of Medieval Song." University of Pennsylvania, February 8, 2008.

Prinet, Max. "L'Illustration héraldique du chansonnier du Roi." In *Mélanges de linguistique et de littérature offerts à M. Alfred Jeanroy par ses élèves et ses amis*, 521–37. Paris: Éditions E. Droz, 1928.

Prou, Maurice. *Manuel de paléographie. Recueil de fac-similés d'écritures du XIIe au XVIIe siècle (Manuscrits latins et français).* Paris: A. Picard, 1892.

Ragnard, Isabelle. "Le *Voir Dit*: Dialogue autour de poésies chantées." In *Guillaume de Machaut, Le Livre du Voir Dit*, edited by Danielle Quéruel, 91–112. Paris: Ellipses Édition, 2001.

Räkel, Hans-Herbert. "Le Chant du roi, le roi du chant : L'invention mélodique chez Thibaut de Champagne." In *Thibaut de Champagne: Prince et poète au XIIIe siècle*, edited by Yvonne Bellenger and Danielle Quéruel, 57–64. Lyon: La Manufacture, 1987.

———. *Die musikalische Erscheinungsform der Trouvèrepoesie.* Publikationen der Schweizerischen Musikforschenden Gesellschaft, ser. 2, vol. 27. Berne: P. Haupt, 1977.

Raynaud, Gaston. *Bibliographie des chansonniers français des XIIIe et XIVe siècles.* 2 vols. Paris: F. Vieweg, 1884.

Reaney, Gilbert. "Concerning the Origins of the Rondeau, Virelai, and Ballade Forms." *Musica Disciplina* 6 (1952): 155–66.

———. "Guillaume de Machaut: Lyric Poet." *Music & Letters* 39, no. 1 (1958): 38–51.

———. "The *Lais* of Guillaume de Machaut and their Background." *Proceedings of the Royal Musical Association* 82 (1955): 15–31.

Recueil de paléographie normande. Edited by Louis Le Roc'h Morgère et al. Caen: Conseil général du Calvados, 1995.

Reeves, Marjorie. *Joachim of Fiore and the Prophetic Future: A Medieval Study in Historical Thinking*. Phoenix Mill, Stroud: Sutton Publishing, 1999.

———. "The Originality and Influence of Joachim of Fiore." *Traditio: Studies in Ancient and Medieval History, Thought, and Religion* 36 (1980); 269–316; repr. in *The Prophetic Sense of History in Medieval and Renaissance Europe*. Brookfield, VT: Ashgate Publishing, 1999.

———."Pattern and Purpose in History in the Later Medieval and Renaissance Periods." In *Apocalypse Theory and the Ends of the World*, edited by Malcolm Bull, 90–111. Cambridge, MA: Blackwell Publishers, 1995.

Rhetorica ad Herennium [pseudo-Cicero]. Translated by Harry Caplan. Cambridge, MA: Harvard University Press, 1954. Reprint 2004.

Richardson, Louise Barbara. "The *Confrérie des jongleurs et des bourgeois* and the *Puy d'Arras* in Twelfth- and Thirteenth-Century Literature." In *Studies in Honor of Mario A. Pei*, edited by Jon Fisher and Paul A. Gaeng, 161–71. Chapel Hill: University of North Carolina Press, 1972.

Robertson, Anne Walters. *Guillaume de Machaut and Reims: Context and Meaning in his Musical Works*. Cambridge: University of Cambridge Press, 2002.

Robinson, Fred C. "Medieval, the Middle Ages." *Speculum* 59, no. 4 (1984): 745–56.

Rohloff, Ernst. *Die Quellenhandschriften zum Musiktraktat des Johannes de Grocheio im Faksimile herausgegeben nebst Übertragung des Textes und Übersetzung ins Deutsche, dazu Bericht, Literaturschau, Tabellen und Indices*. Leipzig: Deutscher Verlag für Musik, 1972.

Rokseth, Yvonne. *Polyphonies du XIIIᵉ siècle*. See entry under *Mo* in the list of facsimiles.

Rosenberg, Samuel N., and Hans Tischler. *The Monophonic Songs in the Roman de Fauvel*. Lincoln: University of Nebraska Press, 1991.

Rosenstein, Roy. "New Perspectives on Distant Love: Jaufre Rudel, Uc Bru, and Sarrazina." *Modern Philology* 87, no. 3 (1990): 225–38.

———. "Retour aux origines du troubadour Jaufre Rudel: 'L'escola n'Eblo." *Studia in honorem prof. M. de Riquer*. 2 vols. 2:603–11. Barcelona: Quaderns Crema, 1987.

Ross, Werner. "Über den sogennanten Natureingang der Trobadours,"*Romanische Forschungen* 65 (1954): 49–68.

Rothenberg, David J. "The Marian Symbolism of Spring, ca. 1200–ca. 1500: Two Case Studies," *Journal of the American Musicological Society* 59, no. 2 (2006): 319–98.

Rouse, Richard H., and Mary A. Rouse. *Manuscripts and their Makers: Commercial Book Producers in Medieval Paris, 1200–1500*. 2 vols. Turnhout: Harvey Miller Publishers, 2000.

Saenger, Paul. *Space between Words: The Origins of Silent Reading*. Stanford: Stanford University Press, 1997.

Said, Edward W. "Adorno as Lateness Itself." In *Apocalypse Theory and the Ends of the World*, edited by Malcolm Bull, 264–81. Cambridge, MA: Blackwell Publishers, 1995.

———. *On Late Style: Music and Literature against the Grain*. New York: Pantheon Books, 2006.

Saltzstein, Jennifer. "Relocating the Thirteenth-Century Refrain: Intertextuality, Authority and Origins." *Journal of the Royal Musical Association* 135, no. 2 (2010): 245–79.

————. "Wandering Voices: Refrain Citation in Thirteenth-Century French Music and Poetry." Ph.D. diss., University of Pennsylvania, 2007.

Sanders, Ernest H. "The Medieval Hocket in Practice and Theory." *Musical Quarterly* 60, no. 2 (1974): 246–56.

Sanders, Ernest H., and Peter M. Lefferts. "Sources, MS, §V: Early Motet." In *Grove Music Online. Oxford Music Online*, http://www.oxfordmusiconline.com/subscriber/article/grove/ music/50158pg5.

Schrade, Leo. *The Works of Guillaume de Machaut. Polyphonic Music in the Fourteenth Century*, vols. 2–3. Les Remparts, Monaco: L'Oiseau-Lyre, 1956.

Schubert, Johann. *Die Handschrift Paris, Bibl. Nat. Fr. 1591: Kritische Untersuchung der Trouvèrehandschrift R.* Frankfurt am Main [n. publ.], 1963.

Schulman, Nicole M. *Where Troubadours Were Bishops: The Occitania of Folc of Marseille (1150–1231).* New York: Routledge, 2001.

Schulze-Busacker, Elisabeth. "Topoi." In *HT*, 421–40.

Schwan, Eduard. *Die Altfranzösischen Liederhandschriften: Ihr Verhältniss, ihre Enstehung und ihre Bestimmung.* Berlin: Wiedmannsche Buchhandlung, 1886.

Seigel, Jerrold. *The Idea of the Self: Thought and Experience in Western Europe since the Seventeenth Century.* Cambridge: Cambridge University Press, 2005.

Shirt, David J. "'Le Chevalier de la Charrete': A World Upside Down?" *Modern Language Review* 76, no. 4 (1981): 811–22.

Sieburth, Richard. Introduction to Ezra Pound, *The Pisan Cantos*, edited by Richard Sieburth, ix–xliii. New York: New Directions Publishing, 2003.

Singleton, Mack. "Spanish *acordar* and Related Words." *Language* 17, no. 2 (1941): 119–26.

Smith, F. Joseph. *Jacobi Leodiensis, Speculum Musicae: A Commentary.* 3 vols. Brooklyn, NY: The Institute of Medieval Music, 1966–83.

Smith, Nathaniel B. *Figures of Repetition in the Old Provençal Lyric: A Study in the Style of the Troubadours.* Chapel Hill: University of North Carolina Press, 1976.

————. "Rhetoric." In *HT*, 400–20.

Snow, Joseph T. "The Iberian Peninsula." In *HT*, 271–78.

Sokel, Walter H. "The Prose of German Expressionism." In *A Companion to the Literature of German Expressionism*, edited by Neil H. Donahue, 69–88. Rochester, NY: Camden House, 2005.

Songs of the Women Troubadours. Edited and translated by Matilda Tomaryn Bruckner, Laurie Shepard, and Sarah White. New York: Garland, 2000.

Songs of the Women Trouvères. Edited and translated by Eglal Doss-Quinby et al. New Haven: Yale University Press, 2001.

Source Readings in Music History. Edited by Oliver Strunk; revised by Leo Treitler. New York: W. W. Norton, 1998.

Spanke, Hans. *Beziehungen zwischen romanischer und mittellateinischer Lyrik, mit besonderer Berücksichtigung der Metrik und Musik.* Abhandlungen der Gesellschaft der Wissenschaften zu Göttingen Philologisch-Historische Klasse, Folge 3, no. 18. Berlin: Weidmannsche Buchhandlung, 1936.

————. "Der Chansonnier du Roi." *Romanische Forschungen* 57 (1943): 38–104.

————. Review of F. Gennrich: *Grundriss einer Formenlehre des mittelalterlichen Liedes* (1932), in *Studien zur lateinischen und romanischen Lyrik des Mittelalters*, edited by Ulrich Mölk, 440–54. Hildesheim: Georg Olms Verlag, 1983.

————. "St. Martial-Studien: Ein Beitrag zur frühromanischen Metrik." In *Studien zur lateinischen und romanischen Lyrik des Mittelalters*, edited by Ulrich Mölk, 1–36. Hildesheim: Georg Olms Verlag, 1983.

————. "Tanzmusik in der Kirche des Mittelalters." In *Studien zur lateinischen und romanischen Lyrik des Mittelalters*, edited by Ulrich Mölk, 104–31. Hildesheim: Georg Olms Verlag, 1983.

Spearing, A. C. *Textual Subjectivity: The Encoding of Subjectivity in Medieval Narratives and Lyrics*. Oxford: Oxford University Press, 2005.

Spence, Sarah. *Rhetoric of Reason and Desire: Vergil, Augustine, and the Troubadours*. Ithaca: Cornell University Press, 1988.

————. *Text and the Self in the Twelfth Century*. Cambridge: Cambridge University Press, 1996.

Spiegel, Gabrielle M. *Romancing the Past: The Rise of Vernacular Prose Historiography in Thirteenth-Century France*. Berkeley: University of California Press, 1993.

Spitzer, Leo. *L'Amour lontain de Jaufré Rudel et le sens de la poésie des troubadours*. University of North Carolina Studies in the Romance Languages and Literature, no. 5, 1944.

————. "Note on the Poetic and the Empirical 'I' in Medieval Authors." *Traditio* 4 (1946): 414–22.

Stevens, John. "The Manuscript Presentation and Notation of Adam de la Halle's Courtly Chansons." In *Source Materials and the Interpretation of Music: A Memorial Volume to Thurston Dart*, edited by Ian Bent, 29–84. London: Stainer and Bell, 1981.

————. *Words and Music in the Middle Ages: Song, Narrative, Dance and Drama, 1050–1350*. Cambridge: Cambridge University Press, 1986.

Stock, Brian. "The Self and Literary Experience in Late Antiquity and the Middle Ages." *New Literary History* 25, no. 4 (1994): 839–52.

Stone, Gregory B. *The Death of the Troubadour: The Late Medieval Resistance to the Renaissance*. Philadelphia: University of Pennsylvania Press, 1994.

Sturrock, John. *Structuralism*. 2nd edn. Oxford: Blackwell Publishing, 2003.

Subotnik, Rose Rosengard. *Developing Variations: Style and Ideology in Western Music*. Minneapolis: University of Minnesota Press, 1991.

Susskind, Norman. "Love and Laughter in the Romans Courtois." *French Review* 37, no. 6 (1964): 651–57.

Swain, Joseph Ward. "The Theory of the Four Monarchies: Opposition History under the Roman Empire." *Classical Philology* 35, no. 1 (1940): 1–21.

Switten, Margaret. "Music and Versification." In *TI*, 141–63.

————. "Versus and Troubadours around 1100." *Plainsong and Medieval Music* 16, no. 2 (2007): 91–143.

Symes, Carol. *A Common Stage: Theater and Public Life in Medieval Arras*. Ithaca: Cornell University Press, 2007.

Tartakovsky, Roi. "E. E. Cummings's Parentheses: Punctuation as Poetic Device." *Style* 43, no. 2 (2009): 215–47.

Thacker, Christopher. *The History of Gardens*. Berkeley and Los Angeles: University of California Press, 1979.

Thibaut de Champagne. *Les Chansons de Thibaut de Champagne, roi de Navarre: Édition critique*. Edited by A. Wallensköld. Paris: Édouard Champion, 1925.

Thomson, S. Harrison. *Latin Bookhands of the Later Middle Ages*. Cambridge: Cambridge University Press, 1969.

Tischler, Hans. *Conductus and Contrafacta*. Ottawa, Canada: The Institute for Medieval Music, 2001.

———. *The Earliest Motets (to circa 1270): A Complete Comparative Edition*. 3 vols. New Haven and London: Yale University Press, 1982.

———. *The Montpellier Codex*. 4 vols. Madison: A-R Editions, 1985.

———. "A Unique and Remarkable Trouvère Song." *Journal of Musicology* 10, no. 1 (1992): 106–12.

Topsfield, L. T. *Troubadours and Love*. Cambridge: Cambridge University Press, 1975.

Toury, Marie-Noëlle. "Les Chansons de Thibaut de Champagne: L'écriture et le livre." In *Thibaut de Champagne: Prince et poète au XIIIᵉ siècle*, edited by Yvonne Bellenger and Danielle Quéruel, 45–55. Lyon: La Manufacture, 1987.

Treitler, Leo. "The Aquitanian Repertories of Sacred Monody in the Eleventh and Twelfth Centuries." 3 vols. Ph.D. diss., Princeton University, 1967.

———. "The Troubadours Singing their Poems." In *The Union of Words and Music in Medieval Poetry*. Edited by Rebecca A. Baltzer, Thomas Cable, and James I. Wimsatt, 15–48. Austin: University of Texas Press, 1991.

Turco, Lewis. *The New Book of Forms: A Handbook of Poetics*. Hanover, NH and London: University Press of New England, 1986.

Uitti, Karl D. "From *Clerc* to *Poète*: The Relevance of the *Romance of the Rose* to Machaut's World." In *Machaut's World: Science and Art in the Fourteenth Century*, edited by Madeleine Pelner Cosman and Bruce Chandler, 209–16. New York: New York Academy of Sciences, 1978.

Ungureanu, Marie. *La Bourgeoisie naissante: Société et littérature bourgeoises d'Arras aux XIIᵉ et XIIIᵉ siècles*. Arras: CdMhPC, 1955.

Van D'Elden, Stephanie Cain. "The Minnesingers." In *HT*, 262–70.

van der Werf, Hendrik. "Cantus coronatus." In *Grove Music Online. Oxford Music Online*, http://www.oxfordmusiconline.com/subscriber/article/grove/music/04794.

———. *The Chansons of the Troubadours and Trouvères: A Study of the Melodies and their Relation to the Poems*. Utrecht: Oosthoek, 1972.

———. Musical Introduction to *Adam*, xxv–xxxviii.

———. *Trouvères-Melodien II: Thibaut de Navarre, Moniot d'Arras, Moniot de Paris, Colin Muset, Audefroi le Bastard, Adam de la Halle*. Monumenta Monodica Medii Aevi, 12. Kassel and Basel: Bärenreiter, 1979.

Van Vleck, Amelia E. *Memory and Re-Creation in Troubadour Lyric*. Berkeley: University of California Press, 1991.

Verger, Jacques. "Patterns." In *A History of the University in Europe, 1: Universities in the Middle Ages*. Edited by Hilde de Ridder-Symoens, 35–76. Cambridge: Cambridge University Press, 1992.

Wack, Mary F. *Lovesickness in the Middle Ages: The* Viaticum *and its Commentaries*. Philadelphia: University of Pennsylvania Press, 1990.

Walsh, P. G. Introduction to *Andreas Capellanus on Love*, 1–26. Translated by P. G. Walsh. London: Duckworth, 1982.

Weintraub, Karl J. *Visions of Culture*. Chicago: University of Chicago Press, 1966.

Weiss, Julian. "On the Conventionality of the *Cantigas d'amor*." In *ML*, 126–45.

Wetherbee, Winthrop. "The Place of Secular Latin Lyric." In *ML*, 95–125.

Wilhelm, James J. *The Cruelest Month: Spring, Nature and Love in Classical and Medieval Lyrics.* New Haven: Yale University Press, 1965.

Wilkins, Nigel, ed. *The Lyric Works of Adam de la Hale.* Corpus Mensurabilis Musicae 44. N.p.: American Institute of Musicology, 1967.

———. "Virelai." In *Grove Music Online. Oxford Music Online,* http://www.oxfordmusiconline. com/subscriber/article/grove/music/29490.

———. *The Works of Jehan de Lescurel.* Corpus Mensurabilis Musicae 30. N.p.: American Institute of Musicology, 1966.

Williams, Sarah J. "An Author's Role in Fourteenth-Century Book Production: Guillaume de Machaut's 'livre où je met toutes mes choses." *Romania* 90 (1969): 433–54.

Wilson, Jean. *The Challenge of Belatedness: Goethe, Kleist, Hofmannsthal.* Lanham, MD: University Press of America, 1991.

Winckelmann, Johann Joachim. *History of Ancient Art.* Translated by G. Henry Lodge. New York: Frederick Ungar Publishing, 1968.

Wolf, Ferdinand. *Über die Lais, Sequenzen und Leiche.* Heidelberg: C. F. Winter, 1841.

Wolinski, Mary E. "The Compilation of the Montpellier Motet Codex." *Early Music History* 11 (1992): 263–301.

———. "Tenors Lost and Found: The Reconstruction of Motets in Two Medieval Chansonniers." In *Critica Musica: Essays in Honor of Paul Brainard,* edited by John Knowles, 461–81. Amsterdam: Gordon and Breach, 1996.

Wood, Michael. Introduction to *On Late Style: Music and Literature against the Grain,* by Edward W. Said, xi–xix. New York: Pantheon Books, 2006.

Yudkin, Jeremy. *Music in Medieval Europe.* Englewood Cliffs, NJ: Prentice Hall, 1989.

Zink, Michel. *The Invention of Literary Subjectivity.* Translated by David Sices. Baltimore: Johns Hopkins Press, 1999.

Zirkle, Conway. *The Beginnings of Plant Hybridization.* Philadelphia: University of Pennsylvania Press, 1935.

Zumthor, Paul. *Essai de poétique médiévale.* Paris: Seuil, 1972.

———. "An Overview: Why the Troubadours?" In *HT*, 11–23.

———. *Speaking of the Middle Ages.* Translated by Sarah White. Lincoln: University of Nebraska Press, 1986.

———. "The Text and the Voice." Translated by Marilyn C. Engelhardt. *New Literary History,* 16, no. 1 (1984): 67–92.

———. *Toward a Medieval Poetics.* Translated by Philip Bennett. Minneapolis: University of Minnesota Press, 1992.

Musical examples are marked with * and page numbers in bold.

MOTETS